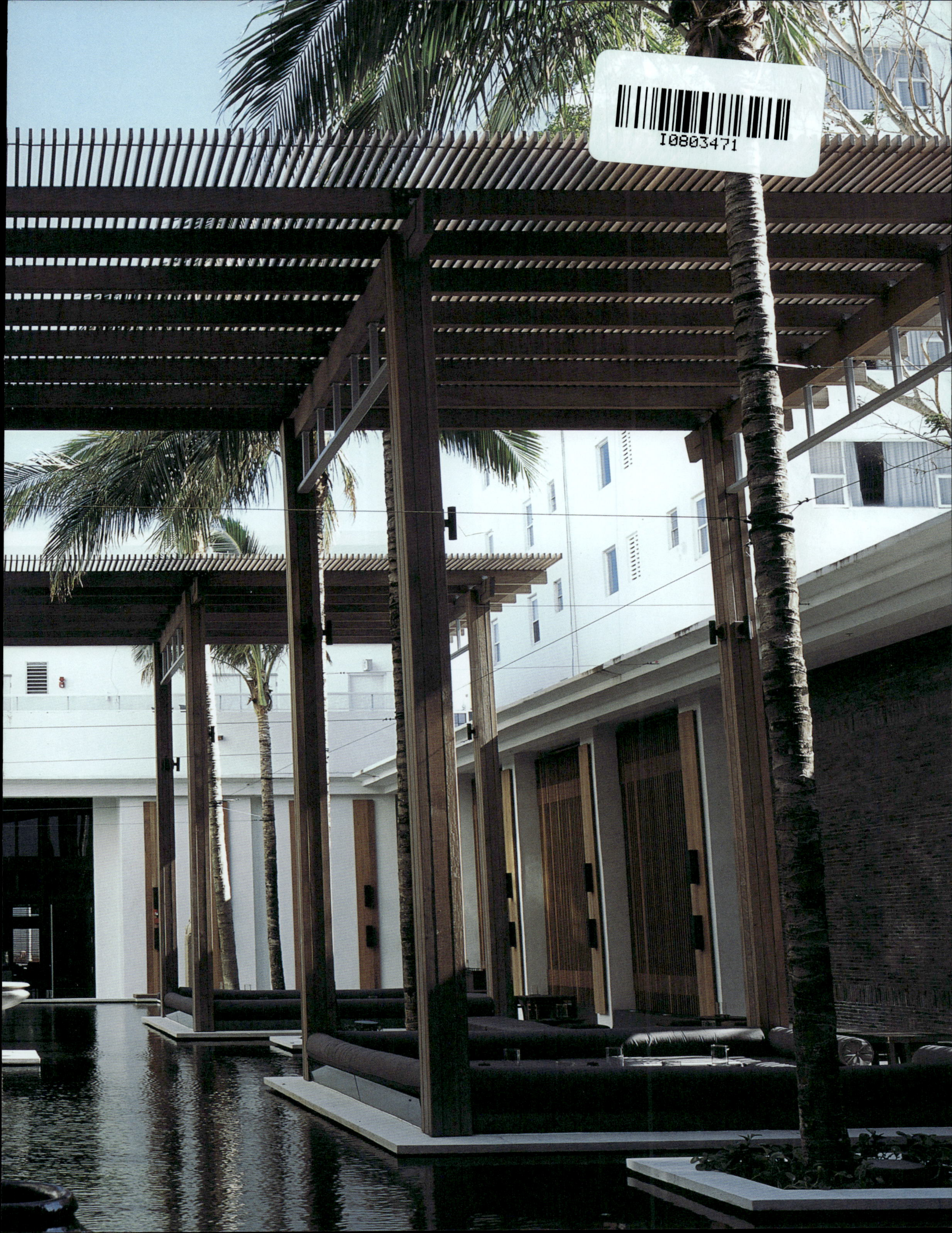

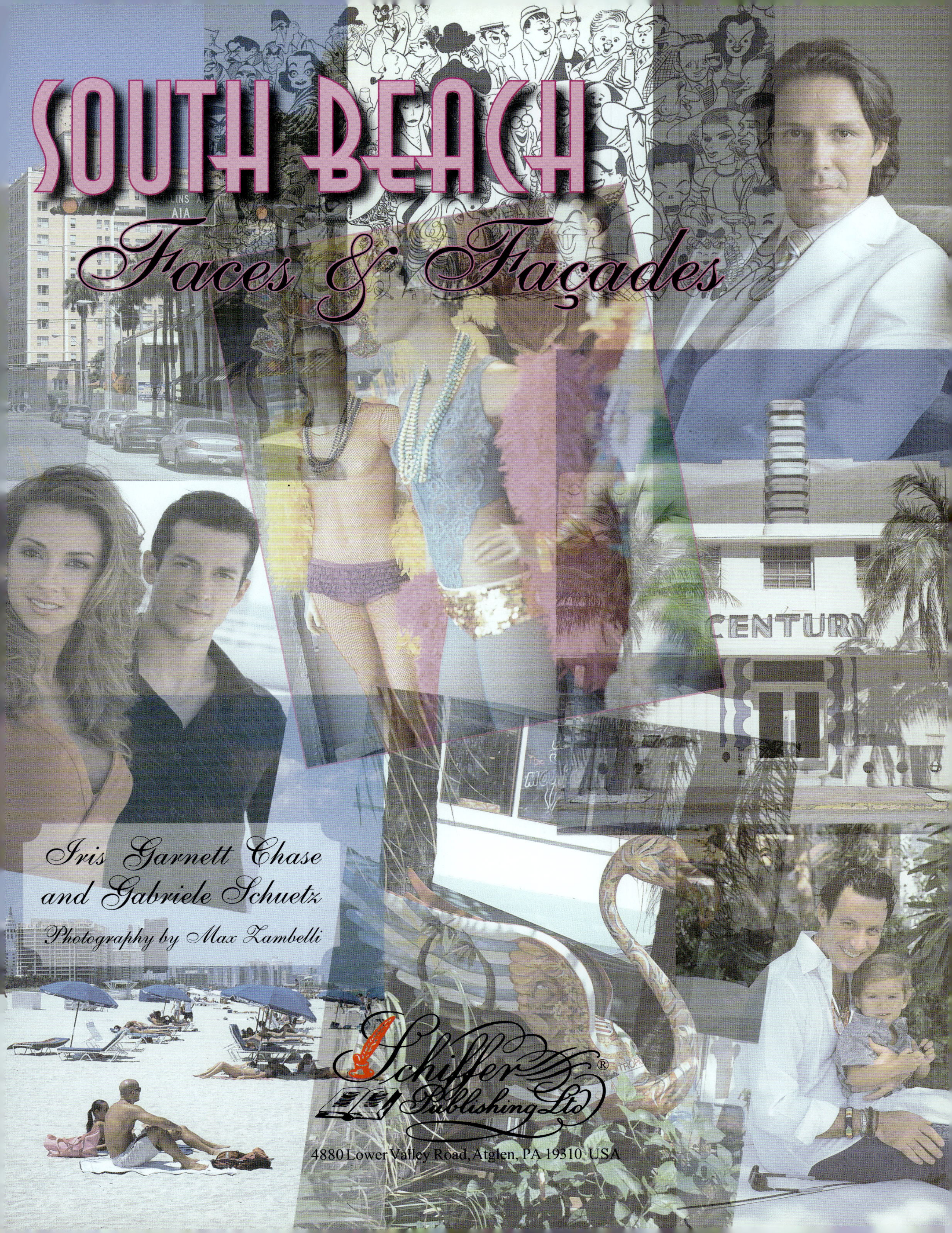

SOUTH BEACH

Faces & Façades

Iris Garnett Chase
and Gabriele Schuetz
Photography by Max Zambelli

Schiffer Publishing Ltd®
4880 Lower Valley Road, Atglen, PA 19310 USA

Dedication

This book is dedicated to my sister, Carol Garnett Abraham, with whom I grew up on a beach, not unlike Miami Beach.

Acknowledgements

Special thanks to James Burns for providing his make-up expertise for so many photo shoots, and to Barry Chase for his merciless editing.

Other Schiffer Books by Iris Garnett Chase

South Beach Deco: Step-by-Step

Other Schiffer Books on Related Subjects

Art Deco Architecture: Miami Beach Postcards, by Paul Clemence

South Beach Architectural Photographs, by Paul Clemence

South Beach: Two Decades of Deco District Paintings by Mark Rutkowski

Miami Memories: A Midcentury Journey, by Mary L. Martin, Tina Skinner, and Nathaniel Wolfgang-Price

Library of Congress Control Number: 2006936013

Designed by "Sue"
Type set in ITC Anna/Novarese Bk BT

ISBN: 0-7643-2593-0
Printed in China

Published by Schiffer Publishing Ltd.
4880 Lower Valley Road
Atglen, PA 19310
Phone: (610) 593-1777; Fax: (610) 593-2002
E-mail: Info@schifferbooks.com

For the largest selection of fine reference books on this and related subjects, please visit our web site at www.schifferbooks.com
We are always looking for people to write books on new and related subjects. If you have an idea for a book please contact us at the above address.

This book may be purchased from the publisher.
Include $3.95 for shipping.
Please try your bookstore first.
You may write for a free catalog.

In Europe, Schiffer books are distributed by
Bushwood Books
6 Marksbury Ave.
Kew Gardens
Surrey TW9 4JF England
Phone: 44 (0) 20 8392-8585; Fax: 44 (0) 20 8392-9876
E-mail: info@bushwoodbooks.co.uk
Website: www.bushwoodbooks.co.uk
Free postage in the U.K., Europe; air mail at cost.

CONTENTS

face

Function: *noun*

Etymology: Middle English, from Old French, from (assumed) Vulgar Latin *facia*, from Latin *facies* form, shape, face

…the front part of the human head including the chin, mouth, nose, cheeks, eyes, and usually forehead

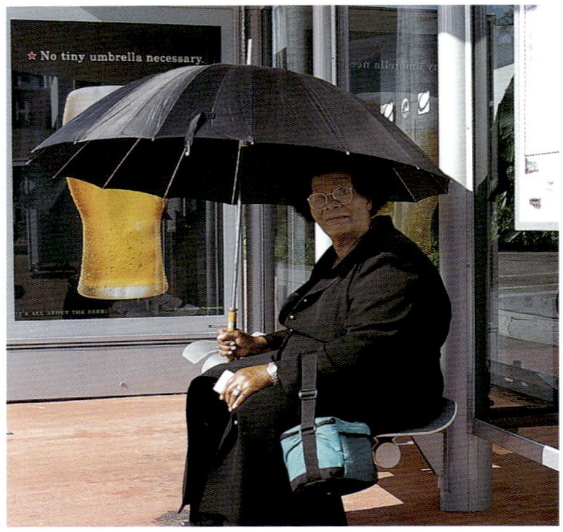

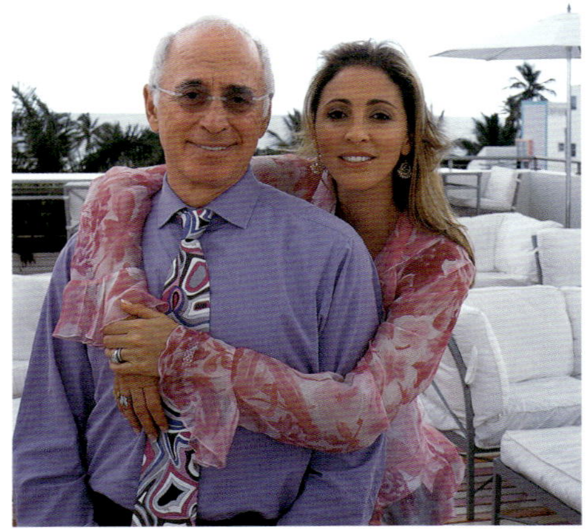

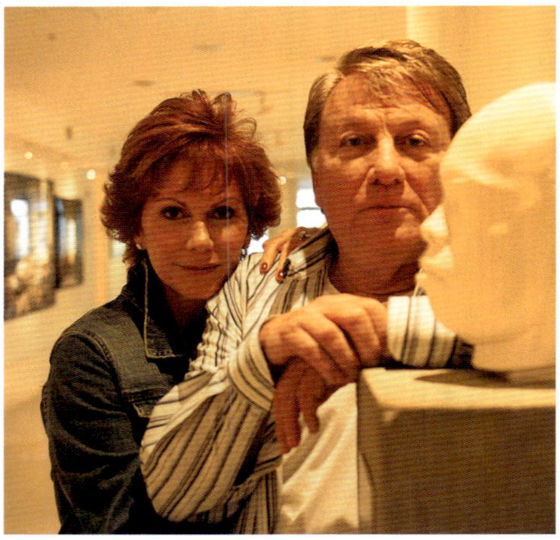

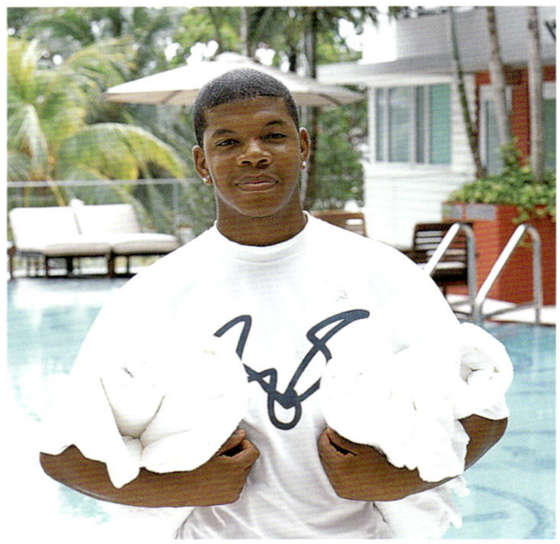

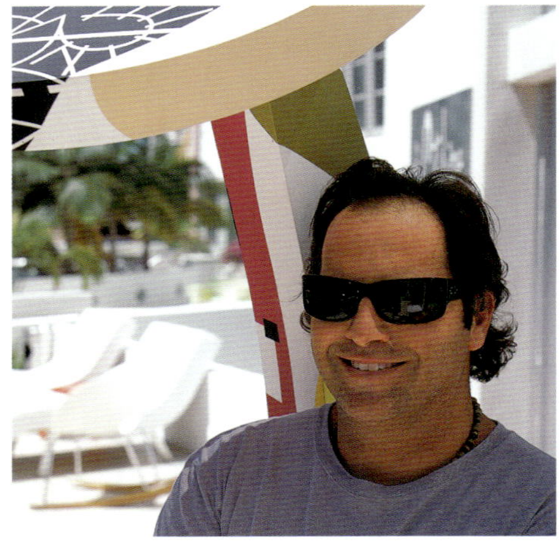

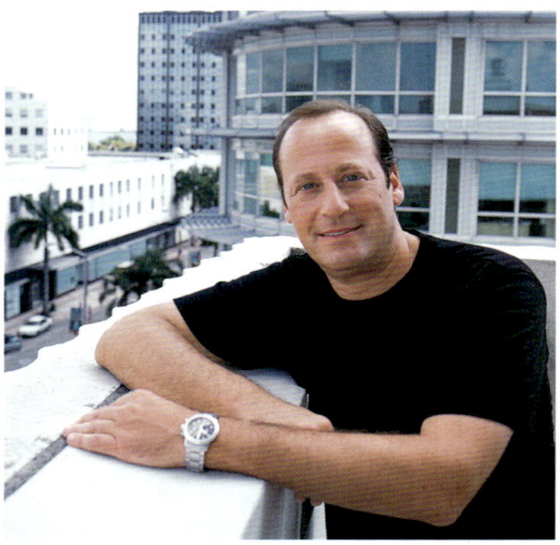

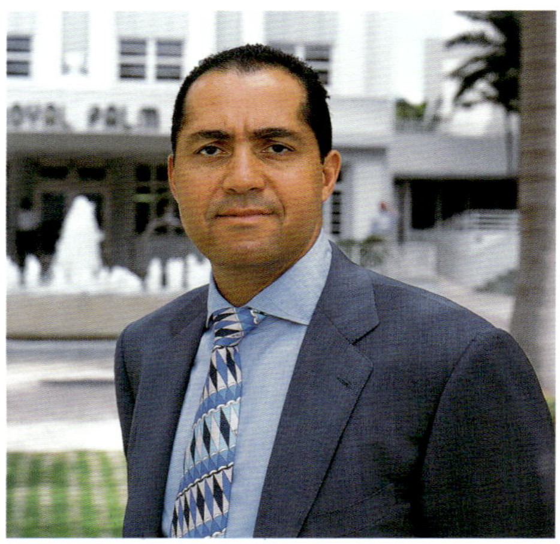

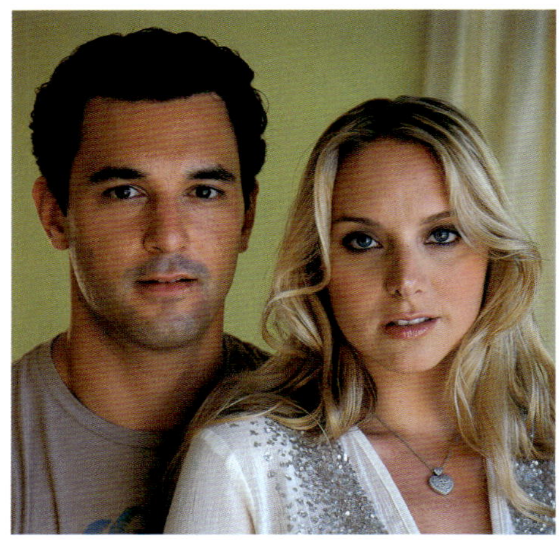

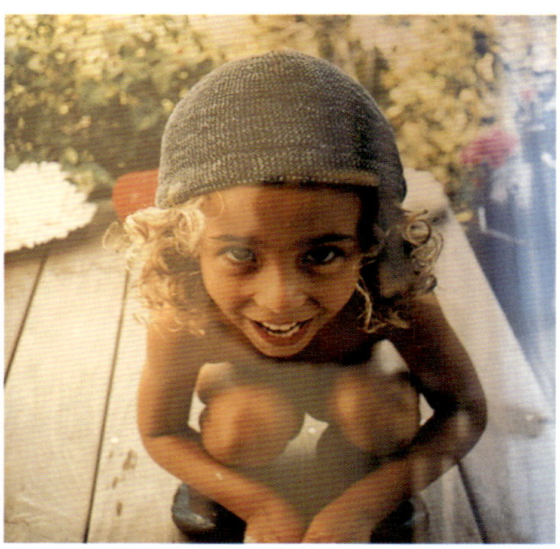

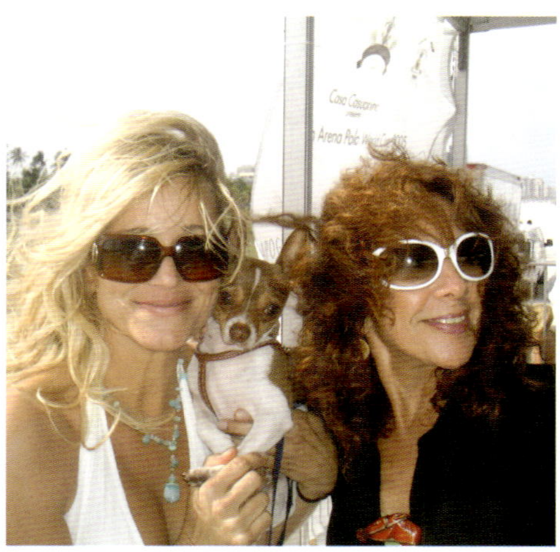

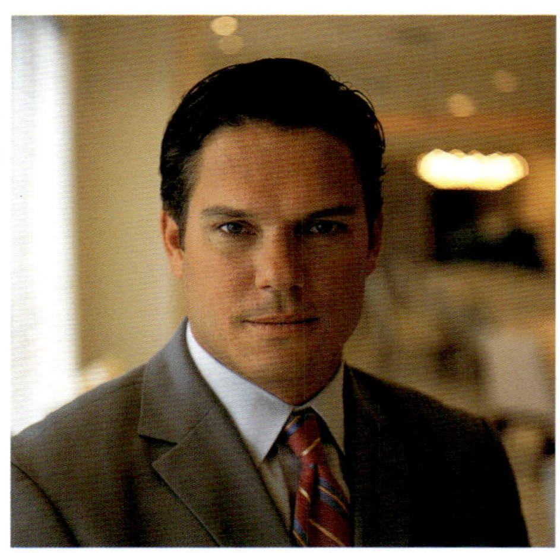

fa·çade

Function: *noun*

Etymology: French *façade,* from Italian *facciata,* from *faccia* face (from—assumed—Vulgar Latin *facia*)

...the front of a building...

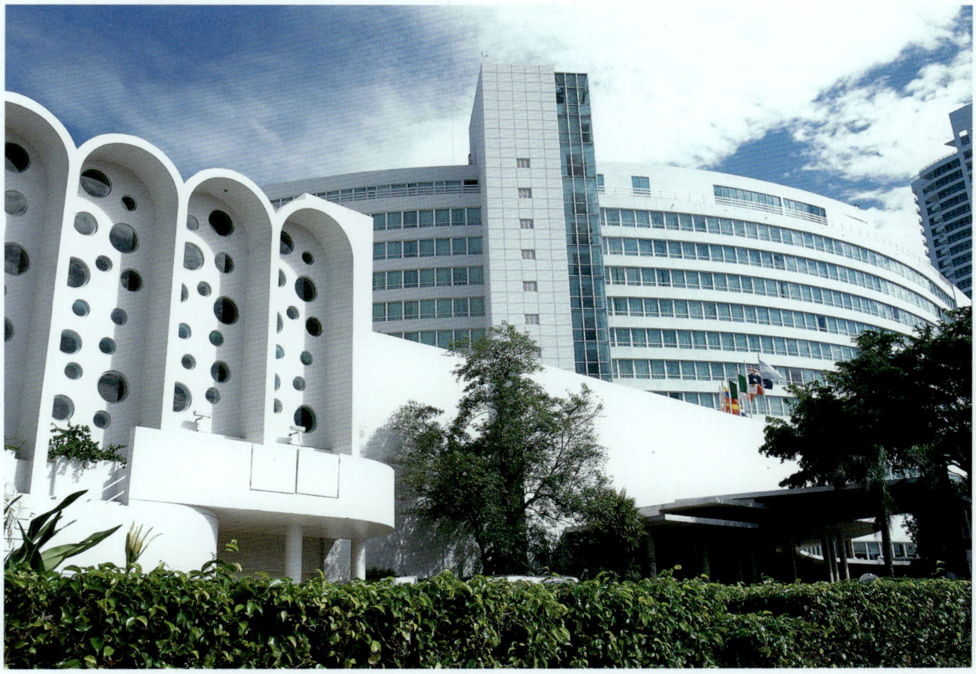

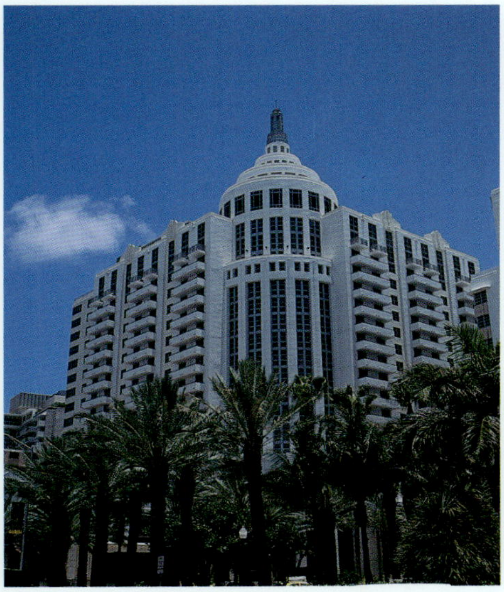

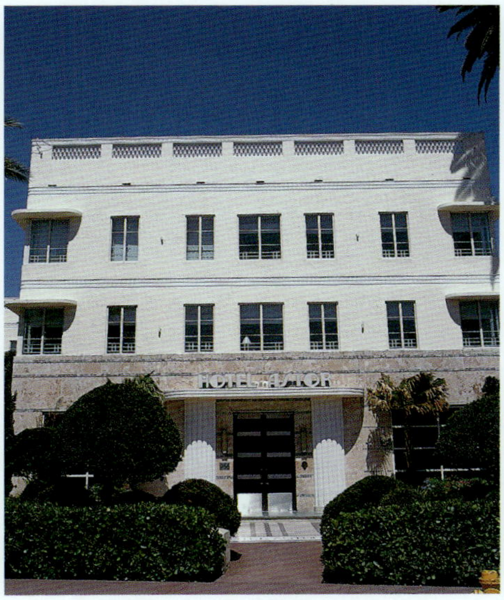

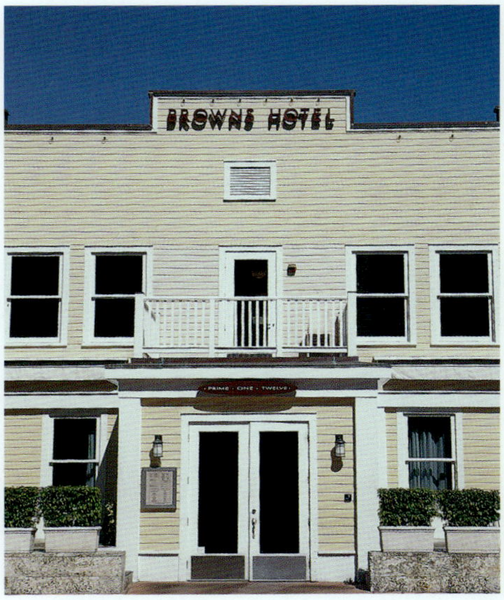

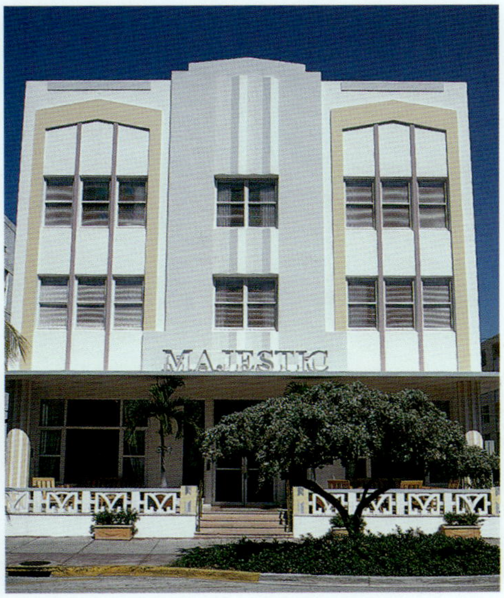

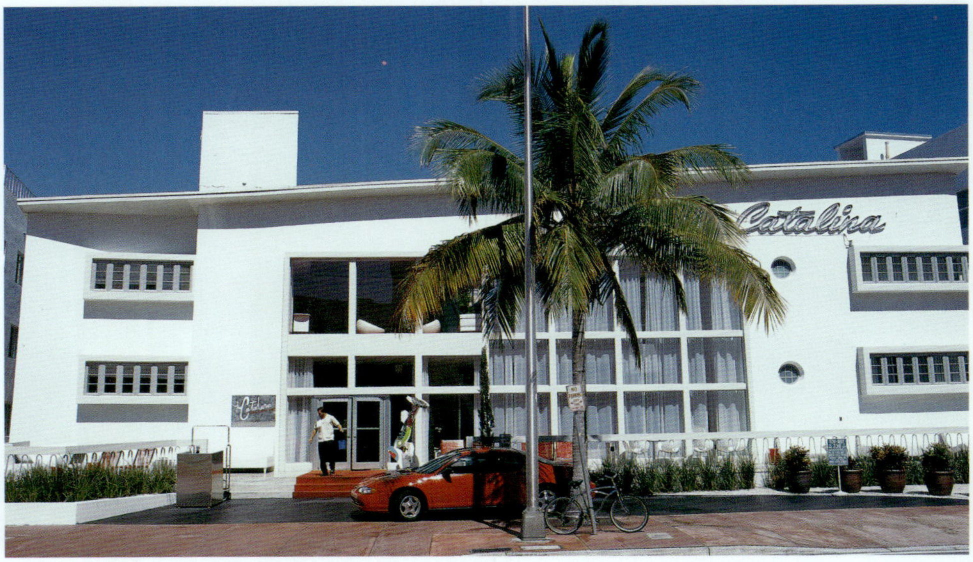

...a face of a building (as a flank or rear facing on a street or court) that is given emphasis by special architectural treatment...

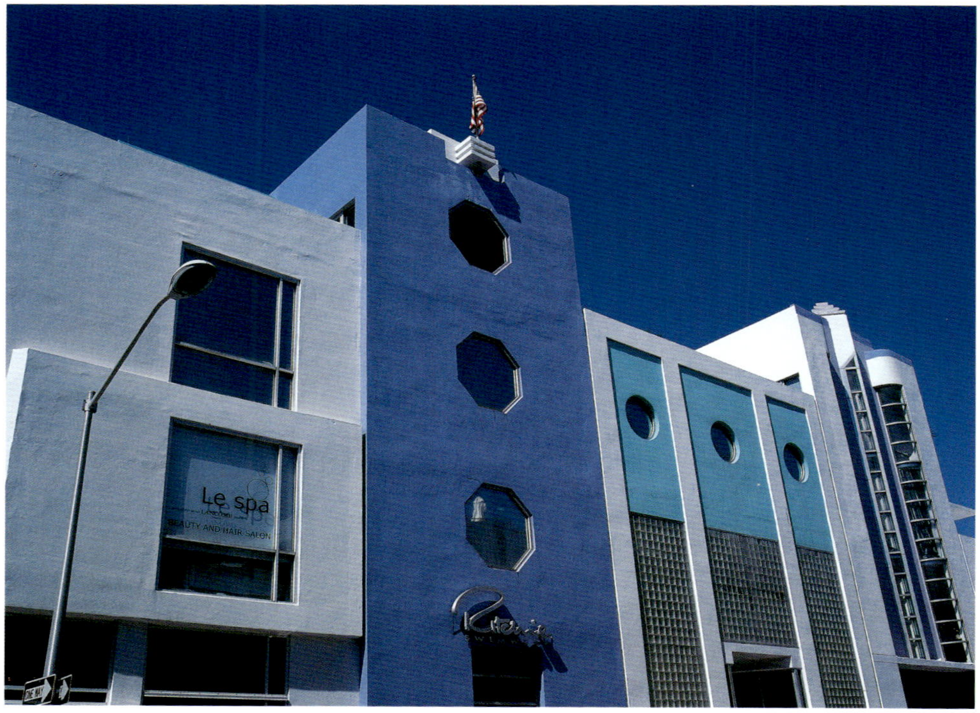

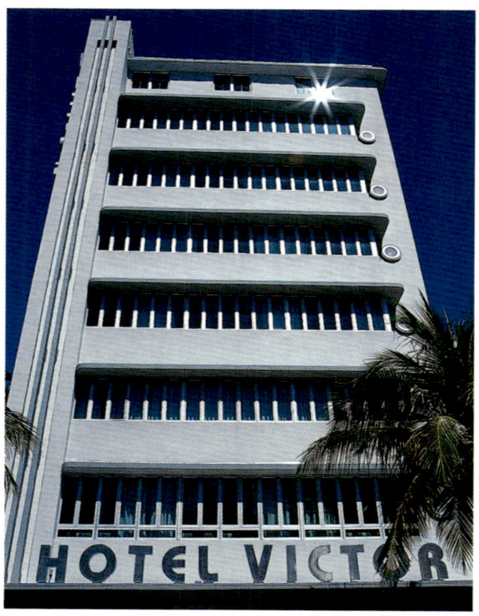

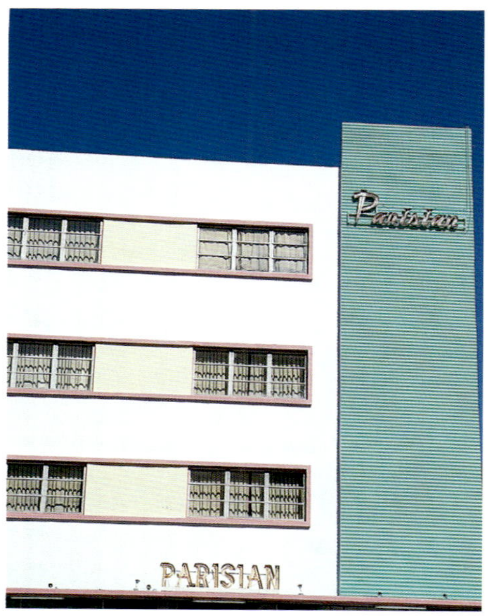

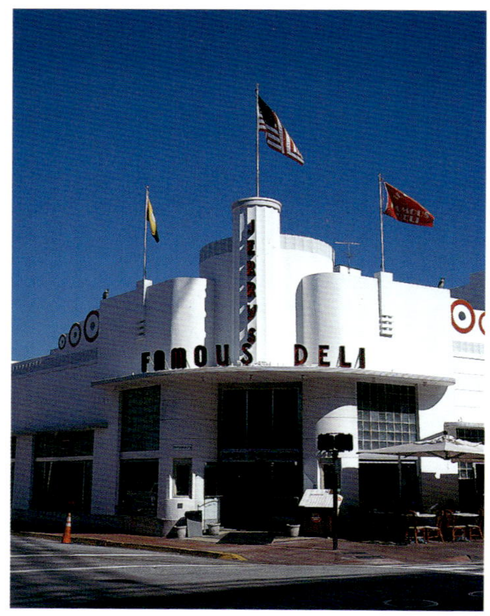

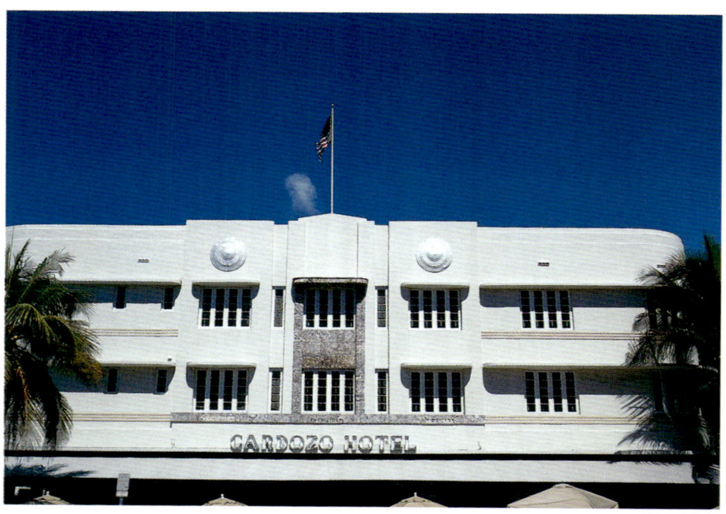

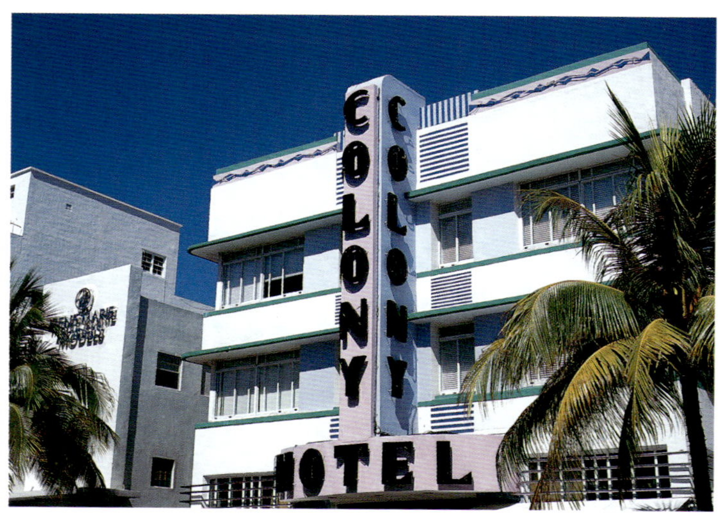

…a false, superficial, or artificial appearance or effect.

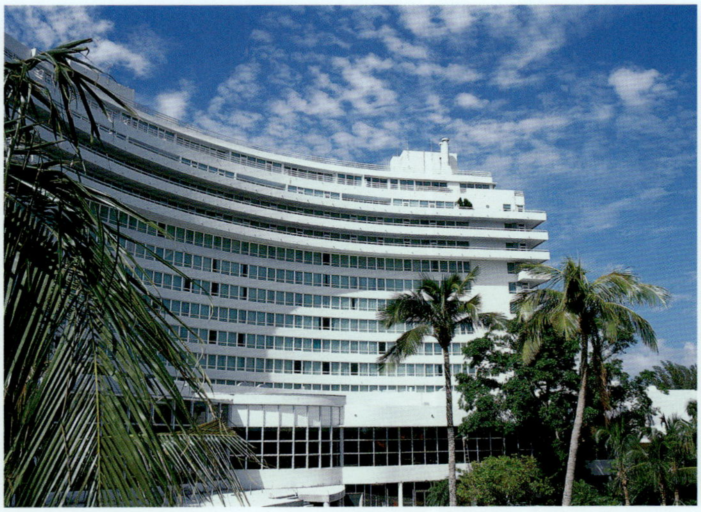

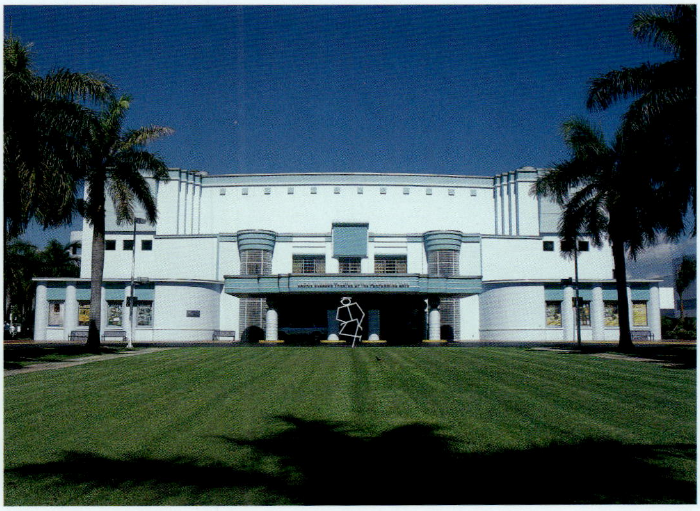

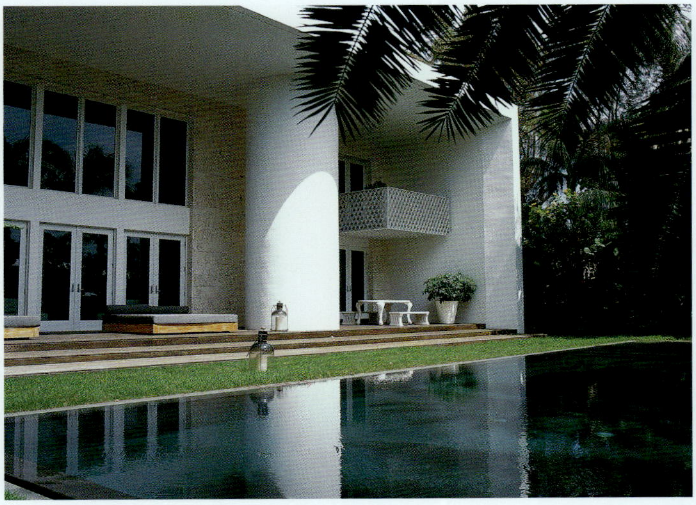

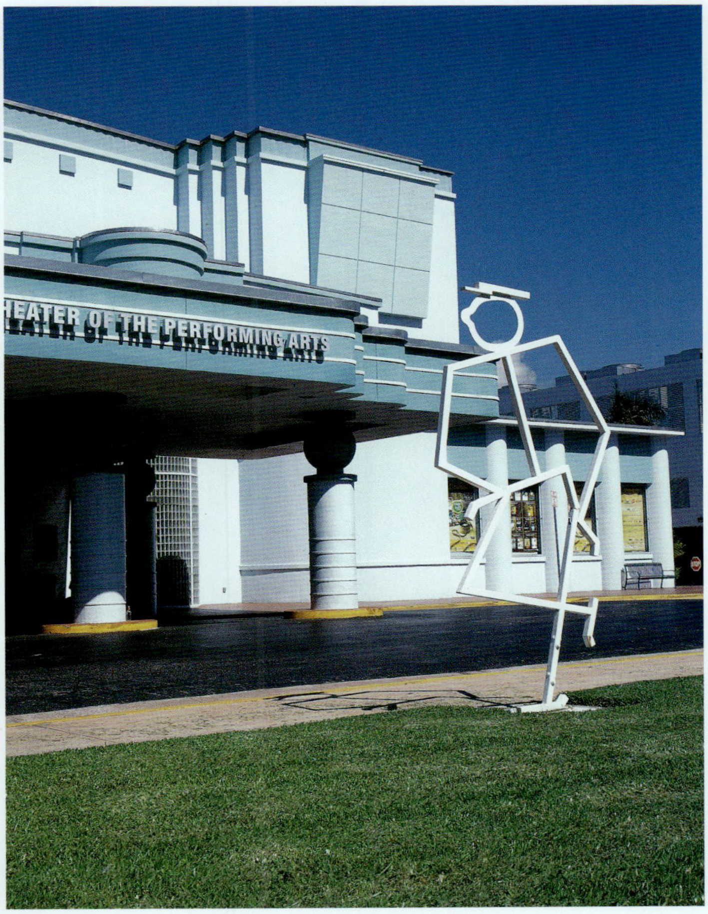

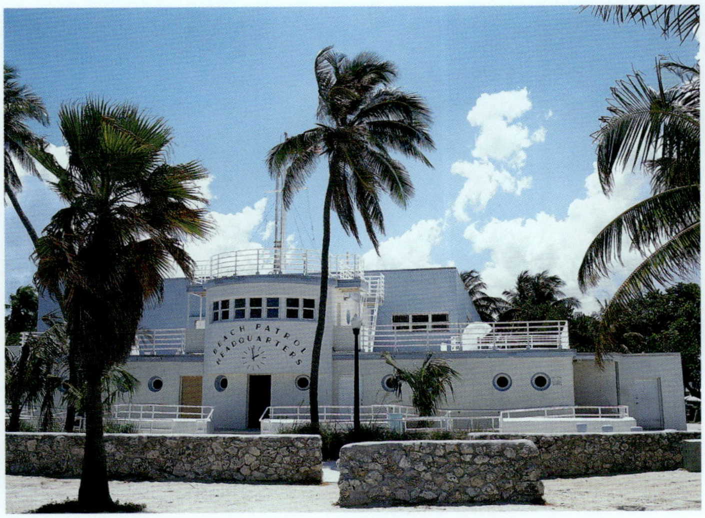

INTRODUCTION

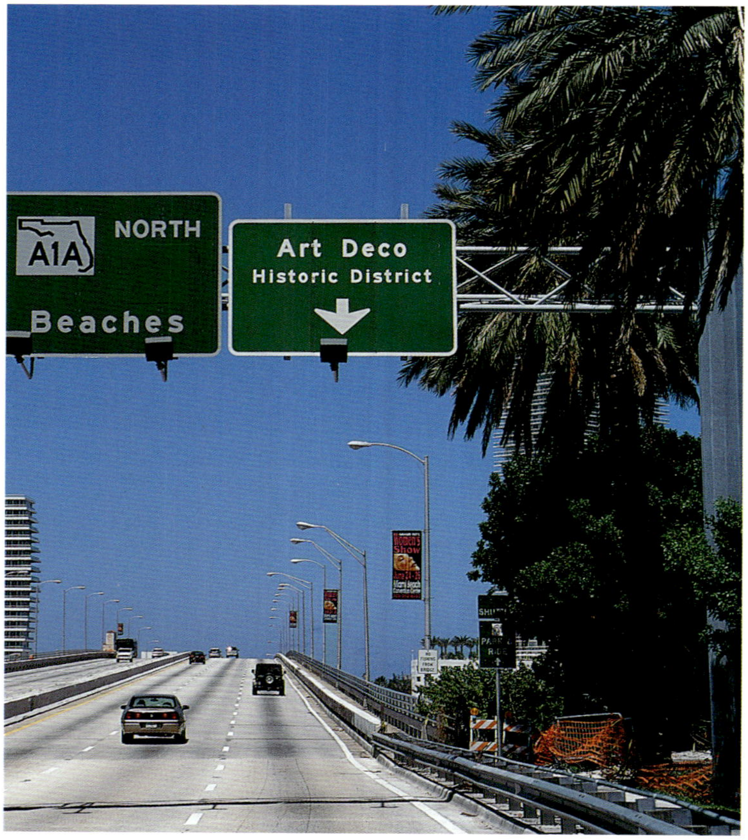

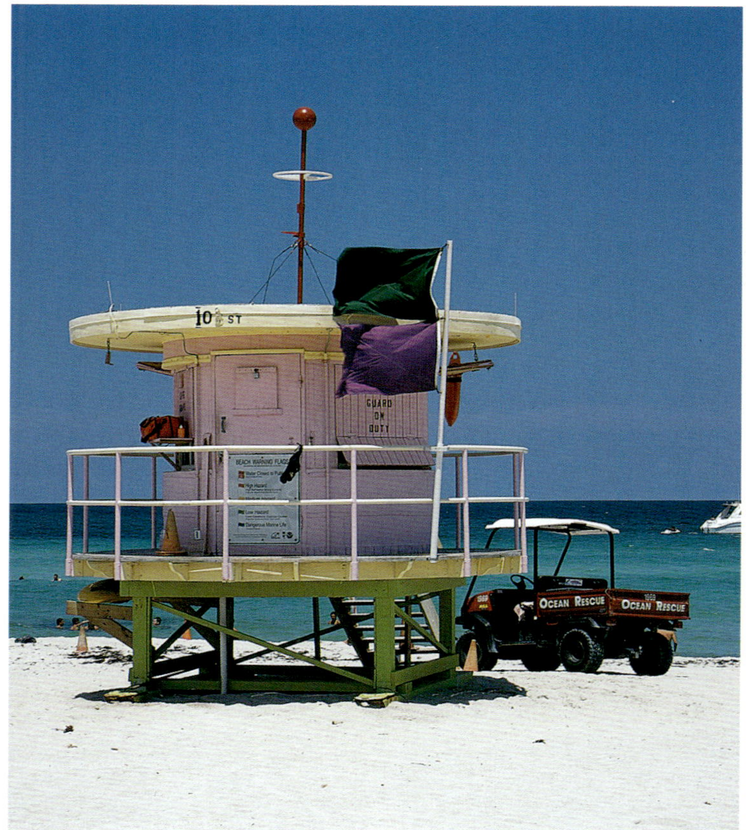

South Beach is the southern part of Miami Beach—about a square mile of palm trees, ocean breezes, and long subtropical days and nights. Its pleasures and treasures are abundant, and rare in the sense that you will find hip urban nightlife, the famous club scene, next to the gentlest of Caribbean-like aqua surf. And to top it off, there's the fabulous Art Deco architecture that showcases its *uber-chic* shops, and not last nor least the glamour of the beautiful-people-parades along Ocean Drive and Lincoln Road. The beauty here is exceptional: the turquoise Atlantic itself, the people and places of South Beach—its faces and façades—are all part of what makes South Beach so special.

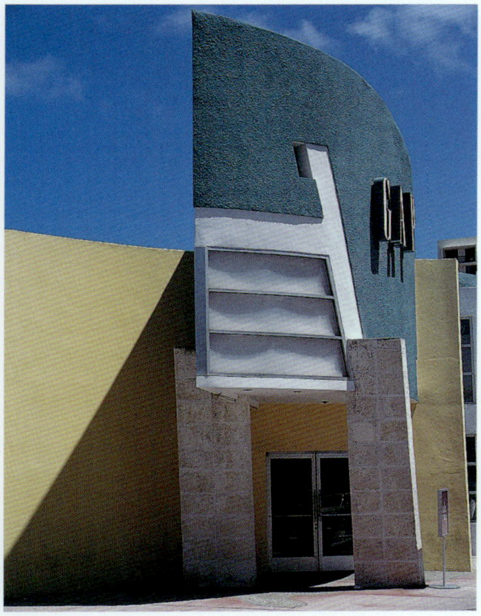

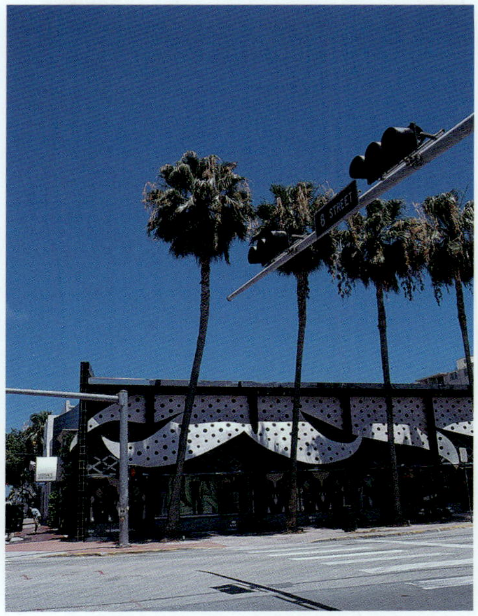

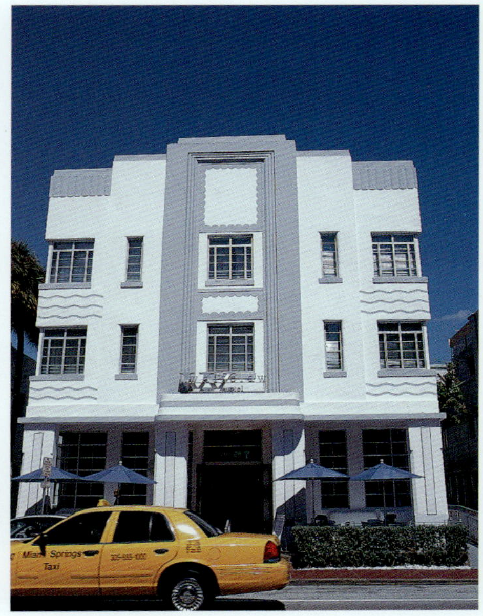
Taxi

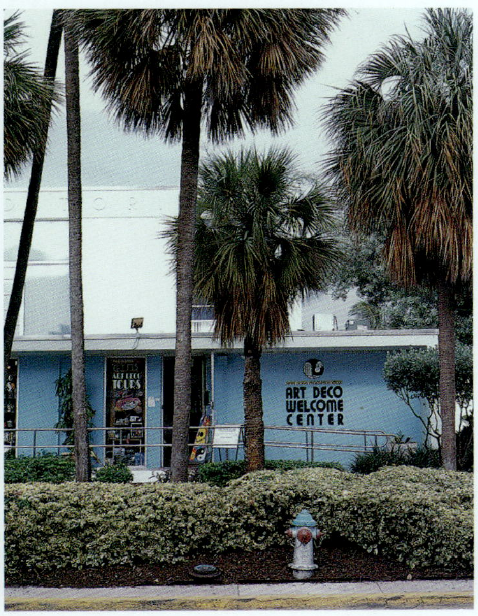
ART DECO
WELCOME
CENTER

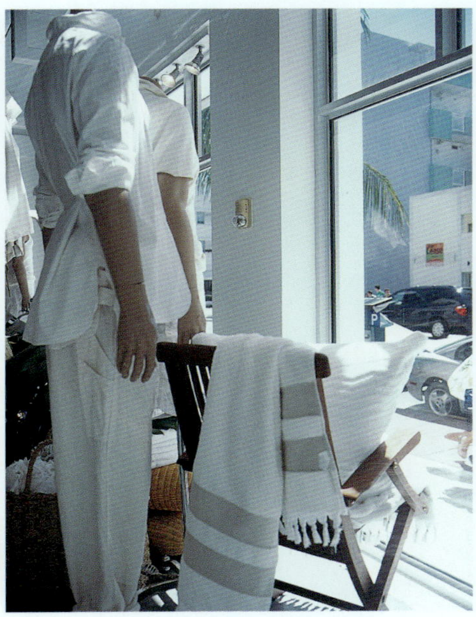

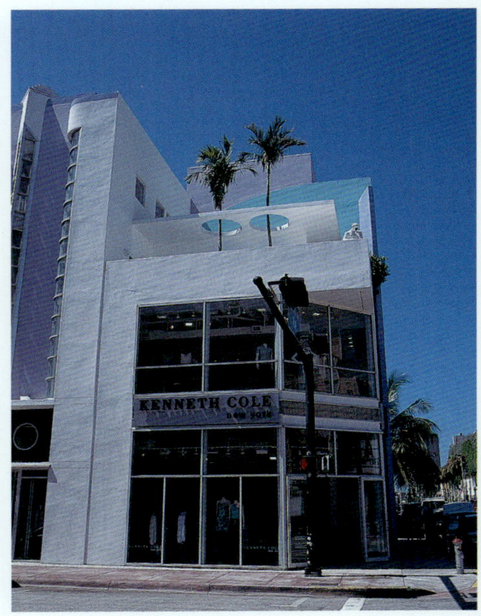
KENNETH COLE

While you're filling your eyes with the architectural treats of Miami Beach, you can also feast on the sights and personalities of the people you'll see and maybe even meet. Obviously a lot of these people will be visitors like you, but the City has a permanent population of something like 90,000. While technically, geographically, and legally part of the United States, South Beach is a unique cultural mix that cannot be found anywhere else in the country. It is, in many ways, temperamentally more like the Mediterranean European coast or parts of Latin America. While walking the streets, you can't help but hear a variety of different languages—Spanish, of course, but also German, French, Brazilian Portuguese, Russian, Hebrew, and lots of British-Empire English. Just listening to the language mix will transport you to a foreign place, a place between the open sea and the City of Miami across Biscayne Bay.

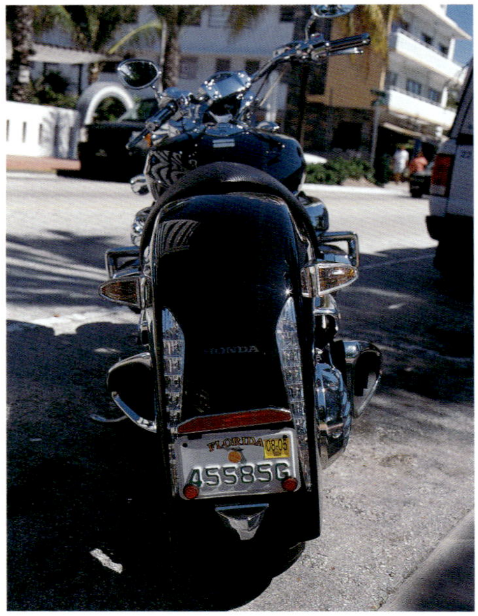

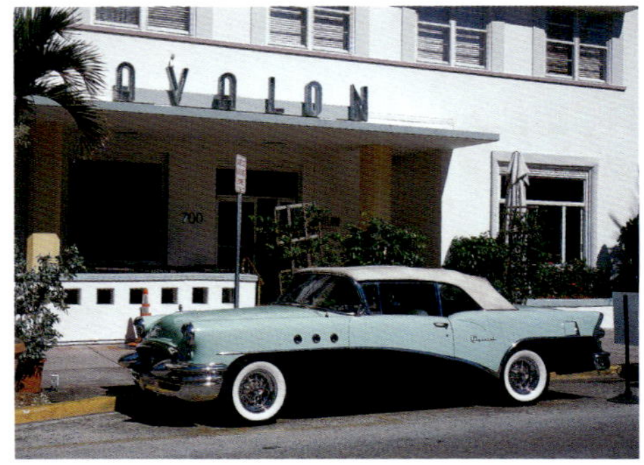

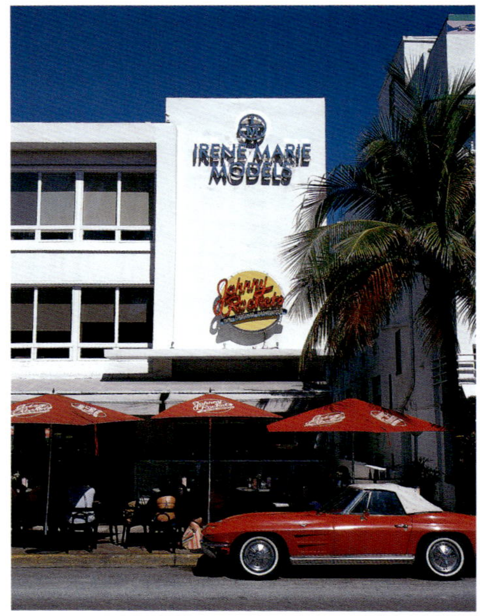

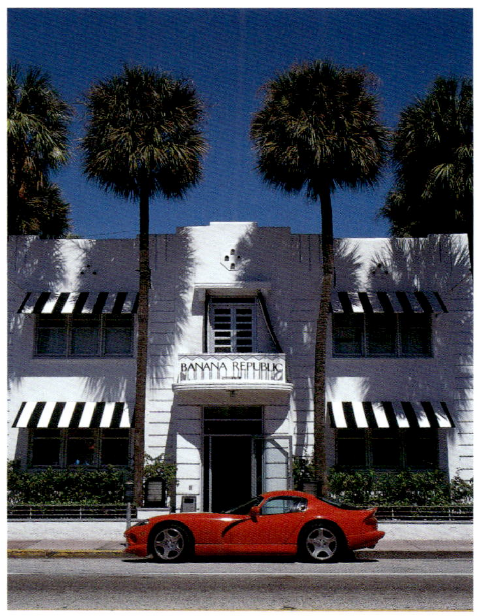

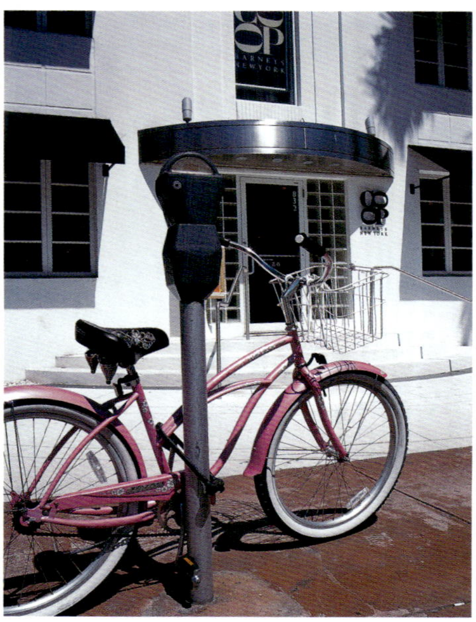

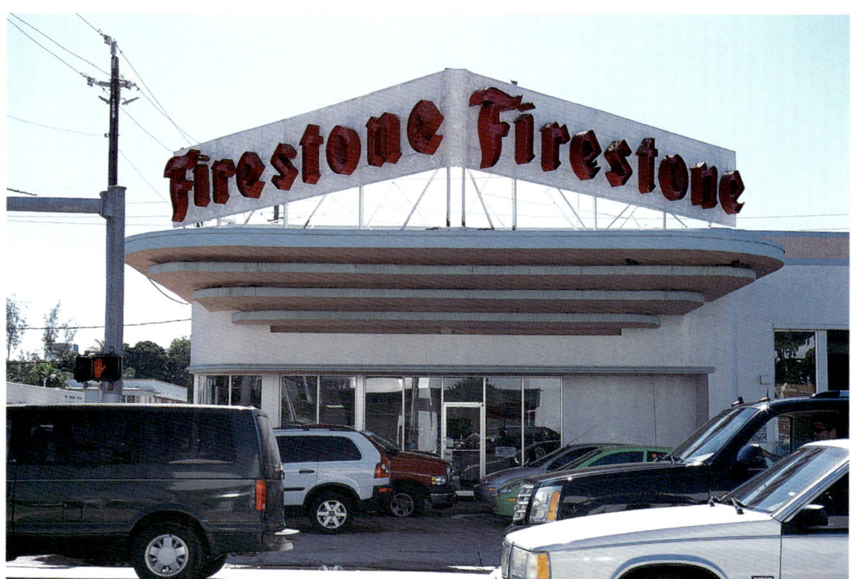

It is these people and places that are the *raison-d'être* of this book.

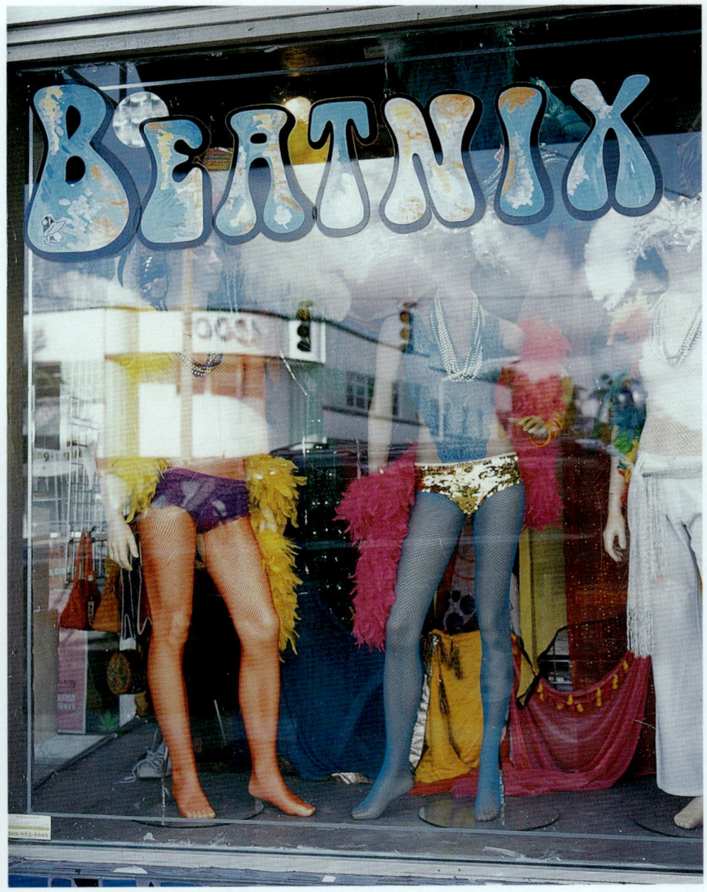

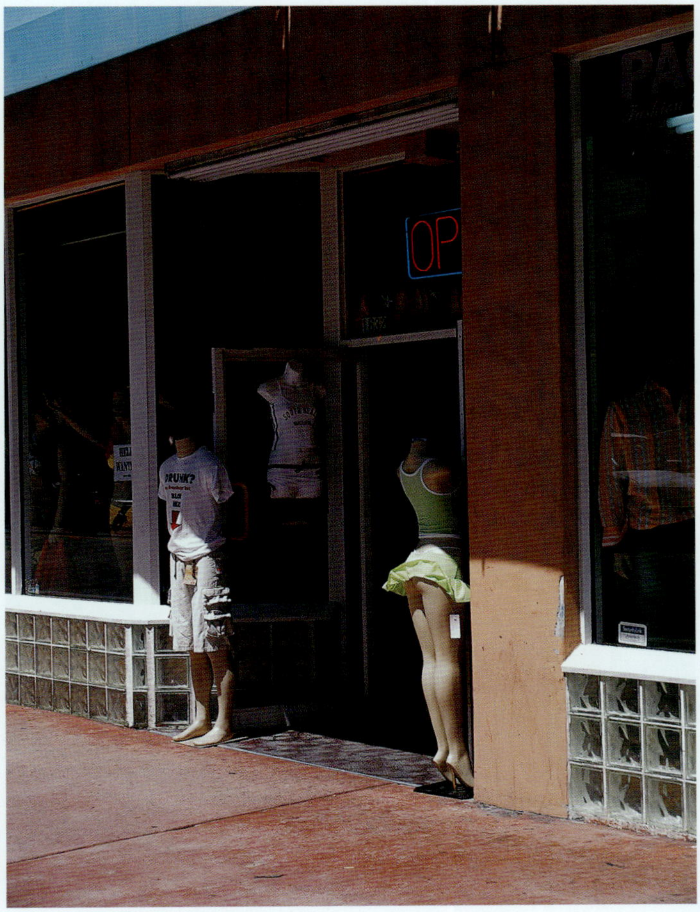

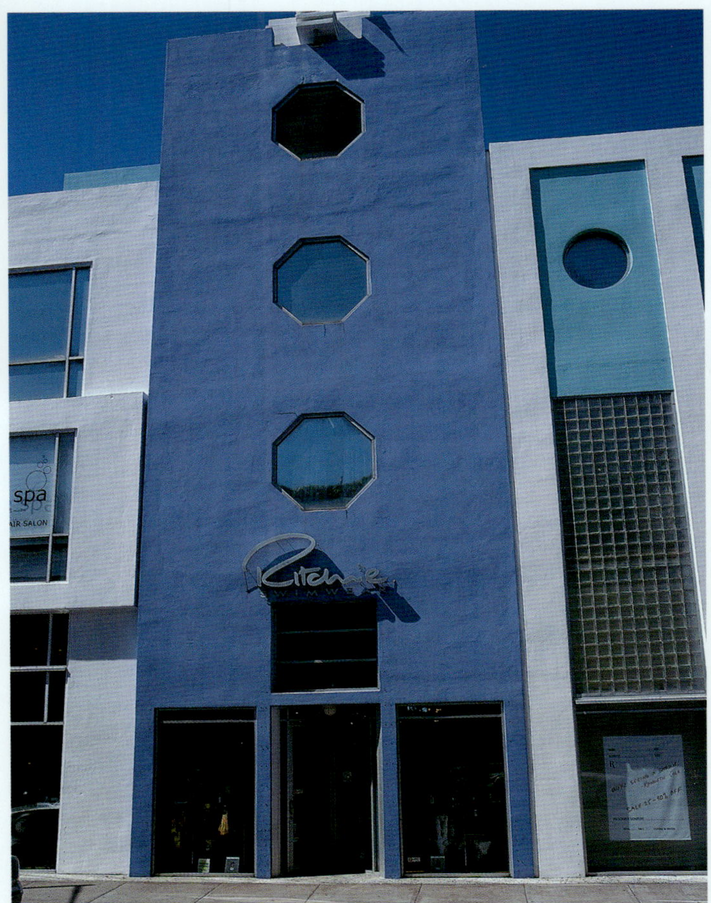

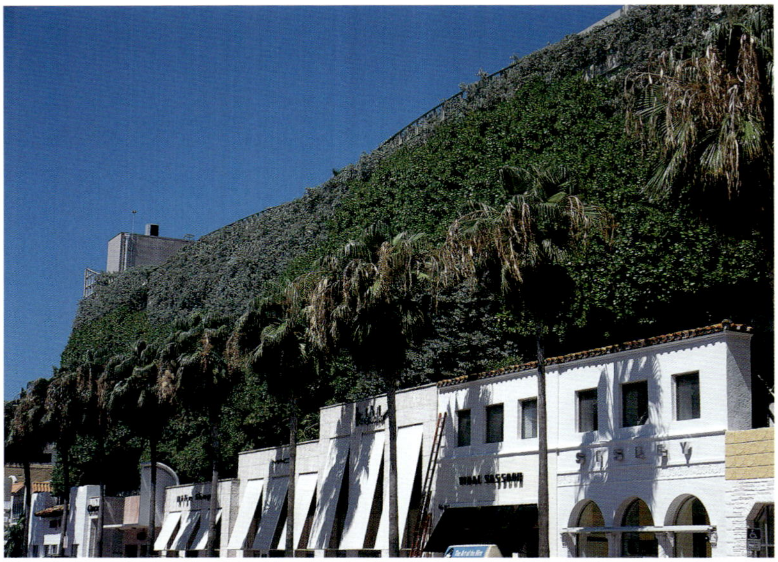

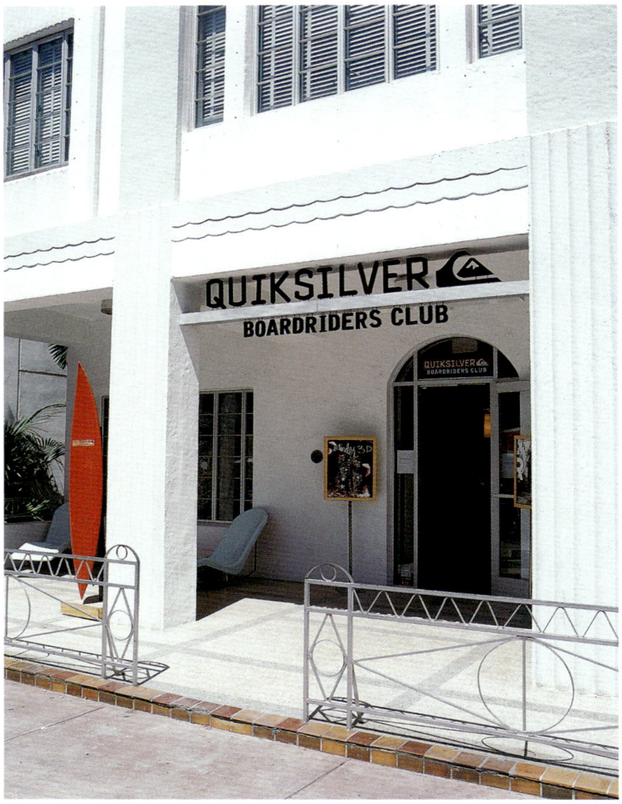
QUIKSILVER
BOARDRIDERS CLUB

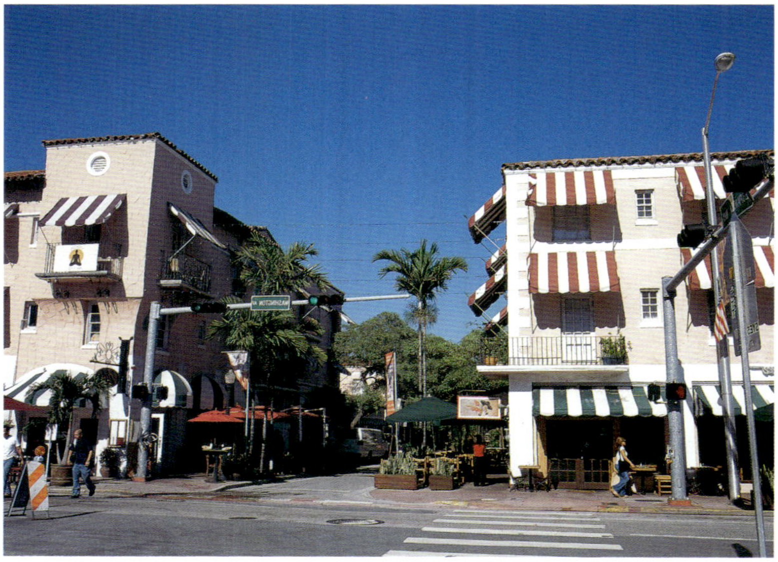

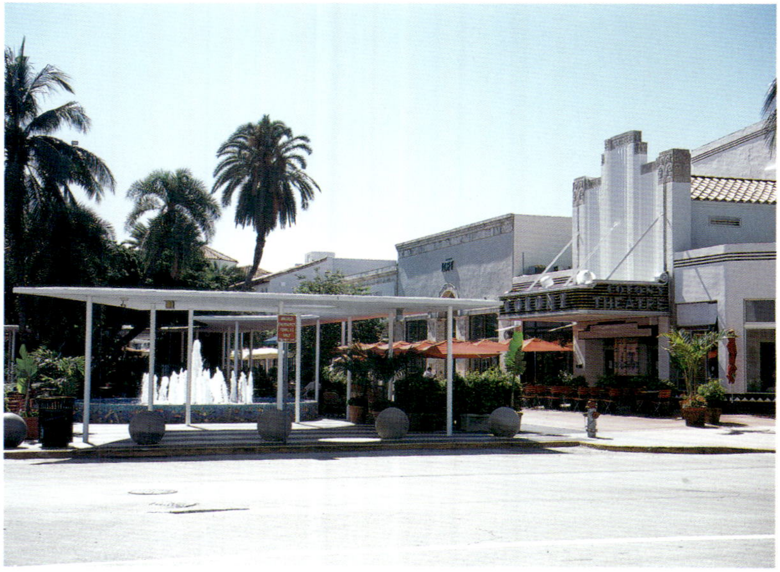

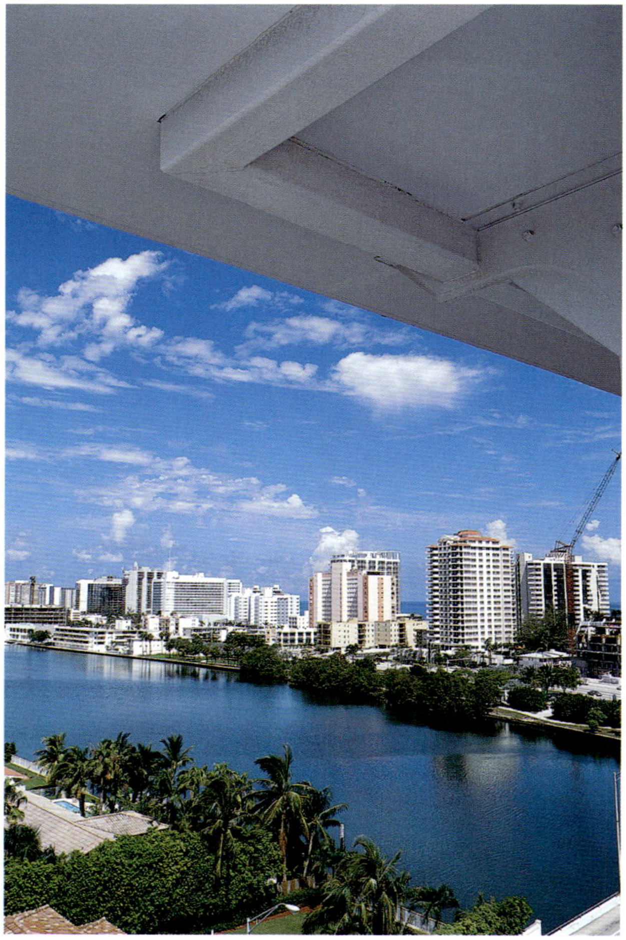

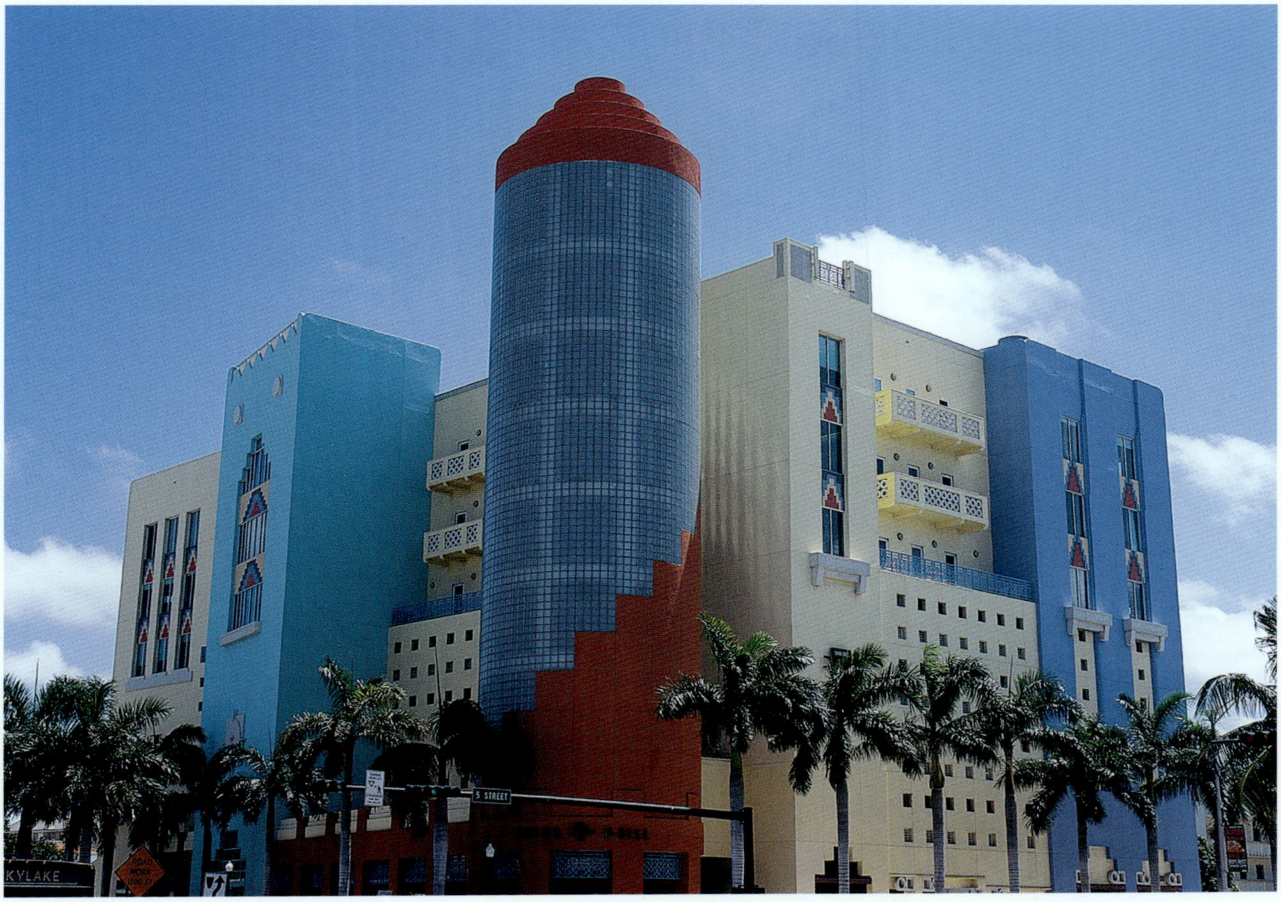
5 STREET

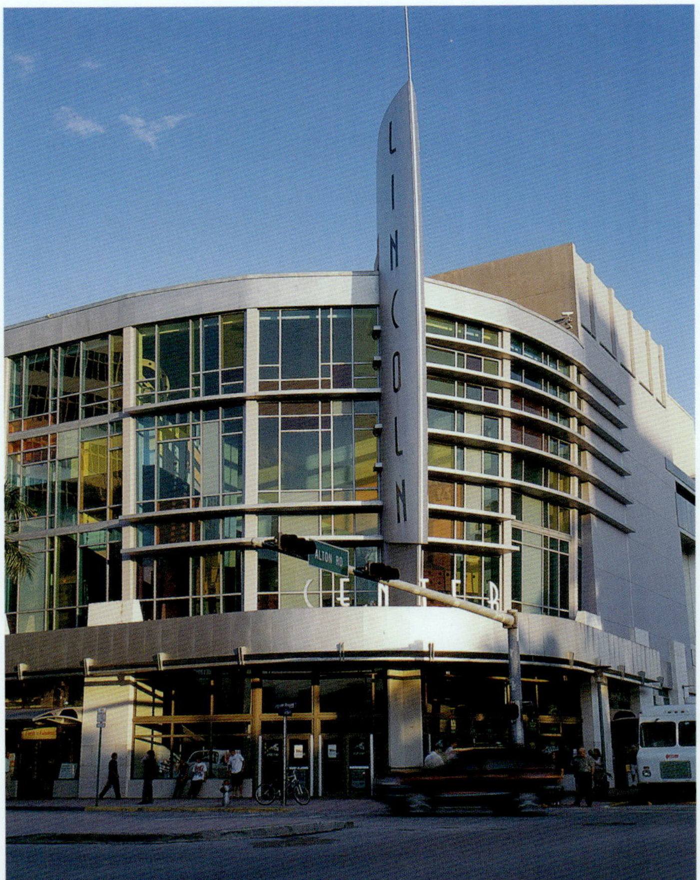
LINCOLN

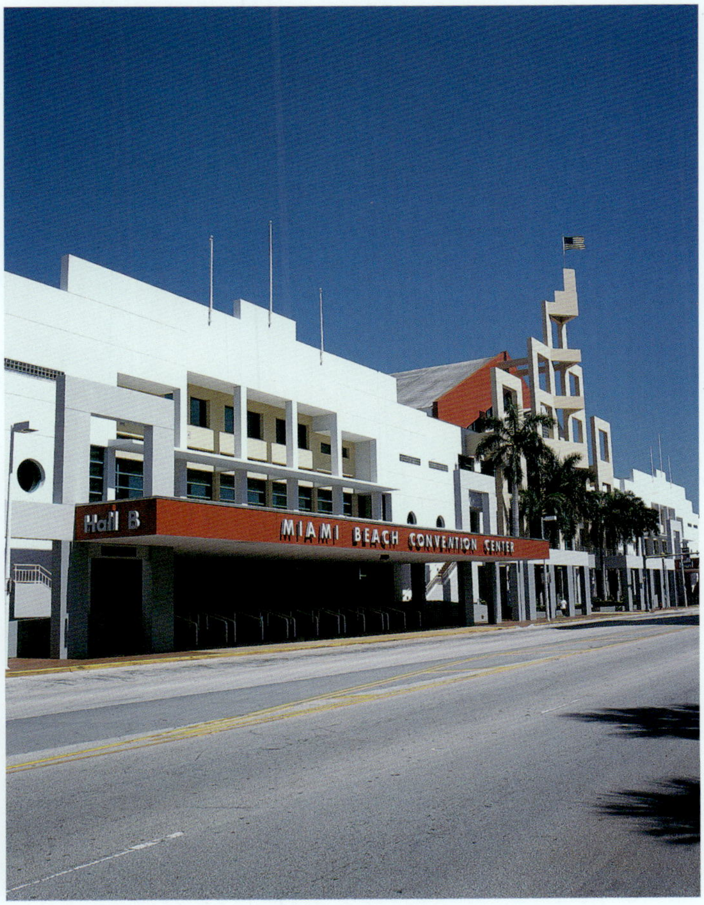
Hall B
MIAMI BEACH CONVENTION CENTER

Chapter 1

GLORIA AND EMILIO ESTEFAN

THE "FIRST COUPLE"

Few, if any, major American cities can fairly be said to have one couple that stands out as "The First Couple." After all, a place like Miami is so large and diverse that it can barely fit on only one ethnic, cultural, or even geographic map.

But Miami does have its acknowledged first couple, of course. Who else but "Gloria and Emilio," a couple whose influence is so broad and appreciated that the conversational use of their last name has, at least locally, become unnecessary.

Everyone knows about the multiple awards that Gloria and Emilio Estefan have received, including Producer of the Year (Emilio), Best Album and Best Performance (Gloria), and Songwriter of the Year (both). And most people know that Gloria has sung for the Pope and Emilio has been a Presidential appointee. But if you're a Miamian, you're also aware and appreciative that Gloria and Emilio have become the First Couple not just of entertainment, but also the First Couple of caring and generosity in their community.

Never having forgotten their Cuban roots, even after conquering North America and the world, the Estefans have also never forgotten the less fortunate. They have played a leading role in the globally significant work of the Miami Project to Cure Paralysis, have established the Gloria Estefan Foundation to help those whom society has otherwise left behind, and are the guiding hands behind the great success of a host of other Latin artists who have followed their lead, including Shakira, Jennifer Lopez, and Ricky Martin. To those who ask what could possibly top the record of achievement that this couple has already attained, they have even more surprises in store. Hints: their latest ventures include a children's book by Gloria, her eagerly awaited screenplay, and an international chain of Cuban restaurants (starting with Miami's own Bongo's Cuban Café in the American Airlines Arena) created by Emilio to spread the rich culture of the native land the Estefans have never forsaken.

Within South Beach itself, Gloria and Emilio are a constant presence, with their corporate headquarters building on Fifth Street, their boutique Cardozo Hotel at 1300 Ocean Drive, and their flagship restaurant, Larios, nearby at 820 Ocean.

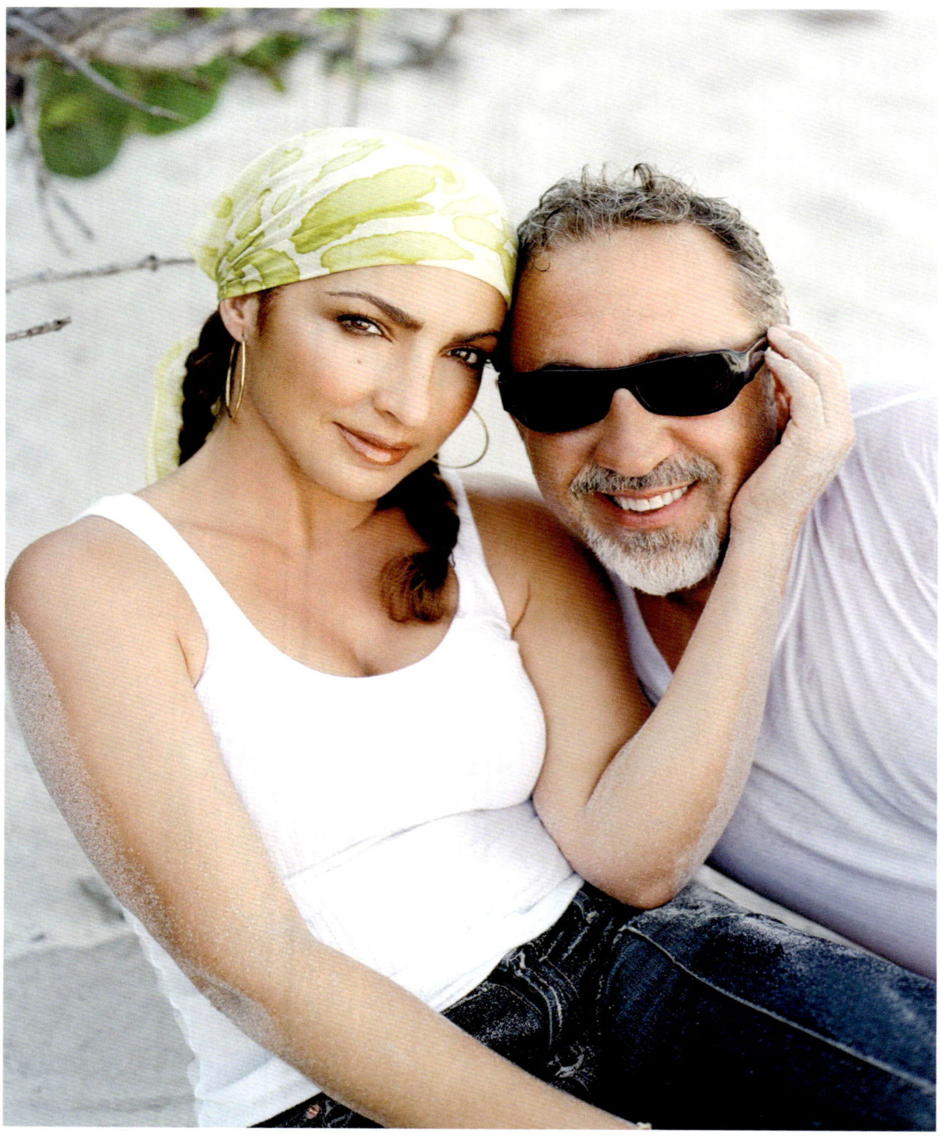

Photo by Alberto Tolot

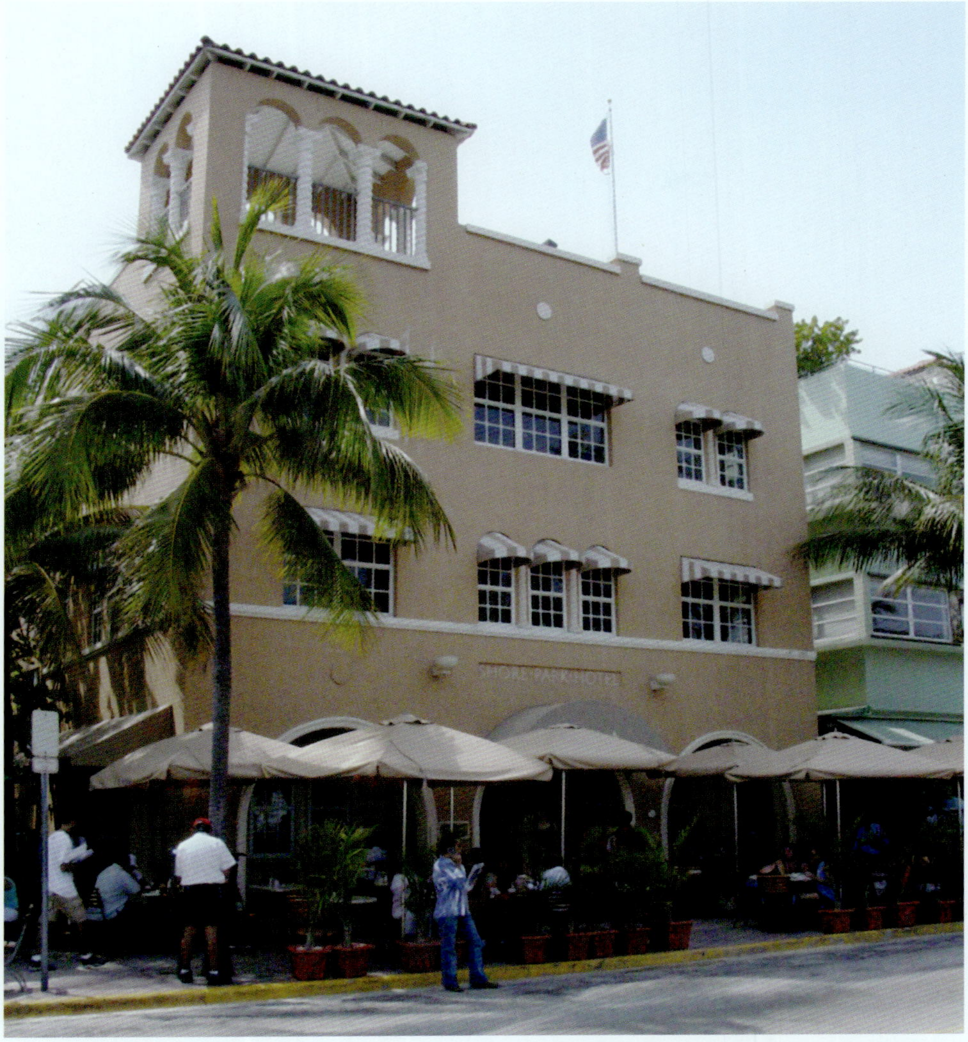

Photo by Dan Forer

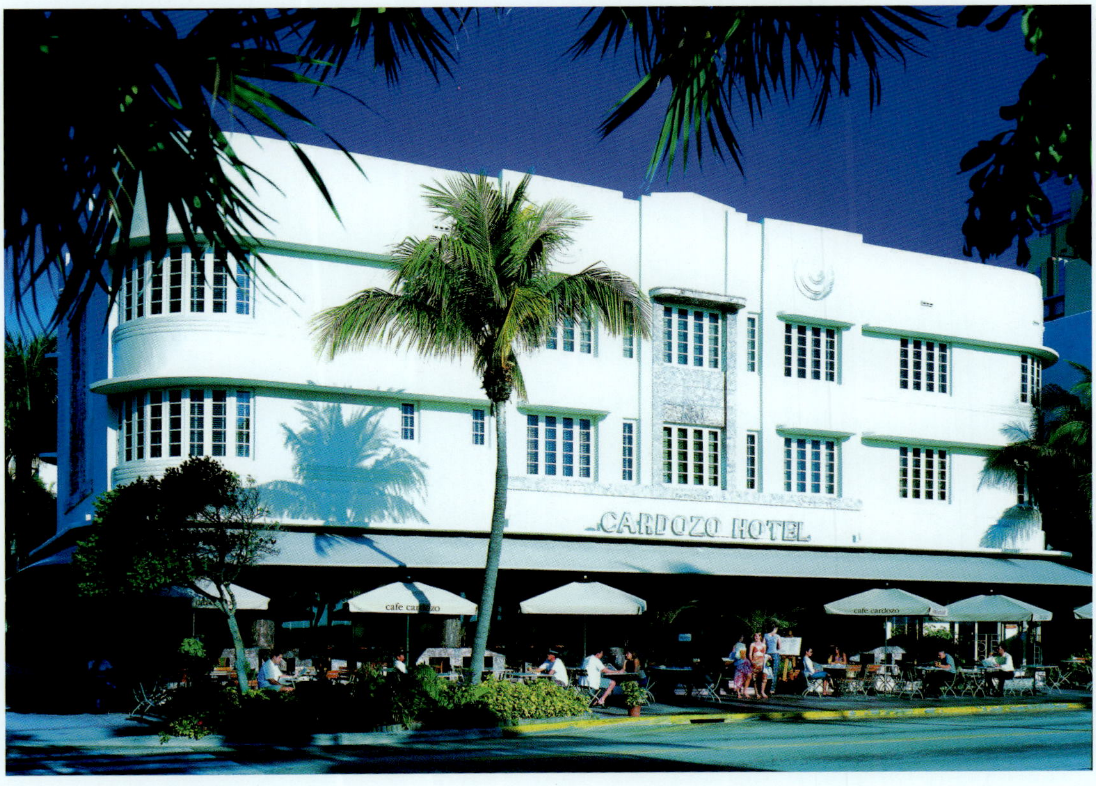

Photo by Marc Sillman

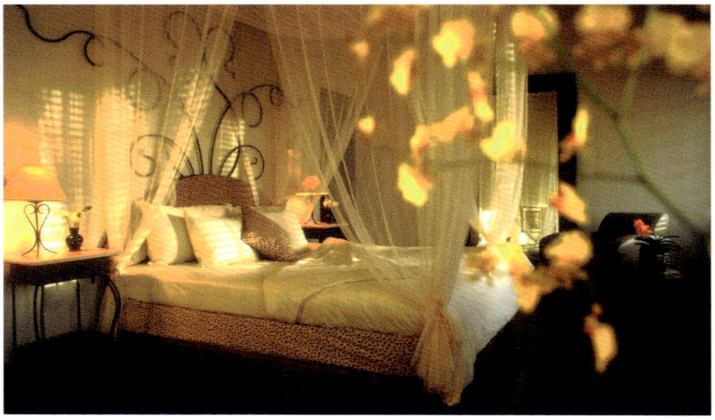

Photo by Cookie Kinkead

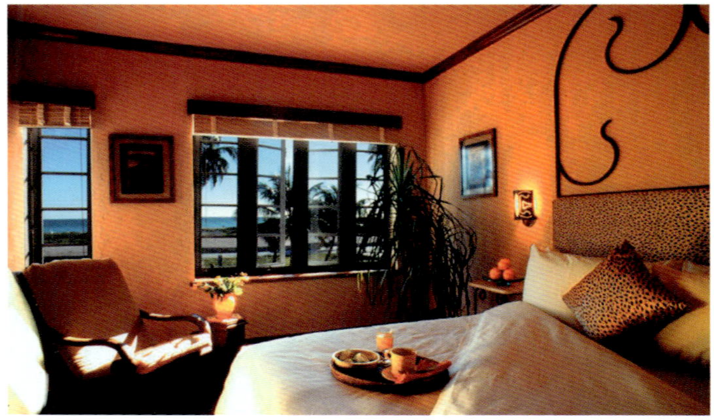

Photo by Cookie Kinkead

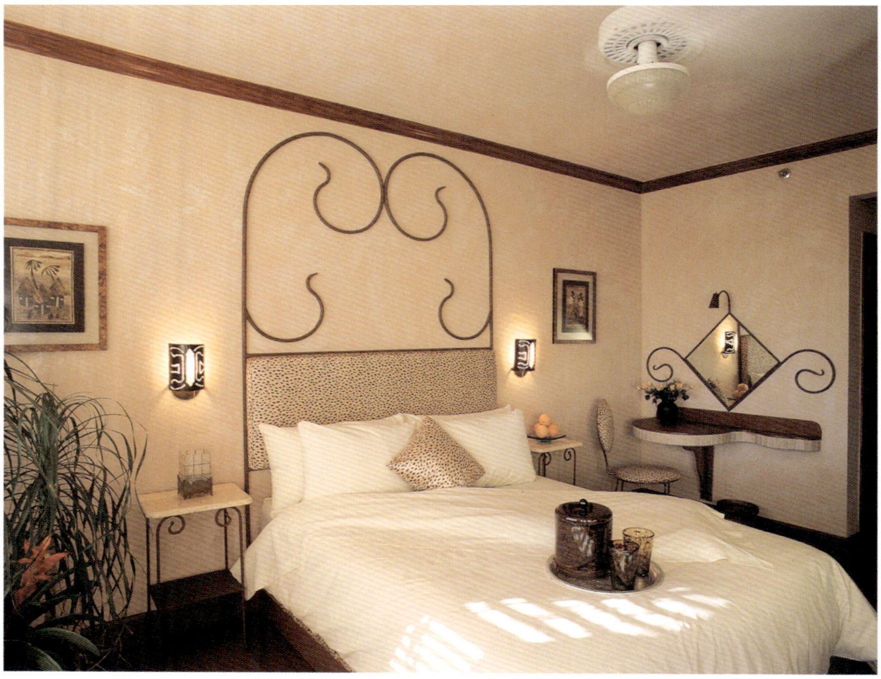

Photo by Cookie Kinkead

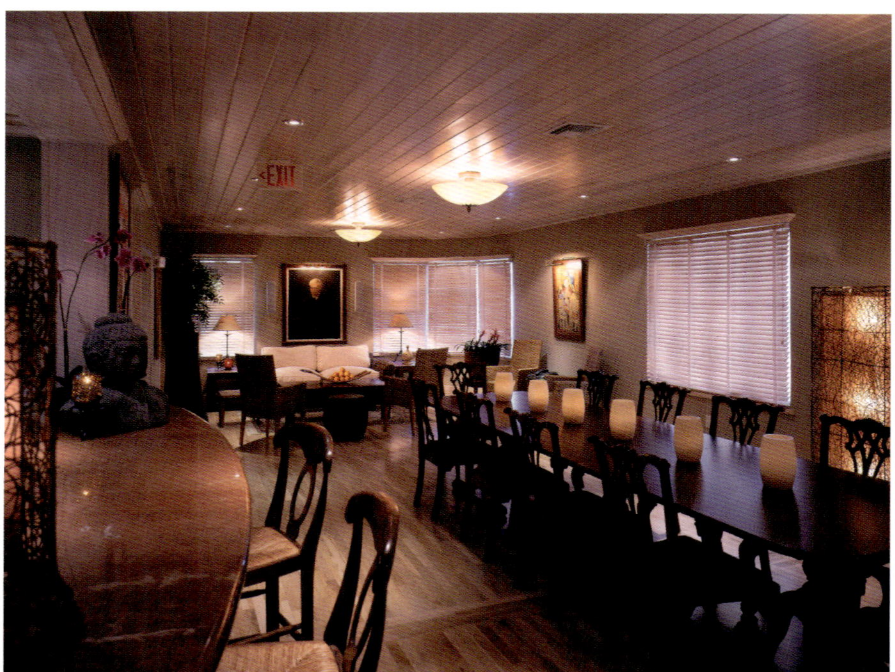

Photo by Marc Sillman

Photo by Dan Forer

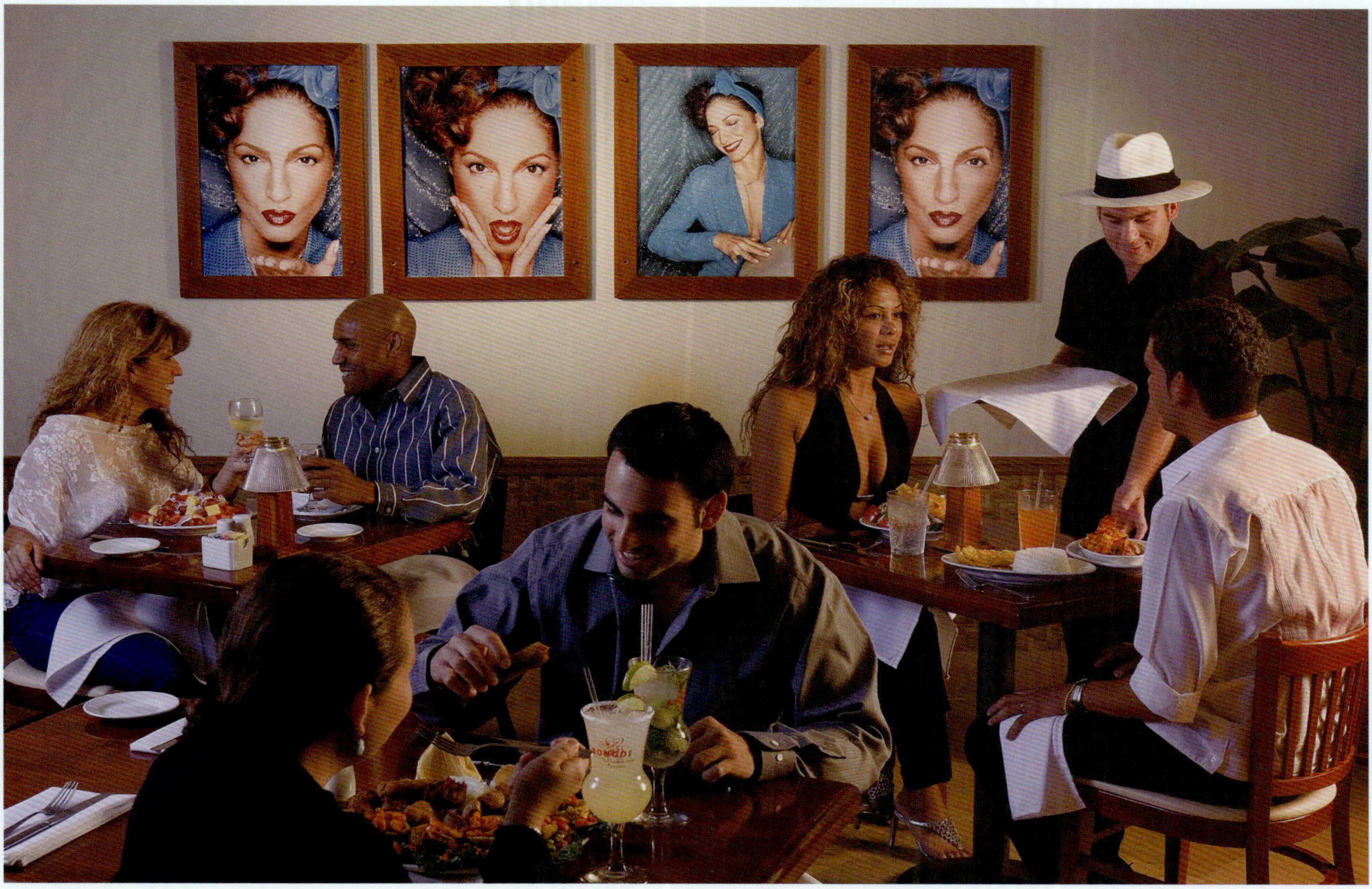

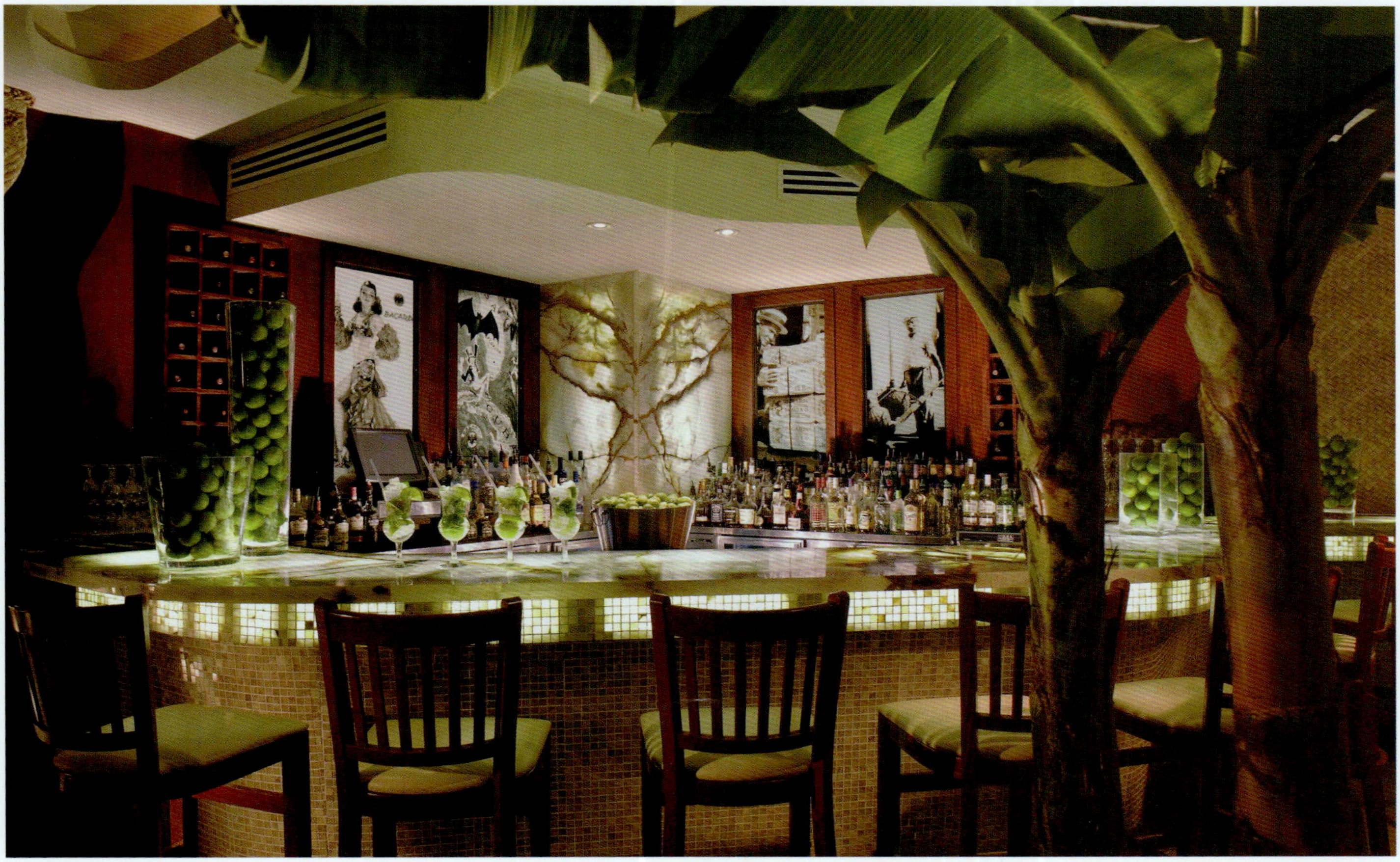

Photo by Dan Forer

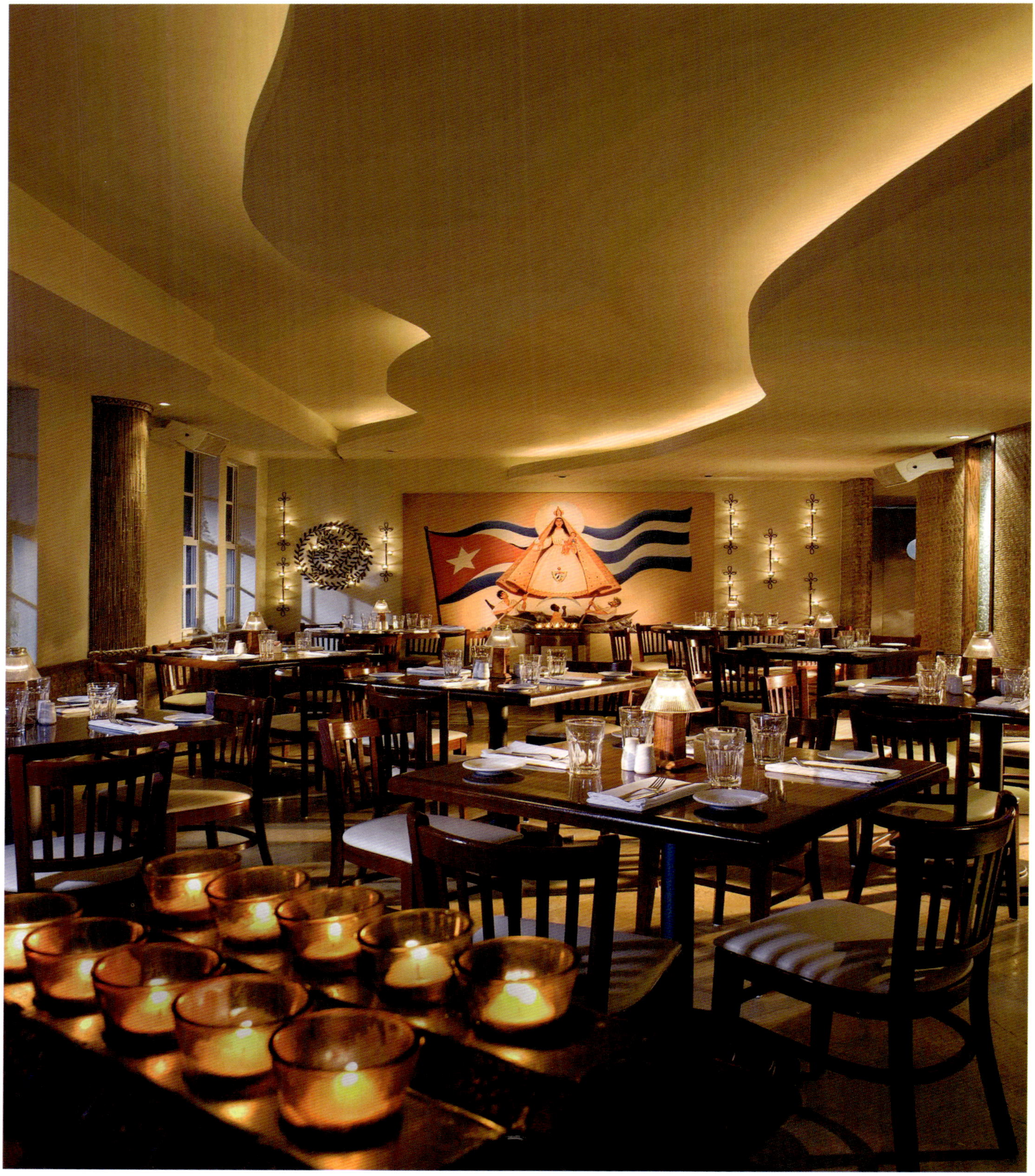

Photo by Dan Forer

Chapter 2

SOUTH BEACH'S TOP COP

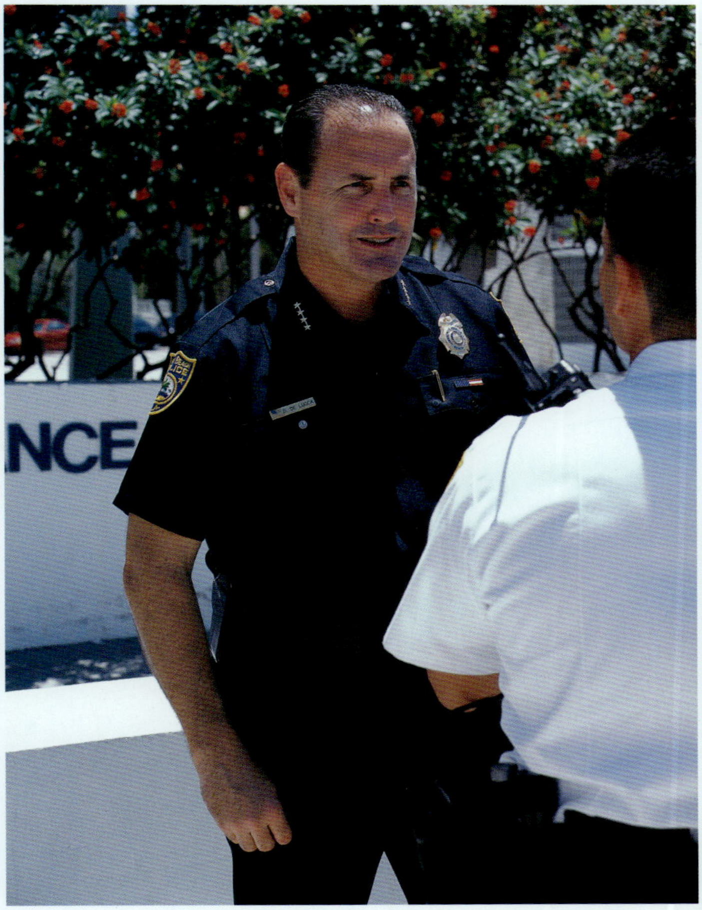

CHIEF DONALD DE LUCCA

Maybe it's no surprise that, in always-surprising South Beach, even the Chief of Police looks as if he could have been chosen for the top-cop role in a movie. And just as amazing is that his police headquarters building seems to have been imagined by a Hollywood set designer for *Miami Vice*.

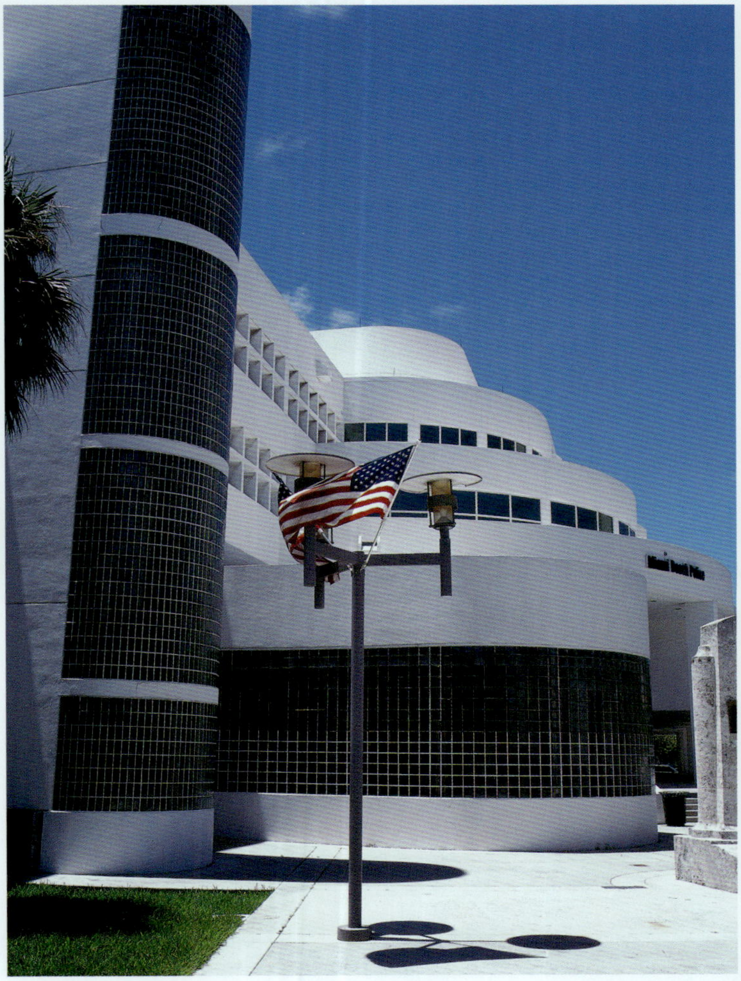

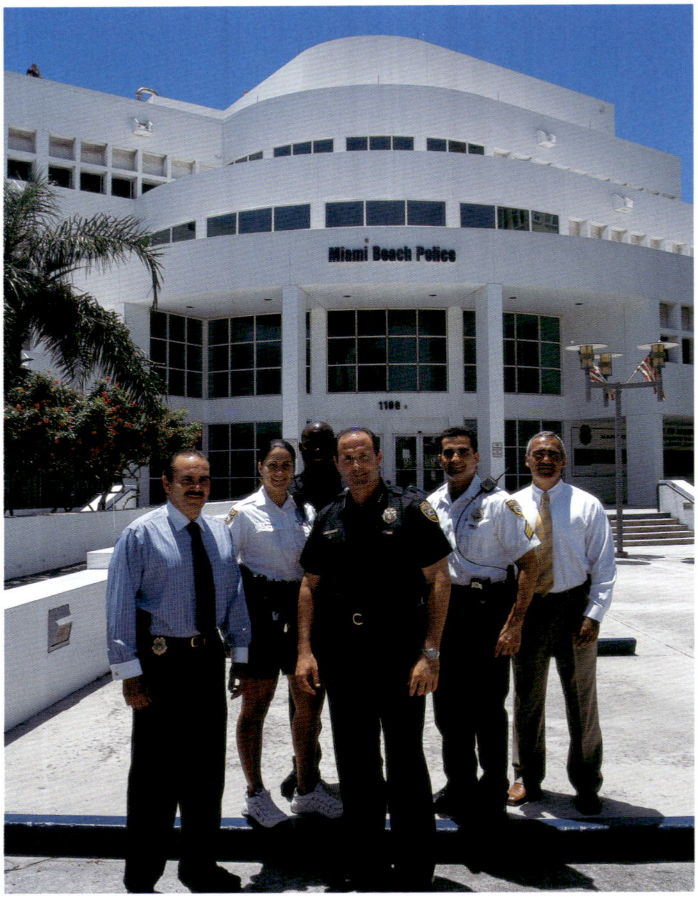

Chief Donald De Lucca, like most others in "South Beach's finest," was born in the United States, but don't let his Latin-sounding name fool you—he's pureblood Italian stallion and proud of it.

In keeping with the "live and let live" spirit of South Beach, Chief De Lucca's department has dedicated itself to maintaining the "human" dimension of police work for the benefit of Miami Beach residents and visitors alike.

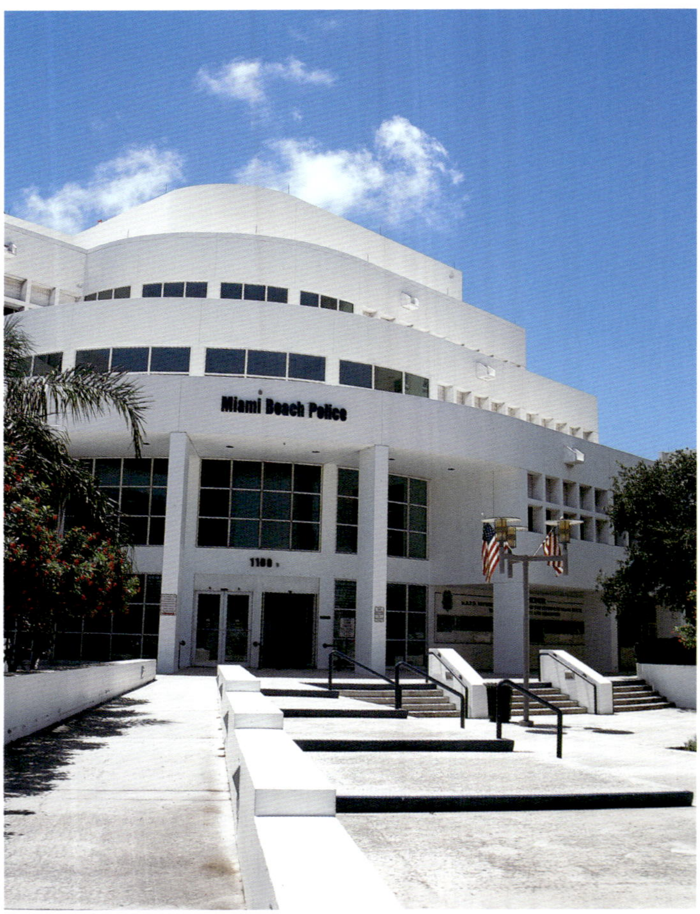

The "with-it" nature of the Police Department's building architecture is a hint about its approach to keeping the peace, as exemplified by its leading role in developing and applying the use of innovative non-lethal weapons in all but the most desperate circumstances. It's an eloquent commentary on all of South Beach that this particular piece of urban architecture is listed as an official "location" site for filmmakers looking to find a sexy cinema backdrop.

Chapter 3

CORNELIUS VICTOR-IOUS

CORNELIUS POLK AND THE VICTOR HOTEL

Recent arrivals along Ocean Drive include the handsome face-and-façade combination of the Victor Hotel and Cornelius L. Polk, II. After many years of abandonment, the Victor has reappeared on South Beach's most glamorous street with more glamour than ever.

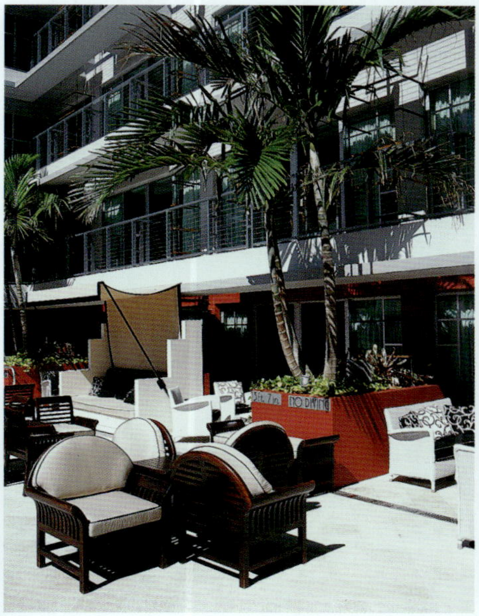

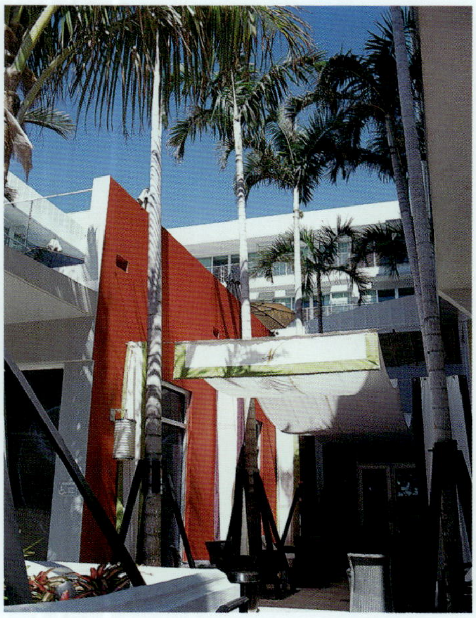

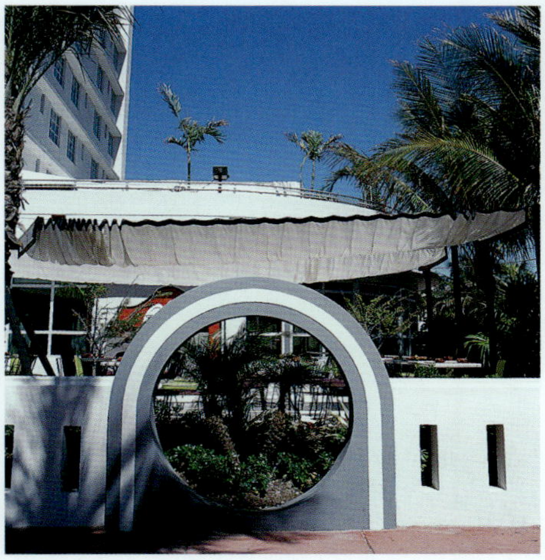

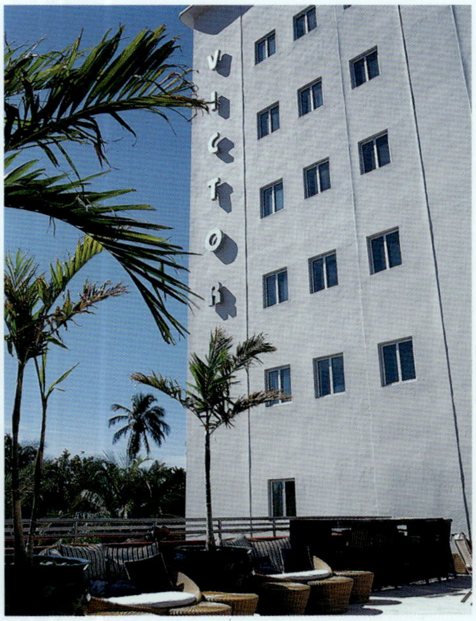

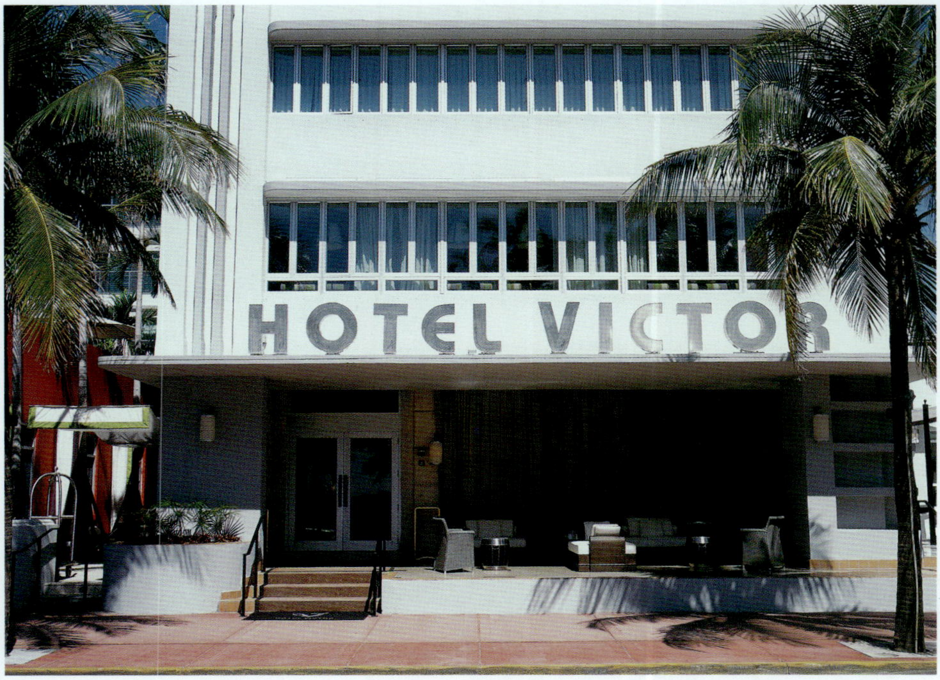

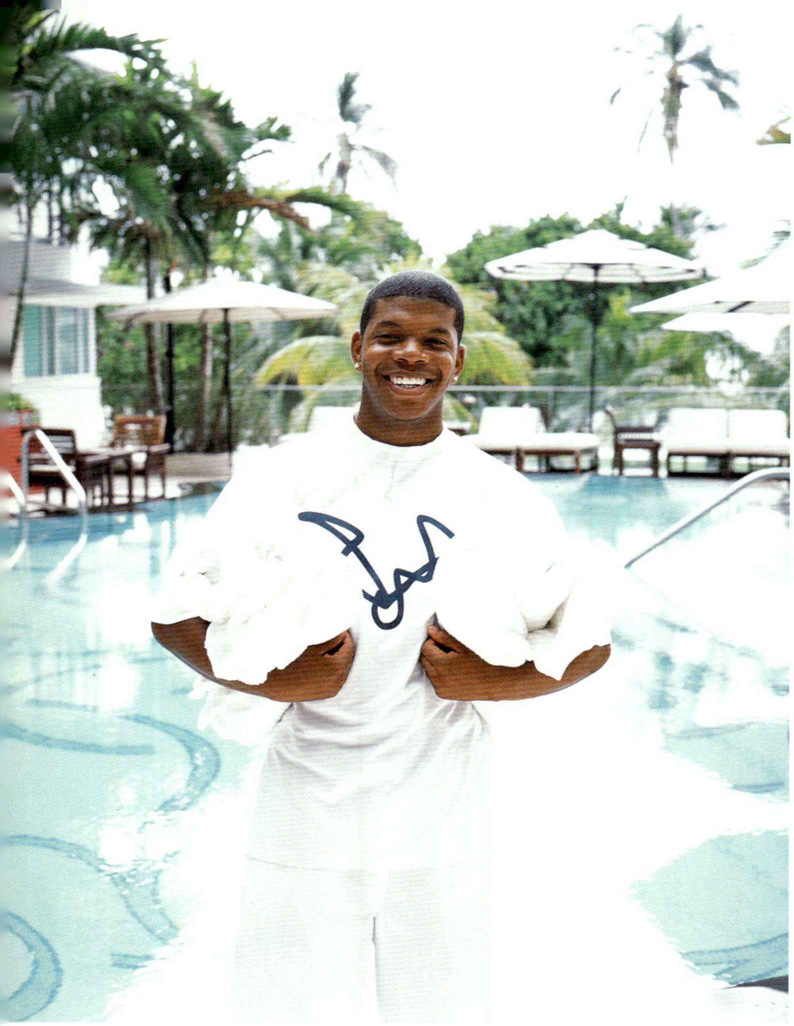
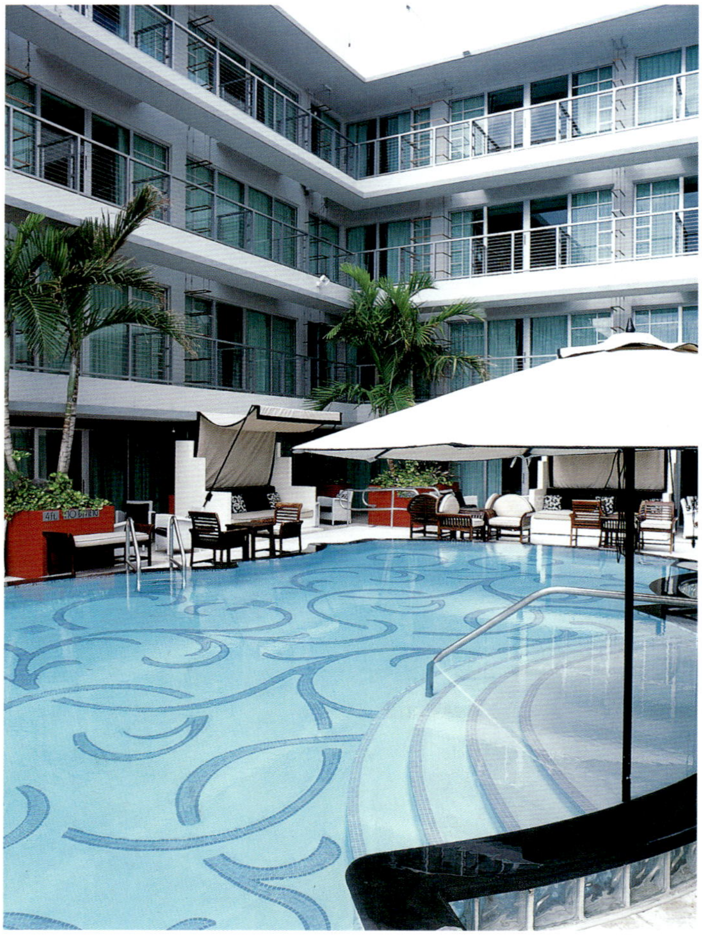
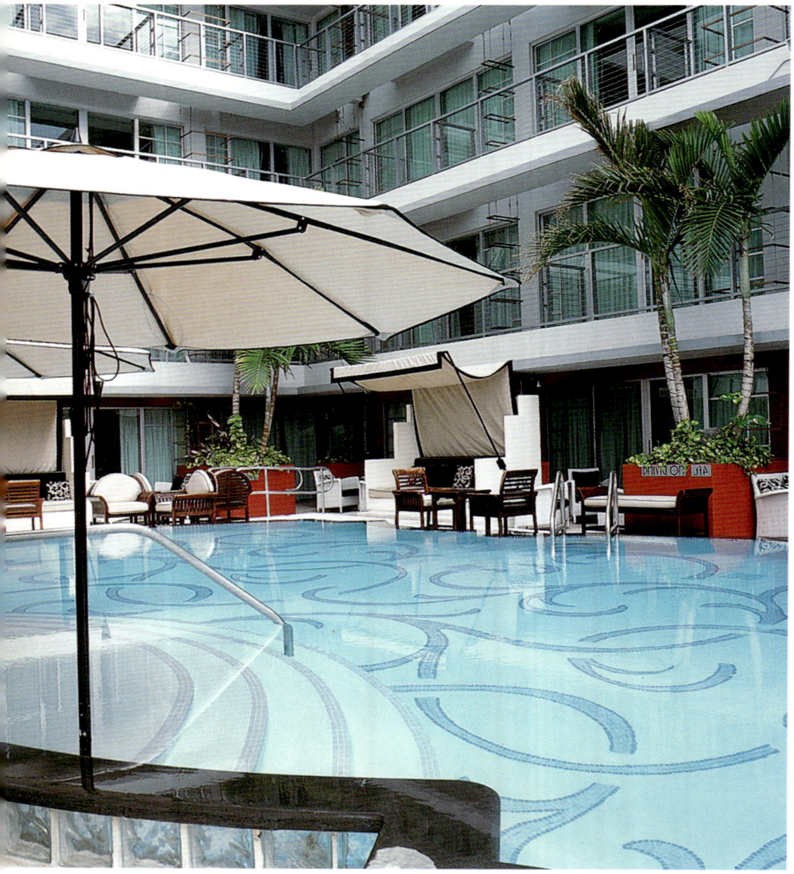
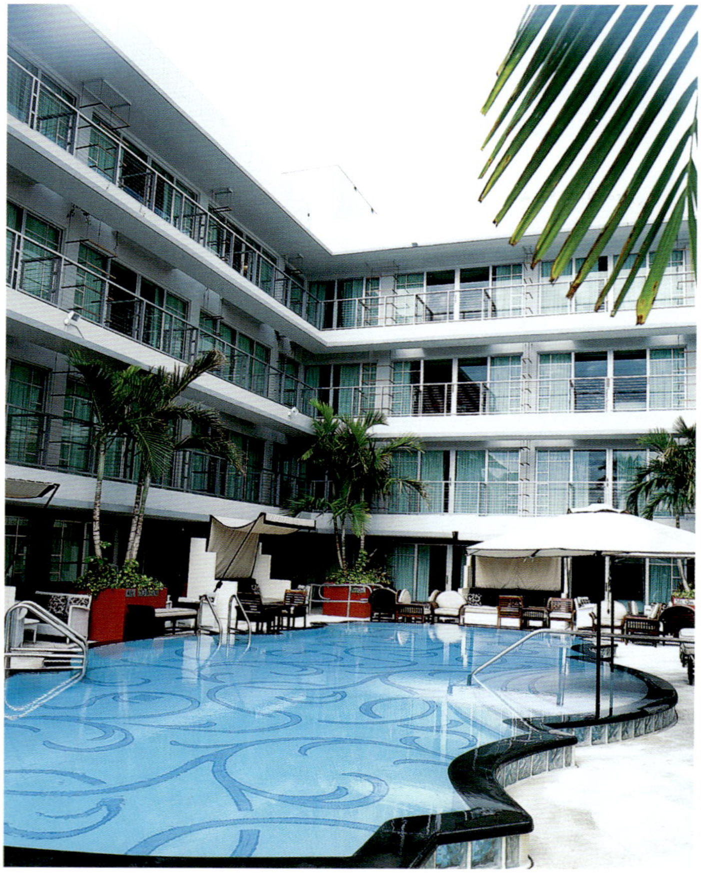

Among its attractive accoutrements is Cornelius Polk, who came from Dallas to Miami to study at Johnson and Wales University and currently works (works?) at the Victor's luxurious elevated pool. It seems as if Cornelius has picked the perfect spot to relish what he and so many others love about South Beach: "Scenery, clubs, and girls." A trifecta of earthly pleasures, inside and out.

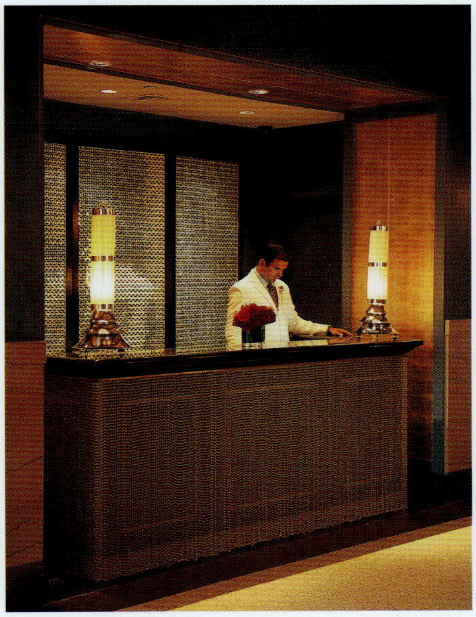

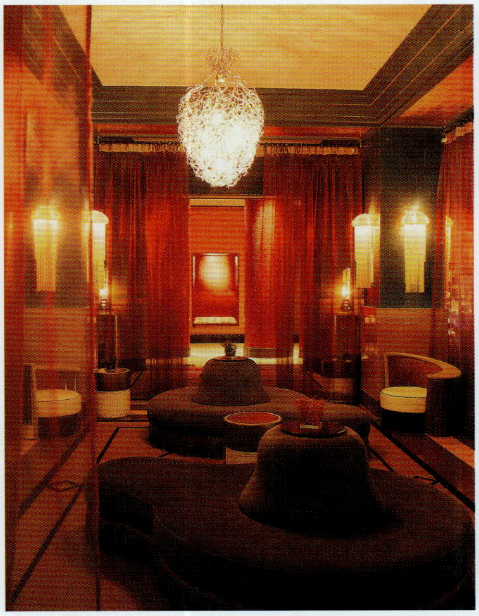

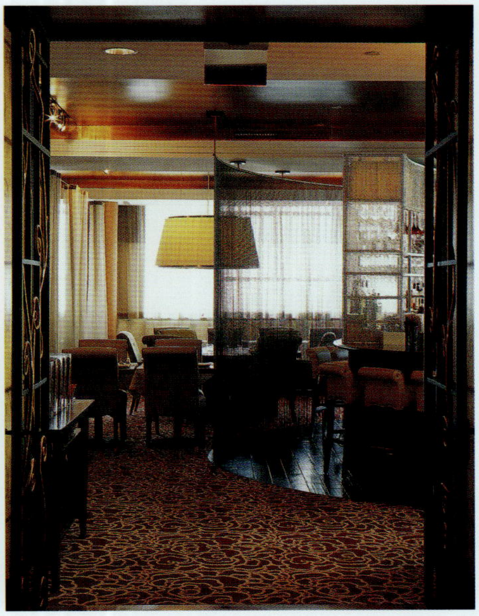

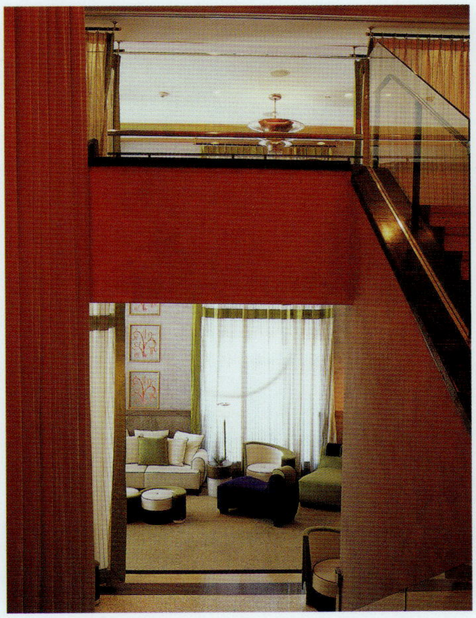

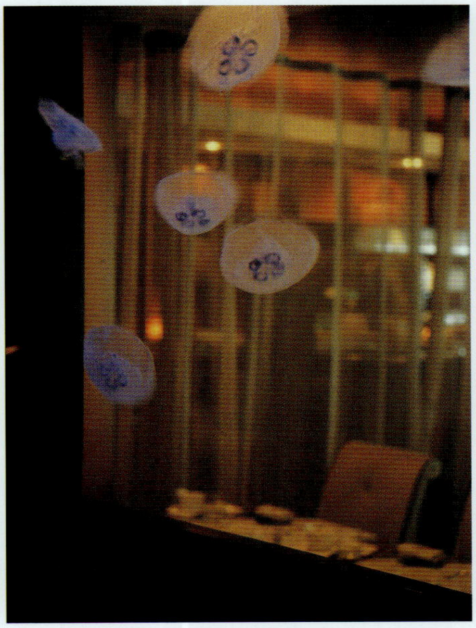

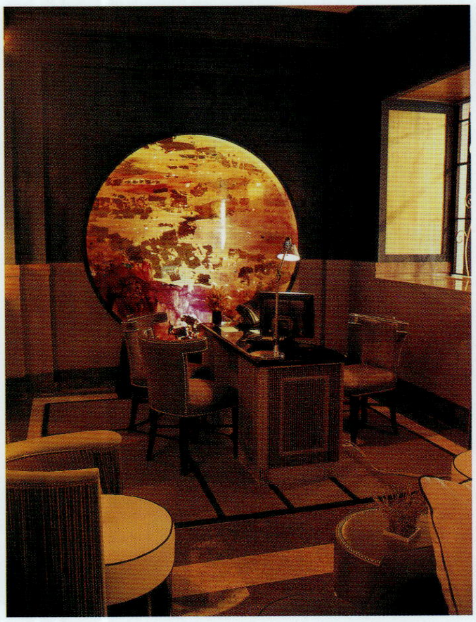

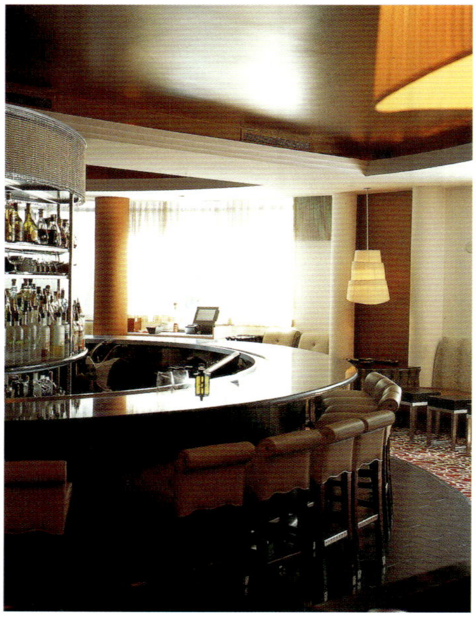

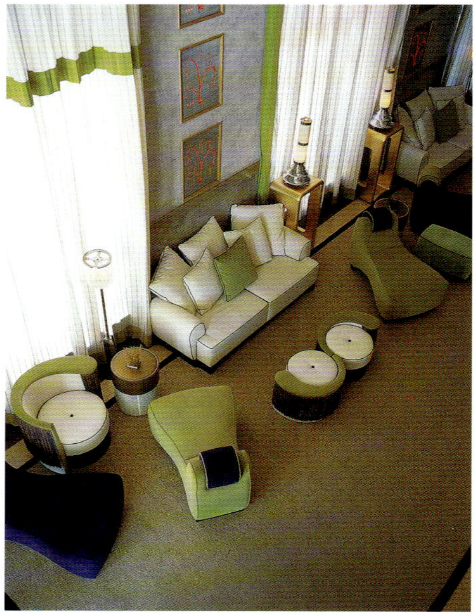

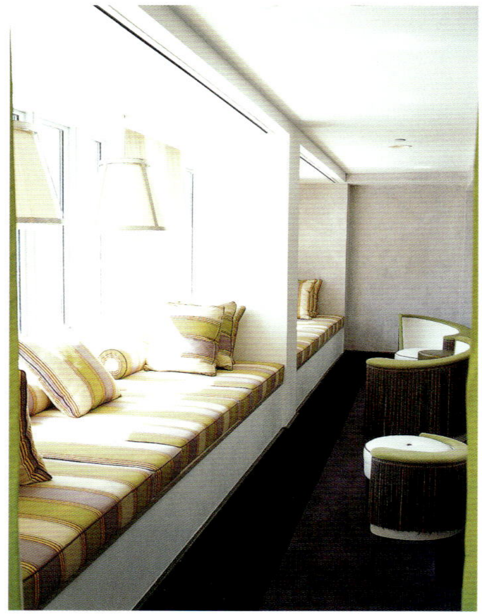

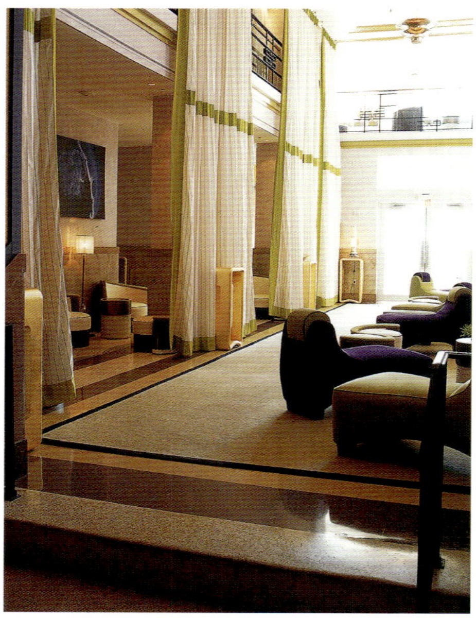

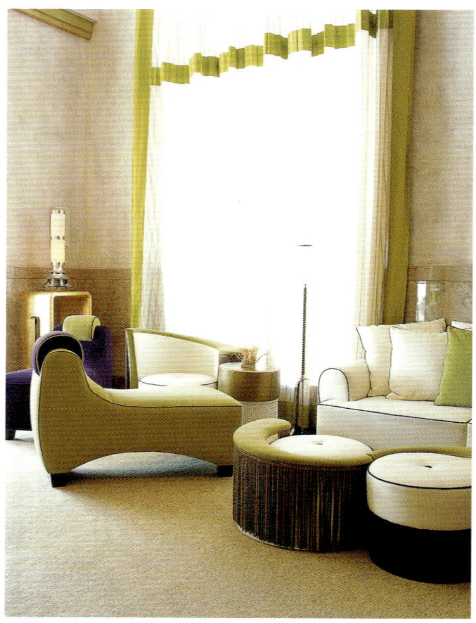

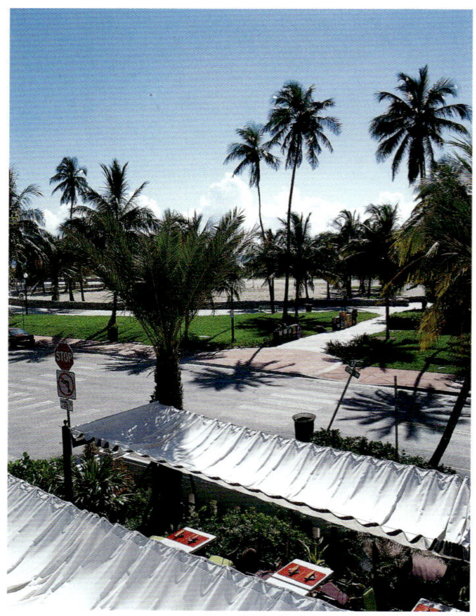

Chapter 4

GODFATHER

TONY GOLDMAN, HIS DAUGHTER, AND THE ECONOMIC RENAISSANCE OF SOUTH BEACH

If Barbara Baer Capitman was (and always will be) the spiritual godmother of the Art Deco District's esthetic, then Tony Goldman, a native and still seasonal New Yorker, is its godfather on the economic side. It was Tony, more and before anyone other than the Dacra Companies, who saw and invested in South Beach as a vibrant present-day economic engine.

If you think about it, part of the special charm of South Beach is not just to observe its visual quaintness from afar, but the fact that you can sleep, eat, drink, dance, and party in those very same quaint surroundings. South Beach is a living economic organism, the farthest thing one can imagine from the museum piece it may have become—and a lot of the credit for that goes to the Goldmans.

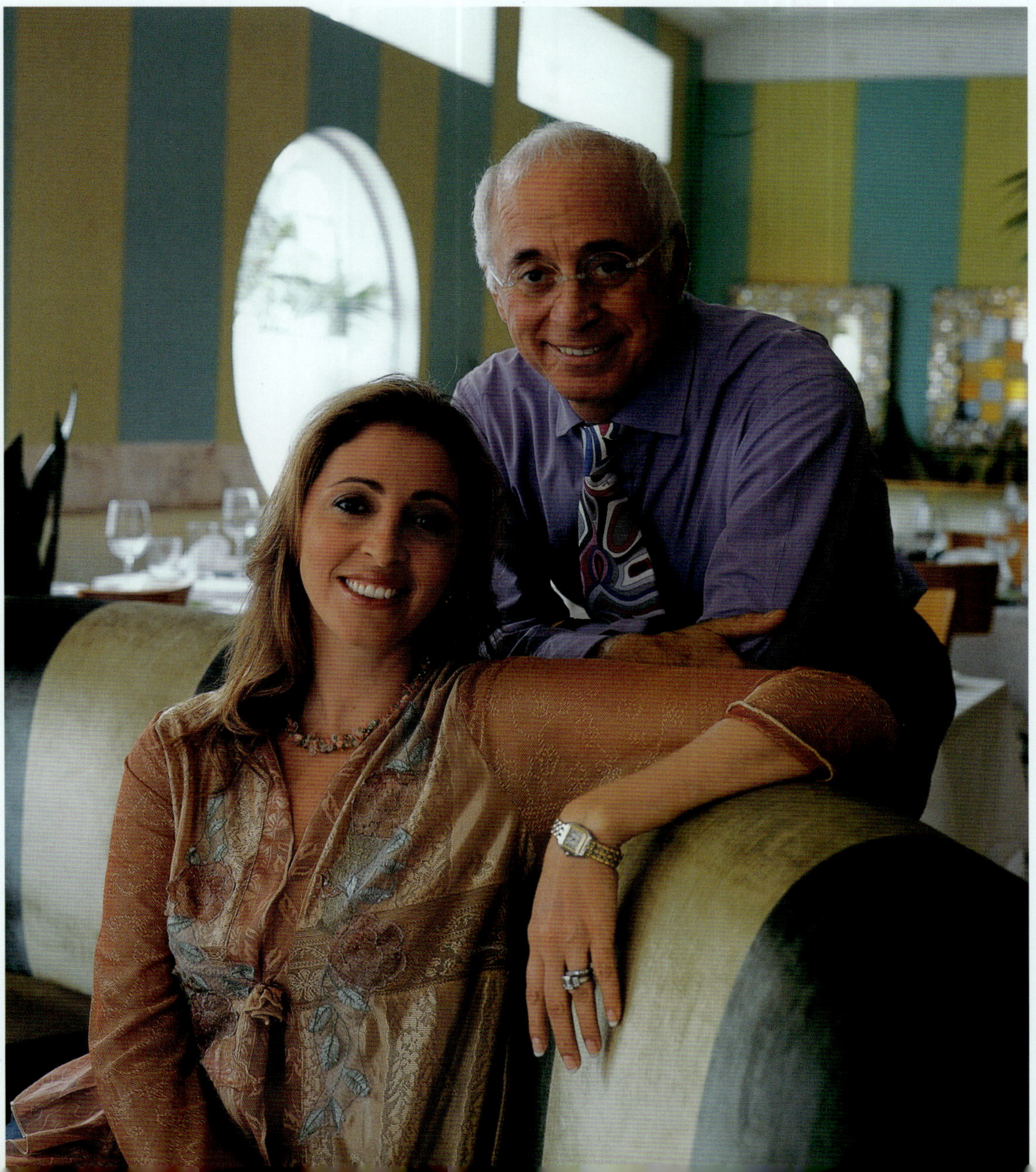

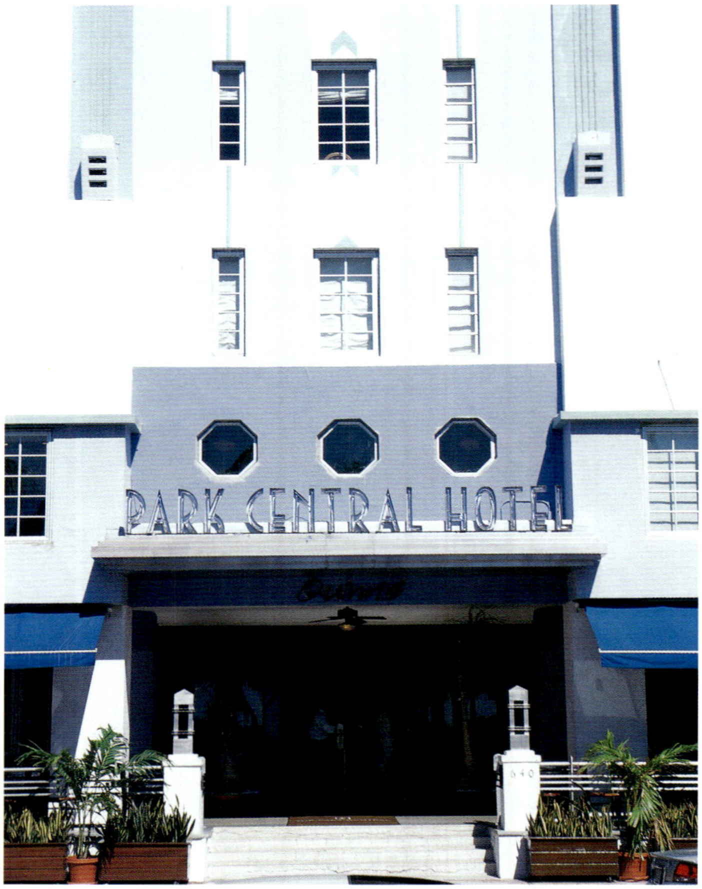

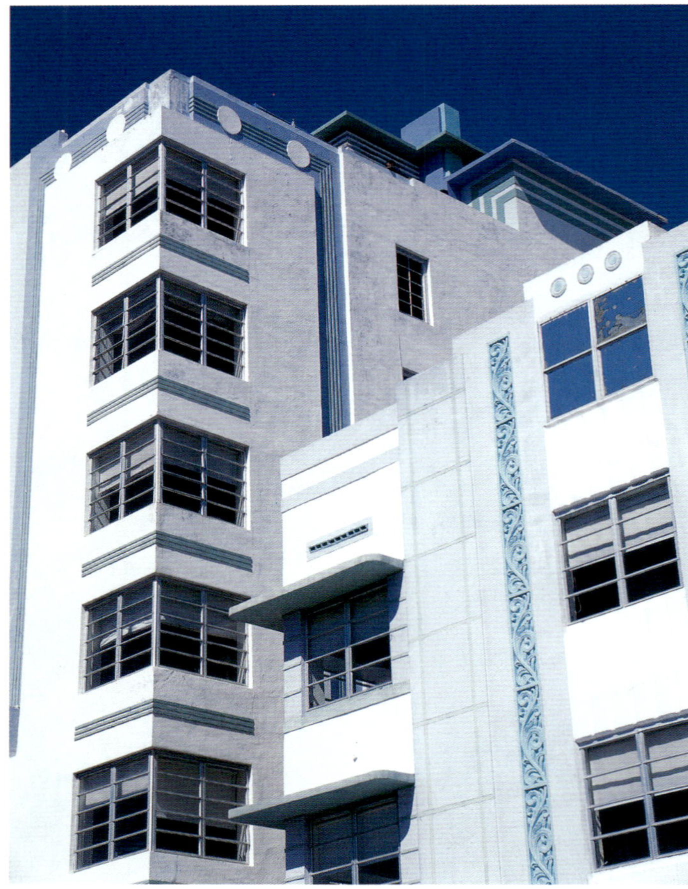

Tony first saw and acted upon his vision of the new South Beach back in the 1980s, and eventually invested in some of its leading "wedding cake hotel" properties. To name a couple: the Park Central at 640 Ocean Drive and "THE" Hotel at 801 Collins (which many locals still call the "Tiffany" Hotel, its name for many years before-the-trade-mark-objection by the famed New York jewelry concern). Both these properties, built in their optimistic style despite being constructed during the dark days of the late 1930s, certainly deserve their status as Art Deco icons.

Jessica Goldman-Srebnick is, like her father, a native New Yorker who splits her time between Gotham and the sea. She runs the family's hotel business and had a lot to do with the successful refurbishment of the Tiffany in 1998.

Tony Goldman's brilliance as a businessman should not be allowed to obscure some very "South Beach" things about him: He is reputed to be a mean crooner in the Frank Sinatra tradition, and he was married for the second time on the beach (literally on the beach)—his second marriage to his first wife Janet. Perhaps they should have been married on the beach the first time. The important thing is they discovered South Beach for them...and for us.

TIFFANY

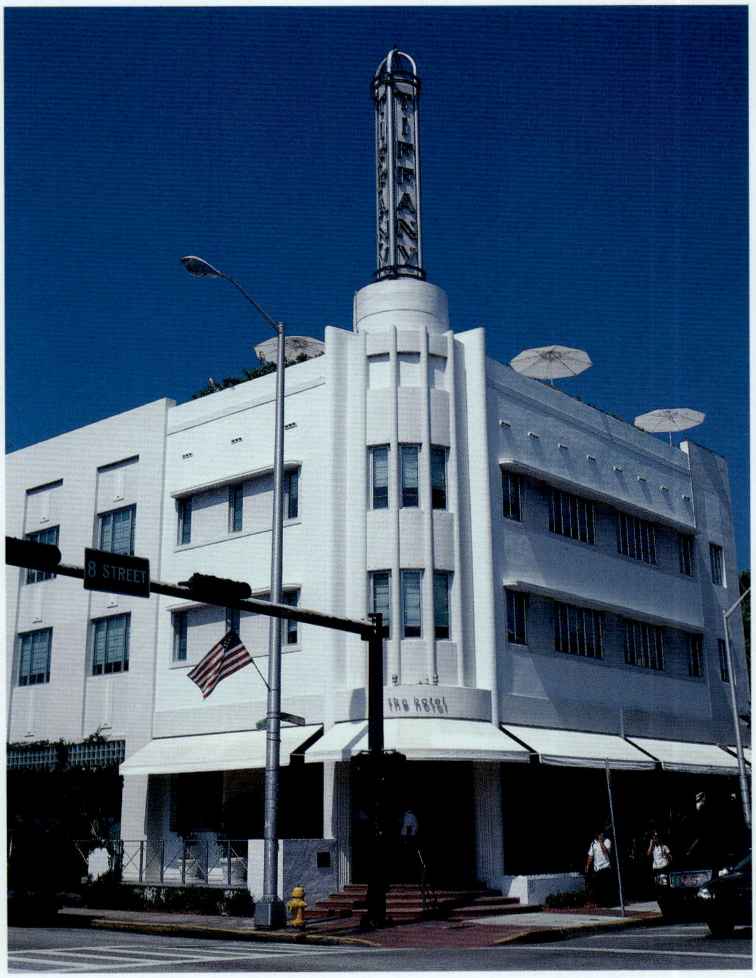
TIFFANY
8 STREET

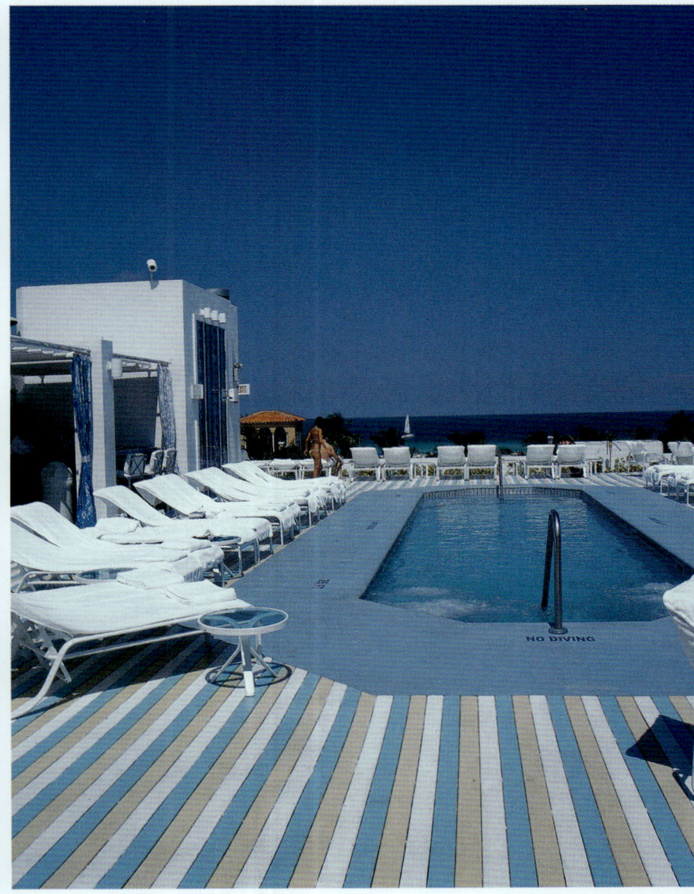
NO DIVING

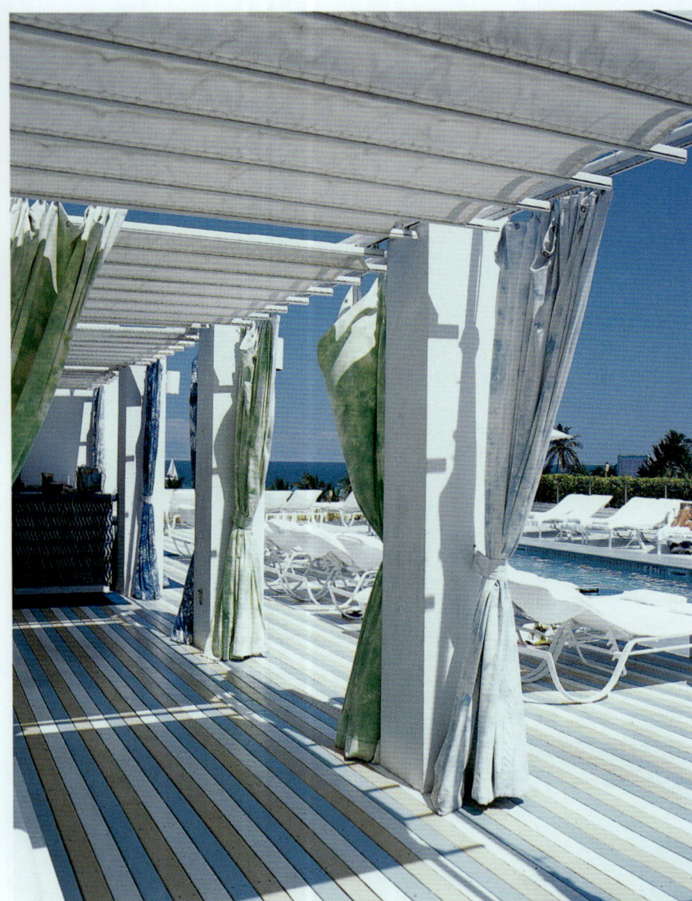

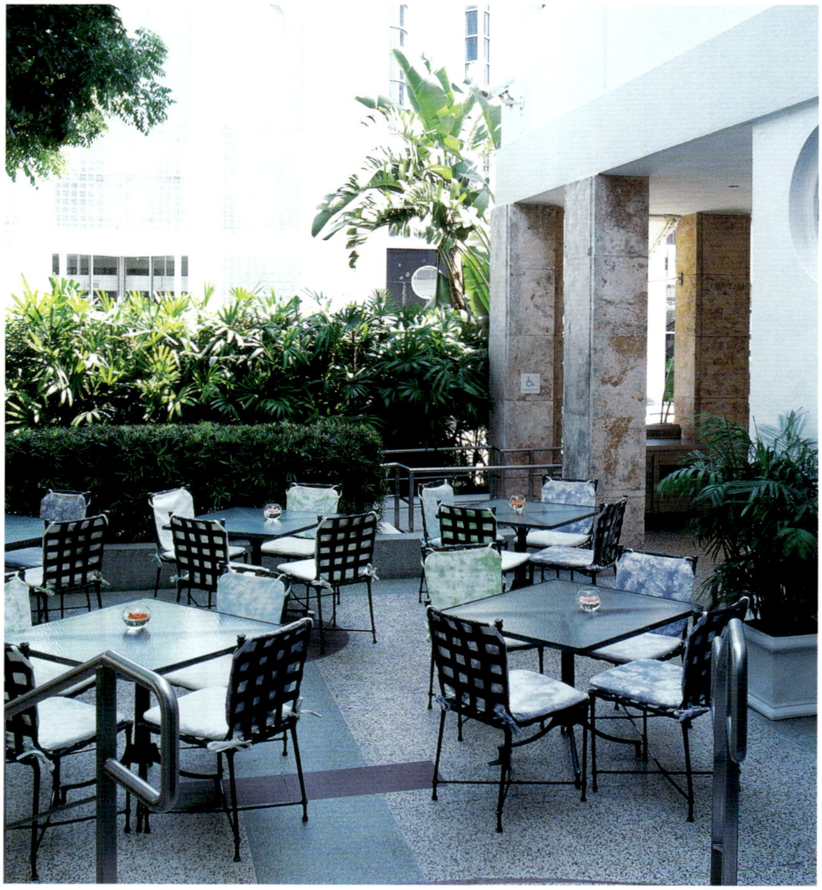

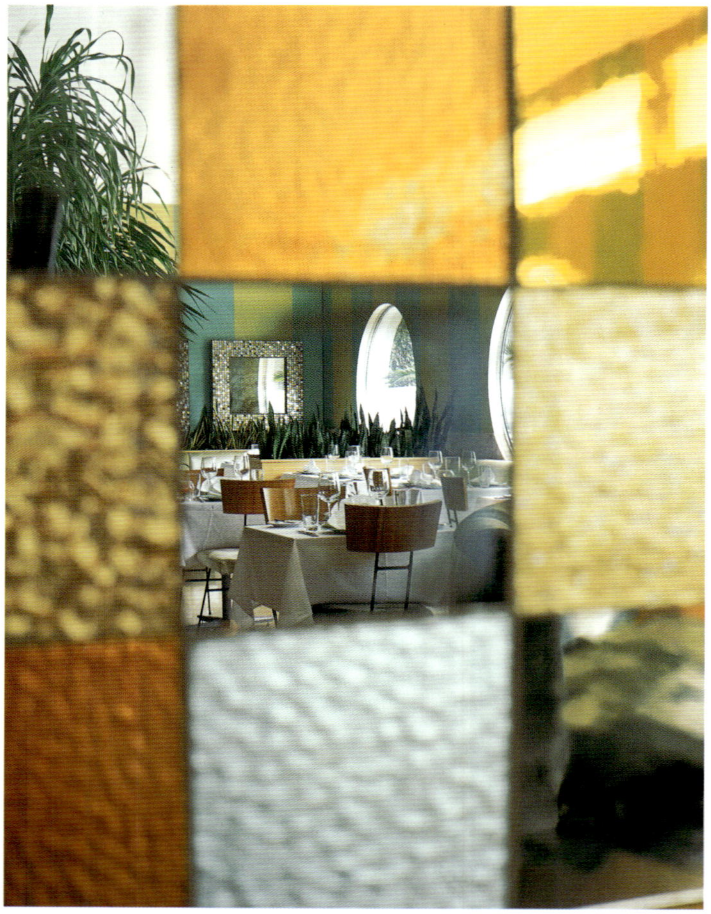

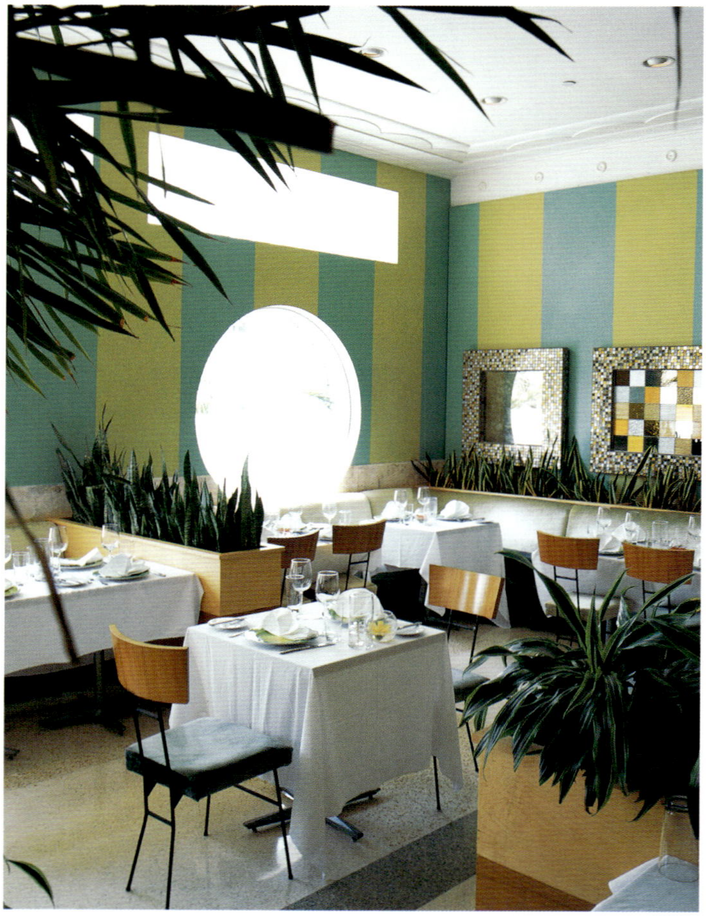

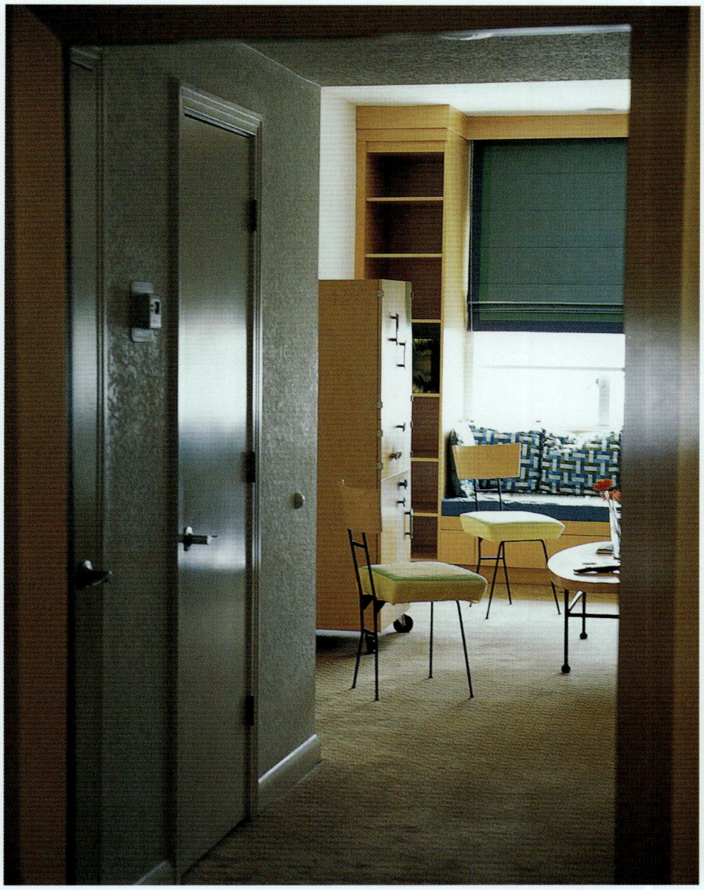
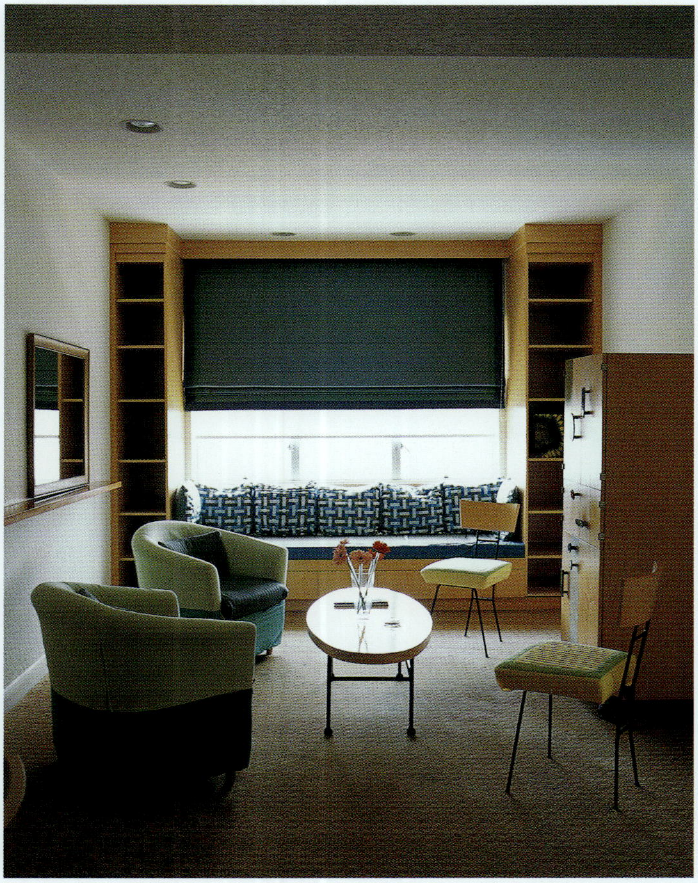
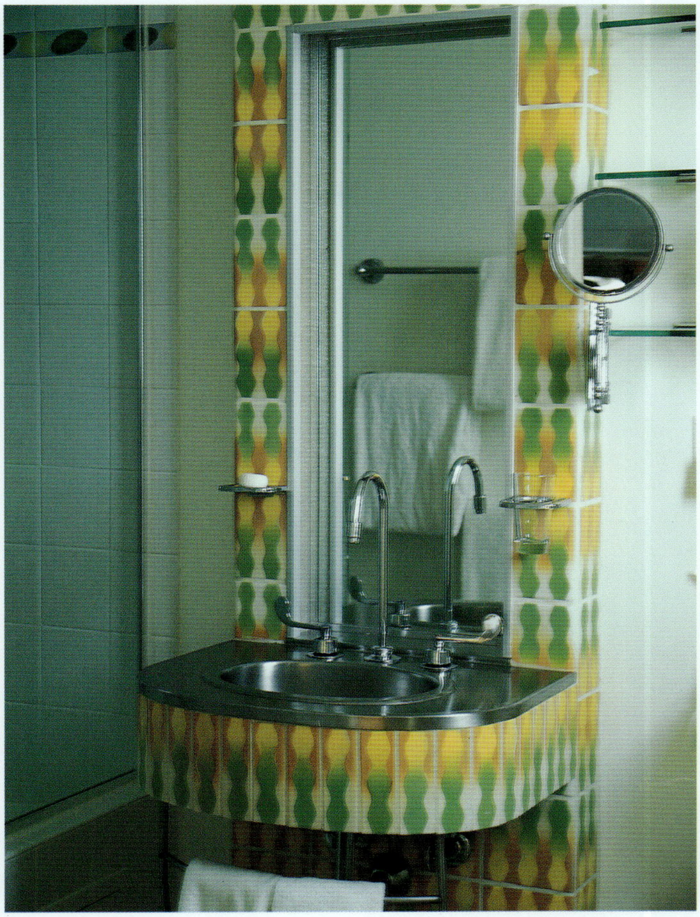
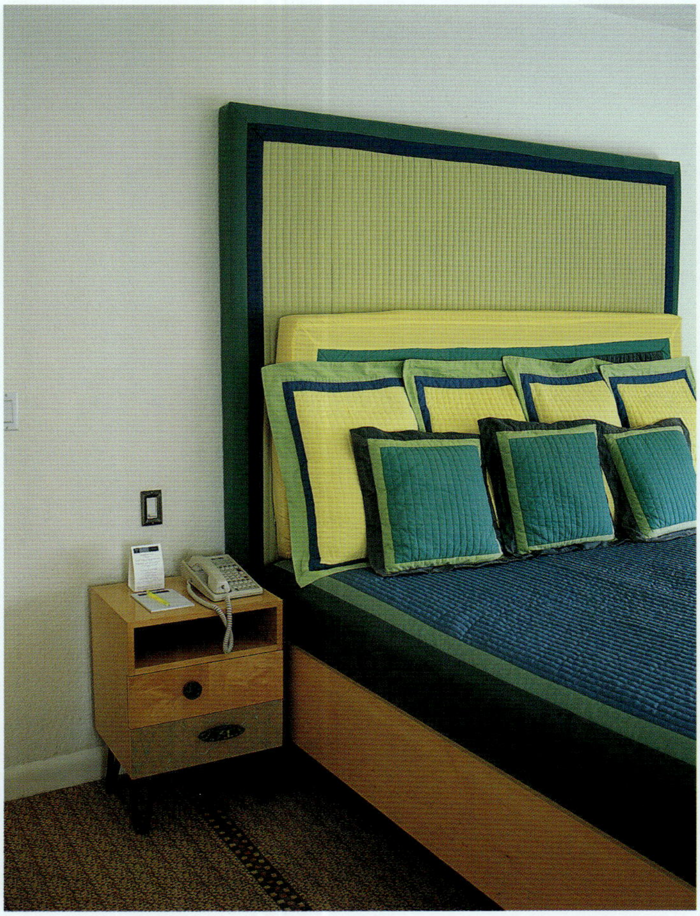

Chapter 5

AT HOME IN "YOUR HOUSE"

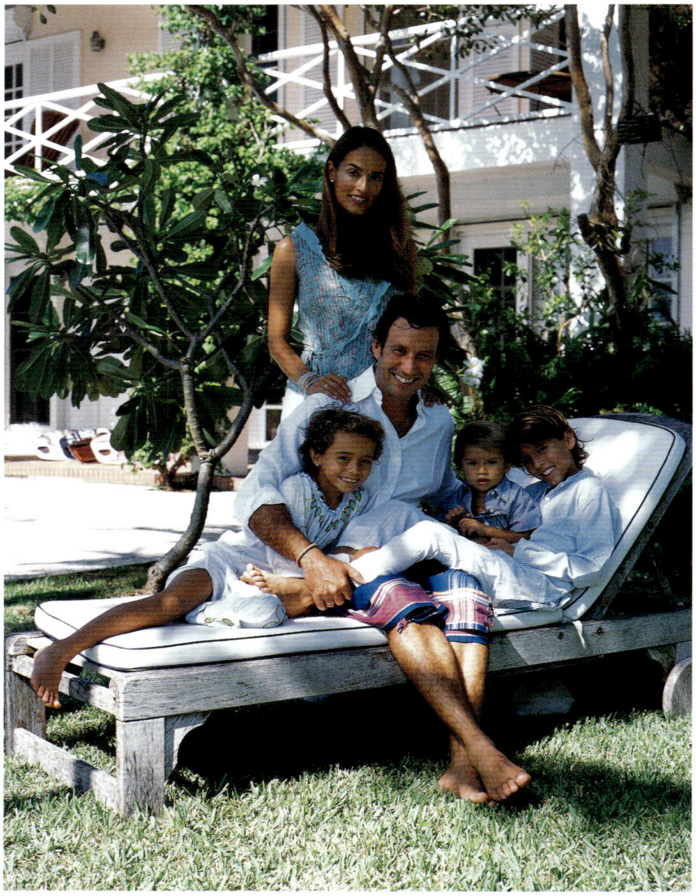

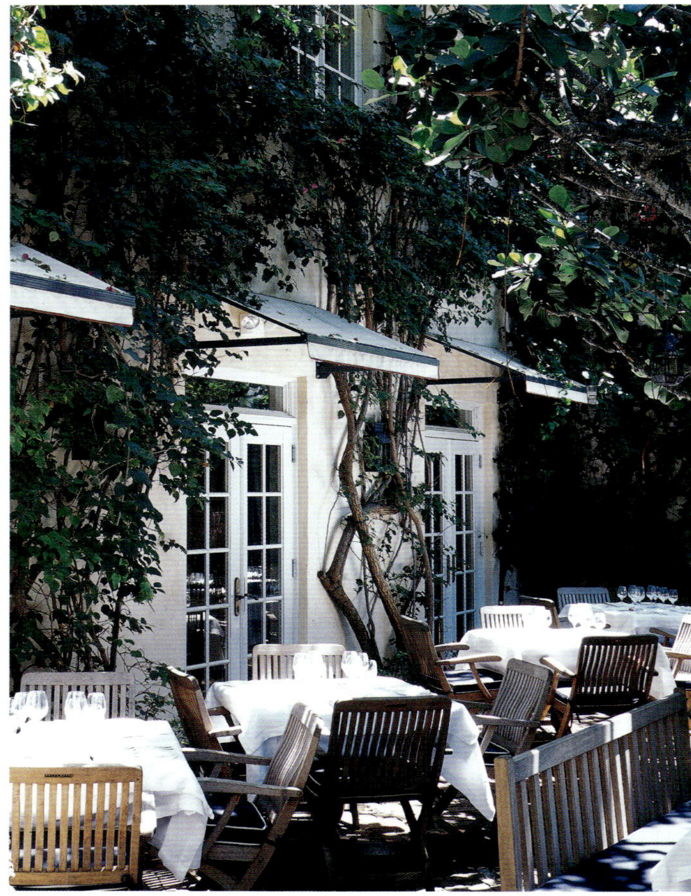

MICHELE & LETICIA GRENDENE (AND FAMILY)... AND "CASA TUA"

Yes, everything you've heard is true: The most beautiful people in the world have flocked to South Beach and made it more beautiful than ever. A prime case in point is this magnificent couple, their magnificent family, and their even more magnificent impact on South Beach. The dashing Michele (known to his friends and employees as "Miky" as in "Mickey" Mantle) and the drop-dead gorgeous love of his life, Leticia, met in Milan and married in Miami Beach. They have been producing more beauty for their adopted city ever since—by raising three beautiful children and, then, by establishing a typically Italian example of family style luxury with their magnificent "Casa Tua" restaurant, which means "Your House" in Italian (and in Spanish too, just for good measure).

Casa Tua, which boasts a dizzying array of famous faces and bodies among its clientele, has become more than a restaurant. It has become a statement about combining the Italians' unique love-of-life with the fascination of the global melting pot that now characterizes South Beach. The restaurant is hidden behind horse-high hedges and a metal gate at 1700 James Avenue, with no external sign that it is anything more than a private dwelling.

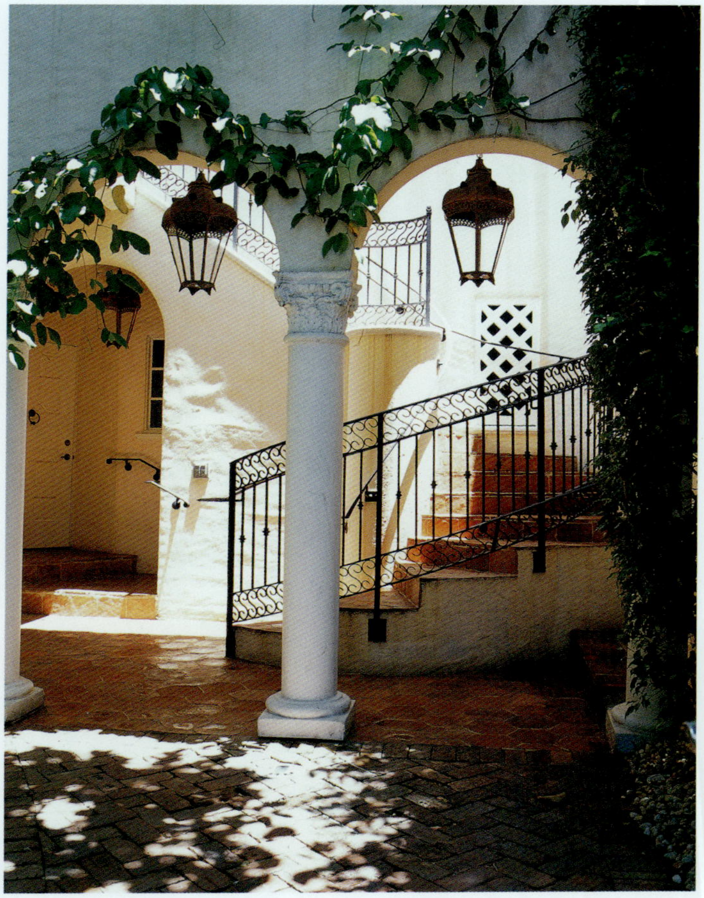

And Casa Tua lives up to it name by creating an "at-home" Italian ambiance even as it coddles its guests with world-class food and service. Its uniquely welcoming atmosphere promises that there is "always room" (well, almost always) for a drop-in pasta and wine dinner at what the Italians call the "Chef's Table" and Miky characteristically calls his "Friend's Table," located within the restaurant's kitchen area. This table is always set with the most creative flower and candle arrangements, which makes it a special table in our eyes.

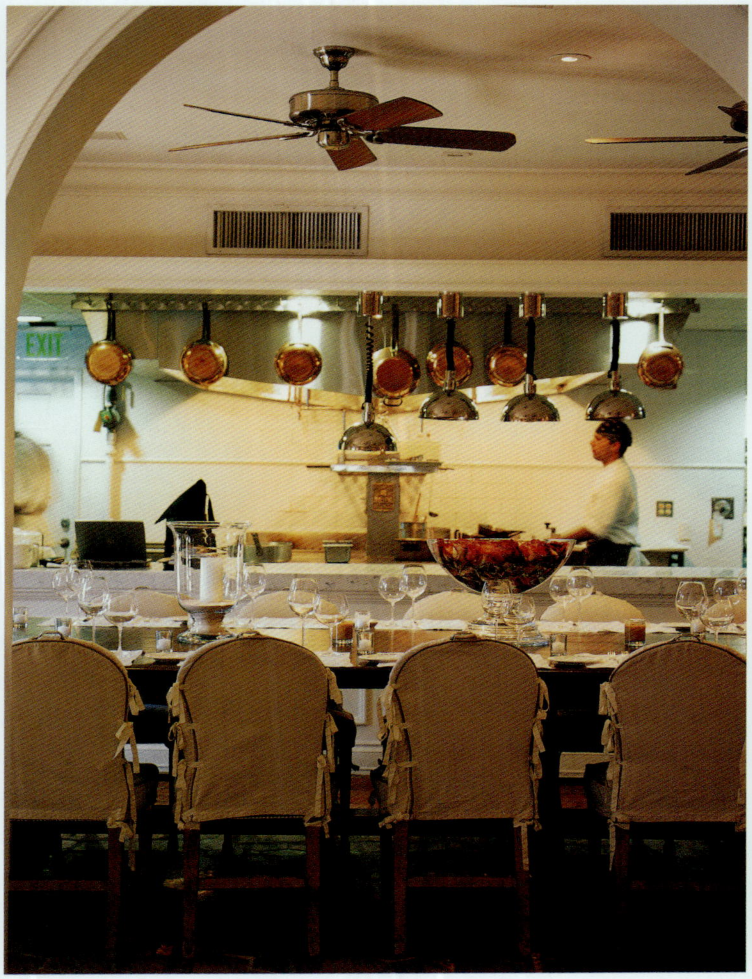

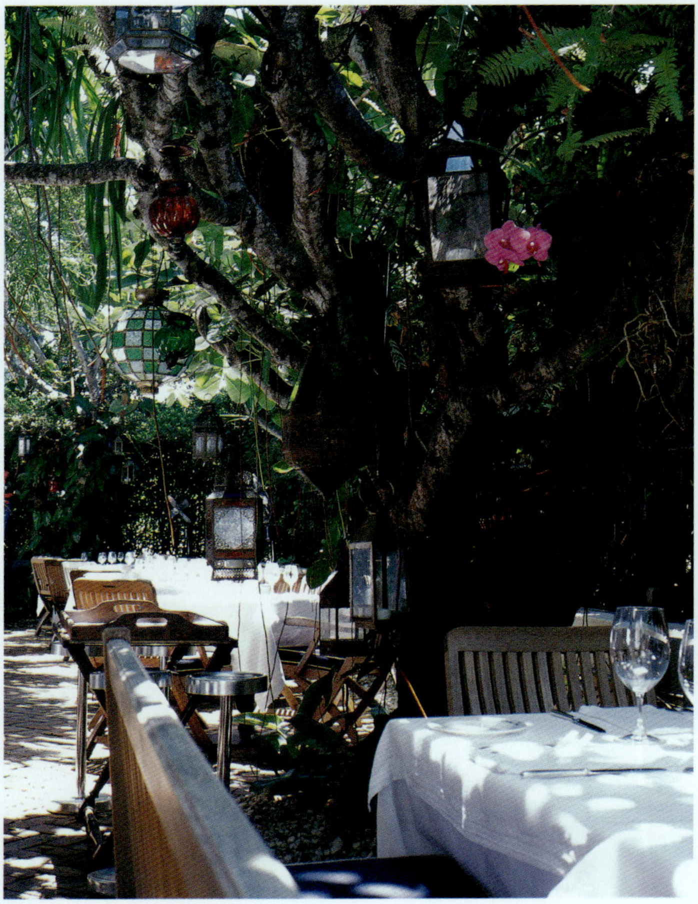

There are specialty dishes and wines at Casa Tua that are available nowhere else in Florida, and there are always beautiful people here that, like the food, seem cast for a fantasy movie set, not a real-life eatery. The furniture and furnishings at Casa Tua (including those in its VERY private "private suites") have all been carefully chosen to accentuate its owner's uniquely South Beach style of Italian enthusiasm, sex appeal, and world-class quality.

Speaking of Casa Tua's private suites, they are as delicious as the dishes served in its restaurant. The extraordinary combination of elegance and comfort has been achieved with mastery. Every detail, from the amber scented signature candle to the extravagant white linens draping the beds, has been carefully thought out and created in such a way as to please as many senses as possible all at once. These surroundings make it a toss-up as to whether to dine in the restaurant or have dinner sent up.

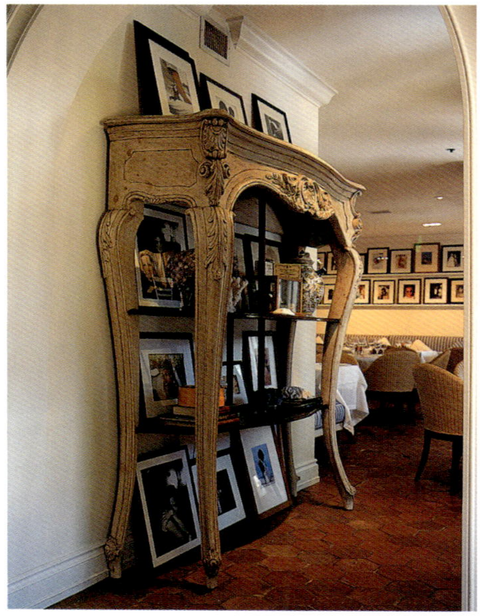

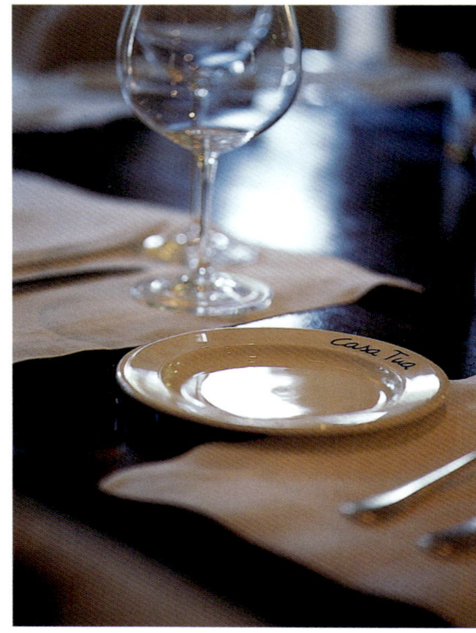

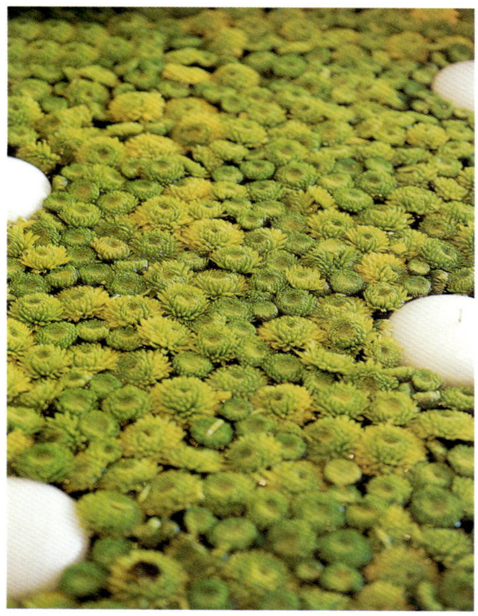

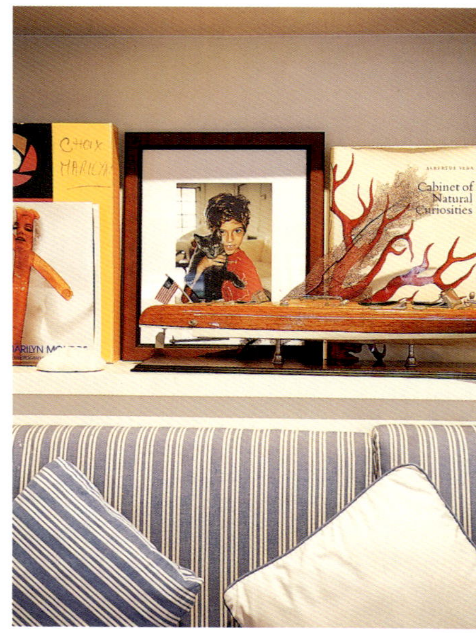

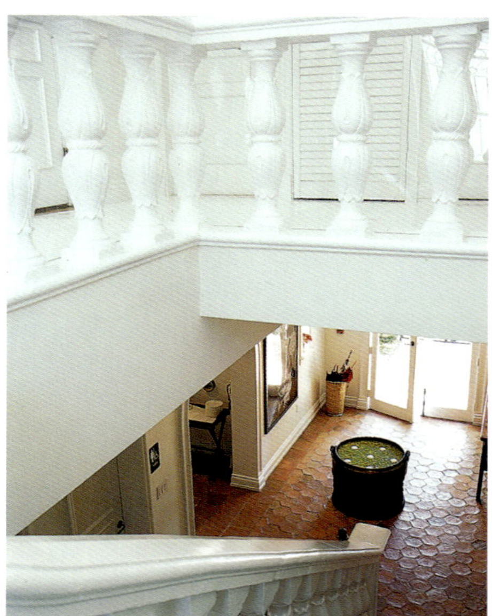

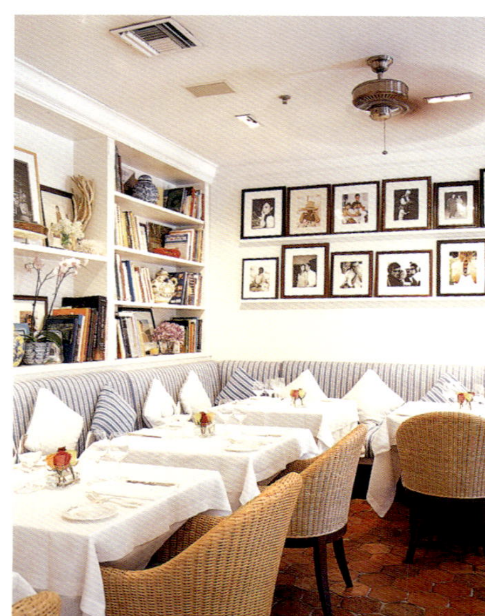

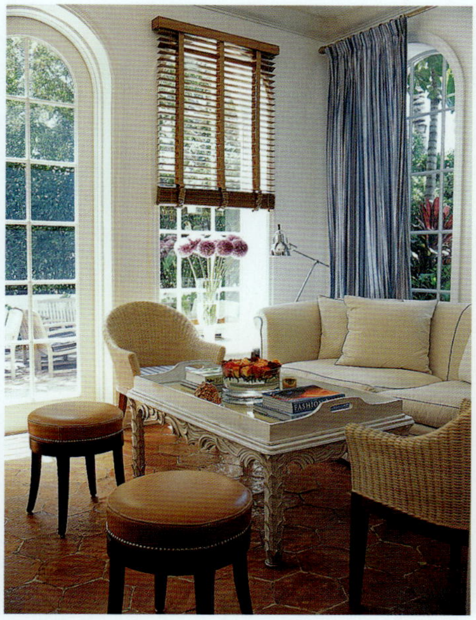
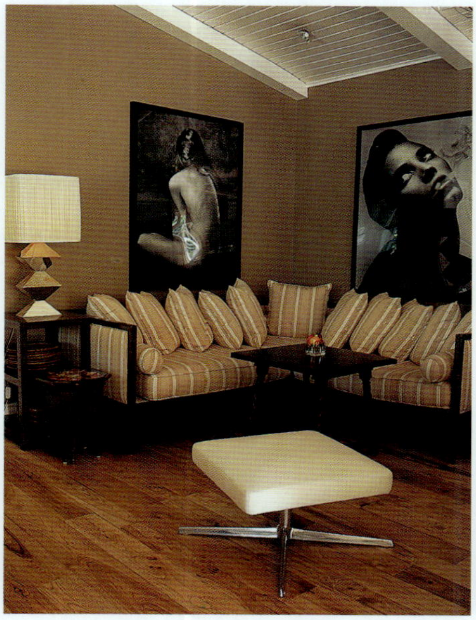
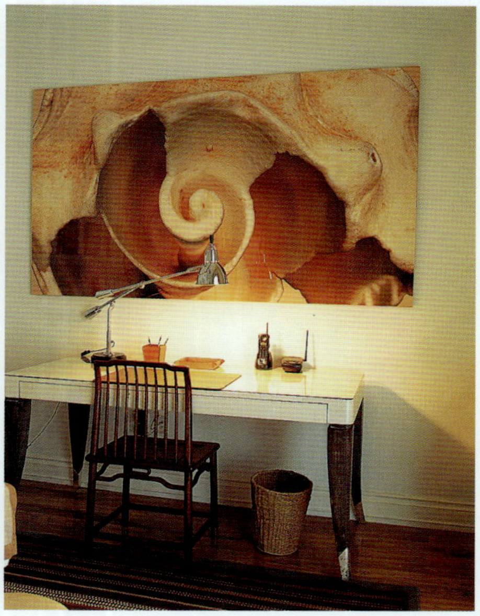
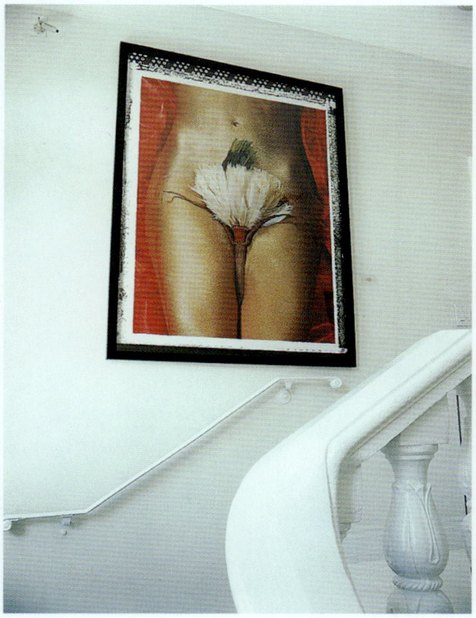
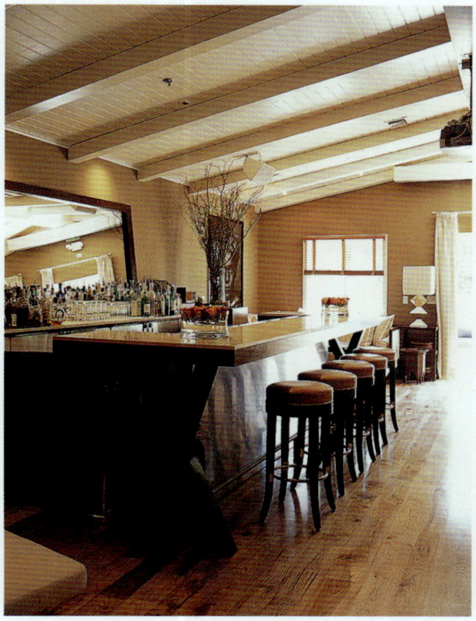
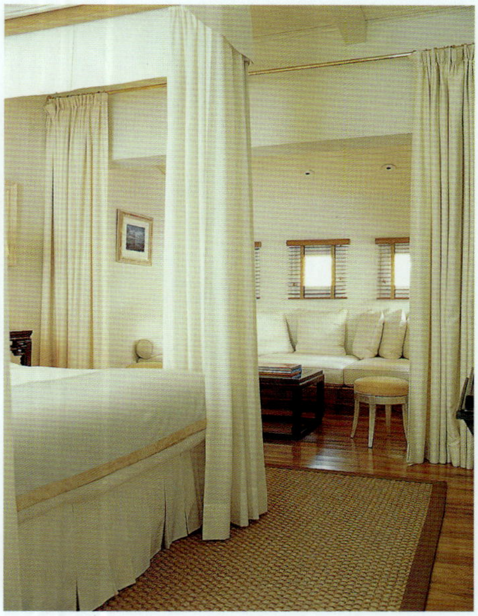
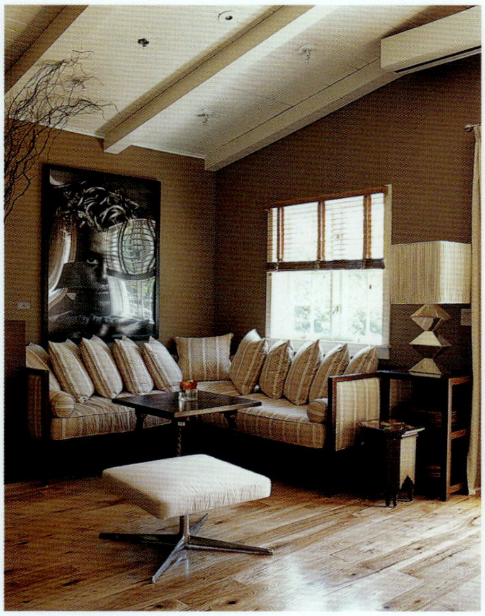
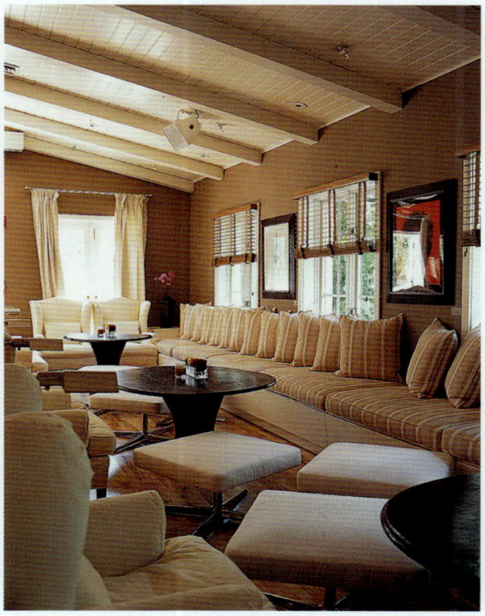
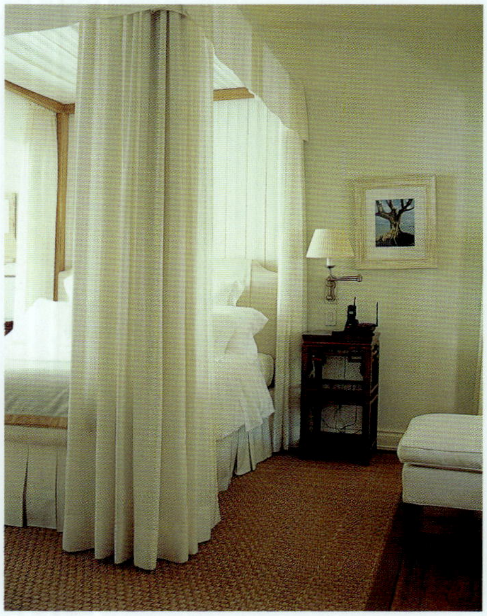

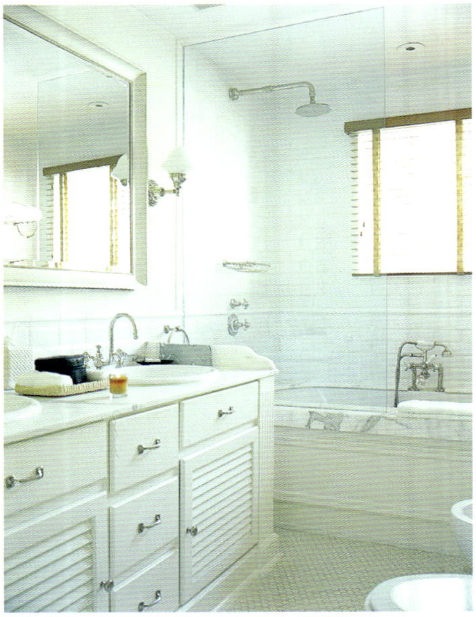
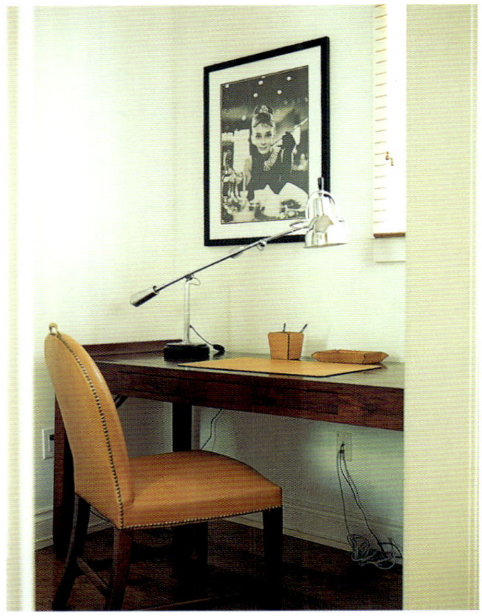
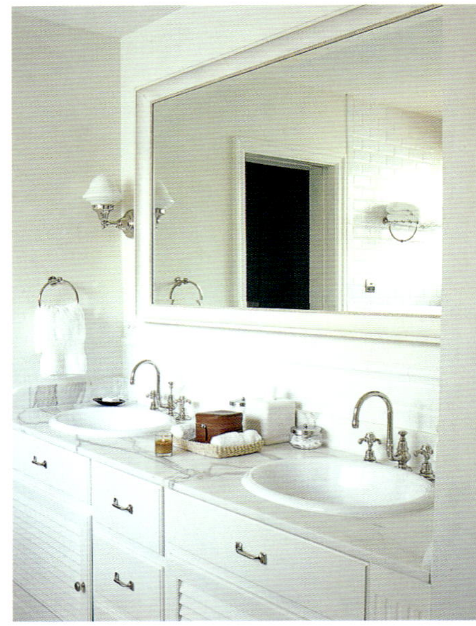
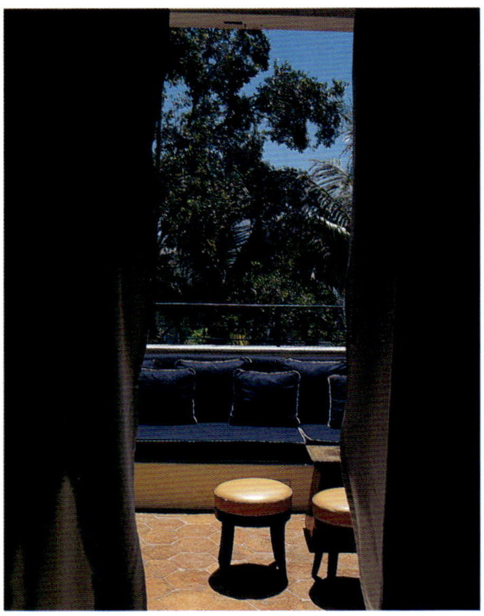
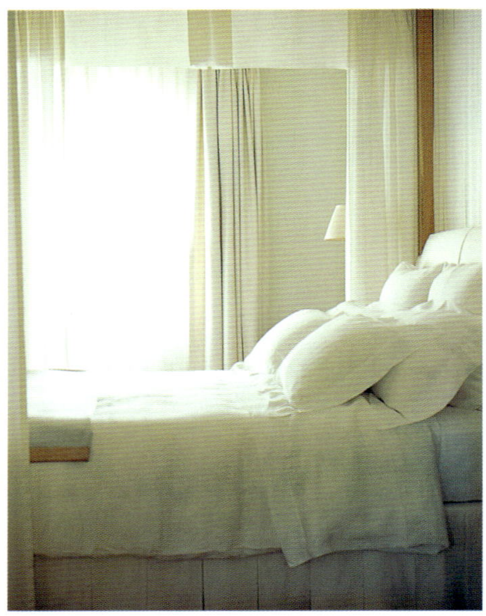
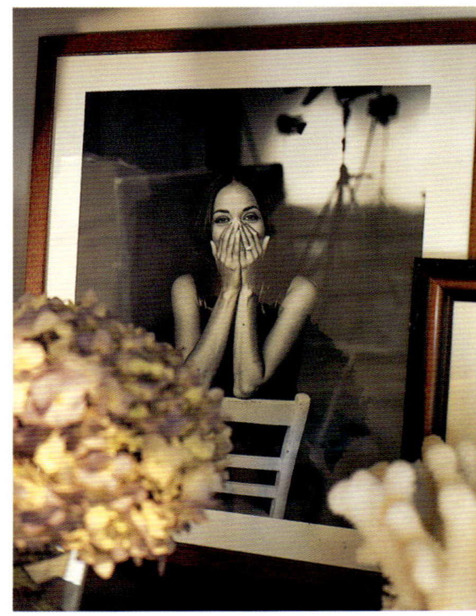
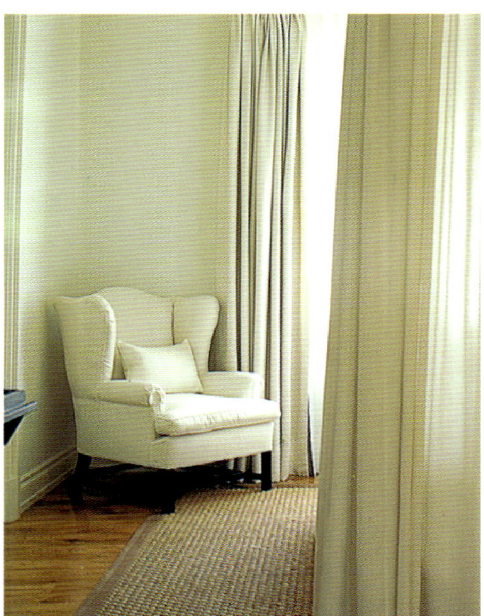
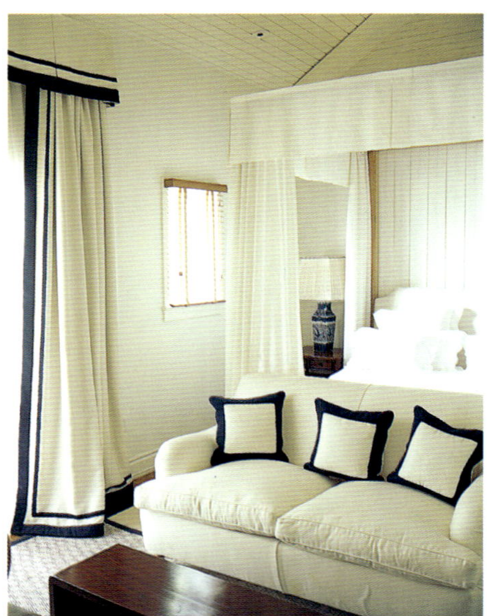
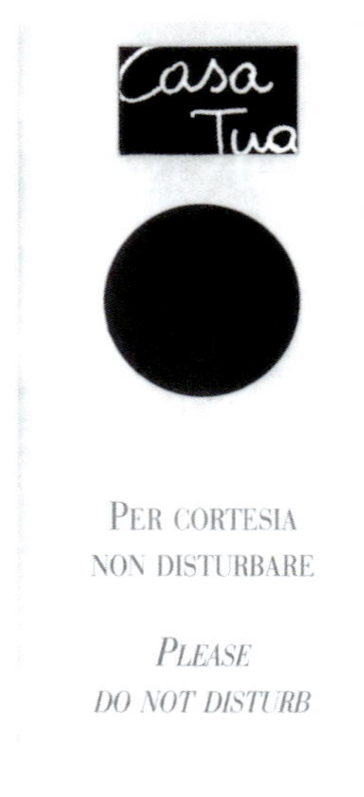
Casa Tua
PER CORTESIA
NON DISTURBARE
PLEASE
DO NOT DISTURB

Chapter 6

"...Just a Small Beach Town..."

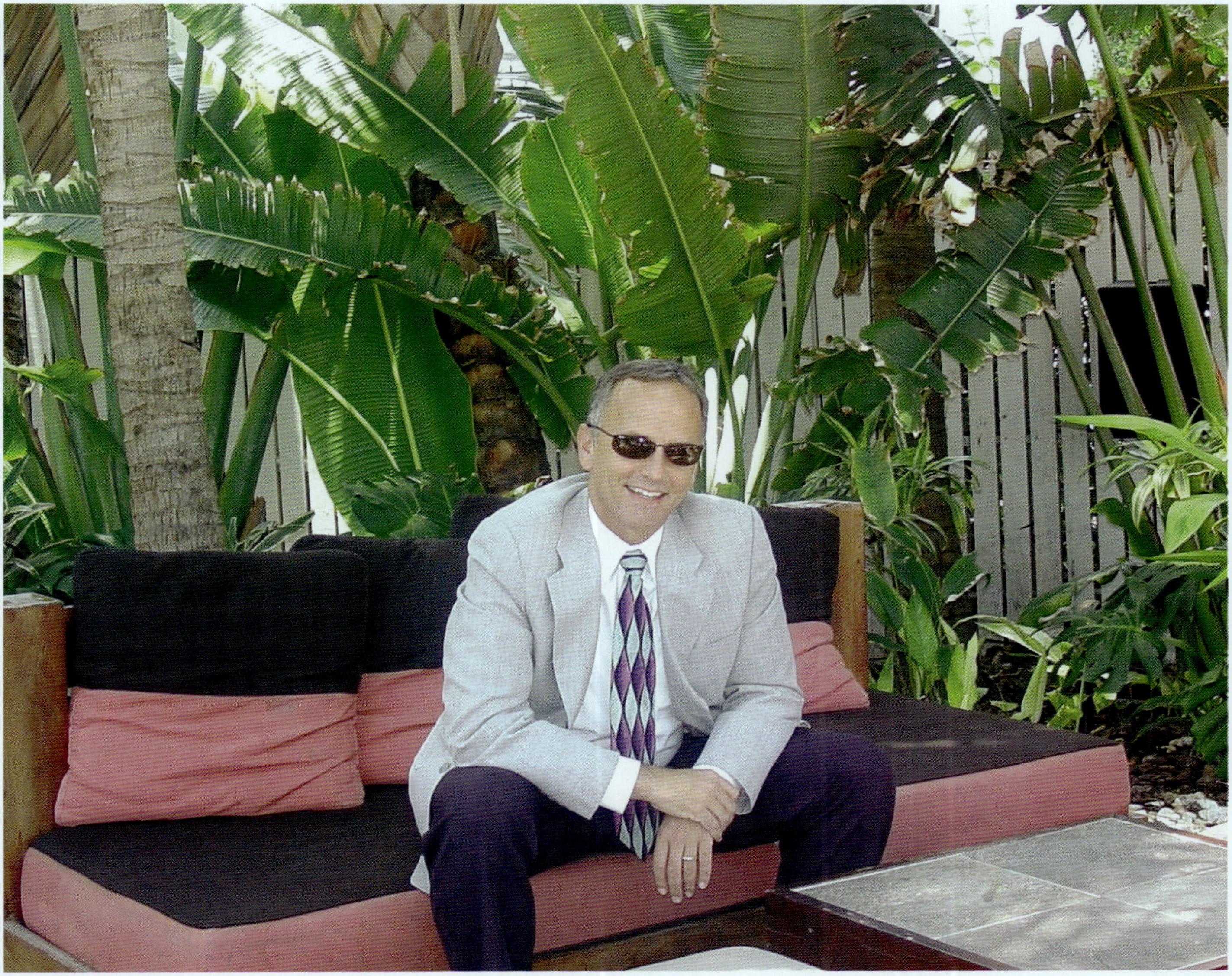

Jeff Lehman and the National Hotel

There is more than one "love-at-first-sight relationship" in Miami Beach. A lot of them are like the affair between Jeff Lehman and what he calls "just a small beach town living life in a big way." LA-born Jeff first saw the new Miami Beach in 1994 while on his way to board a cruise ship: "I quit my job and moved here within a month and have been here ever since."

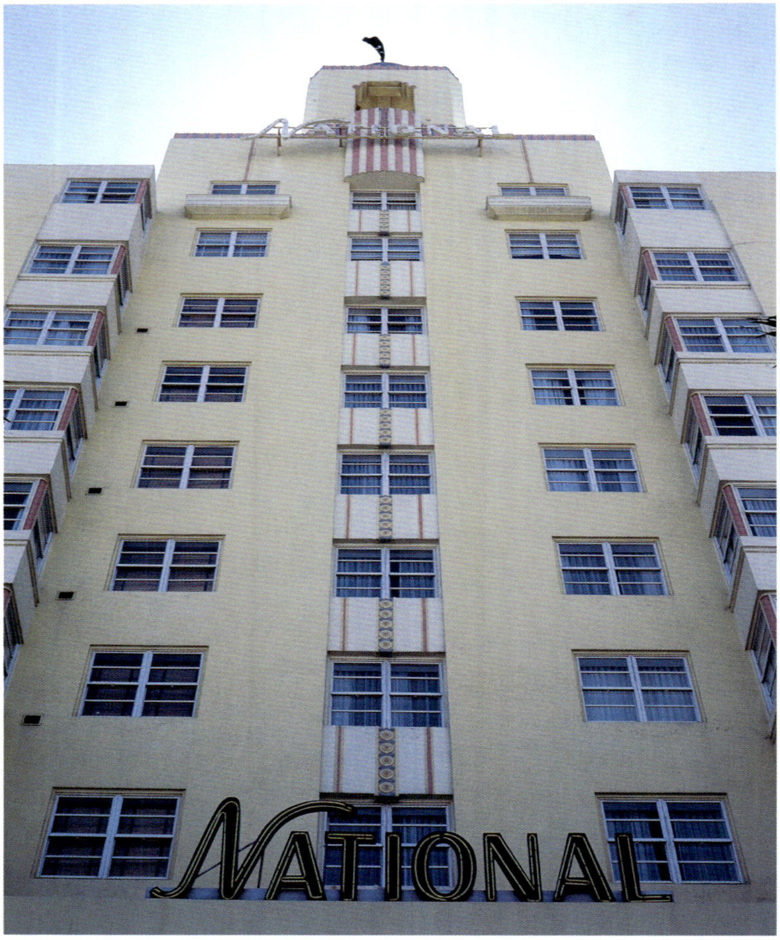

Two years later, Jeff began working for the National Hotel, where he is now Manager. Located at 1677 Collins Avenue, the National is widely regarded as being among South Beach's most faithful Art Deco architectural renovations. Its 1996 restoration added high-quality elements (like the hotel's new front sign featuring its signature "Swimming N" shape). The building's façade and its 1939-vintage interior maintain a special "That's the way it was" atmosphere that whispers "Casablanca."

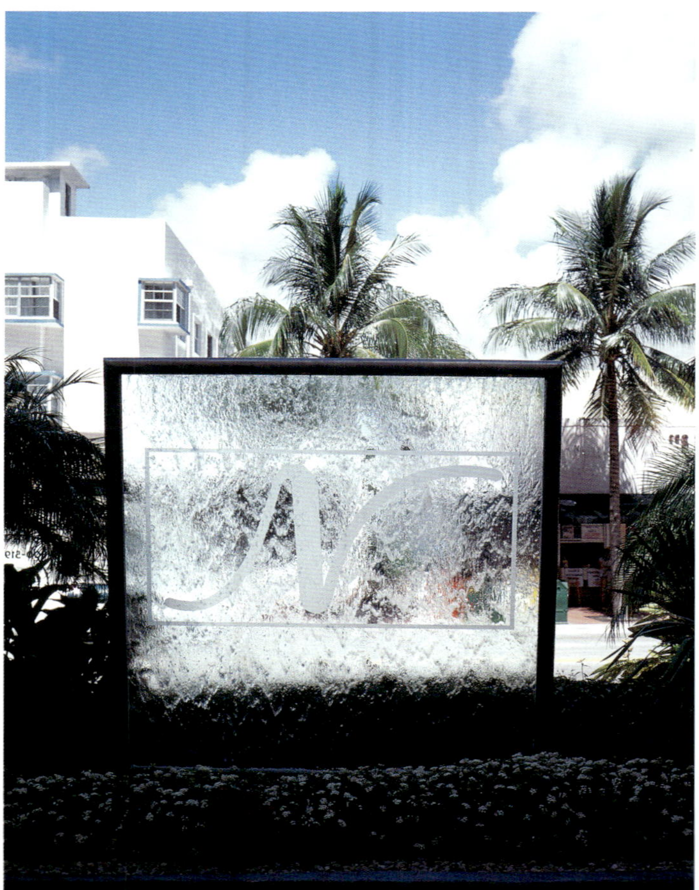

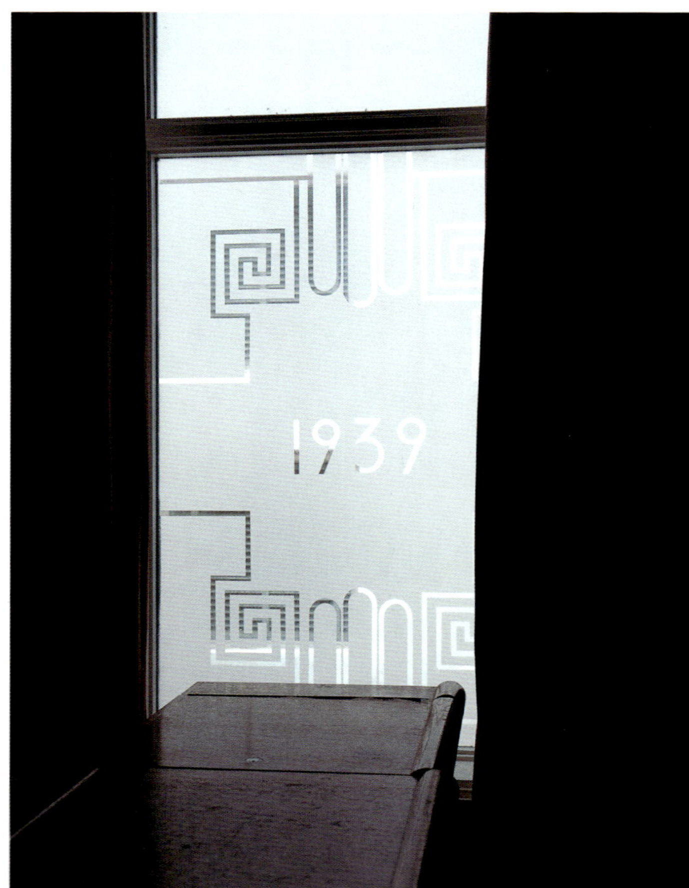

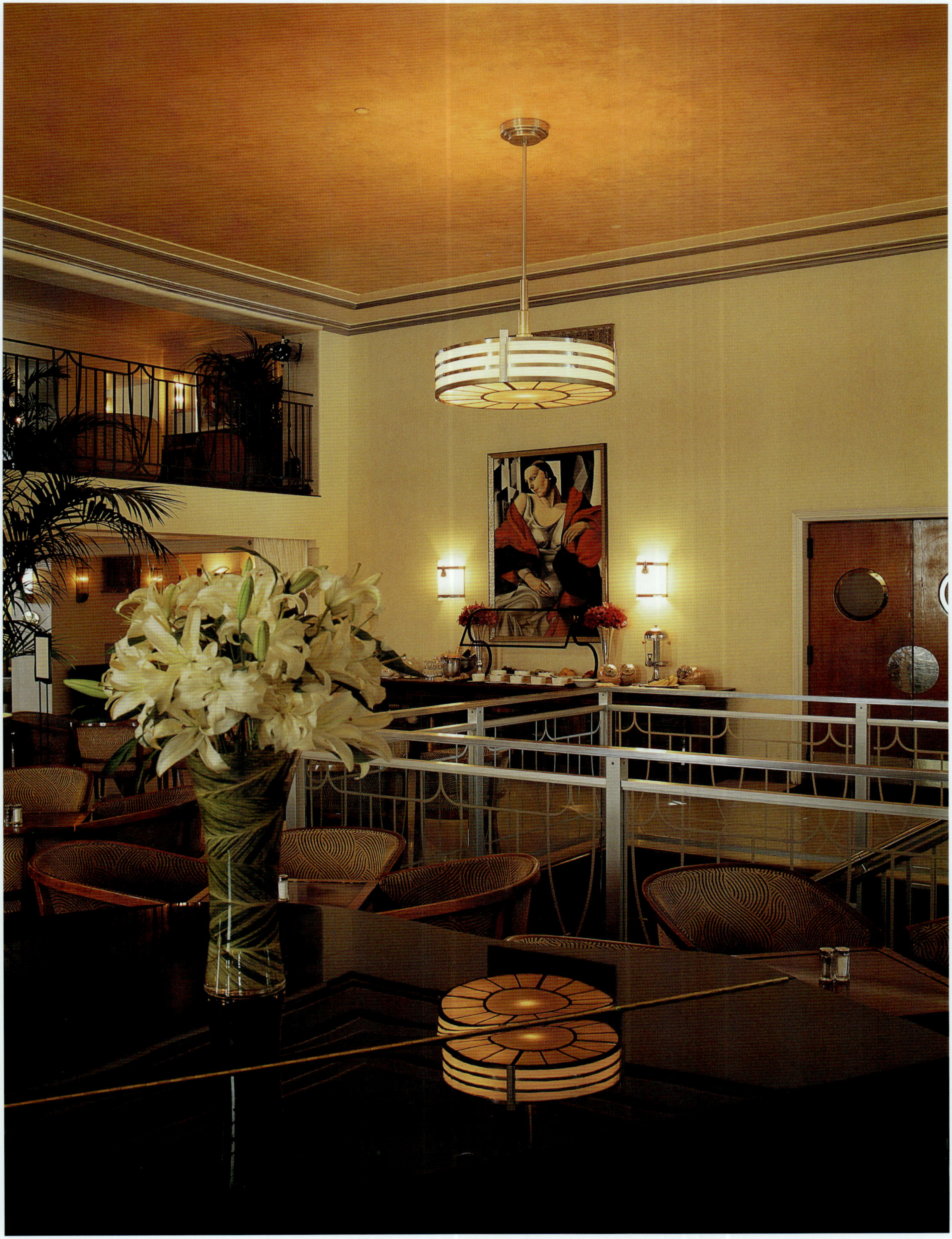

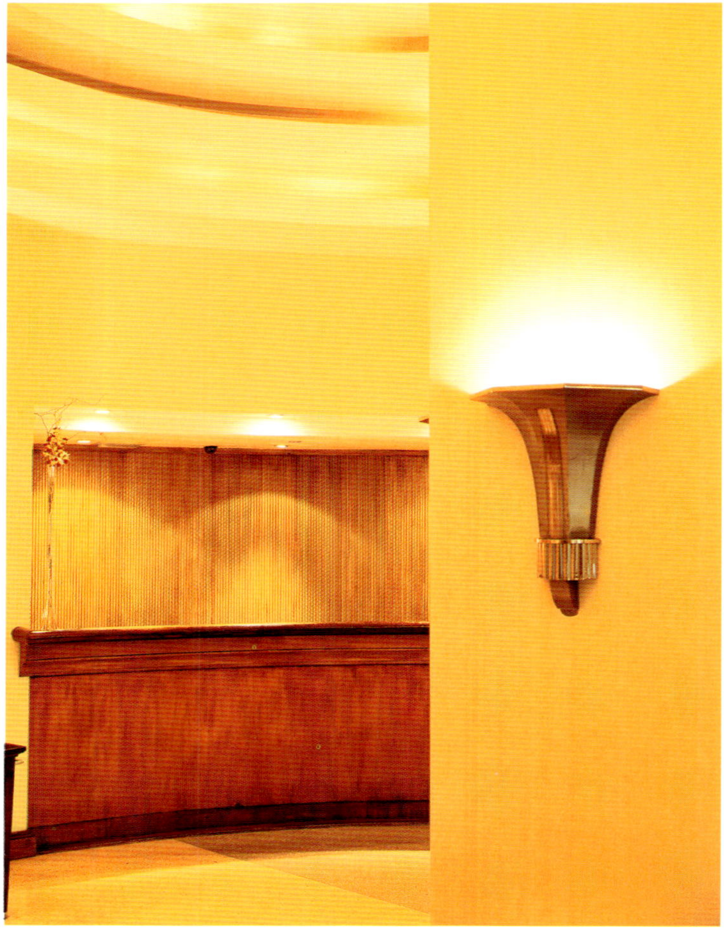

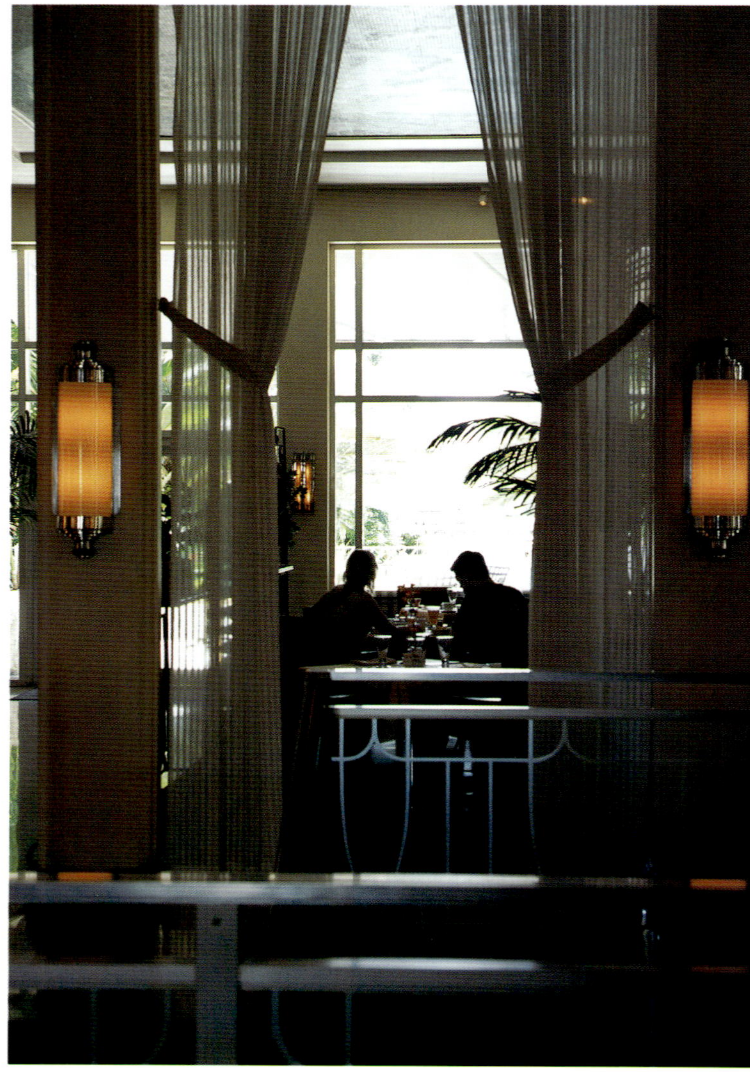

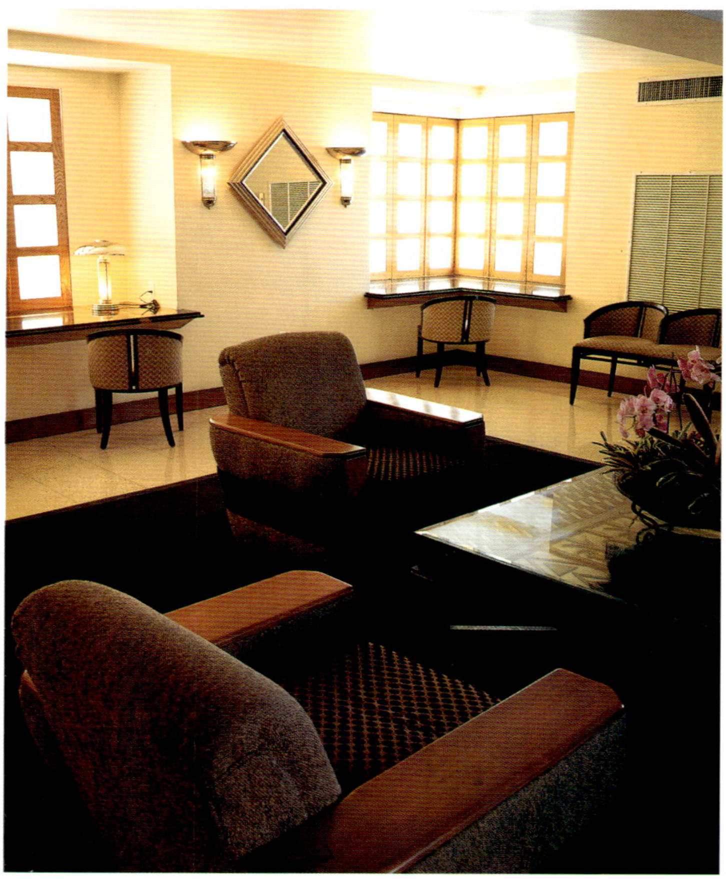

The hotel's oceanside ambiance is, if anything, even more striking, with its longer-than-Olympic length pool leading from the beach up to the building's classic bell-tower shape (see following page).

Despite his demanding work schedule, Jeff finds time to enjoy not only the National's own cuisine at "Tamara," its elegant in-house restaurant, but also to frequent a list of other eateries. His favorites read like a "What's what" of South Beach's eclectic social dining scene: "Tuscan Steakhouse...Smith & Wollensky on a Sunday afternoon, Touch on Friday nights, Sushi Samba, Nobu, Larios on Ocean Drive on a Saturday afternoon, the Front Porch for breakfast...I could go on and on."

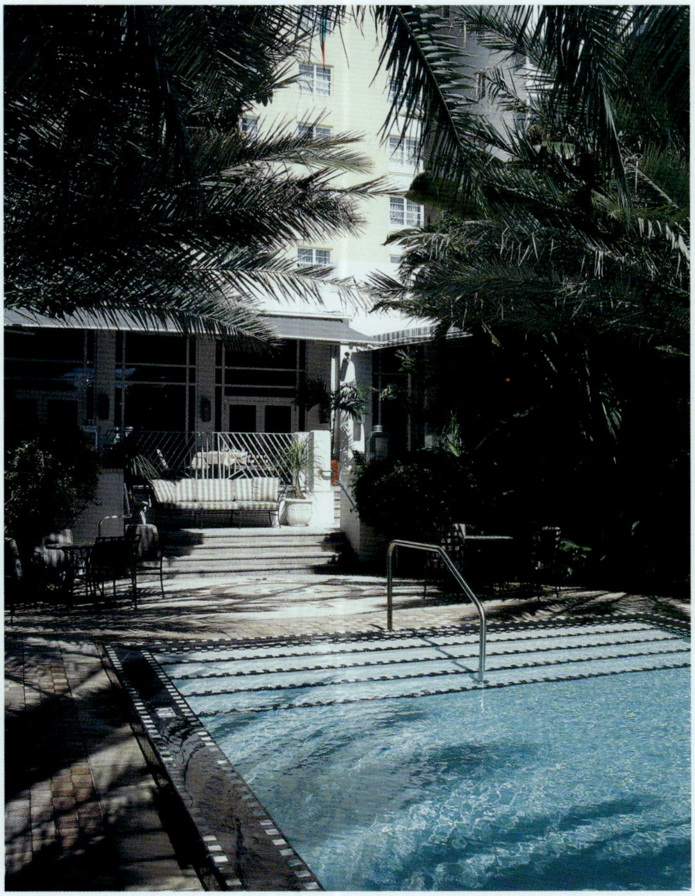

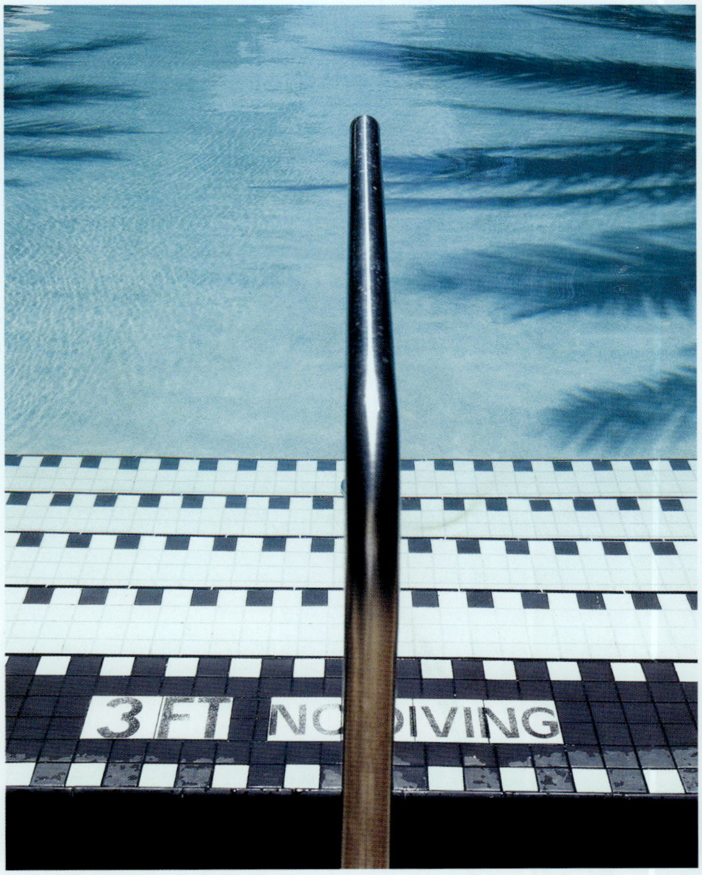

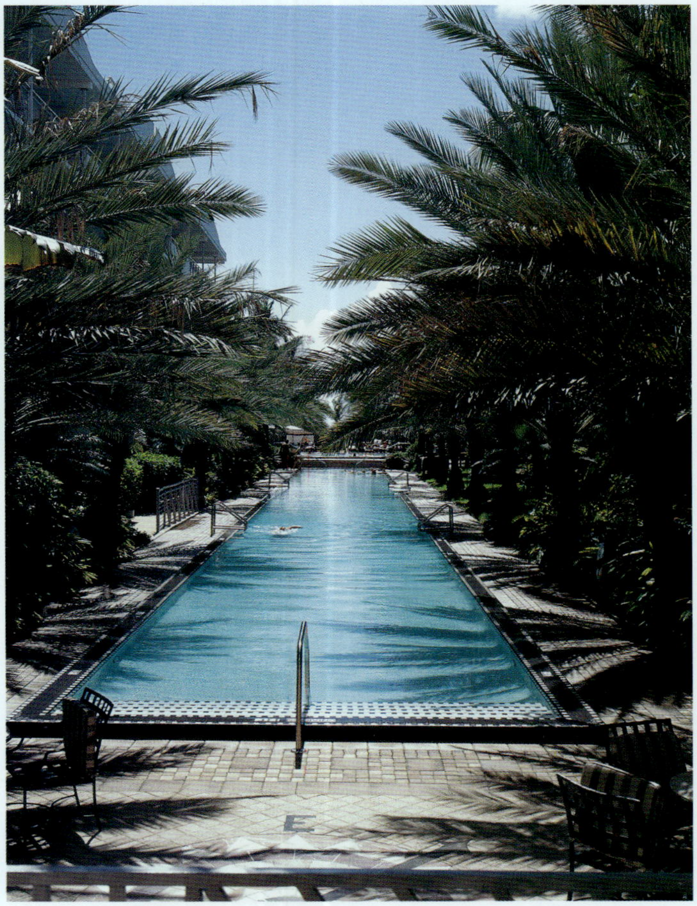

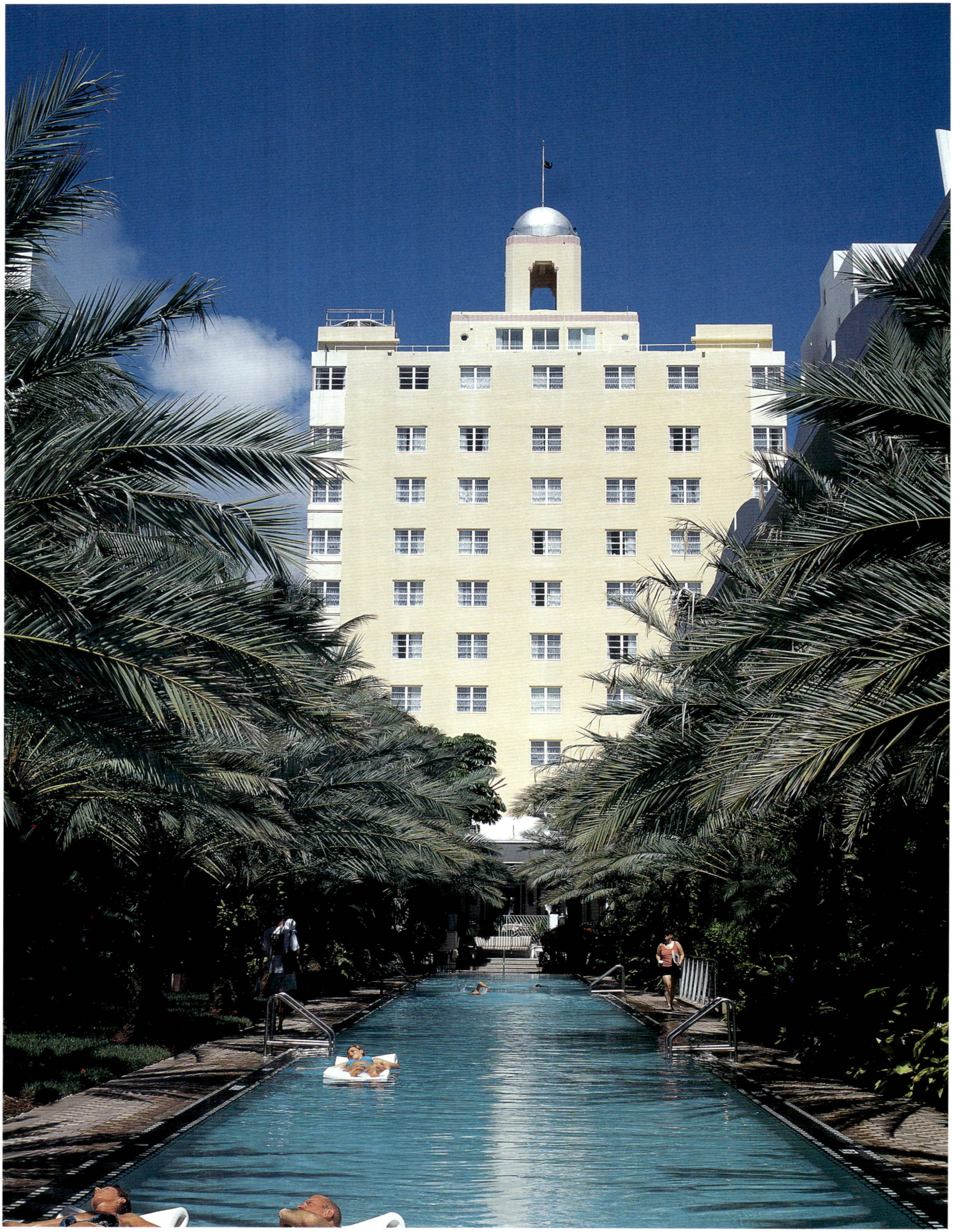

Chapter 7

GODFATHER TOO

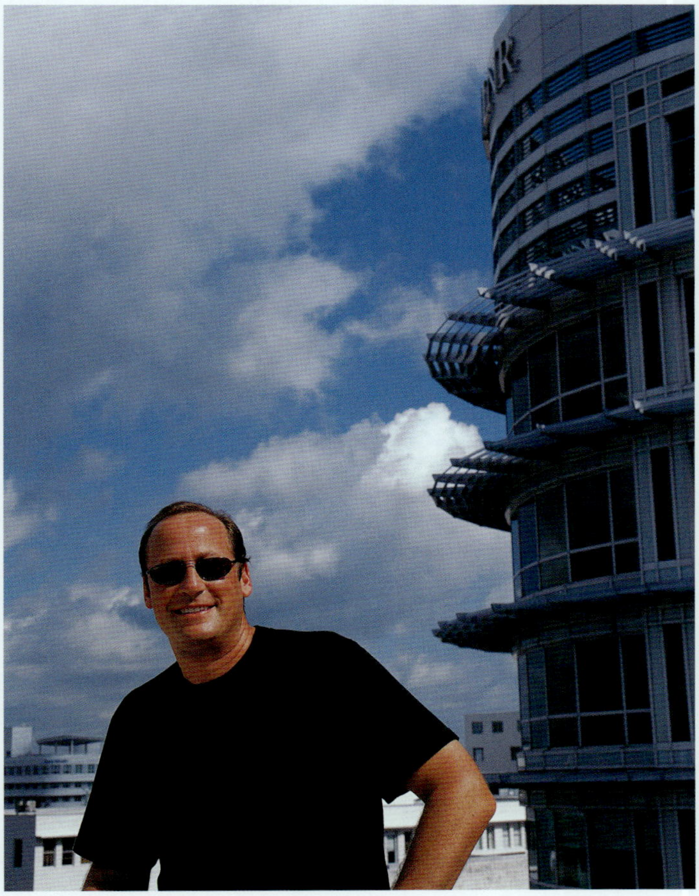

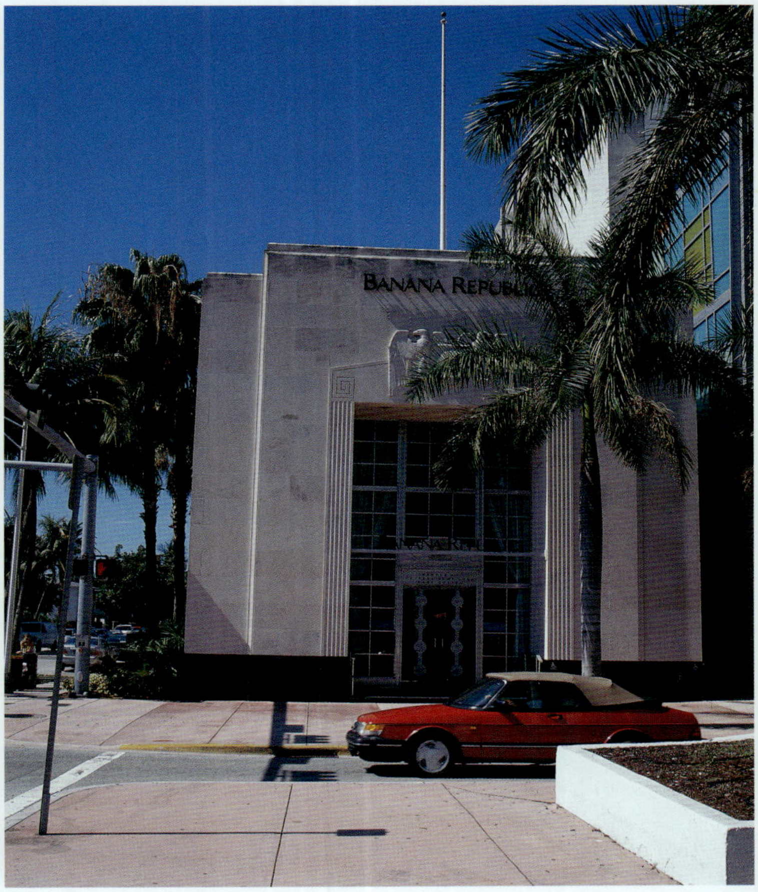

MICHAEL COMRAS AND LINCOLN ROAD (ETC.)

Prominent among the forward-thinking risk-takers that have meant and made so much in the recent history of South Beach is Michael Comras, a native New Yorker who came here to seek his future in the early 1990s. Comras has been a major force behind the development and marketing of the explosively successful Lincoln Road experiment.

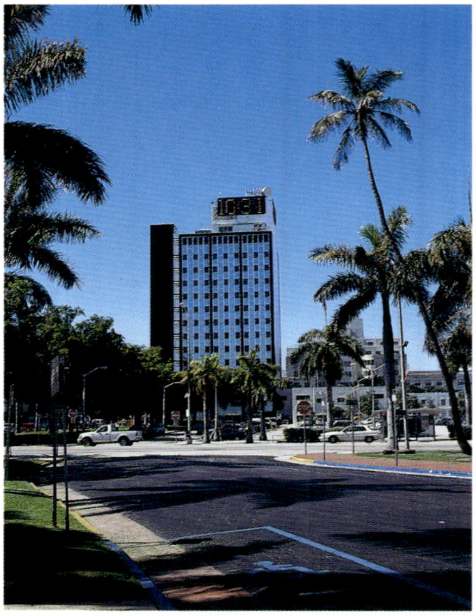

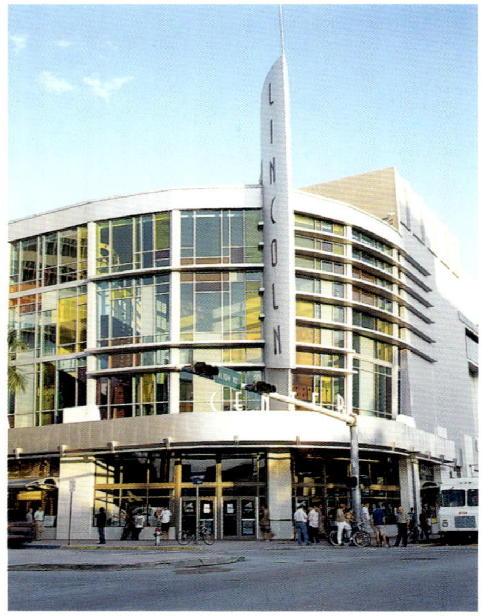
LINCOLN

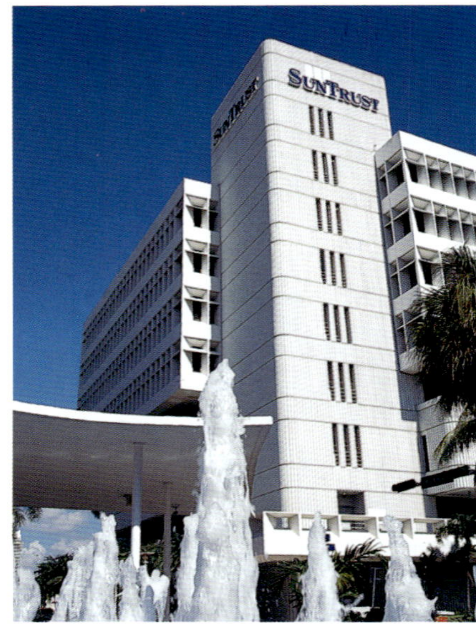
SunTrust

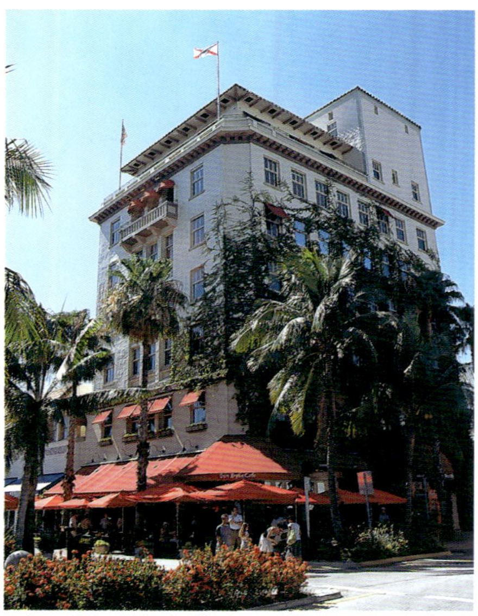

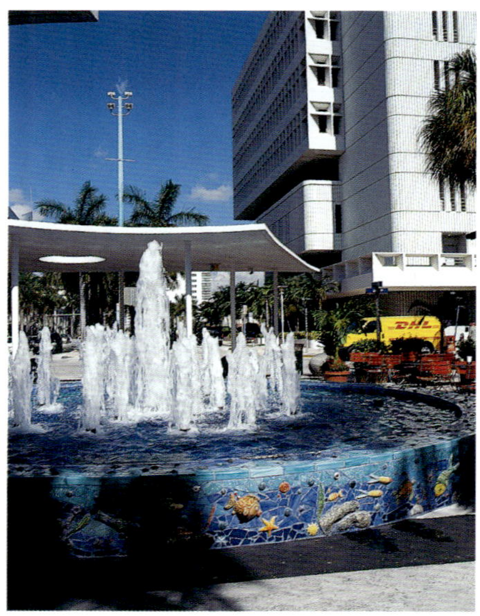
DHL

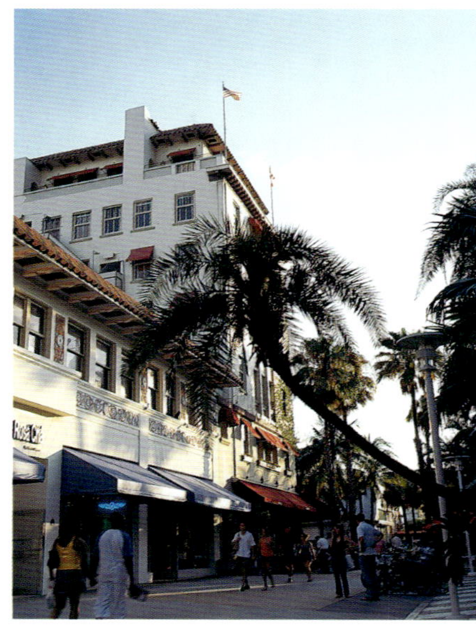

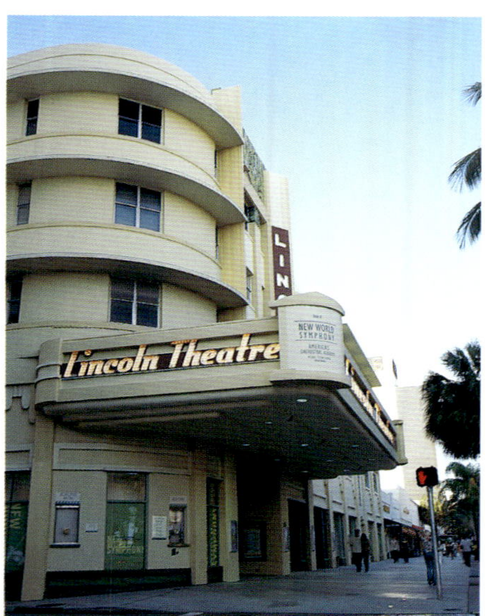
LIN
Lincoln Theatre

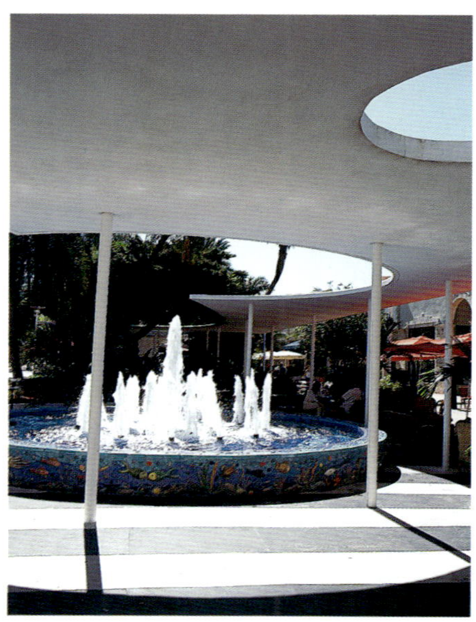

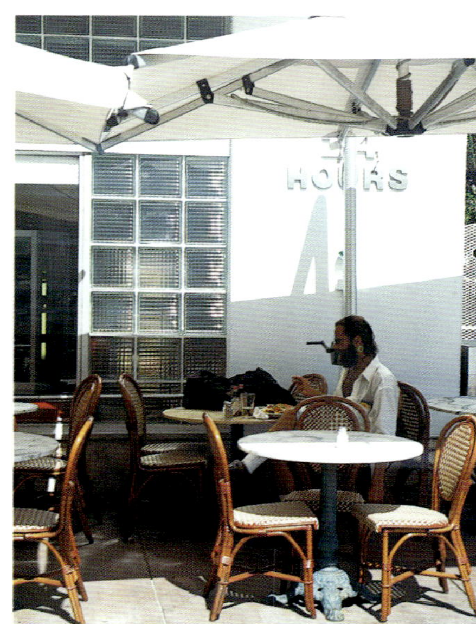
HOURS

Many of the retail and office spaces that now fill the Deco buildings of South Beach are there because of Comras' vision and successful entrepreneurship. His well-received "Lincoln Place" office building at the corner of Washington Avenue and 16th Street is thought by many to herald a new generation of quality commercial architecture for the Deco District.

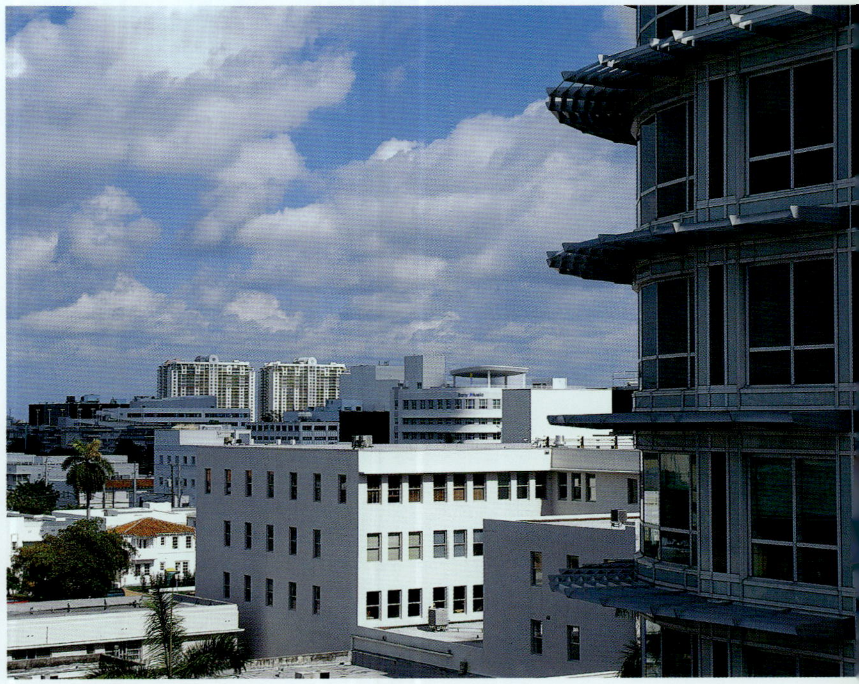

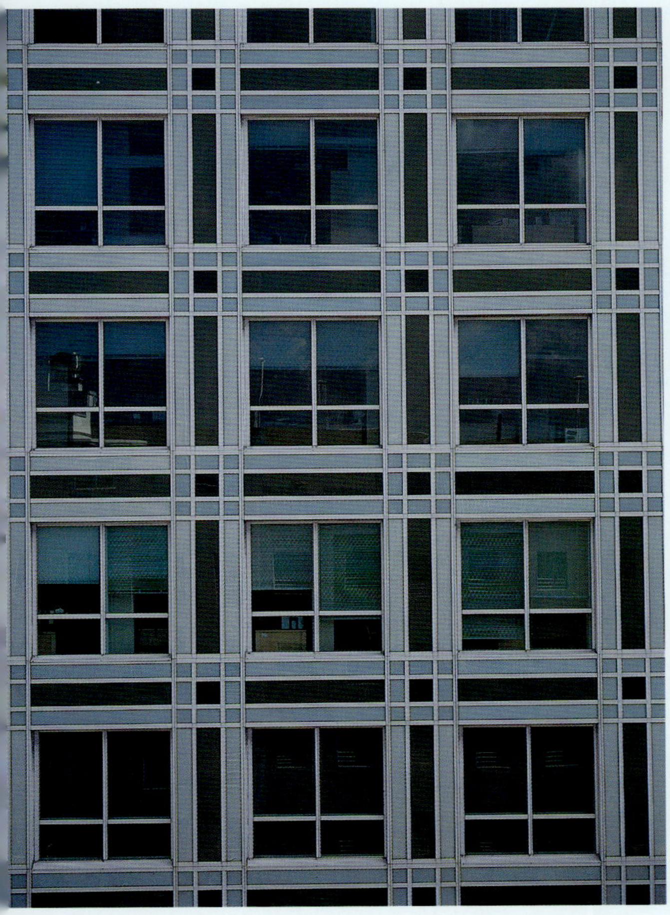

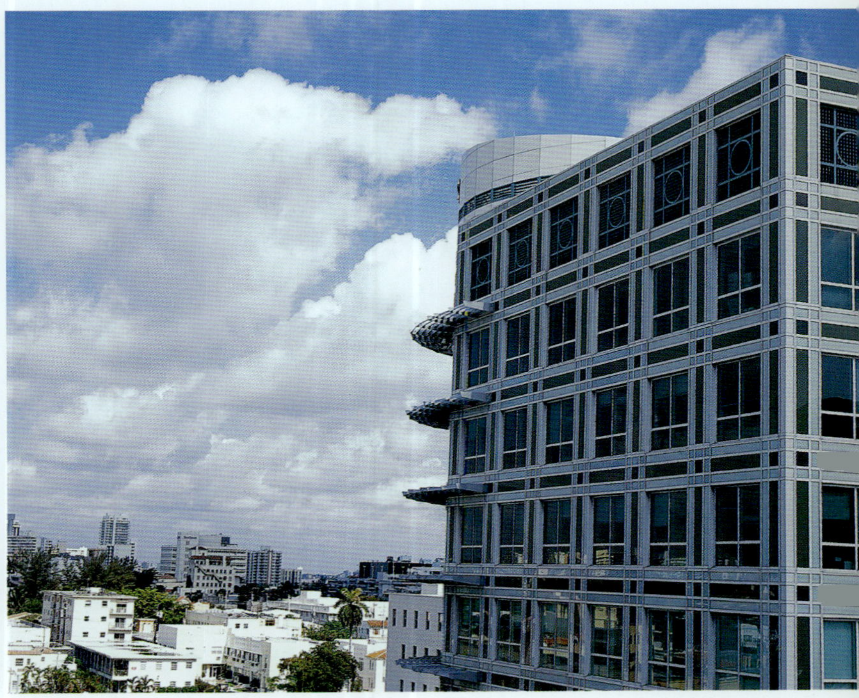

He has also headed up a public-private partnership to capitalize on the revitalized Lincoln Road, where cafés full of happy diners (and drinkers, of course) now line the length of what used to be a forlorn strip of "once-upon-a-time" pedestrian mall. Many of America's favorites stores are housed in Comras' South Beach buildings. The Gap, Ralph Lauren, Sephora, and The Pottery Barn are just a few that rent space from Michael.

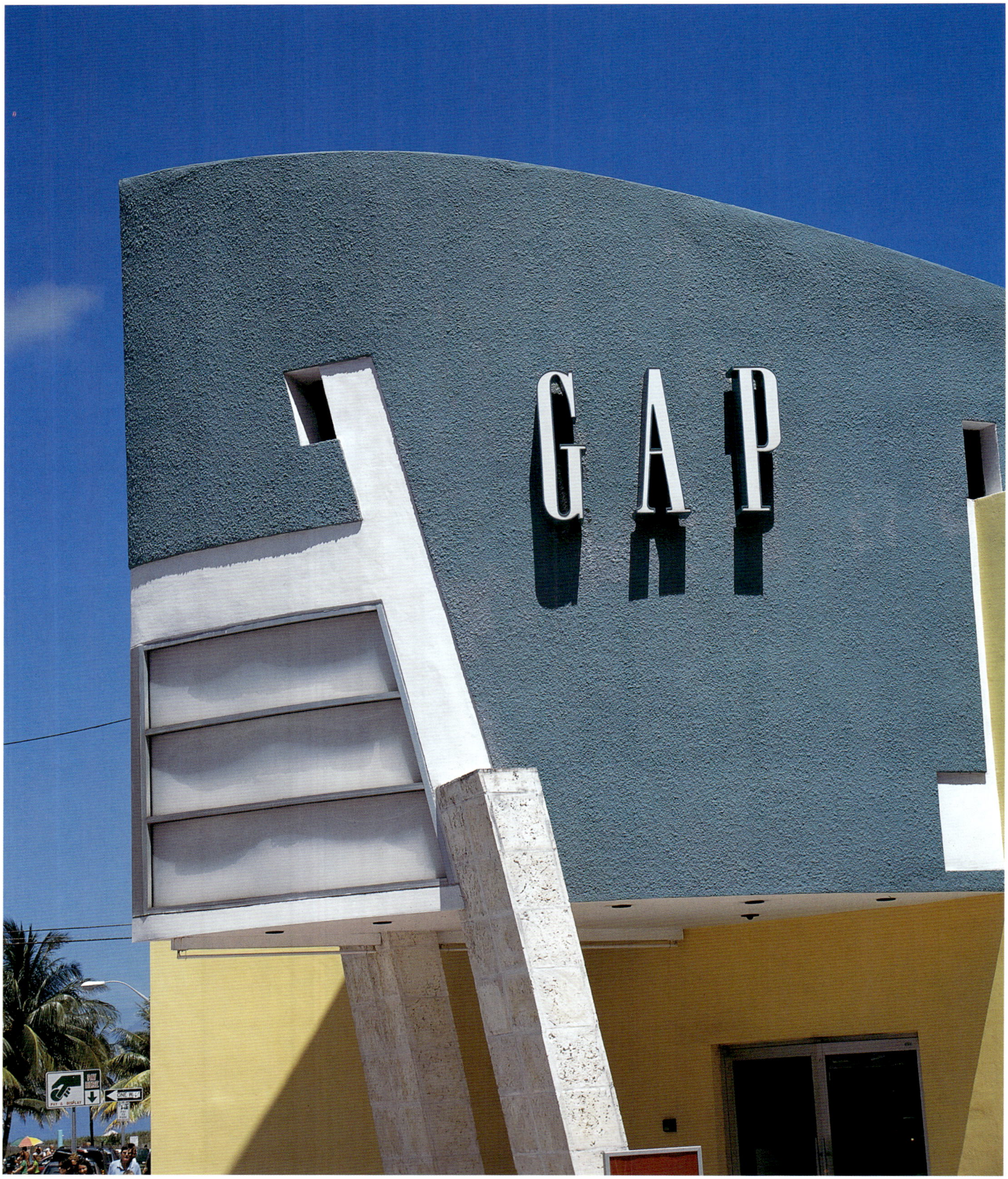

But the serious business side of Michael Comras is, as with so many South Beach faces, only part of the story. He knows why he is here: "The weather and quality of life;" he knows the beauty of the Deco-lined beaches: "...they have beautiful sand and colors;" and he knows what matters most to so many South Beach residents: "Freedom." But his serious business side comes out again when the stakes get high: If he had only $100 to spend, he'd spend it partying, with "4 drinks at Nobu [Restaurant in the Shore Club Hotel]." And with unlimited money? Why, that would go into buying as much additional South Beach property as possible.

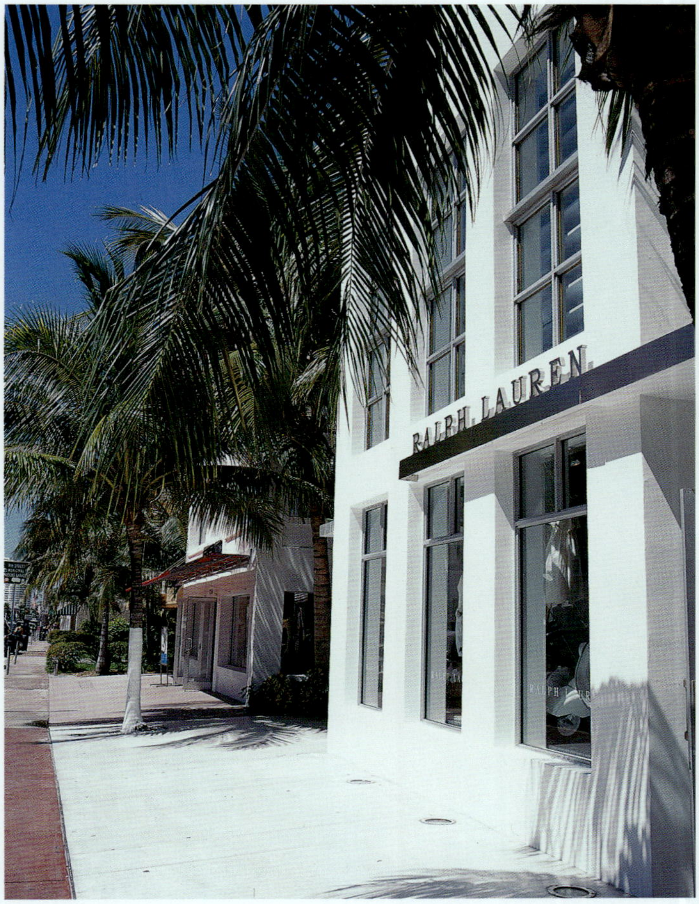

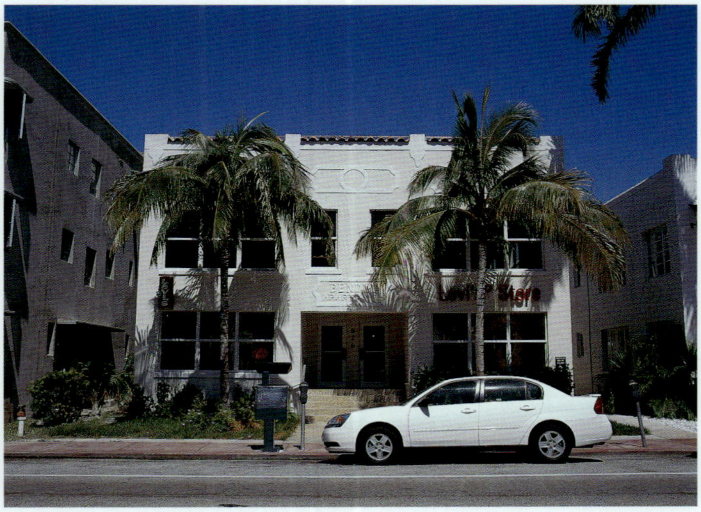

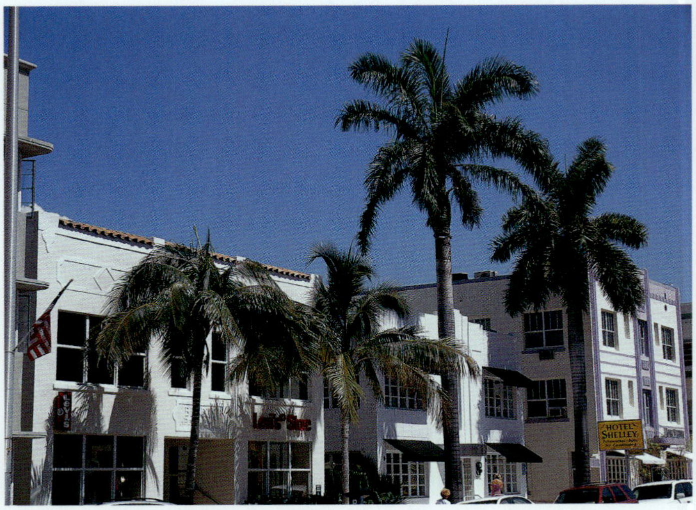

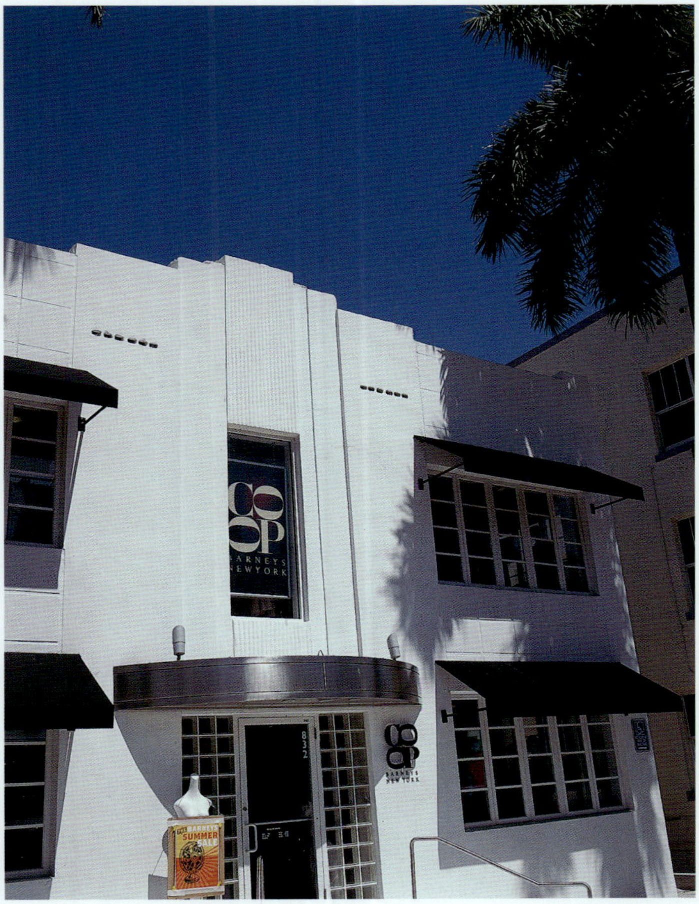

Chapter 8

LANDMARKS BY THE SEA

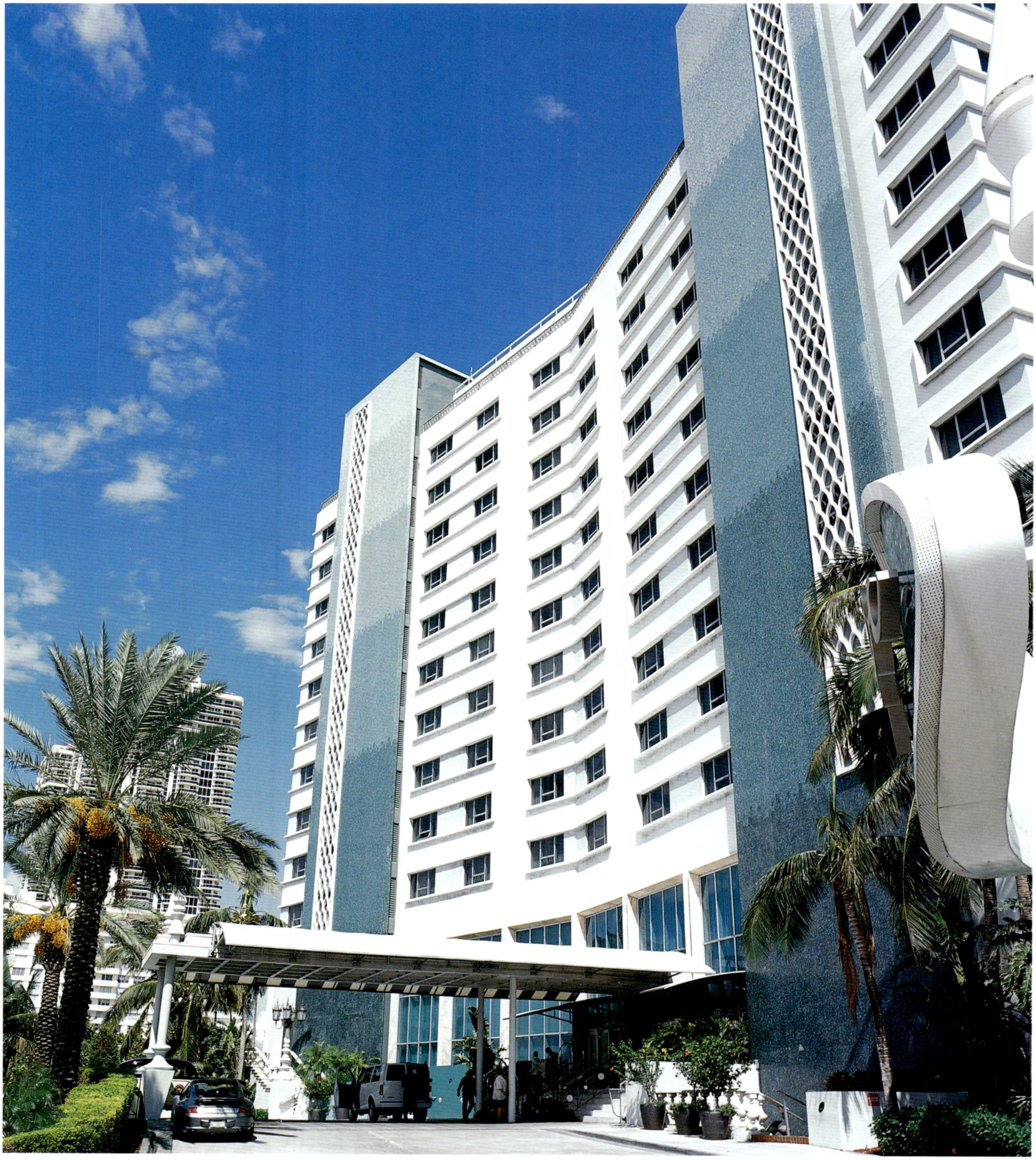

ALEX BATISTA AND THE EDEN ROC

A mid-Beach landmark for over half a century, the Eden Roc has been the backdrop for feature films, frenzied real estate battles, and, of course, countless fashion-photo shoots. It is a signature "Miami-Modern" creation of famed architect Morris Lapidus.

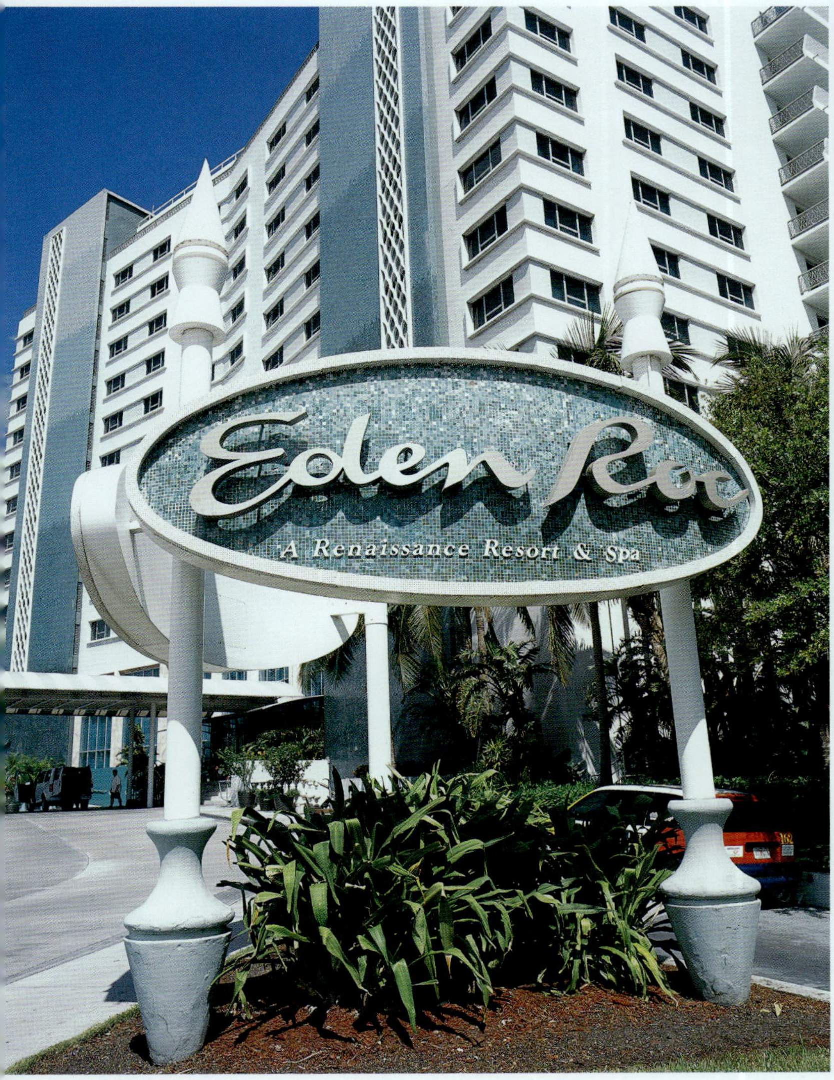

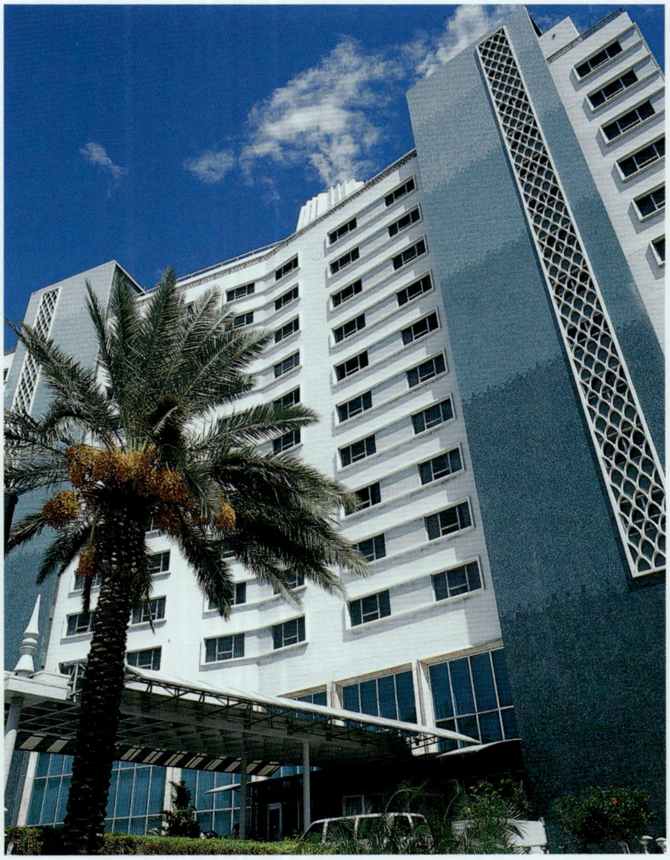

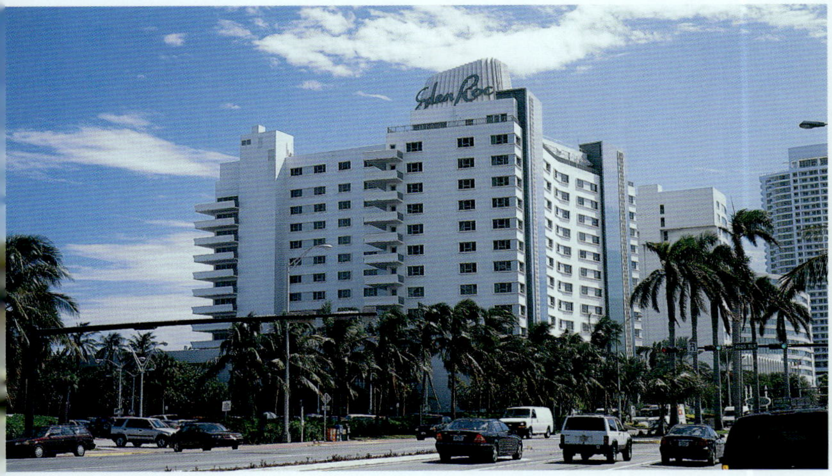

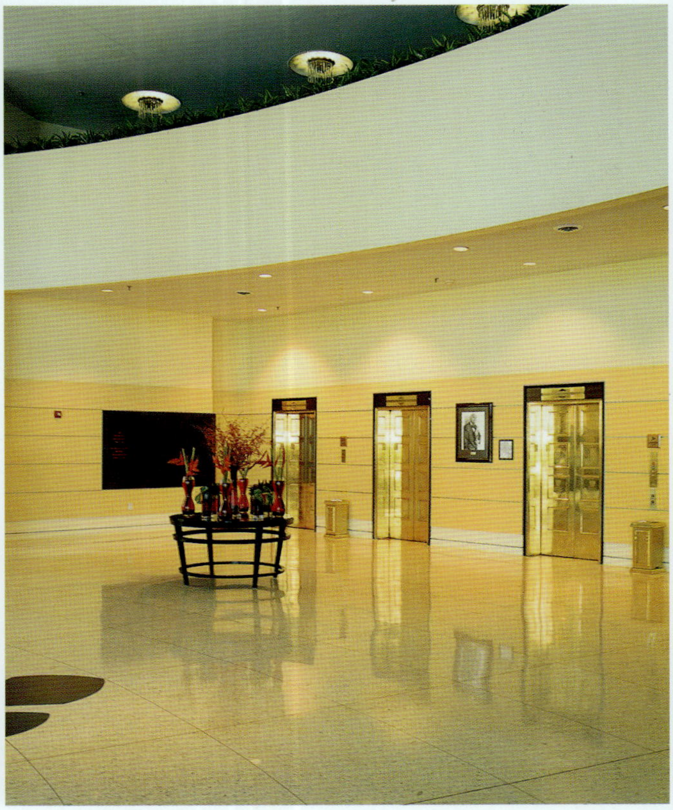

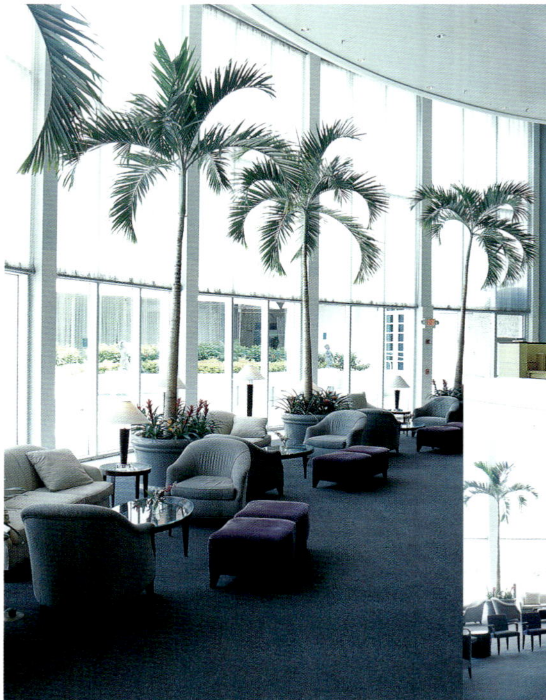

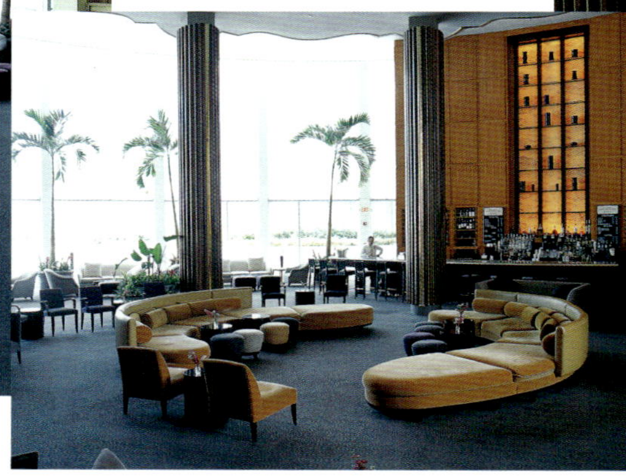

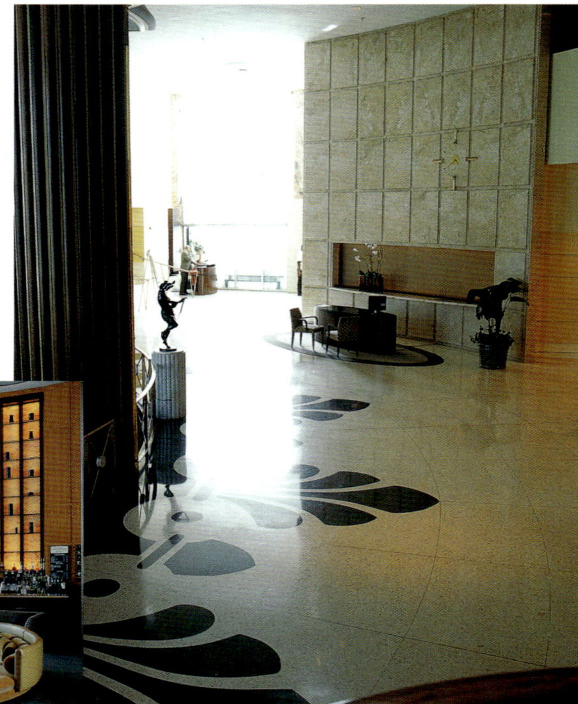

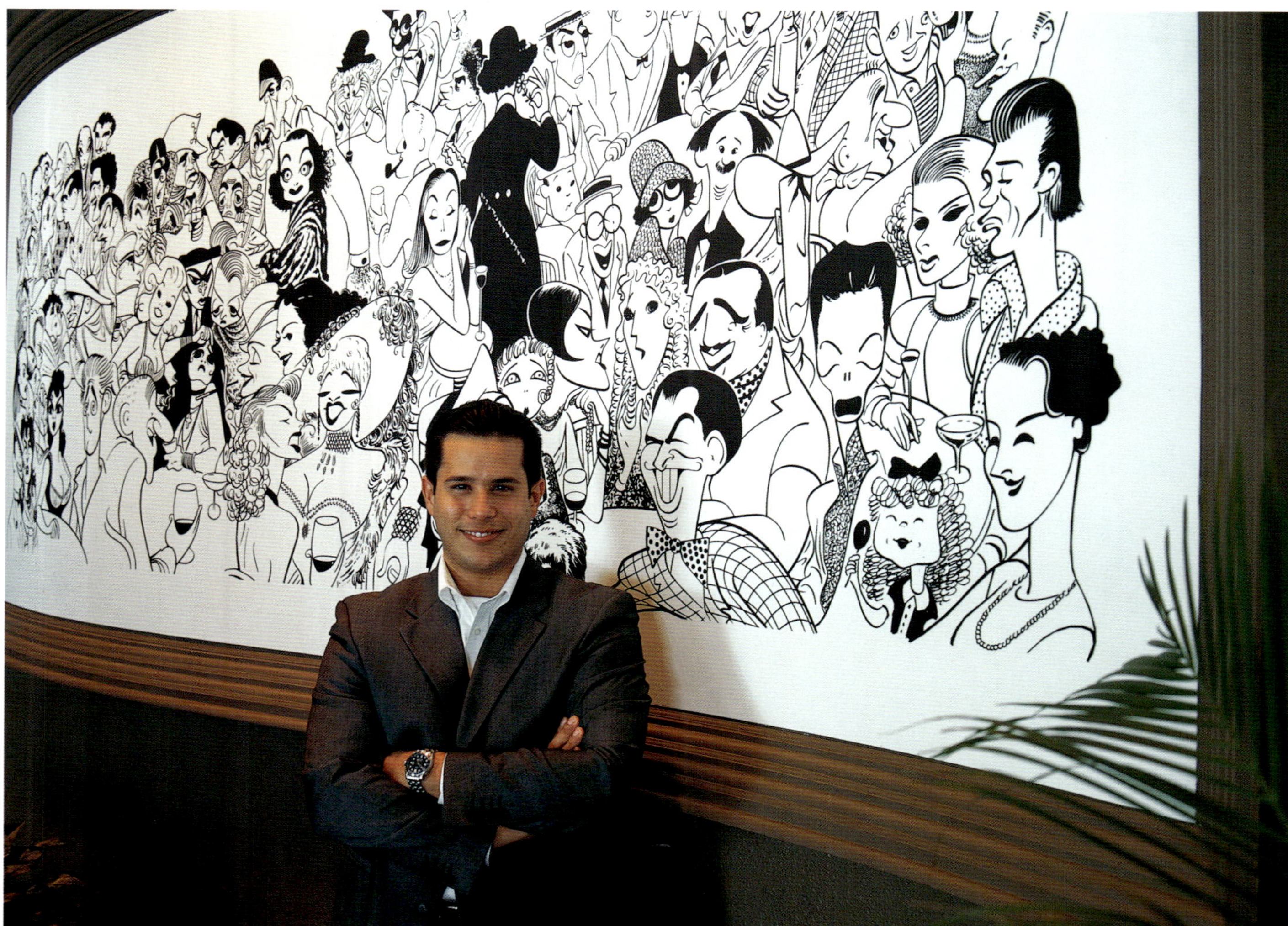

Among "The Roc's" longest-serving faces is Alex Batista, one of the resort's "senior" executives despite his baby-faced looks. Like so many other Miamians, Alex is a native of Cuba. And like so many faces in South Beach, Alex's beaming presence adds sex appeal to what South Beach offers, which he describes as "Everything: architecture, culture, character." His recommendation for living the good life in Miami Beach? "Buy real estate. It is booming."

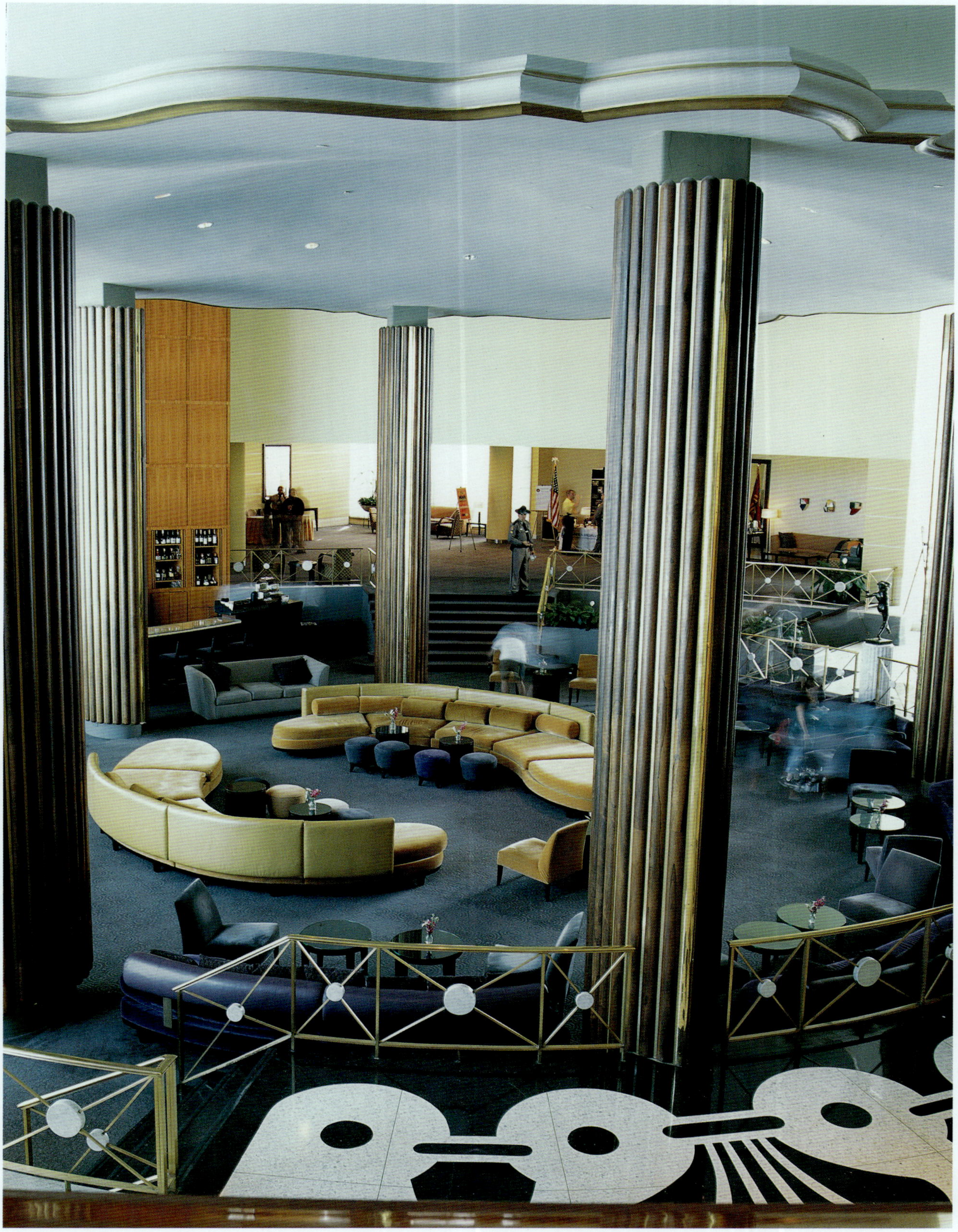

Chapter 9

Riches to Riches

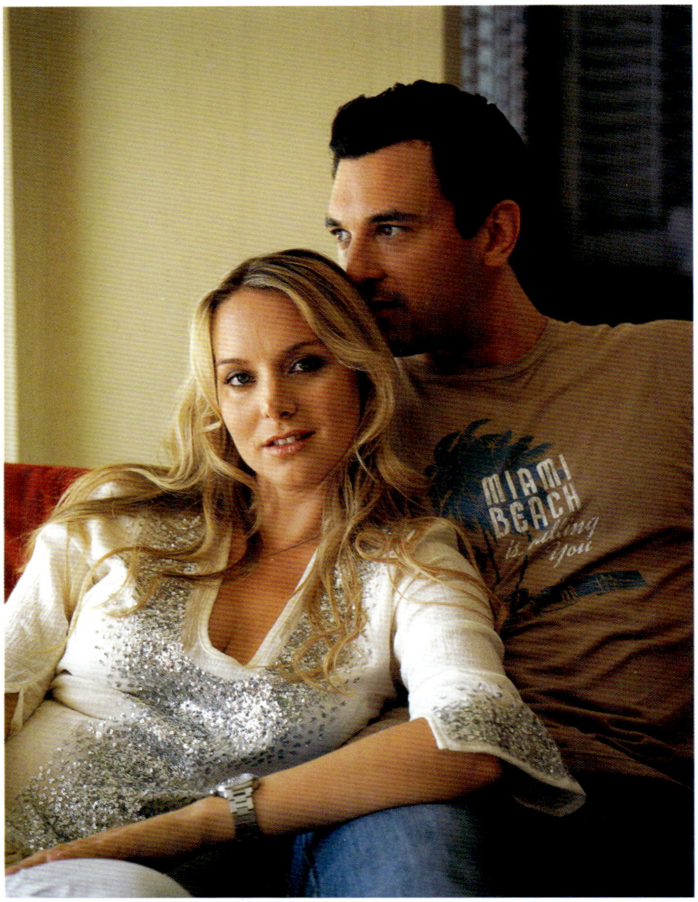

Christina Getty Maercks and Arin Maercks

It's true. South Beach has captivated, and captured, some of the most beautiful people in the world.

A prime example is this globe-trotting couple, Christina and Arin Maercks. Residents of one of South Beach's tonier island neighborhoods, the Maercks, who were expecting the arrival of a new family member when these photos were taken, are literally jet-setters who could spend their precious time together anywhere. More and more, worldly-wise attractive young professional families are finding South Beach a place where you can live and raise children, as well as party.

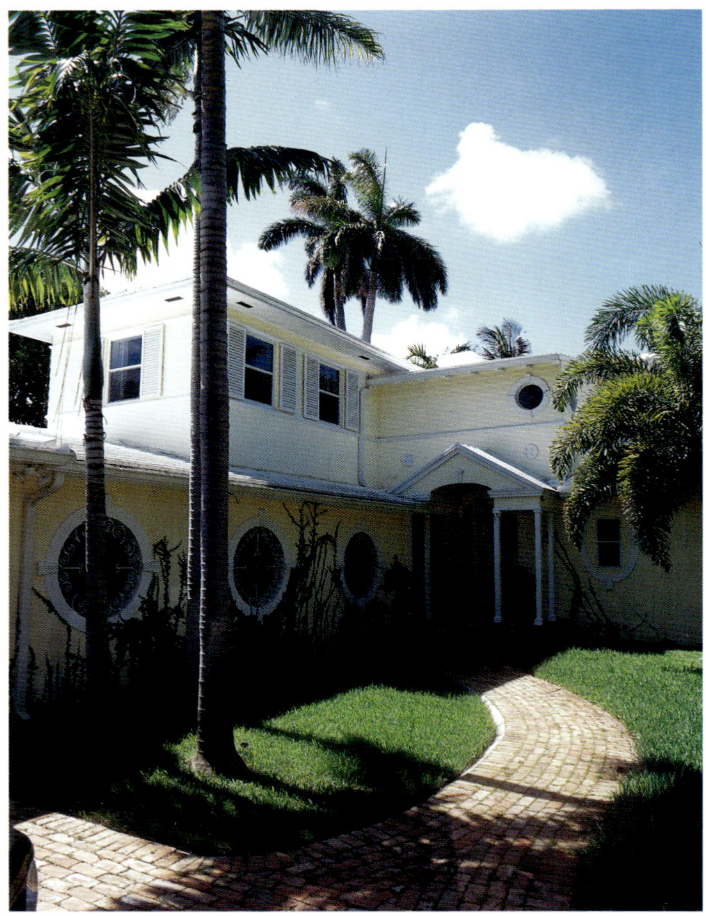

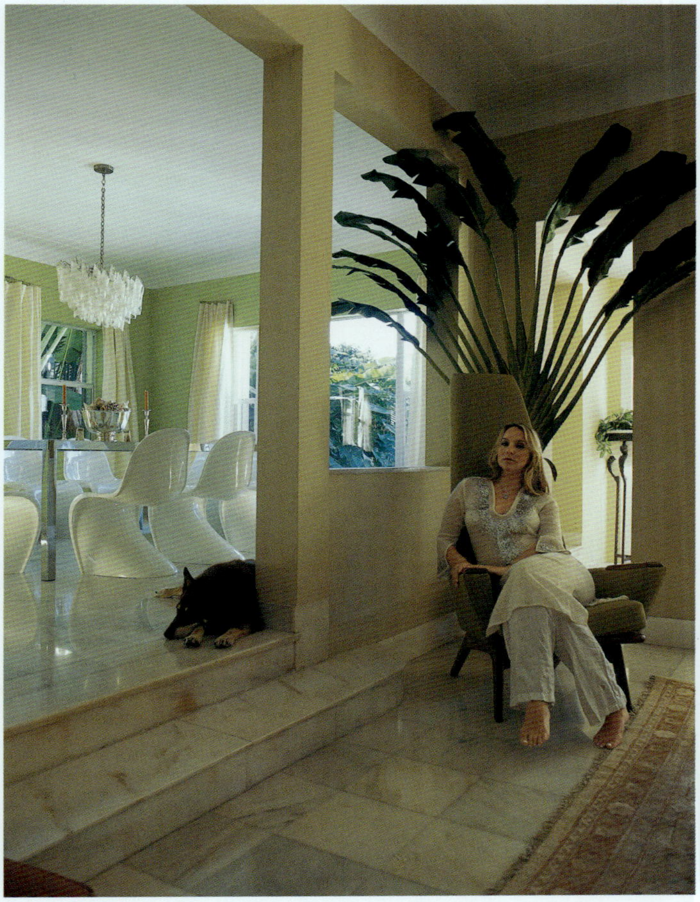

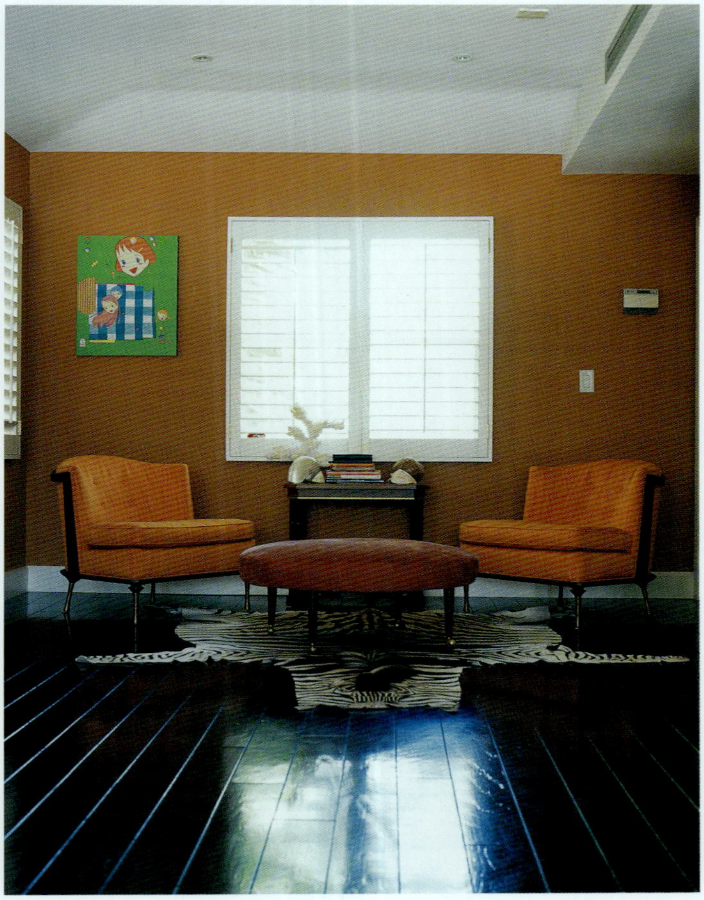

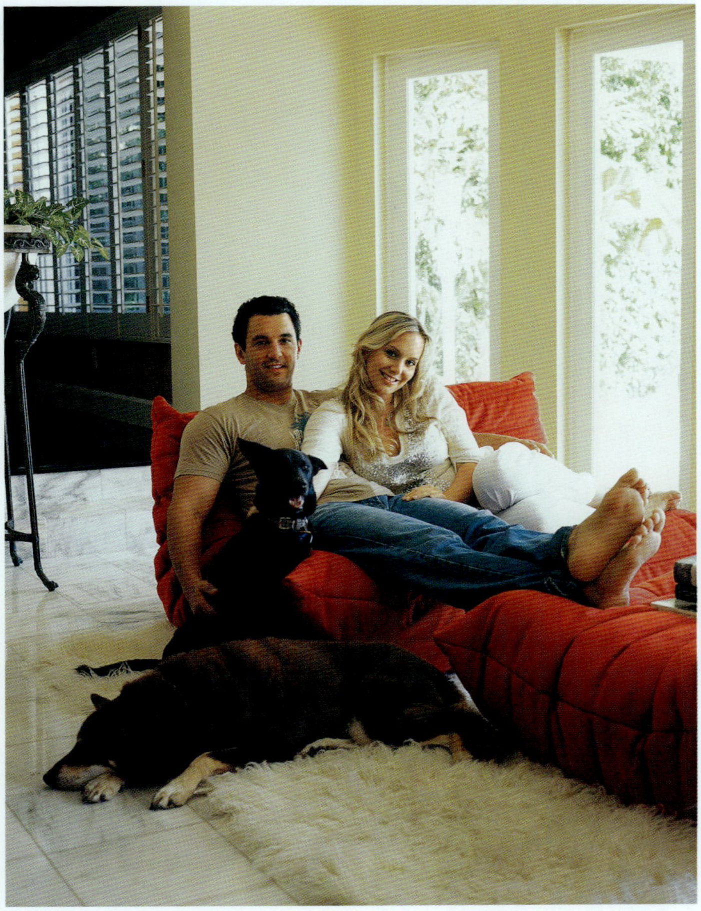

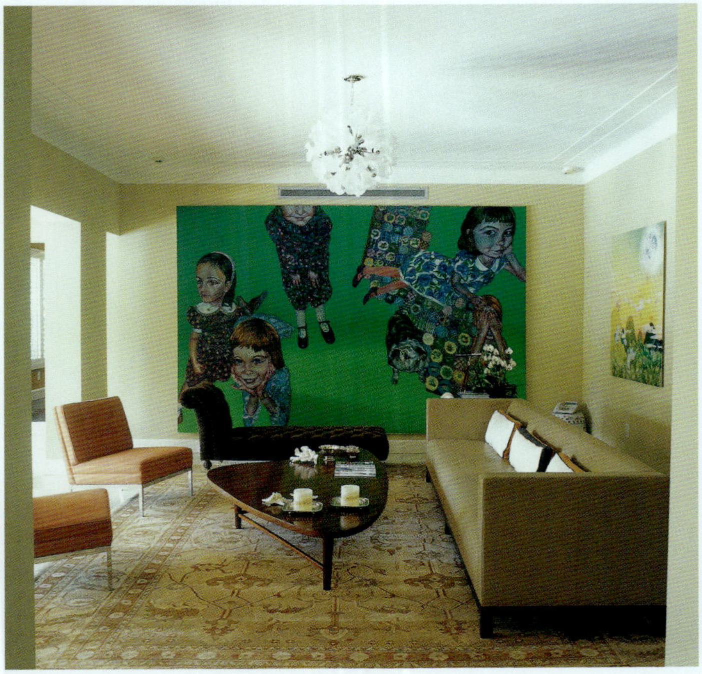

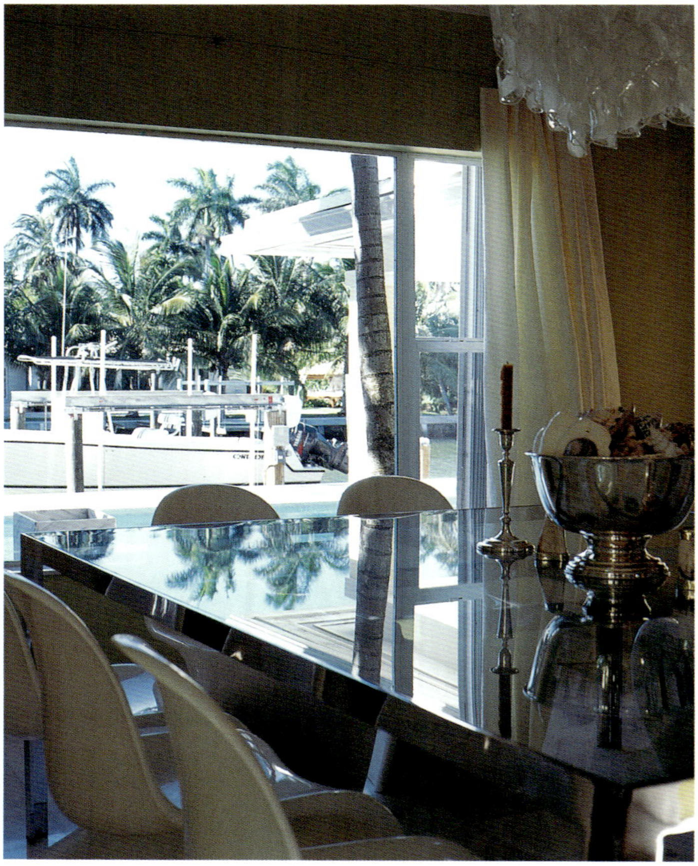

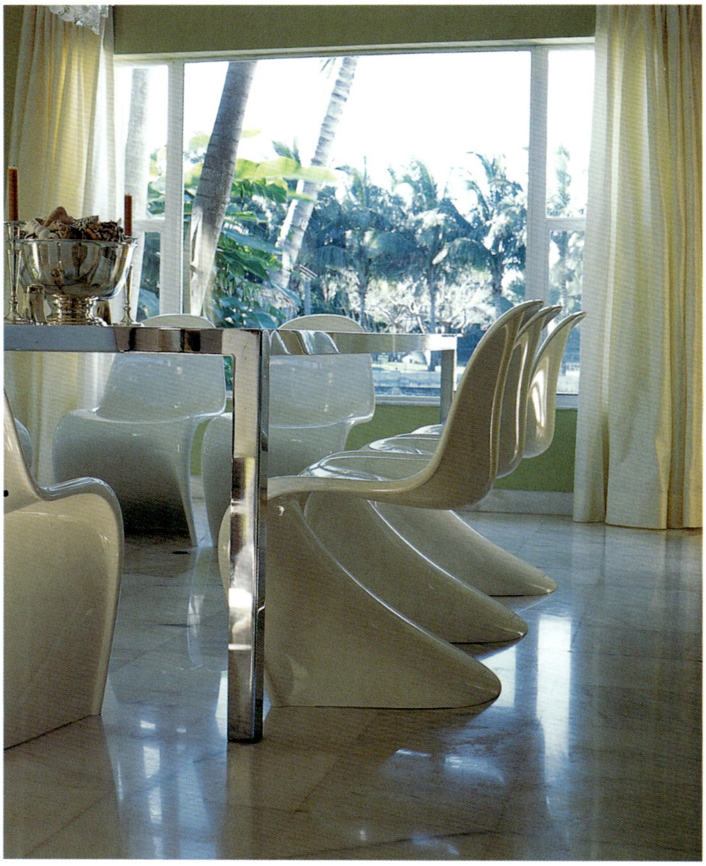

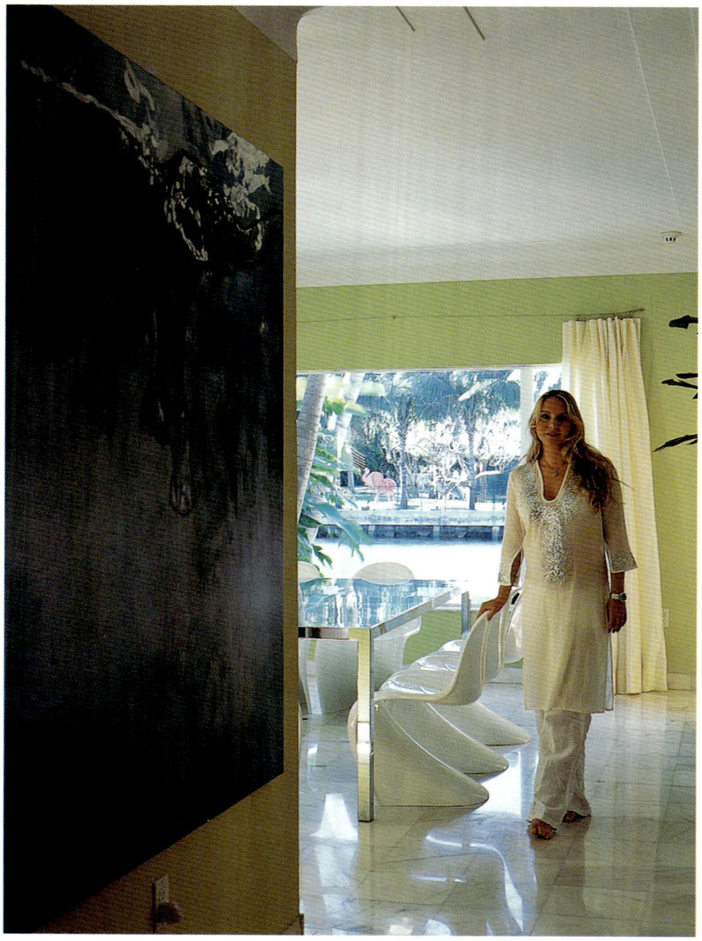

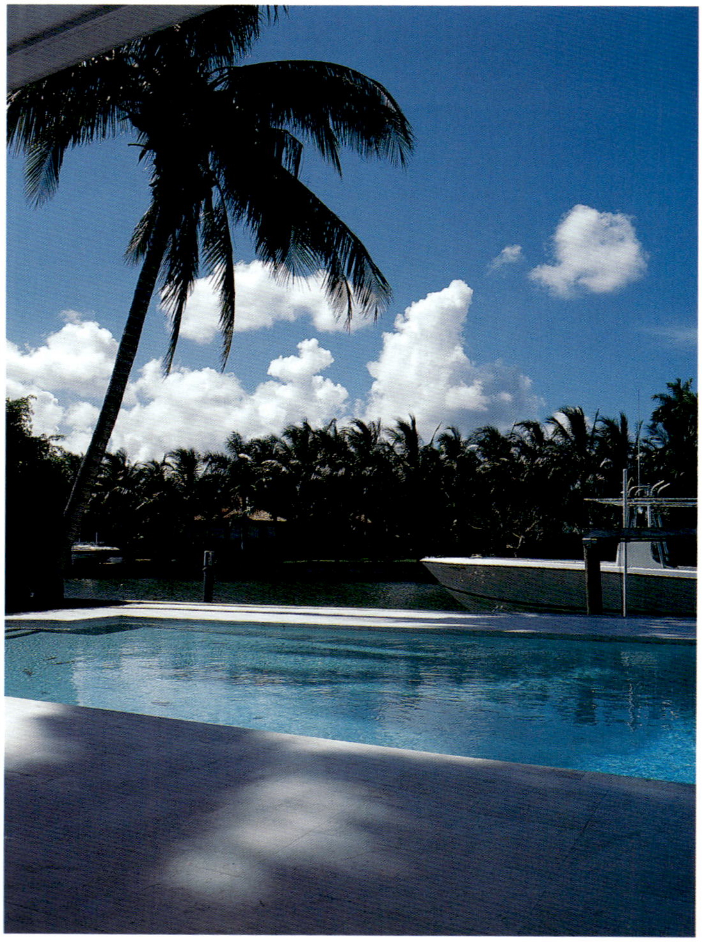

Christina, a public relations professional, is also heavily involved in the Miami and international arts scene, and she travels worldwide to oversee her family's real estate interests. She is at much at home taking in the Lincoln Road people parade (cost: zero) as throwing an elegant onboard party and after-party champagne supper at Casa Tua, one of South Beach's truly fine eateries (cost: considerable).

If you're looking for superlatives, Christina is a woman who can afford to see and live anywhere she wants, and here's how she sums up her prescription for a first-time visitor: "Take a tour of the city by boat...There is no city that has the kind of beauty Miami has by water."

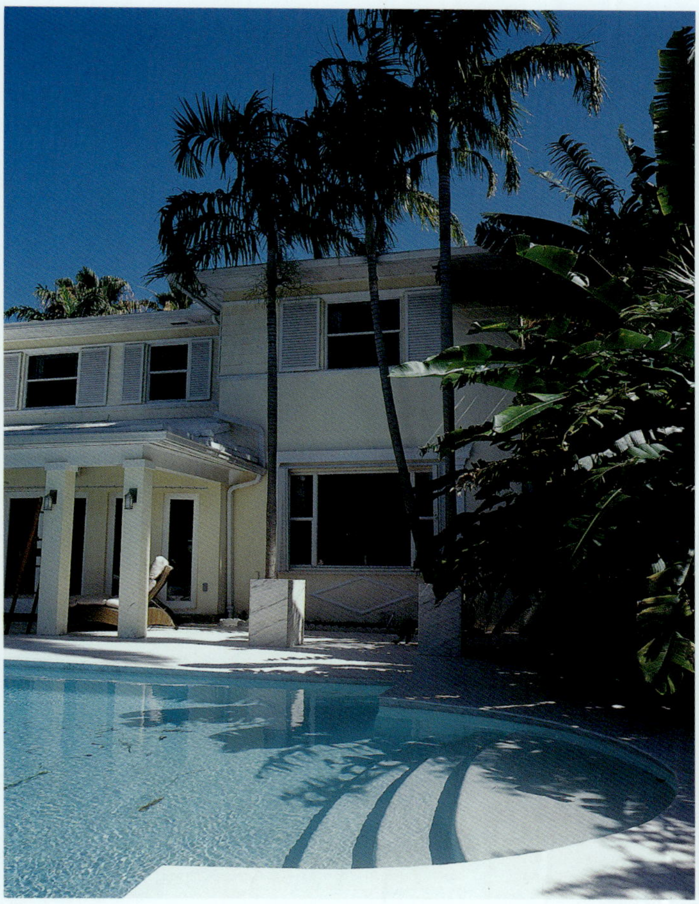

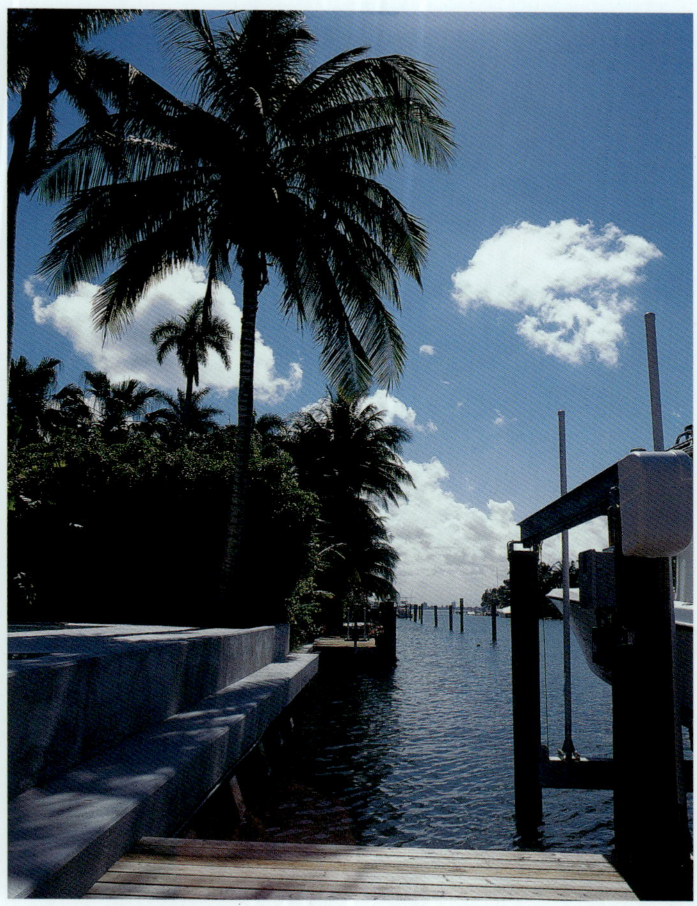

Chapter 10

ART ON THE BEACH

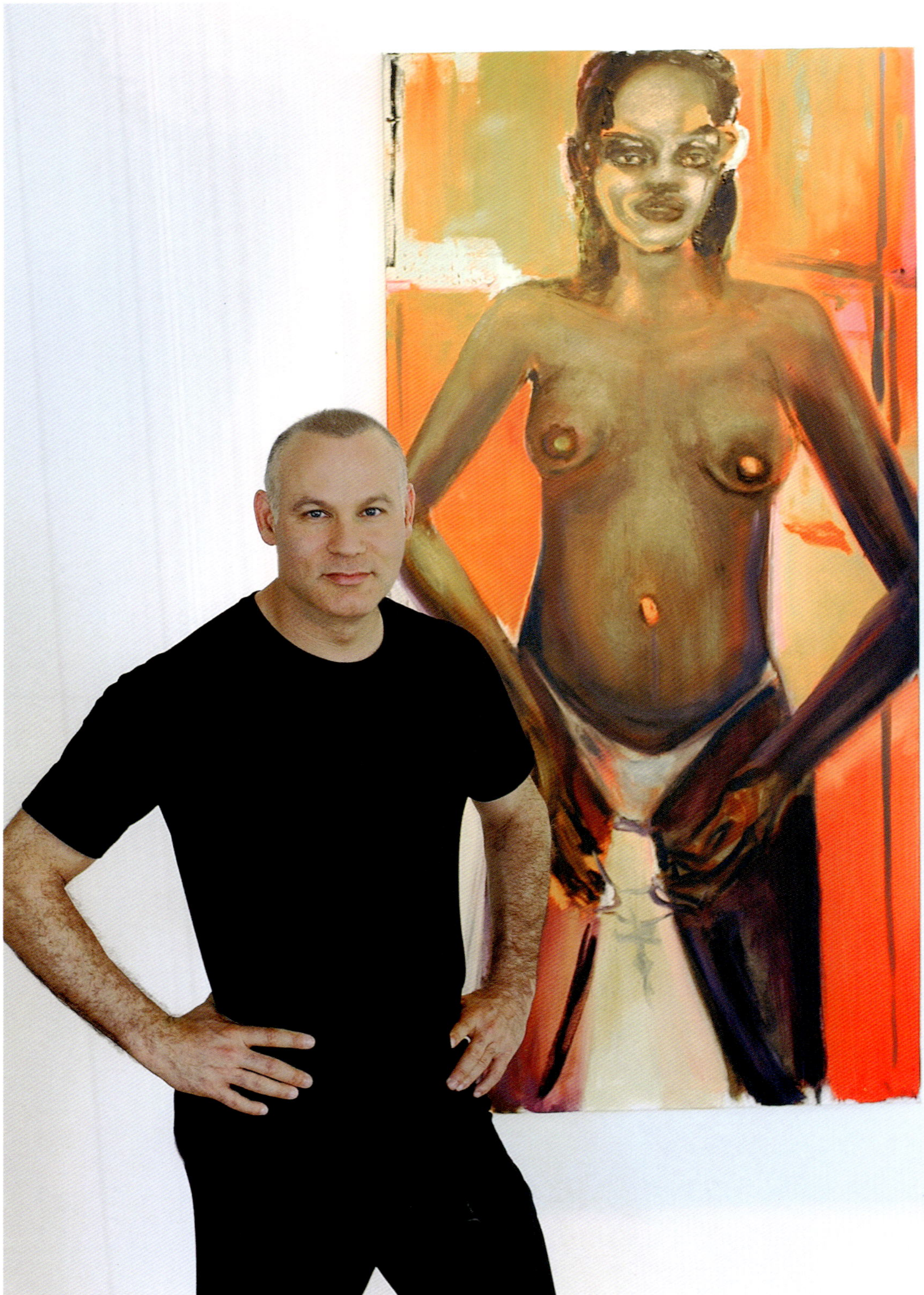

CRAIG ROBINS AND DACRA DEVELOPMENT

There aren't many places where you can be a young man who is already a legend, but Craig Robins comes about as close as you can get. Since graduating from law school, this Miami Beach native has (1) changed the face of the previously derelict South Beach area with his early risk-taking Art Deco development projects; (2) almost single-handedly revived the previously rundown "Design District" on the mainland; and (3) redefined "island living" with his breakthrough Aqua community, recently built on previously vacant mid-Beach property at Allison Island.

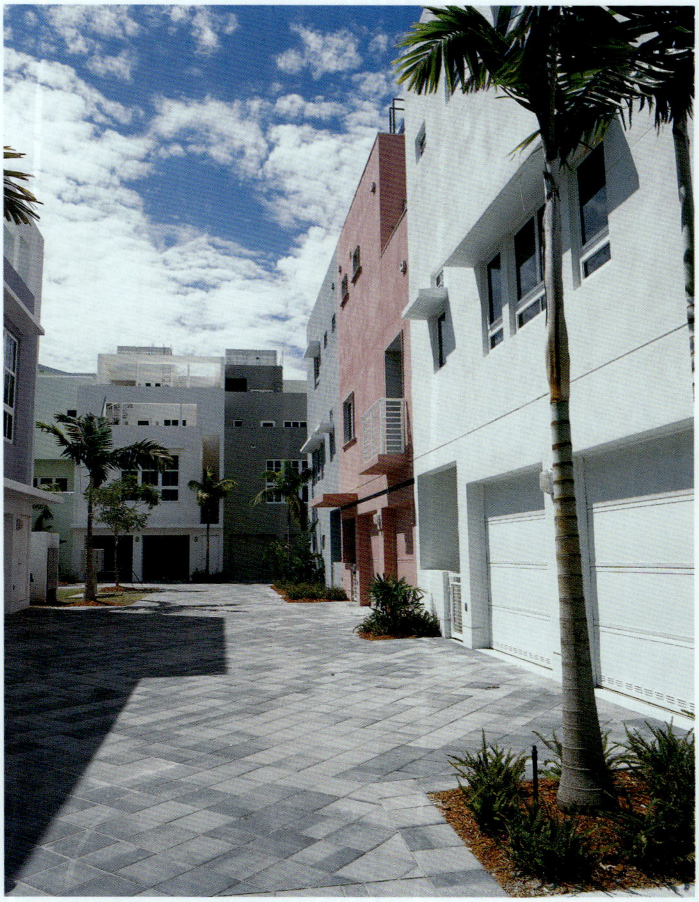

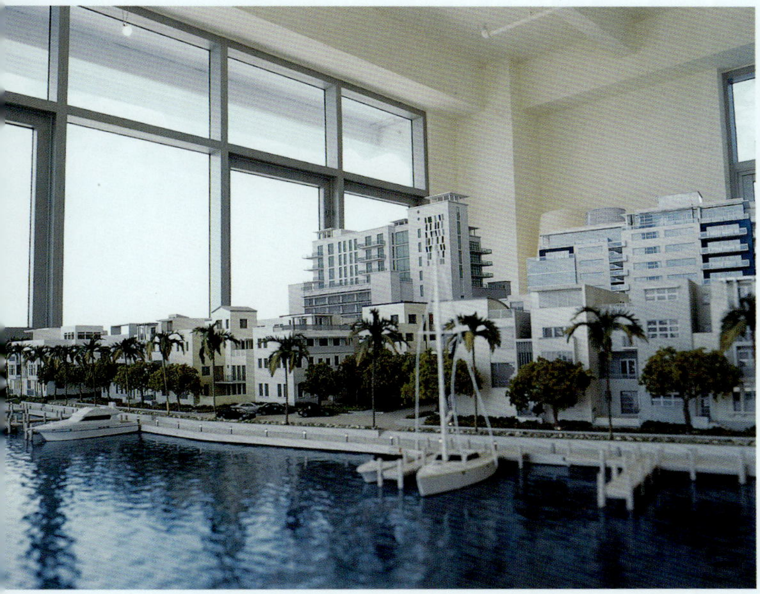

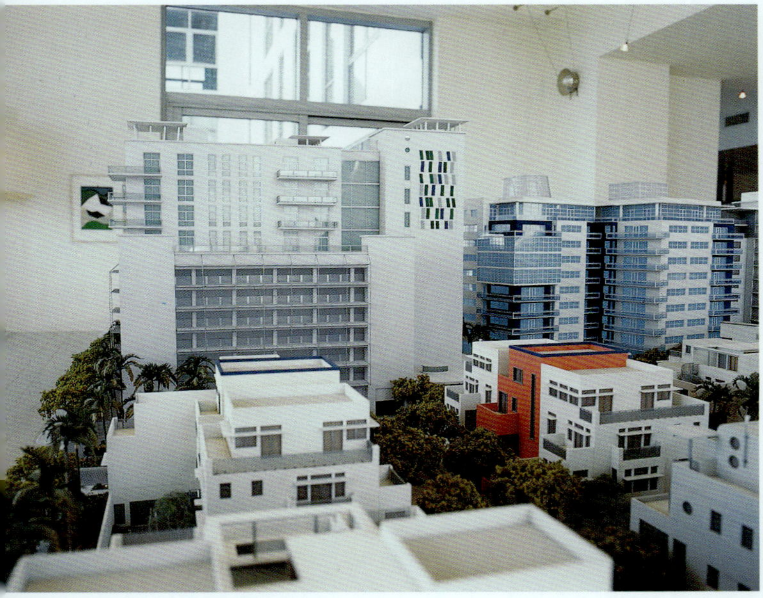

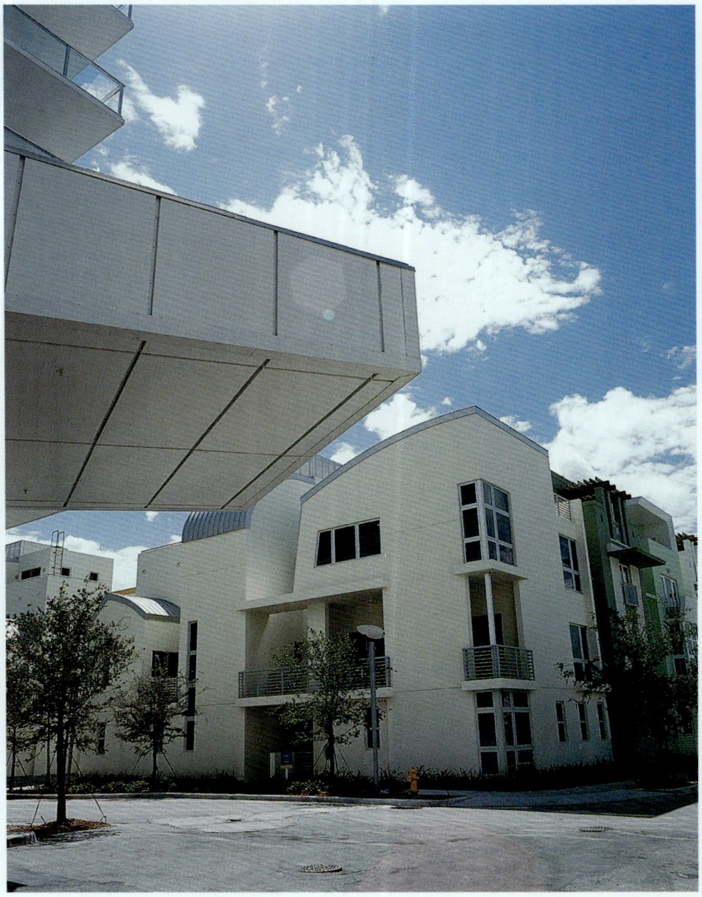

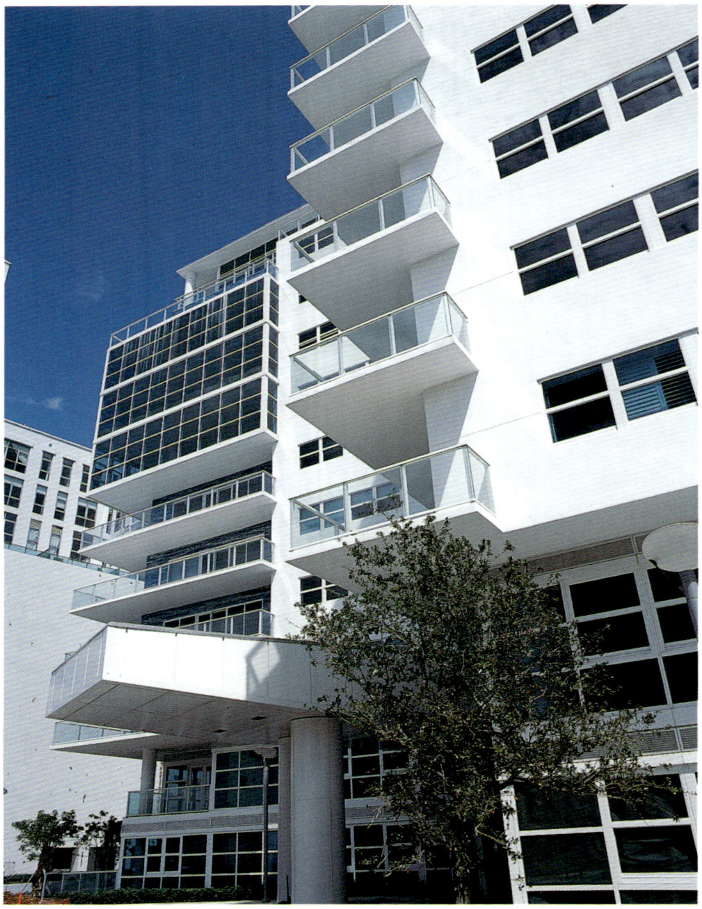
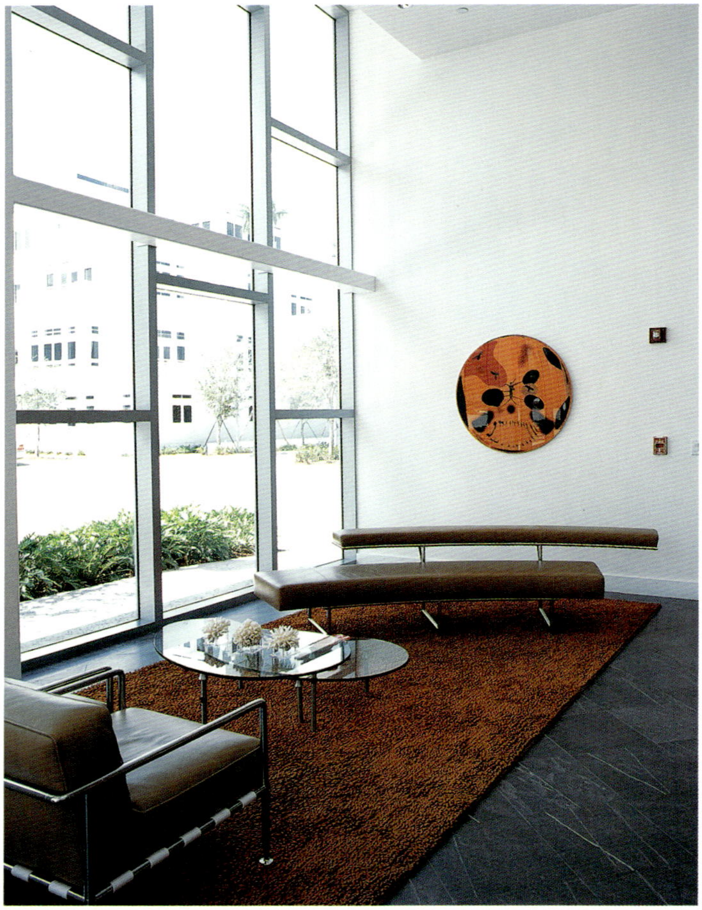
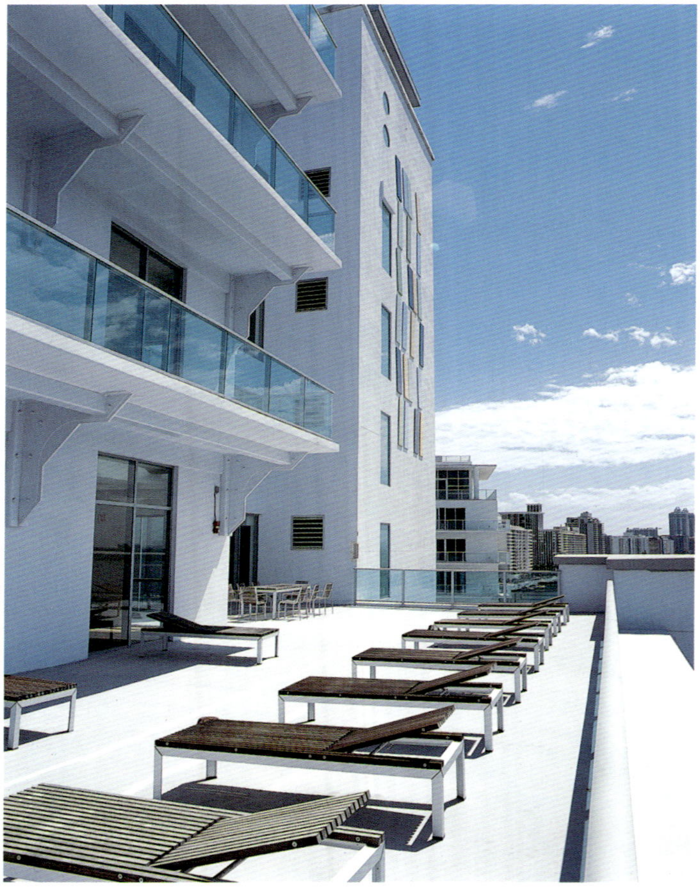
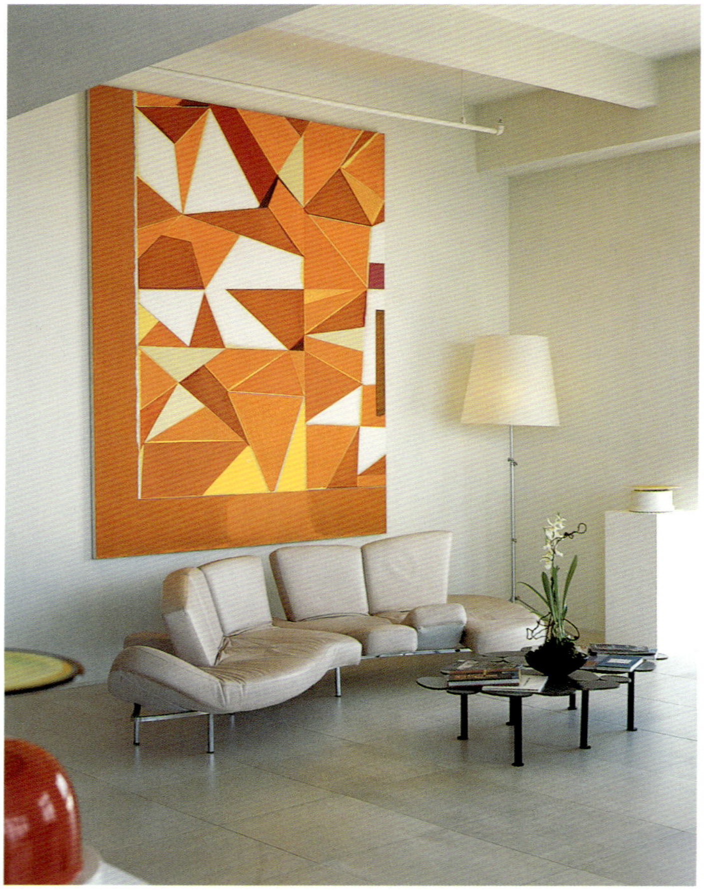

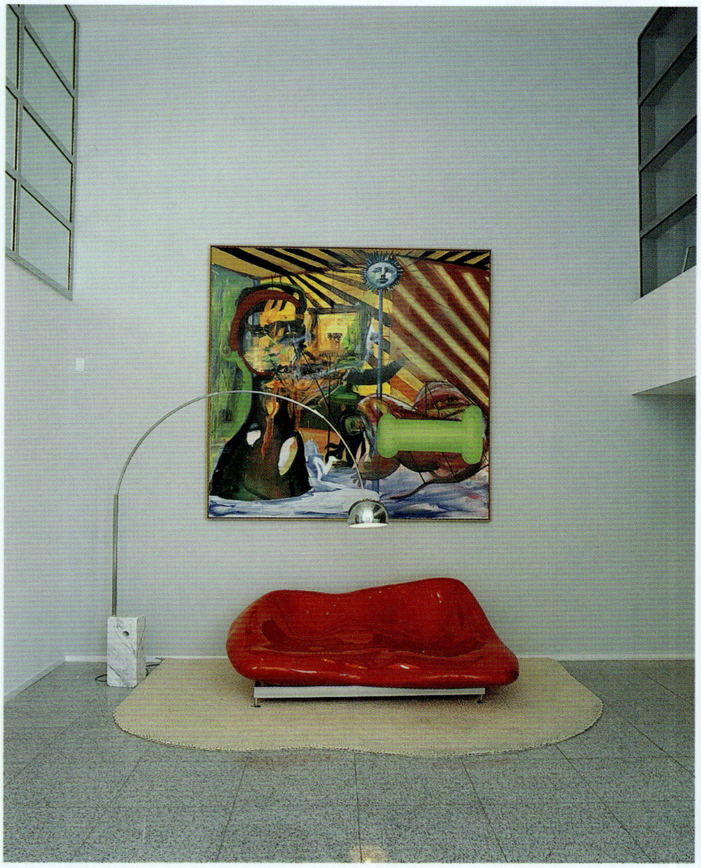

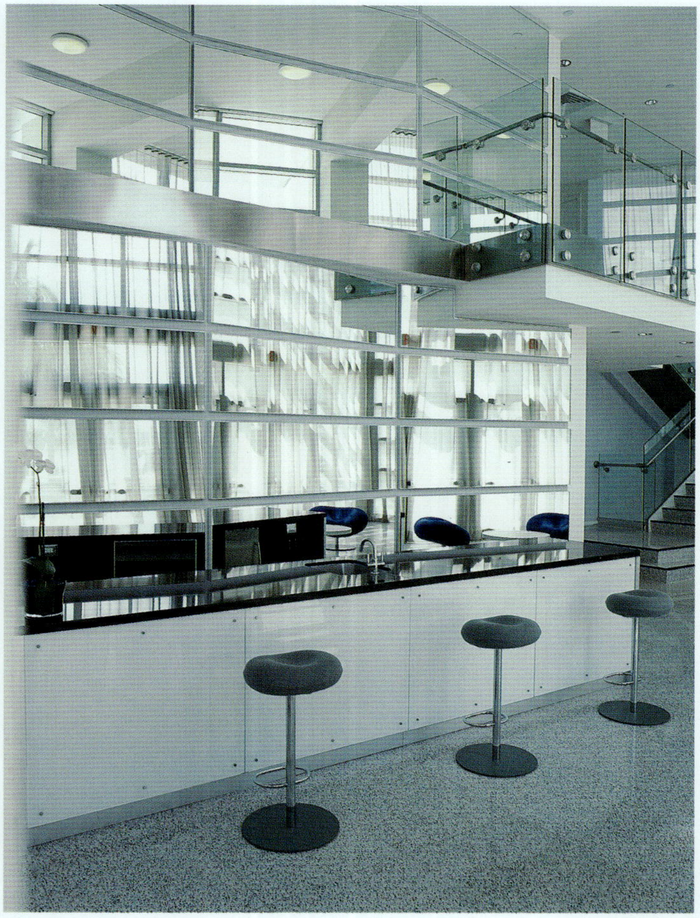

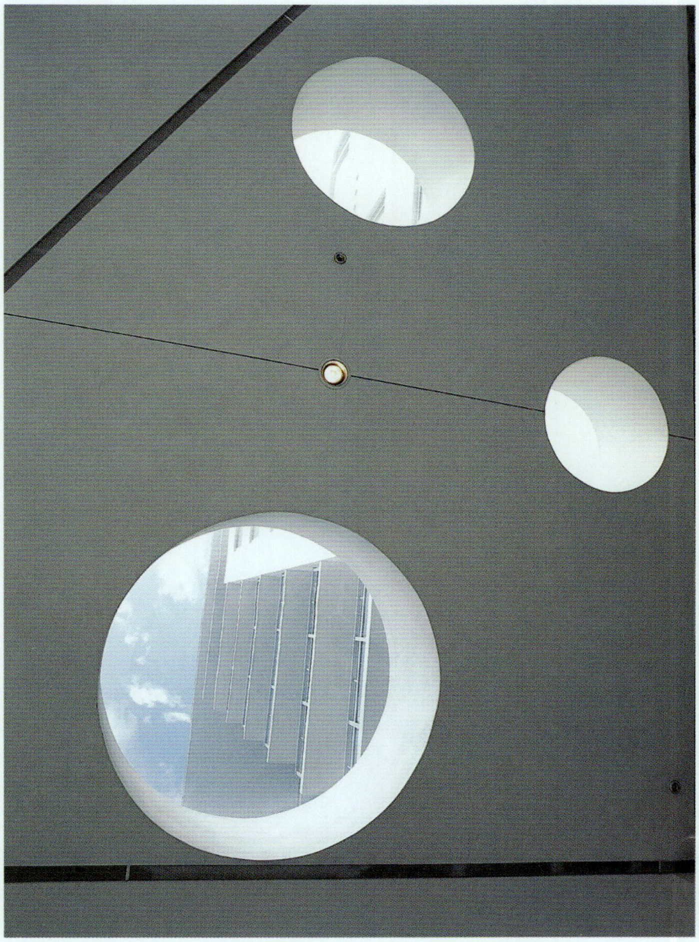

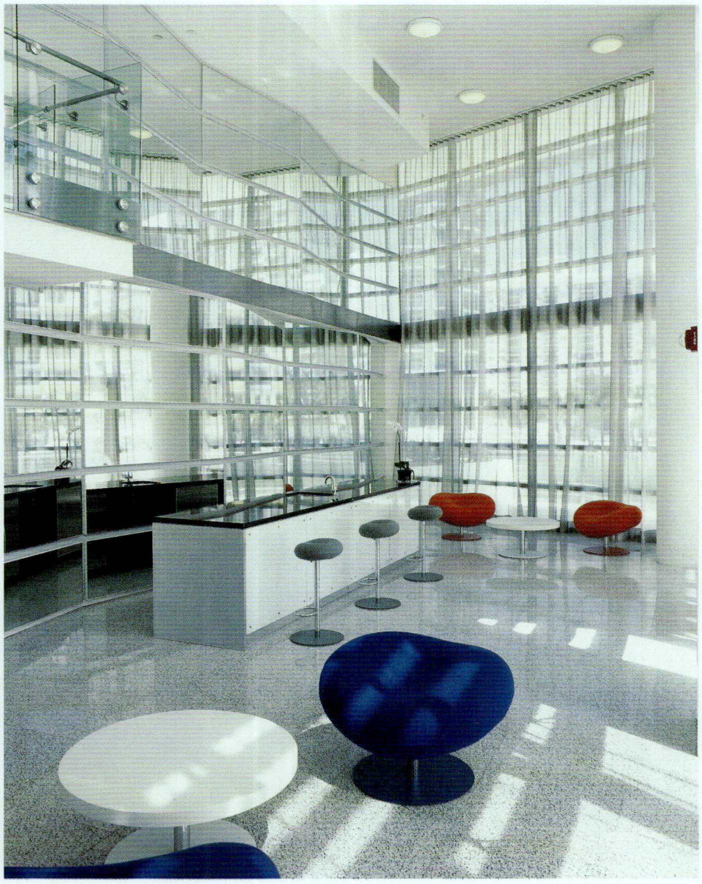

In the meantime, Craig has amassed a world-class art collection and still calls Miami Beach home while spending part of his time in New York City. His prescription for the first time visitor says everything about the love affair between South Beach and its residents: "...walk—Ocean Drive, Collins and Washington Avenues from South Pointe to Lincoln Road—and just watch the extraordinary mix of people." Another great benefit of Miami's climate and gentle waters is that Craig can "go kayaking with my kids twelve months a year."

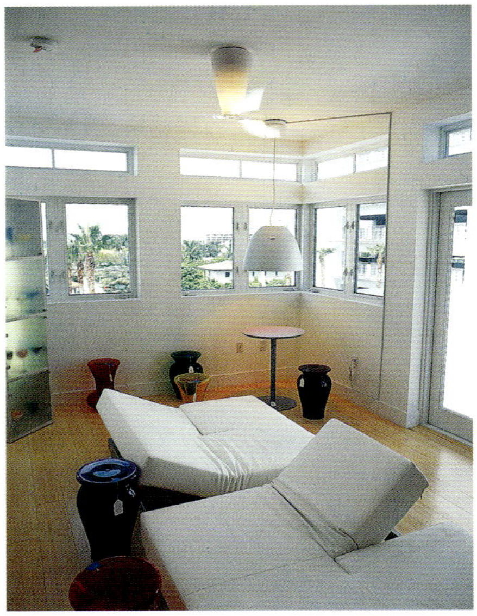

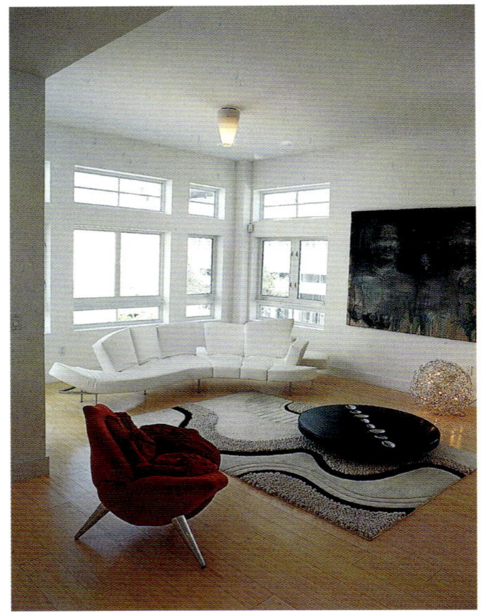

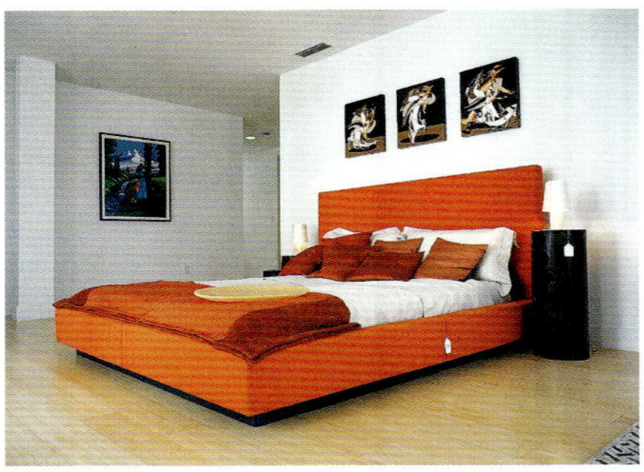

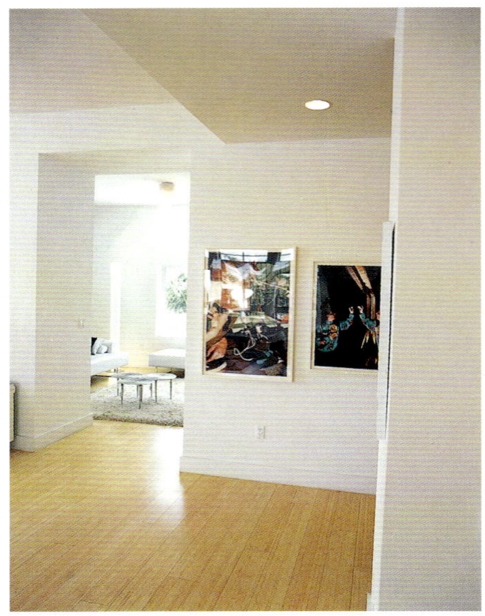

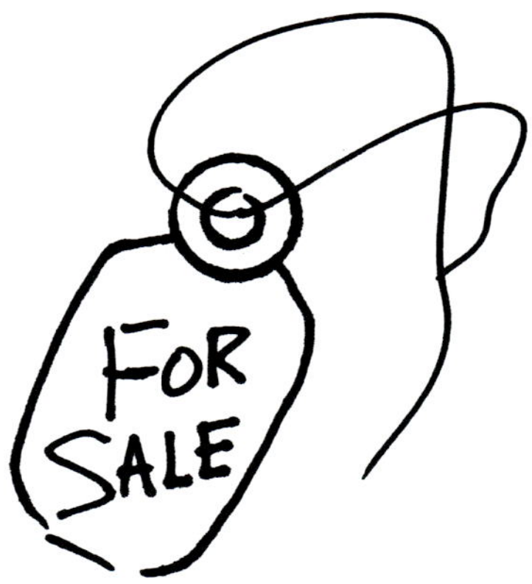

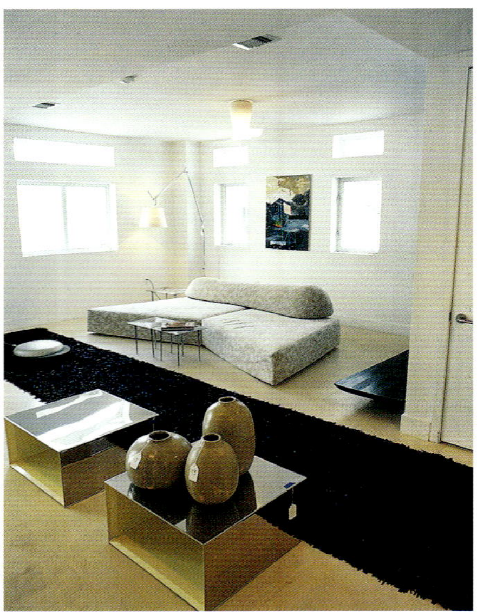

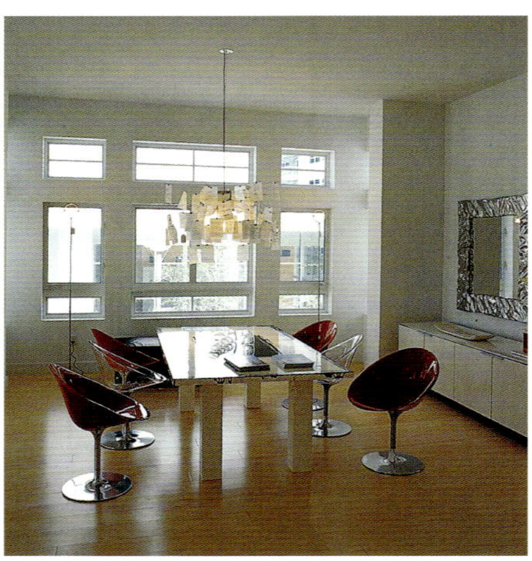

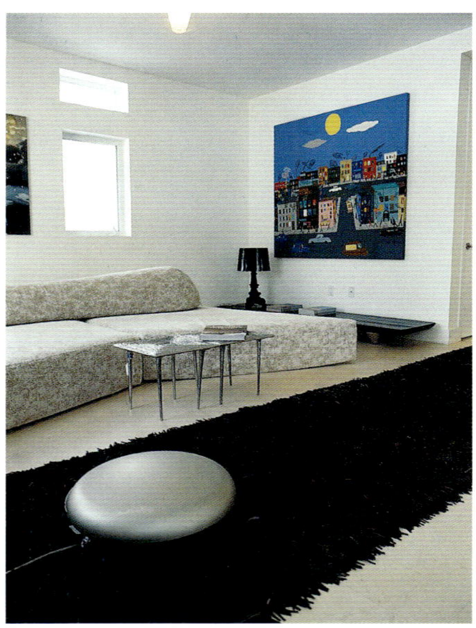

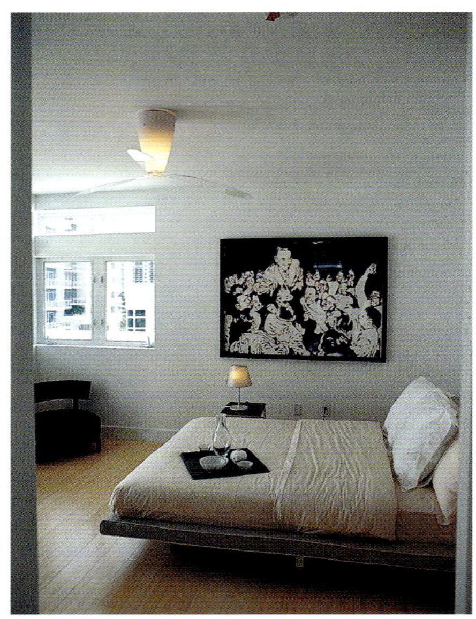

Chapter 11

Heart and Architecture

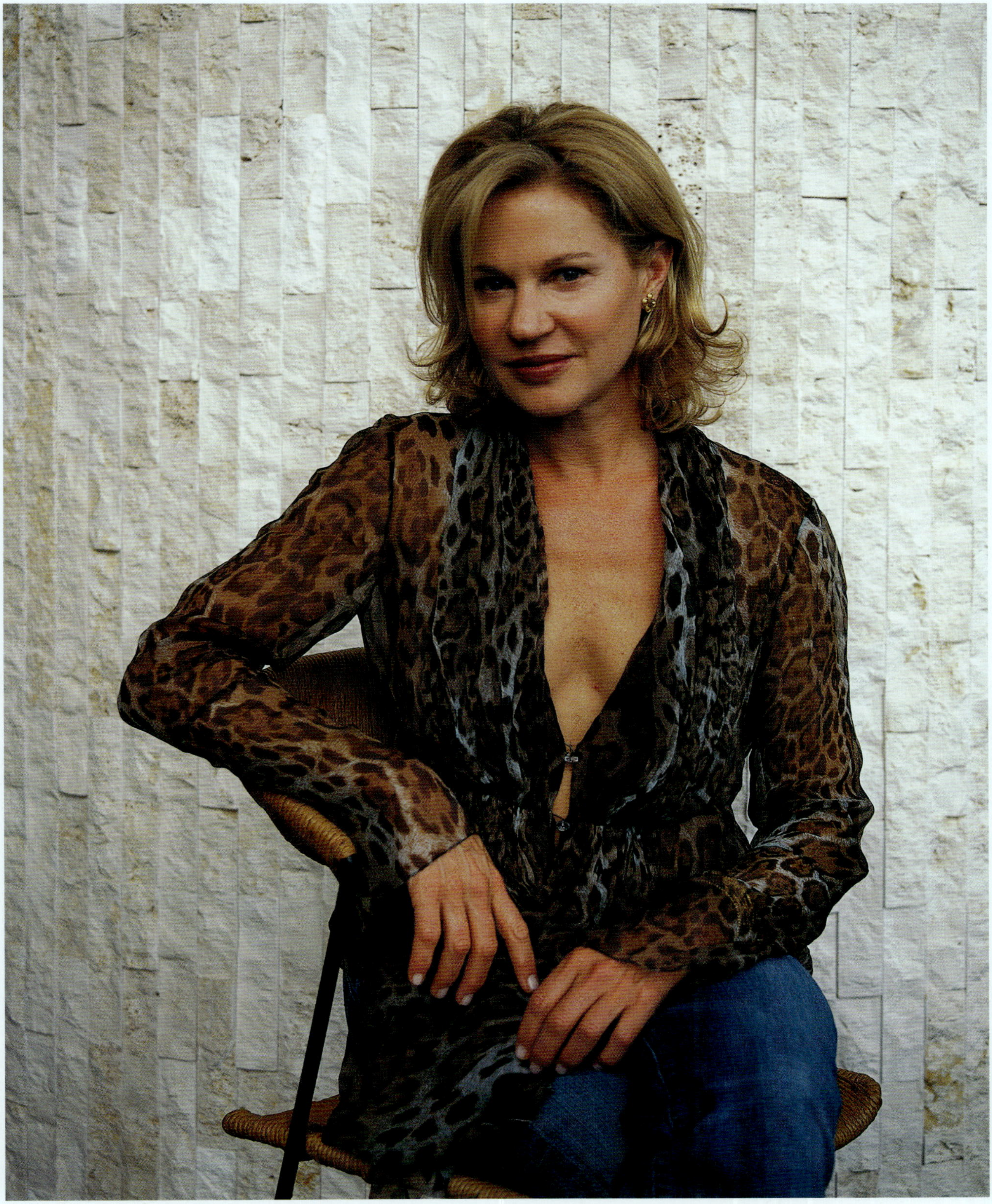

ALISON SPEAR

Unlike the typical "New-Yorker-Discovers-Miami" story-line, Alison Spear's journey to South Beach has been a return to her own roots. Born and raised in Miami, but educated in the Big Apple, Spear became a world-class designer and architect in New York before bringing her world-class self back to her home town. She's already had enough time back home to make an important impact on the design renaissance of Miami and South Beach.

Her influence in Miami Beach includes a building designed by her and "branded" in her name (the "Spear Building") at the ultra-chic Aqua community on Allison Island (no relation); the redesign of the Lido Spa Hotel (now the "Standard") on one of South Beach's island communities; and the breakthrough "Meridian Lofts" condominium near Lincoln Road.

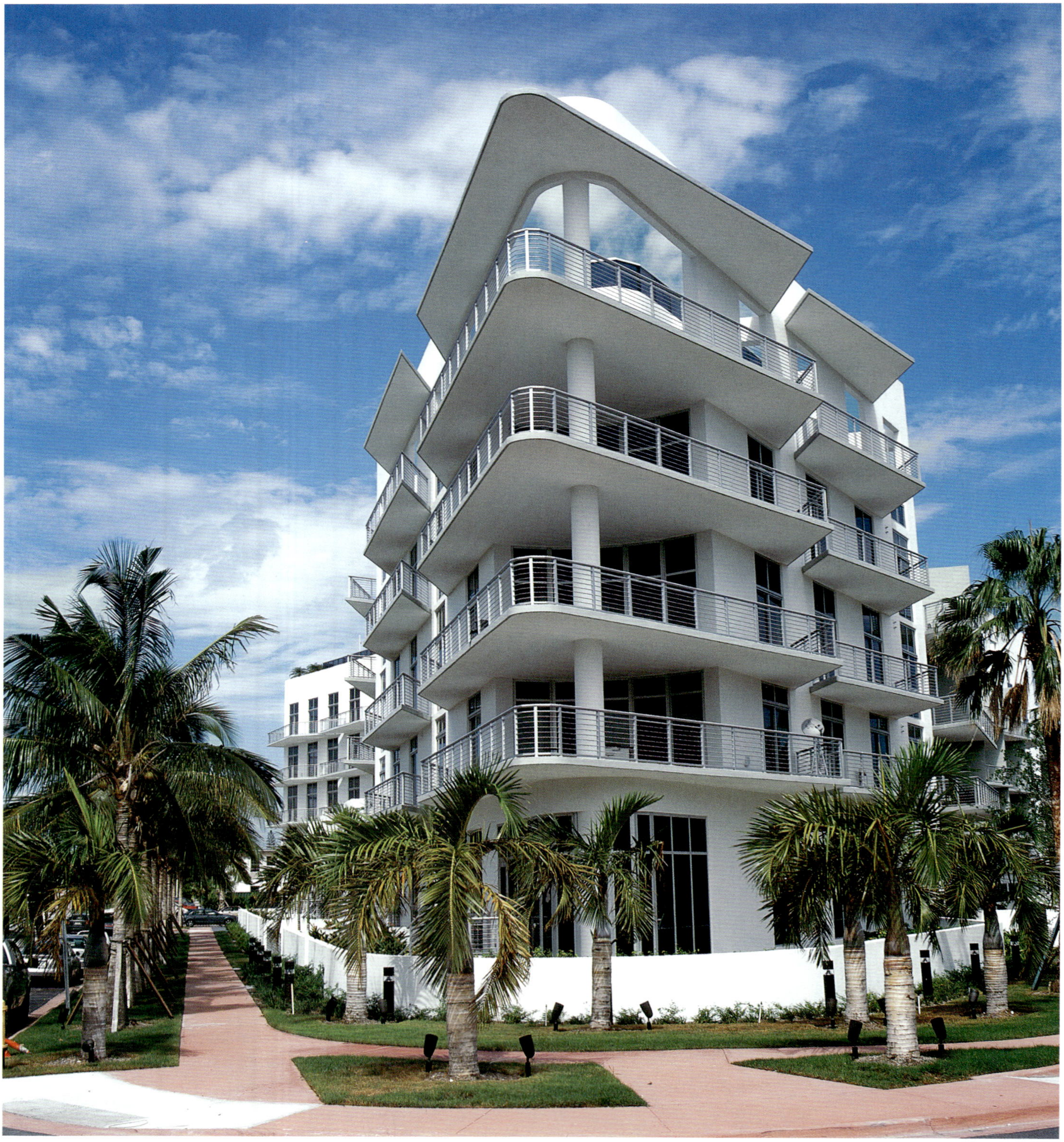

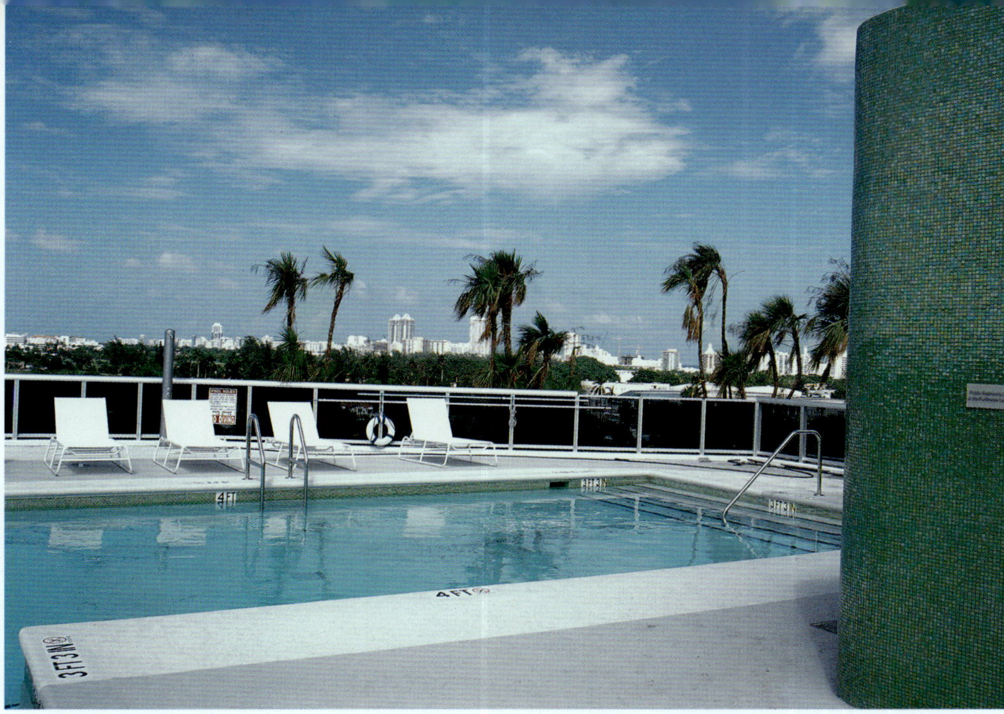
4FT
4FT

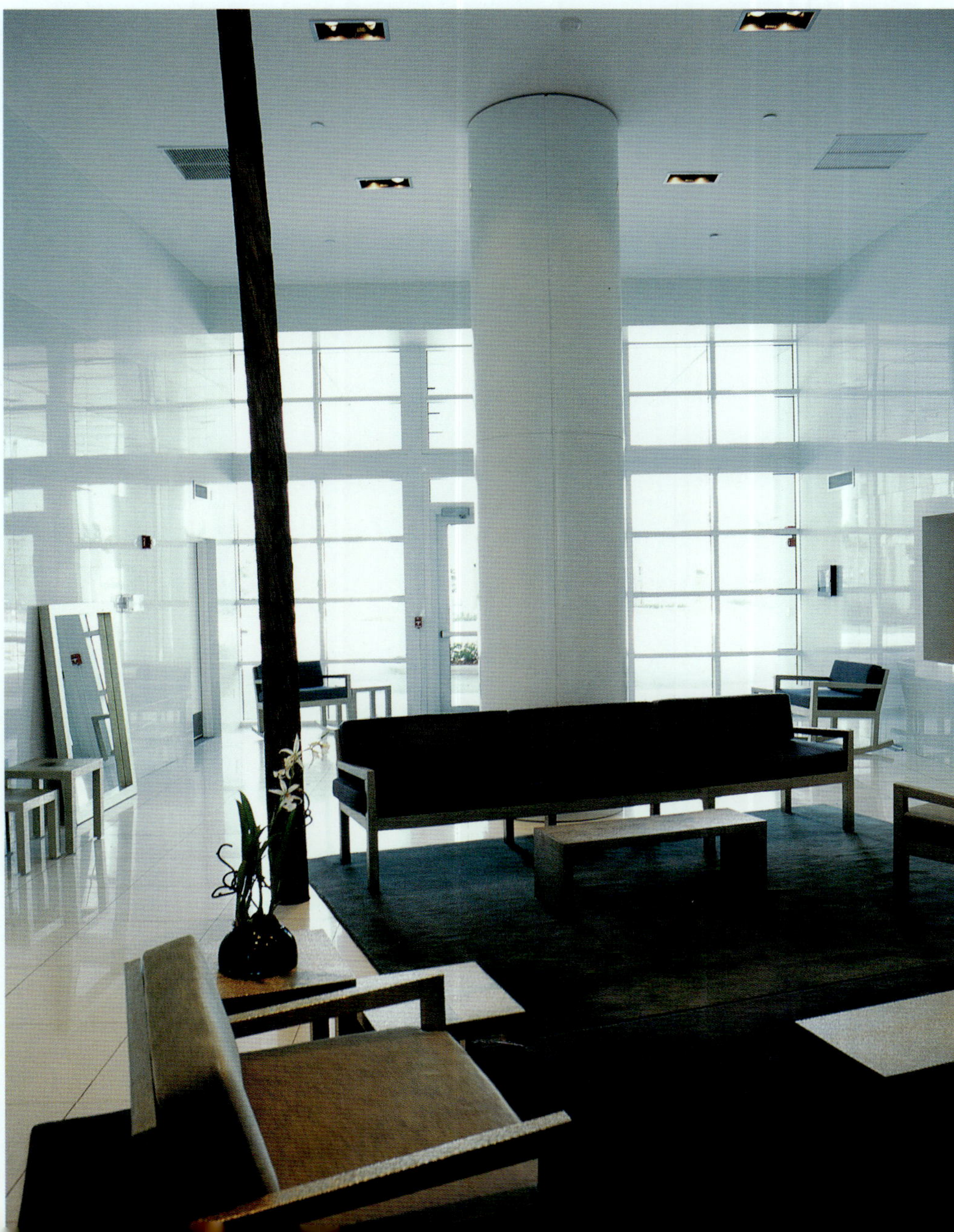

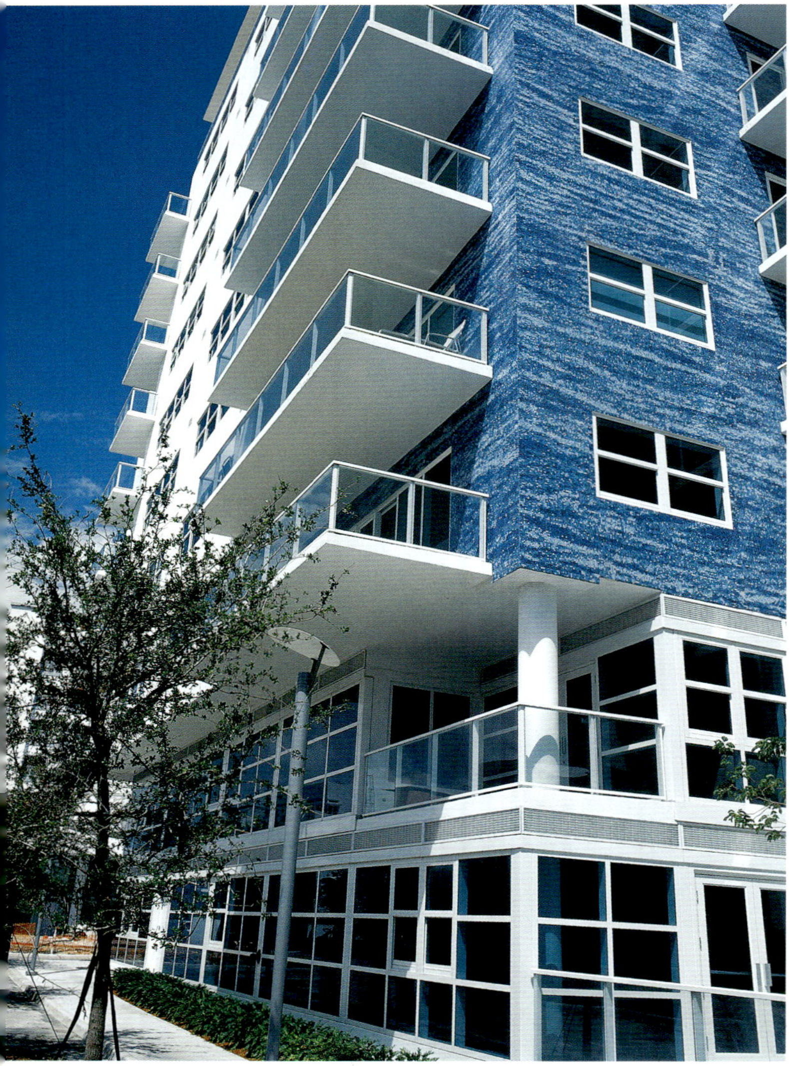

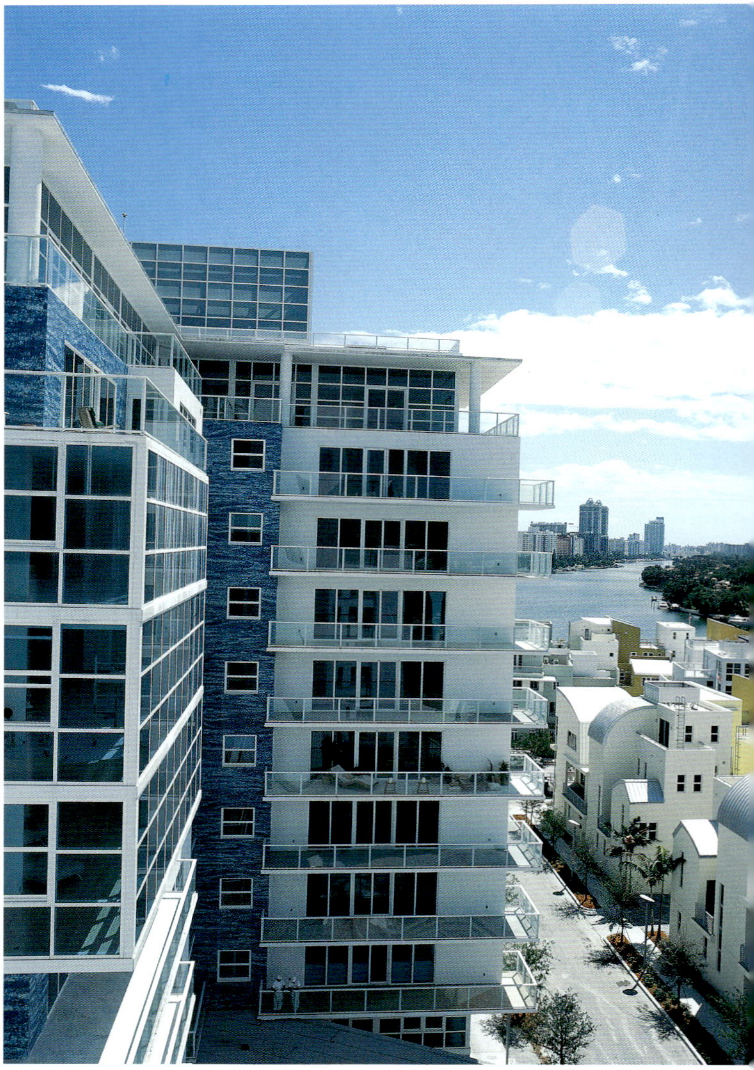

While this celebrity-level architect maintains a professional presence in New York and travels north frequently, Miami is now the city that she and her children call home. Why? "The energy—the air—the diversity—the lack of formality." As might be expected, Alison urges a first-time visitor to bathe in the Art Deco and other architectural history of South Beach and its environs ("It's great to see its history"), and spends her own days and nights involved in what she characterizes as "so many amazingly different experiences (both visual and emotional) in a day." Her personal pastimes, "dancing, surfing, and eating of course," testify to that range of experiences. "The coolest thing about living in Miami," says Alison, "is the diversity that I can have in *one* day." And another of the coolest things about Miami is having an alluring professional woman like Alison as your neighbor.

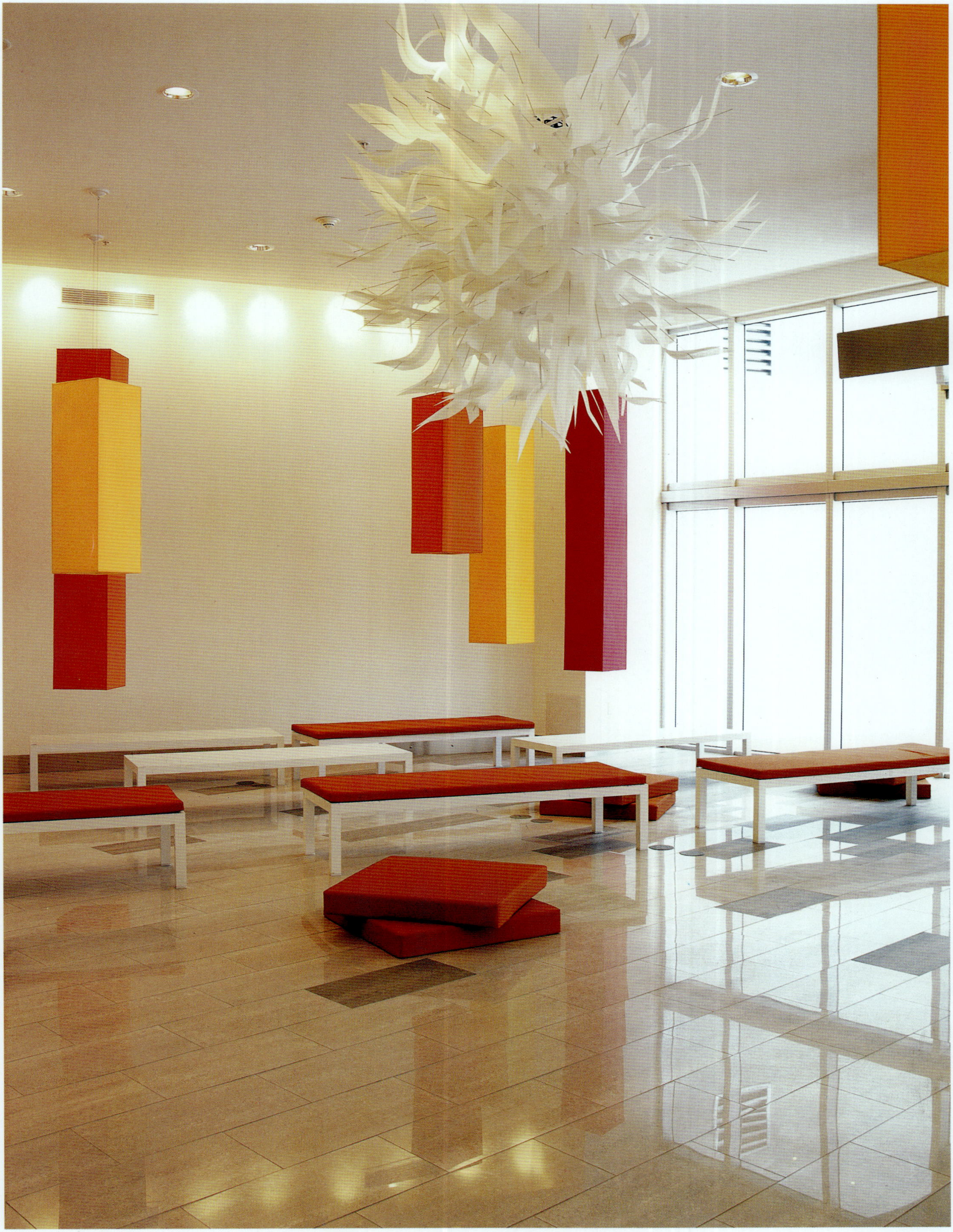

Chapter 12

A Lifetime of Sanctuary

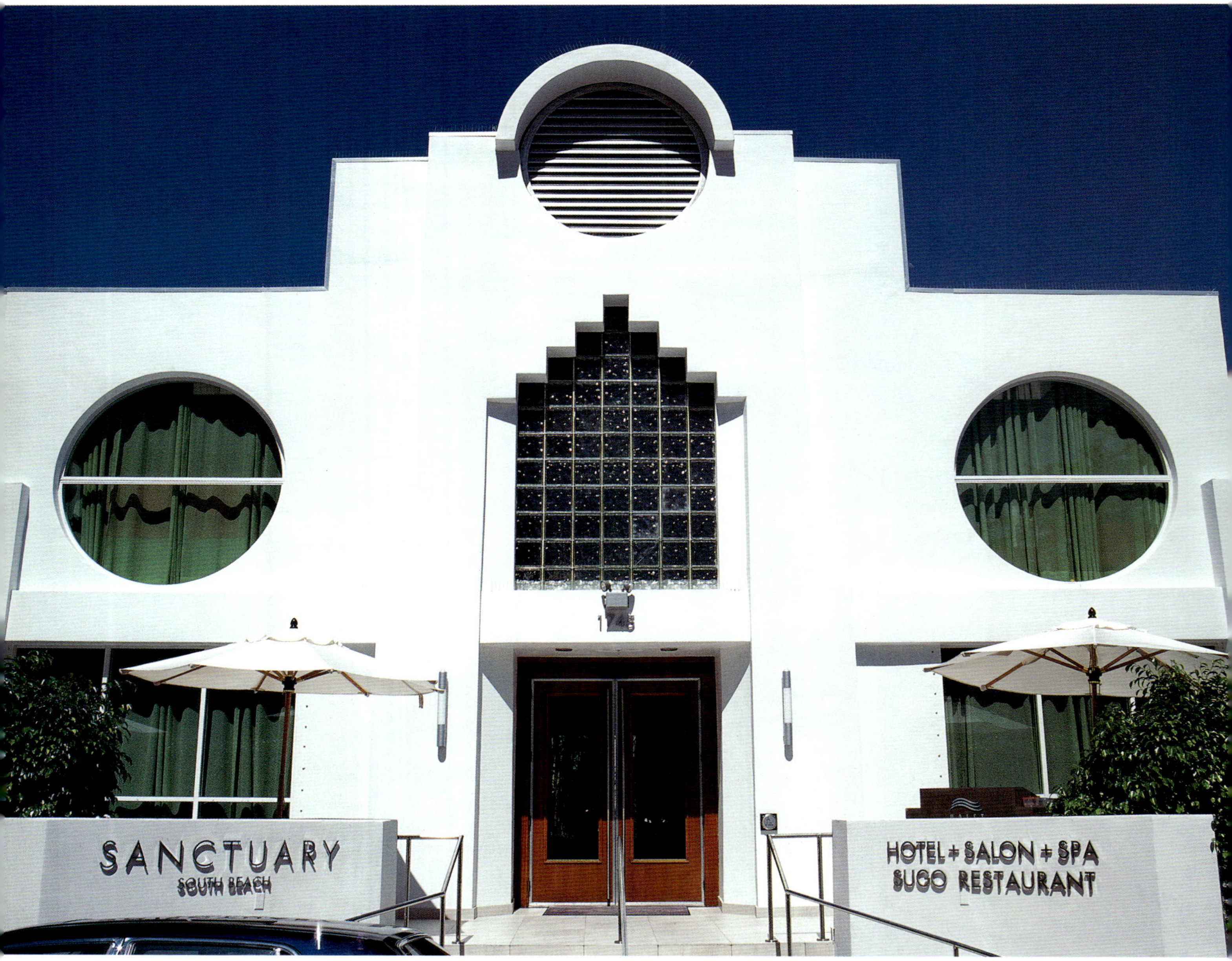

Keith Menin

Here is one of the most unexpected things about the people of Miami Beach: a lot of them were actually born here. In one sense, that is not surprising, since a place like South Beach is enough to keep anyone committed to a long-term geographic relationship. A case in point is Keith Menin, owner of "The Sanctuary," a new and very hot hotel, bar, and spa, where the "pretty, pretty people play."

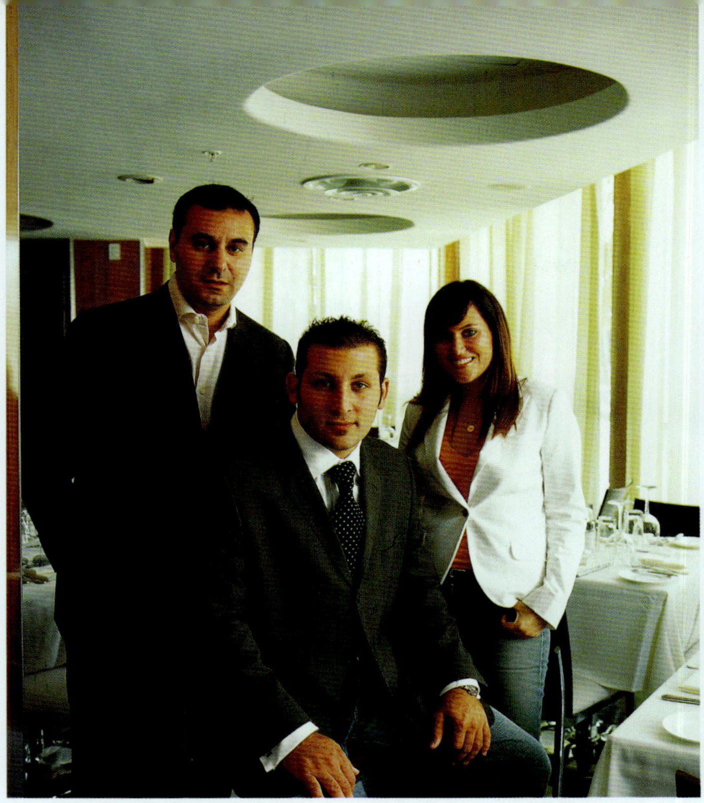

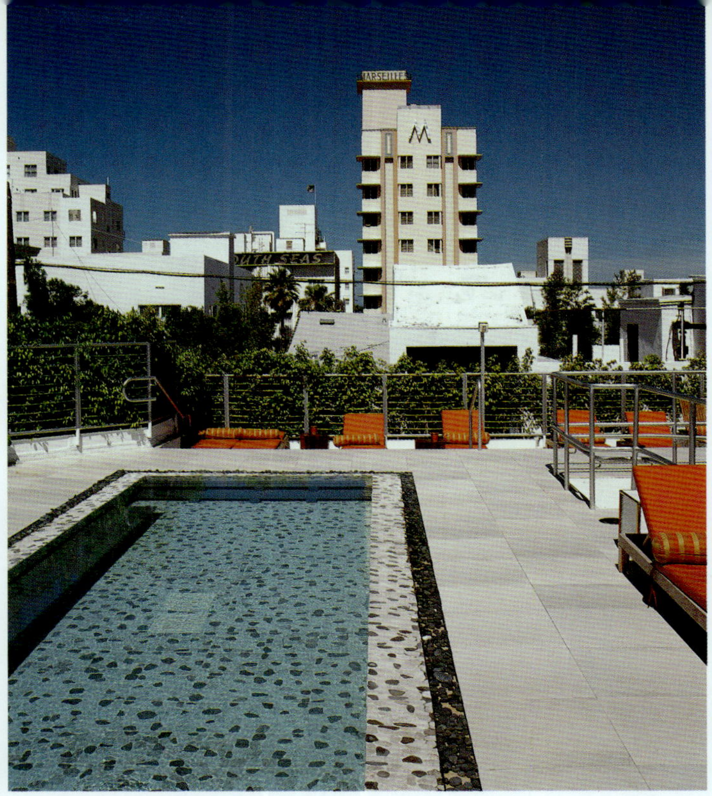

Menin is the great grandson of Al Galbut, a "founding father" of the South Beach melting pot. He was born and brought up in the real estate and hospitality business, and he has never outgrown his love for the sheer beauty of his hometown. Keith's description of what he "loves the most" about Miami Beach: "Driving on the Julia Tuttle causeway going eastbound [toward Miami Beach], when you get to the top of the bridge and you see the skyline."

The architecture of The Sanctuary is an example of renovation-as-improvement. The central Art Deco-themed feature was added to combine two undistinguished 1950s-era structures. It once housed a retirement home, but now, like most of South Beach, has become a Mecca for younger revelers, having been reincarnated as The Sanctuary only in the last few years.

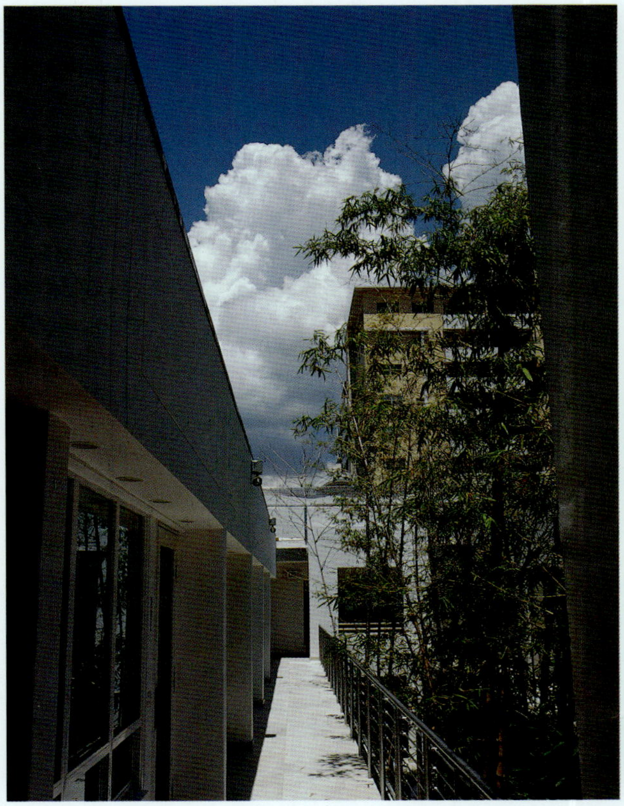

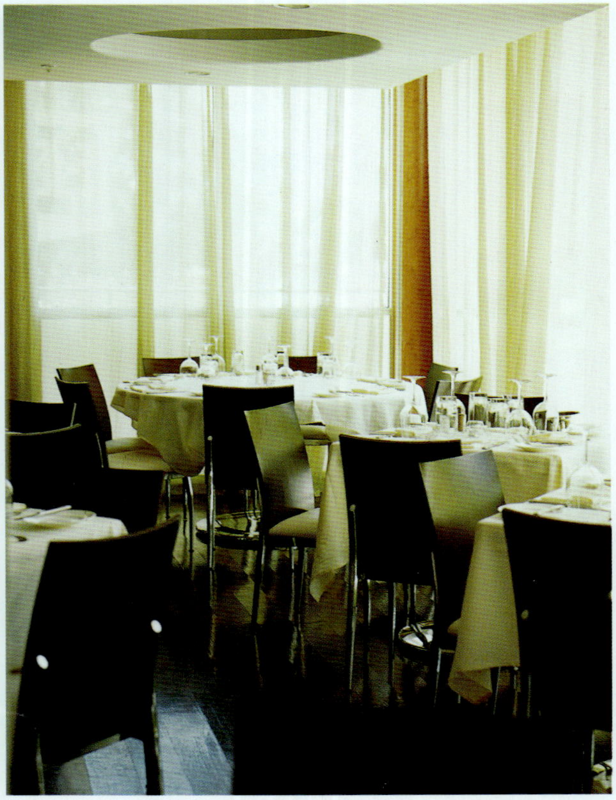

Chapter 13

SEDUCED BY SEA AND JET-SKI

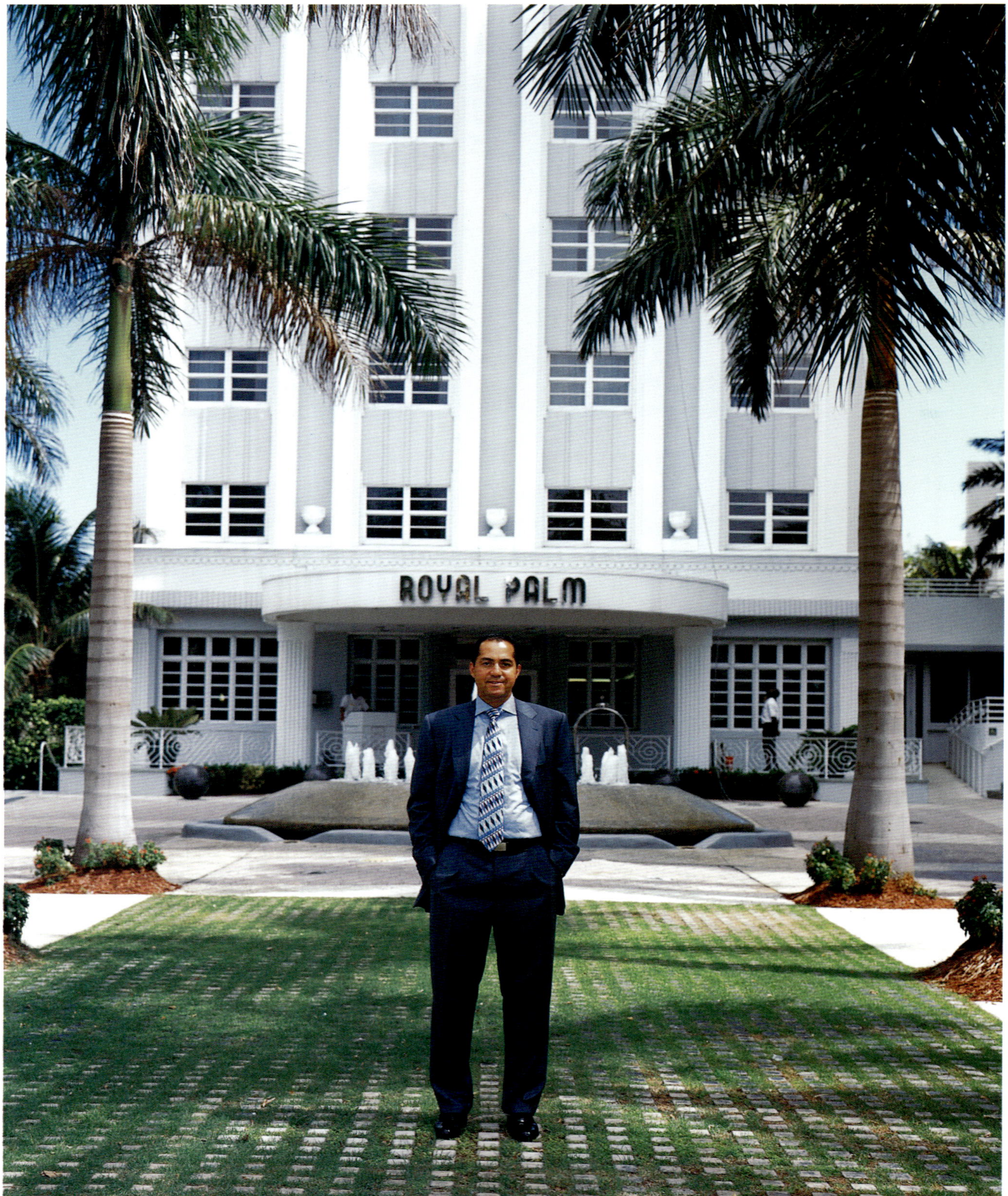

Don Peebles and the Royal Palm Hotel

What do you do for an encore when you've already succeeded as a real estate mogul in the white hot competition of Washington, D.C.? If you're R. Donahue Peebles ("Don" to his friends, and he has lots of friends), you fall in love with your vacation location and redirect your business so you can s-t-r-e-t-c-h your vacation time to fill a lifetime. After purchasing a subtropical vacation home, Peebles and his famously striking wife, Katrina, set up shop (and principal residence) in Florida and have become important people on the South Beach scene as well as in the commercial and social life of greater Miami.

A past Chairman of the Greater Miami Convention and Visitors Bureau, Peebles earlier played a key role in attracting and hosting the African-American celebrities and beautiful people who are the latest generation of South Beach aristocracy. In fact, without his ability to help bridge a festering dispute among South Florida racial and ethnic groups, South Beach might not be the uniquely loved tourist and convention beacon that it has become. His magnificent, meticulous replication of the Royal Palm Hotel on Collins Avenue made Peebles the first African-American resort hotel owner in South Beach and changed the face of the entire Miami area. And while making this important contribution, he created and has maintained a relationship with Art Deco preservationists that is almost unmatched in South Beach. He has even received awards from the Miami Design Preservation League for his faithfulness to the Art Deco style in his preservation of the Royal Palm's original spirit.

So what does a VIP like Don Peebles tell you he'd do with anything from a hundred to a million dollars to spend on a single blowout in the new South Beach? He'd spend it all...on Jet-Skis. Where else do you find a genuine civic leader like this who would spend all of his spare cash on Jet-Skis? That says something.

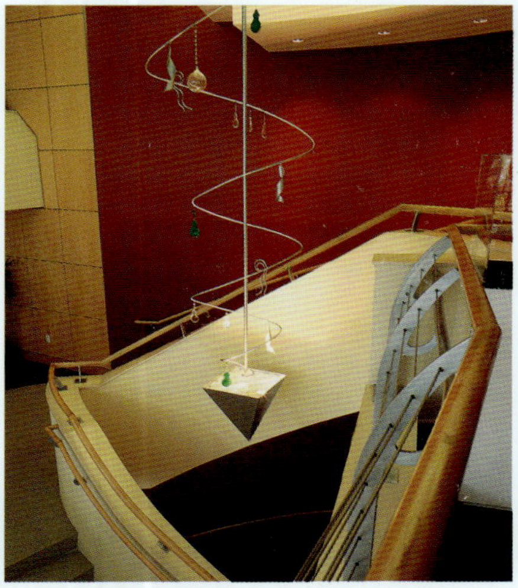

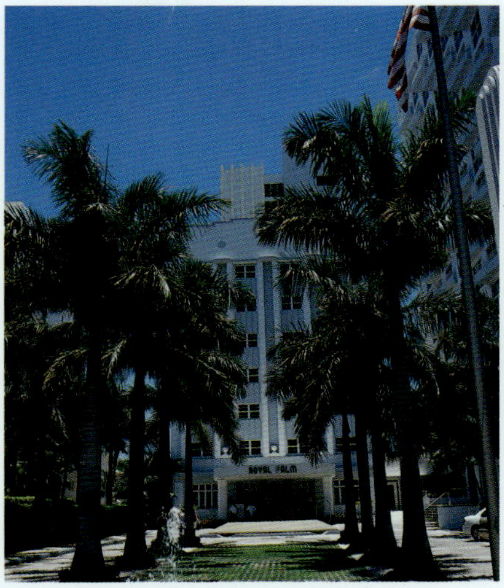

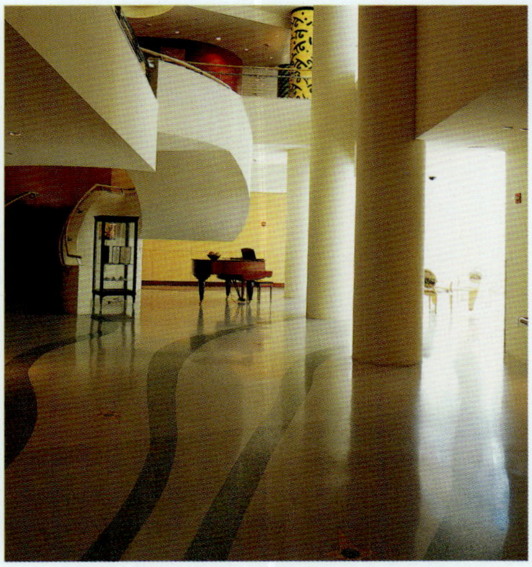

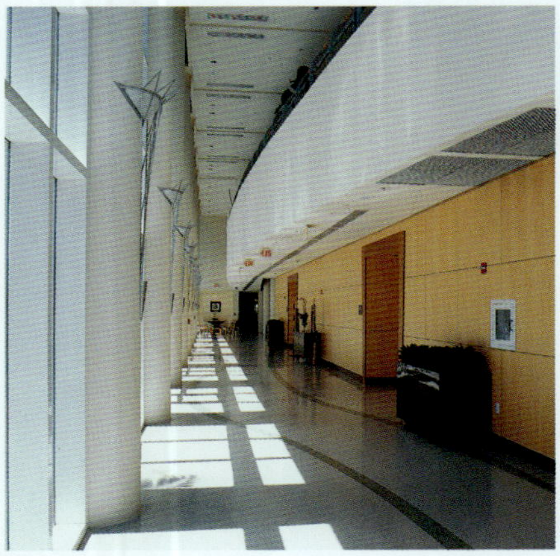

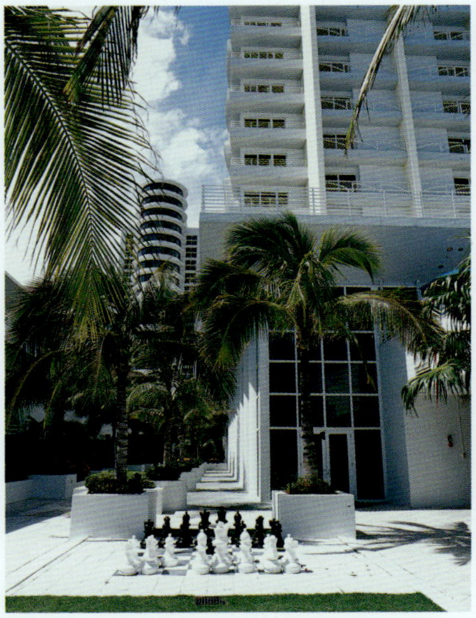

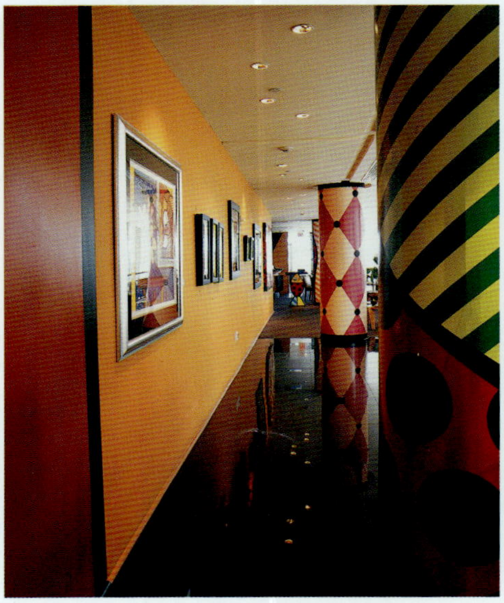

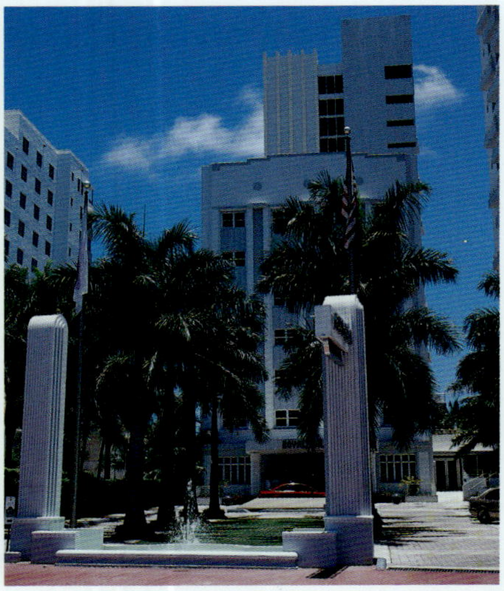

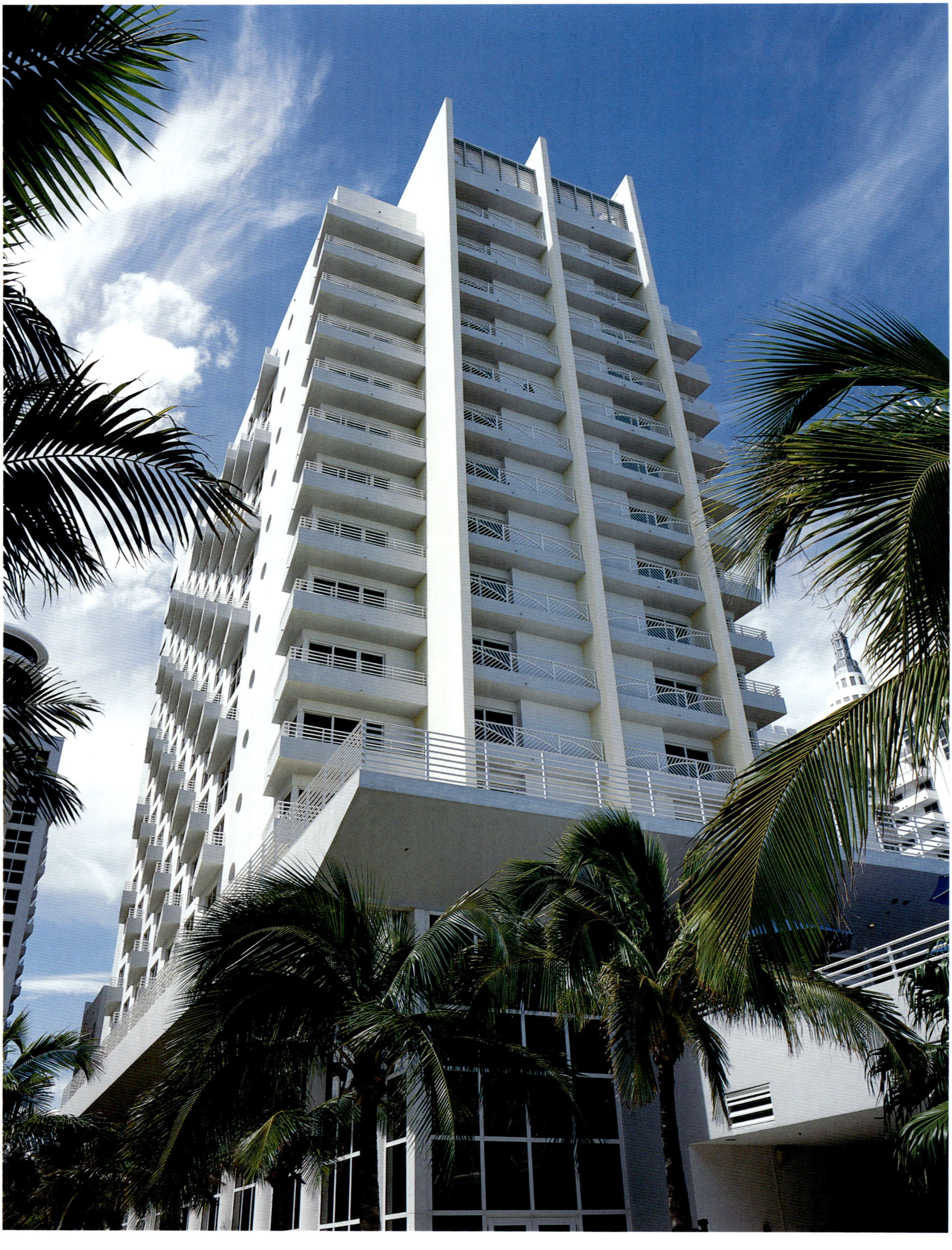

Chapter 14

RESCUE ME

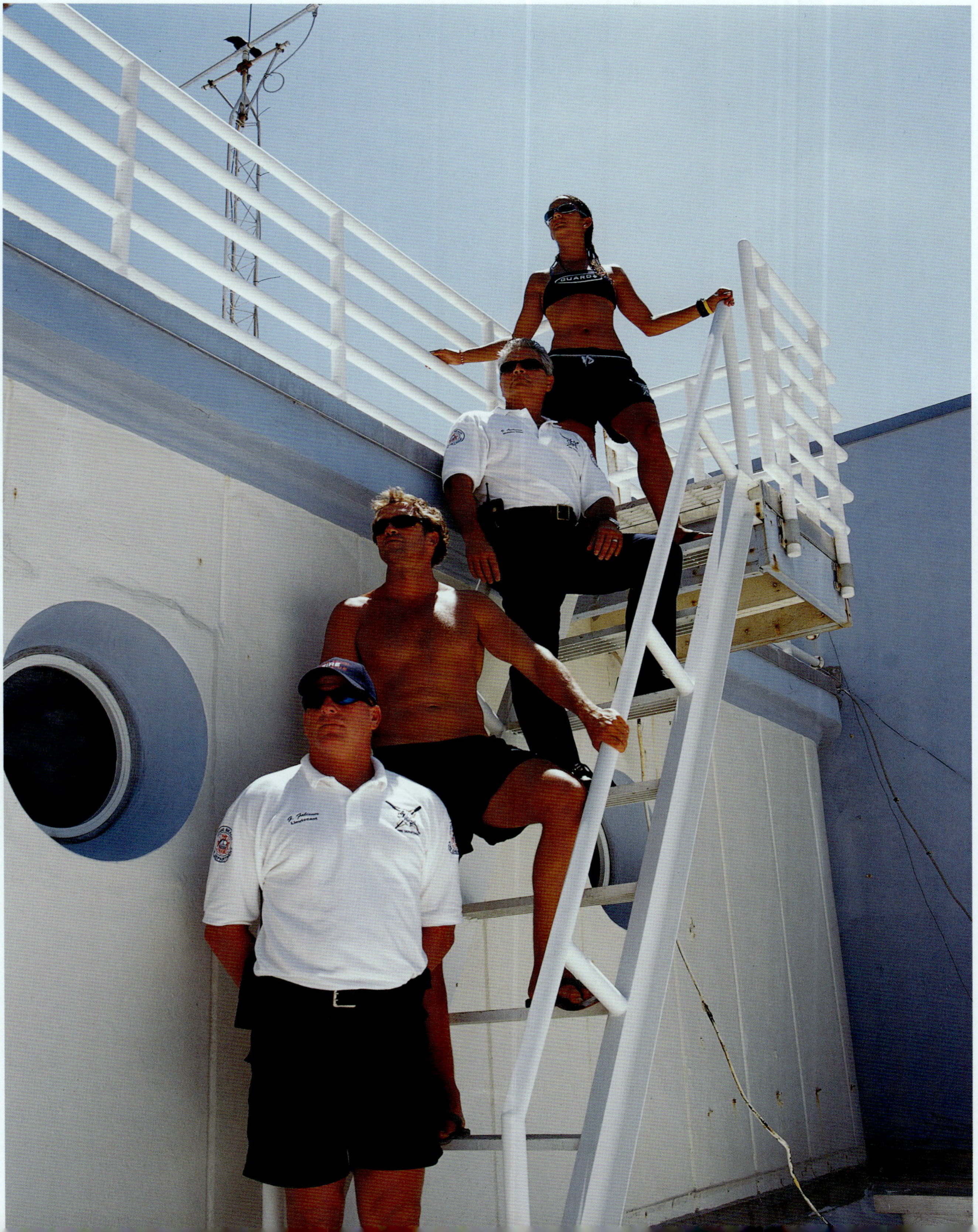

VINCENT ANDREANO AND THE BEACH PATROL

Okay, the last thing you want to think about while frolicking in the warm South Beach surf is the need to be rescued. But won't you take that carefree jump into the Atlantic's waves a little more happily knowing that Vincent Andreano and his band of beautiful lifeguards are there for you, just in case? Right at Ocean Drive and Tenth Street, in the heart of the Deco District and sharing the beach side of a building with the Art Deco Welcome Center.

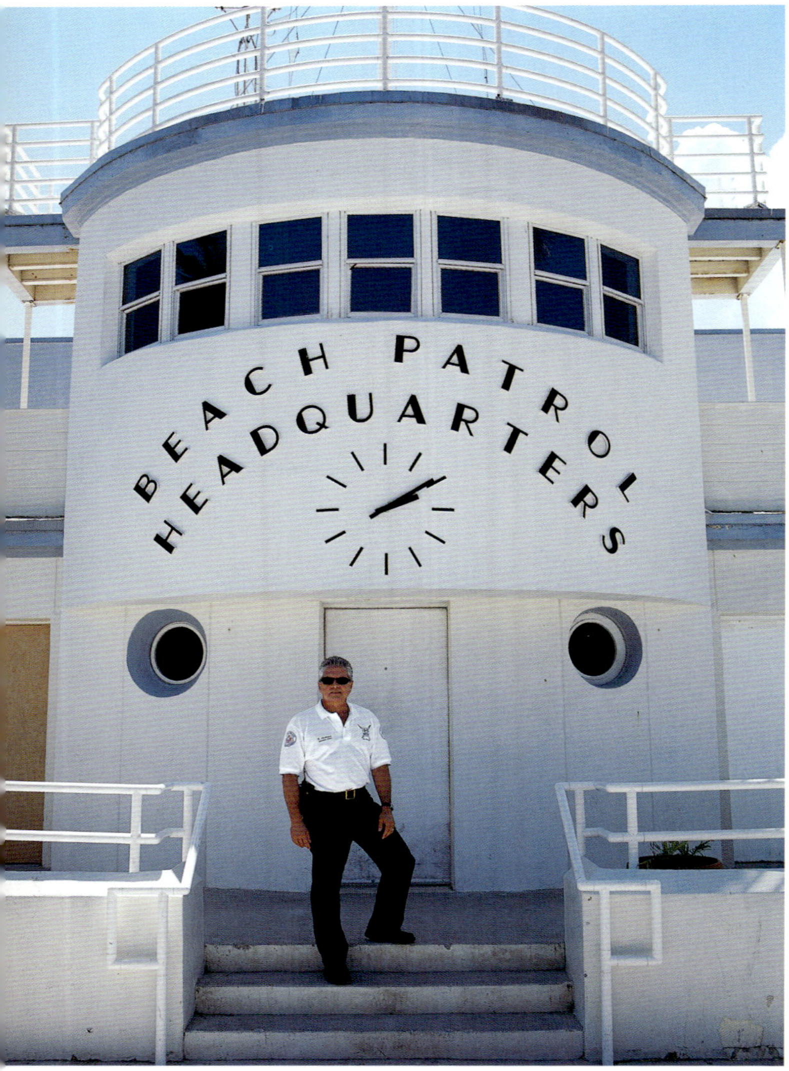

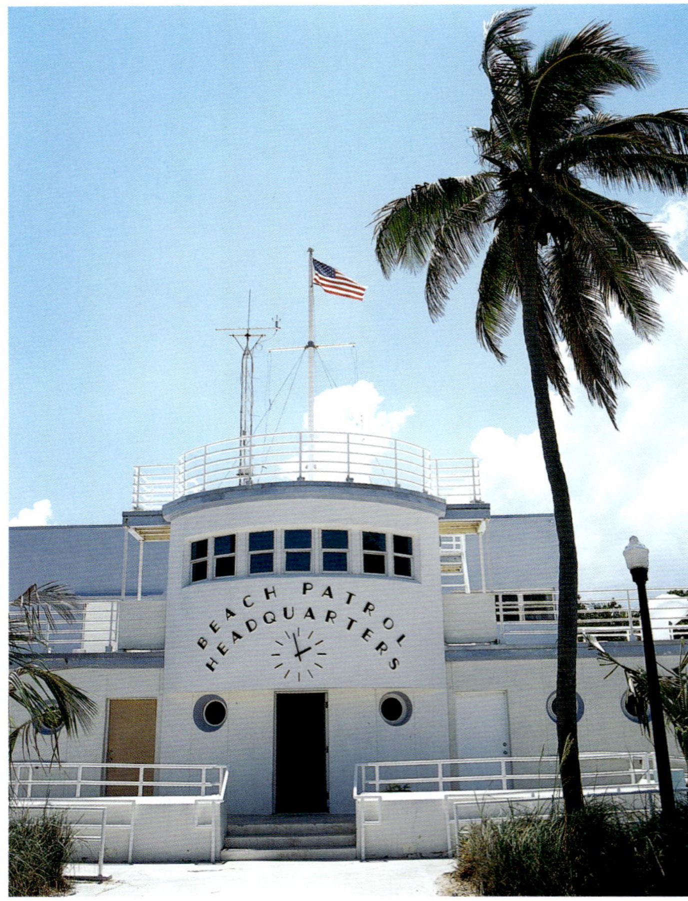

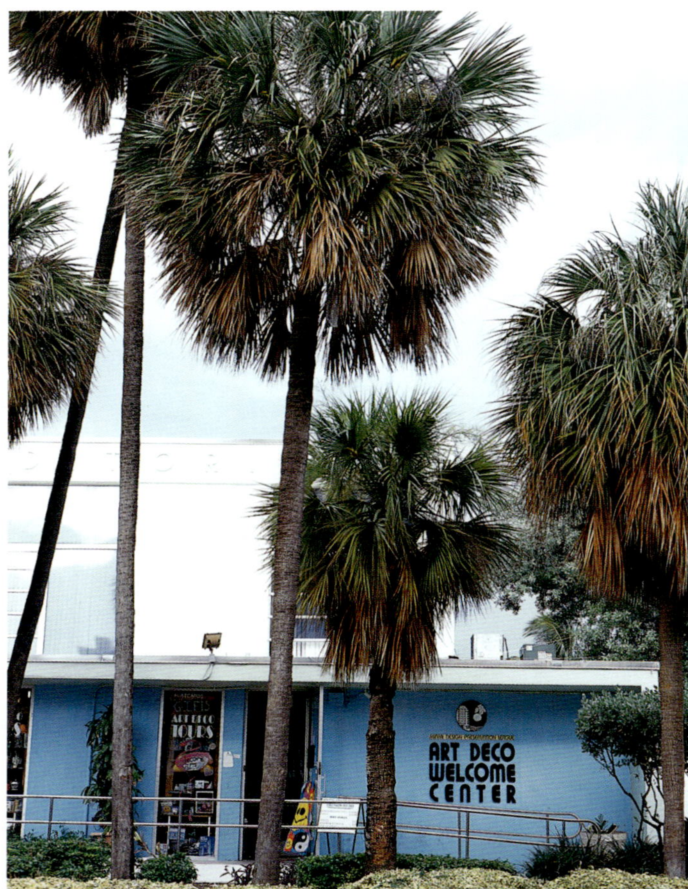

Andreano, who has worked in Miami Beach for more than a quarter-century, was born in the Staten Island borough of New York City but moved south for the "warm weather and great ocean conditions." As Chief of Ocean Rescue, he is the guy who stays on top of the latest in rescue equipment and technology, as well as making sure that the lifeguard you need is there when you need him—and in the kind of physical shape that will assure a happy ending for you. Of course, he doesn't scrimp on his own physical training, including running and, needless to say, swimming.

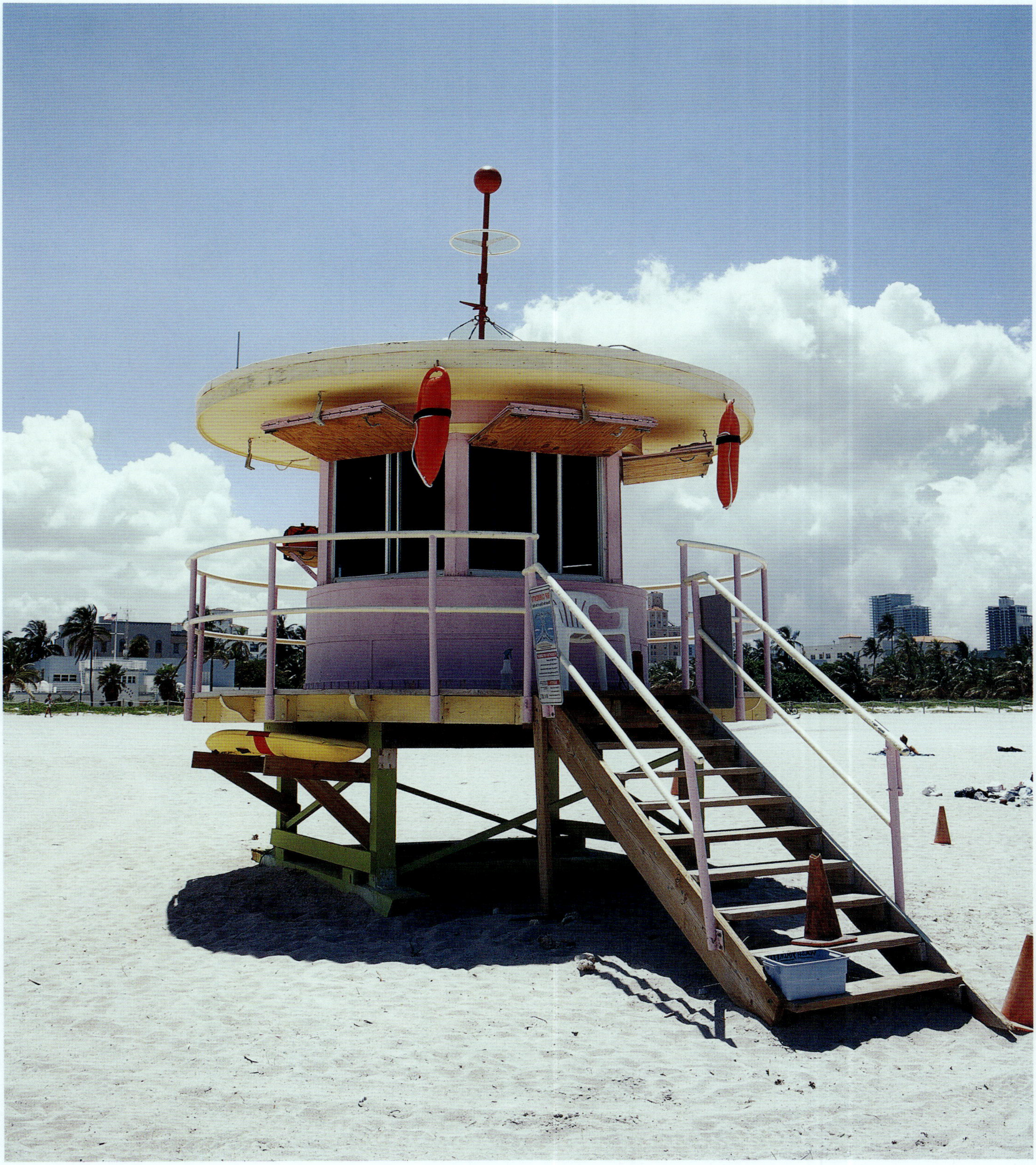

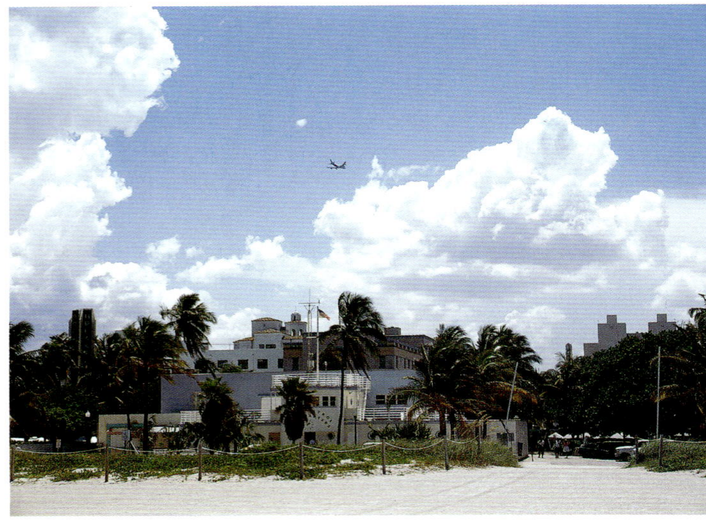

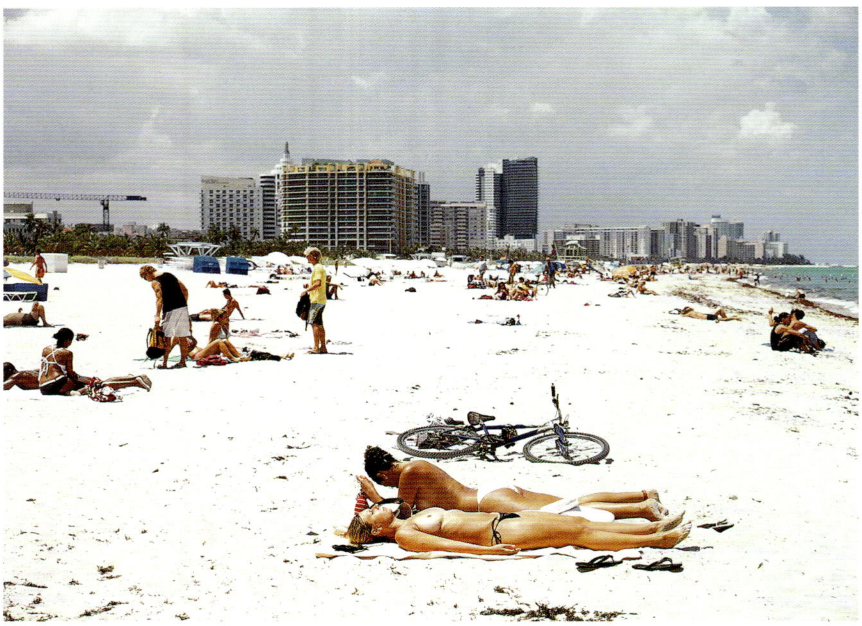

This being South Beach, though, he doesn't hesitate to reward himself with "good food and a glass of wine" (his favorite haunt, like that of so many others in South Beach, is The News Café). How does he describe his South Beach domain? "It has both the small beach town atmosphere and the quality services of a larger city." We might add that it also enjoys the rescue services of a world-class capital of sun and fun, thanks to Vincent Andreano and his band of ocean rescue heroes.

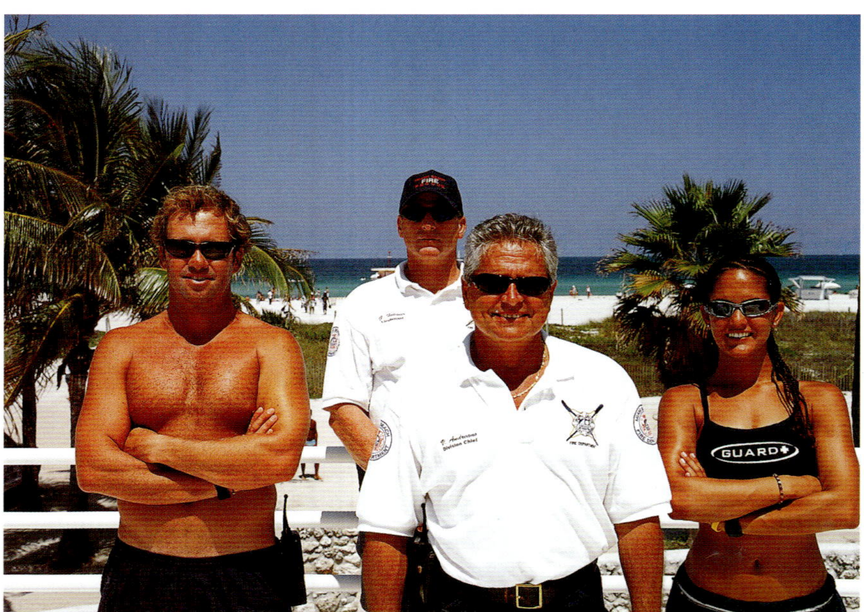

Chapter 15

MIAMI "MIMO"

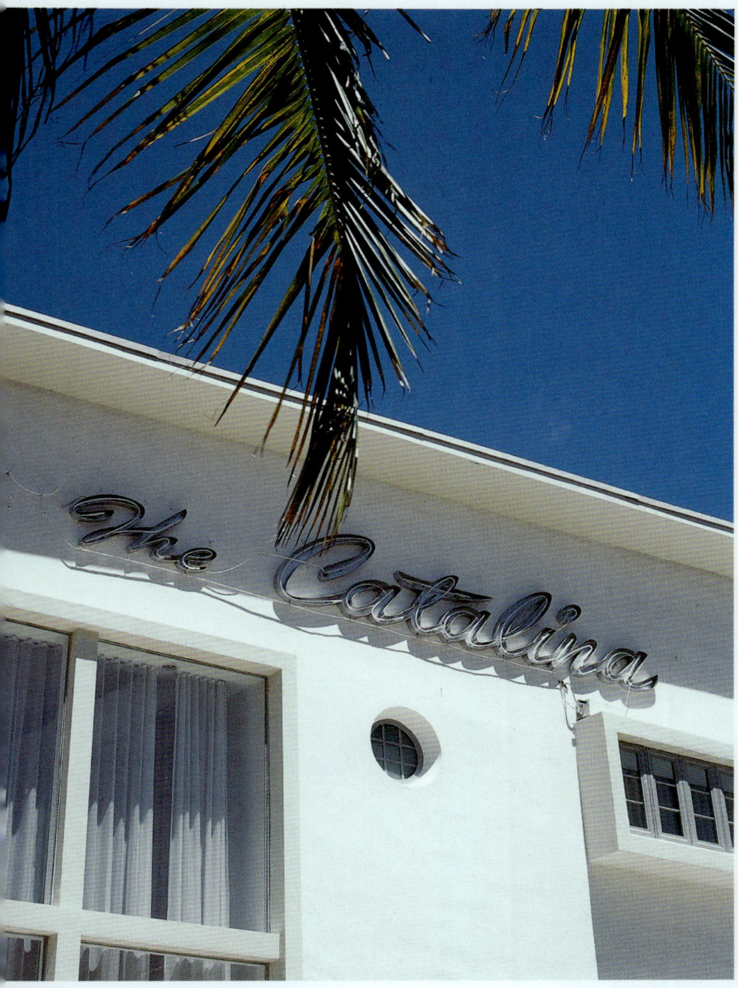

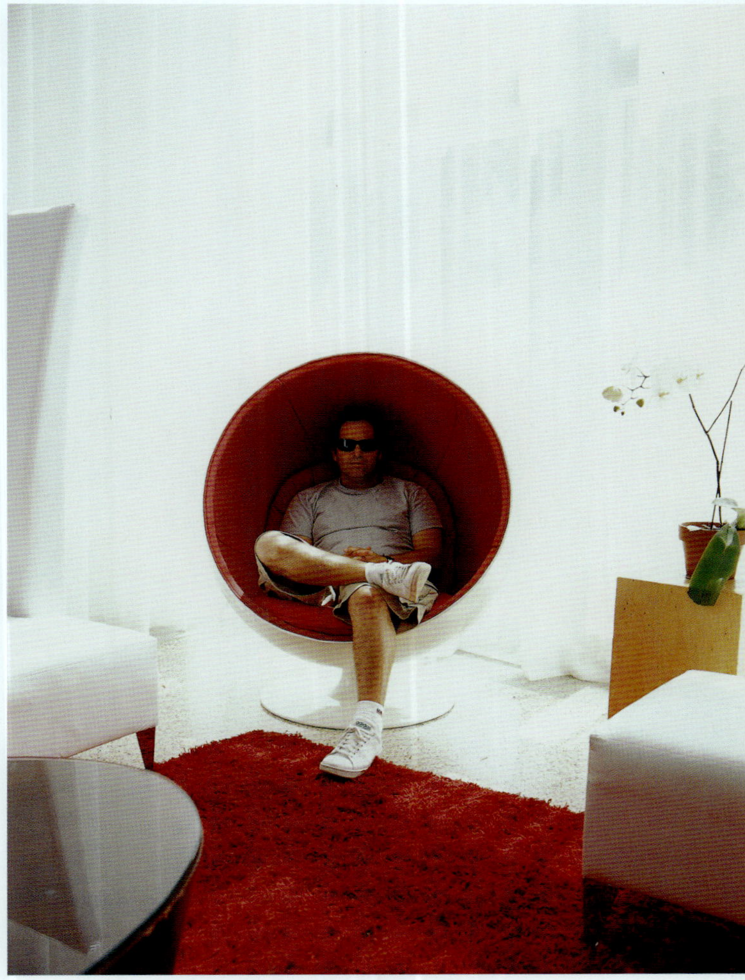

TODD GLAZER

Like a surprising number of serious players on the Miami Beach scene, Todd Glazer, co-owner of the Catalina Hotel at 1732 Collins Avenue, is practically a "native." Brought here from Minnesota as an infant with an asthma condition, Glazer has been a resident of Miami Beach since the sixties. Along with his partner, Alan Lieberman, Glazer is a principal in the South Beach Group of hotel properties, which has made a specialty of taking "tired" hotels and adding them to the South Beach Renaissance.

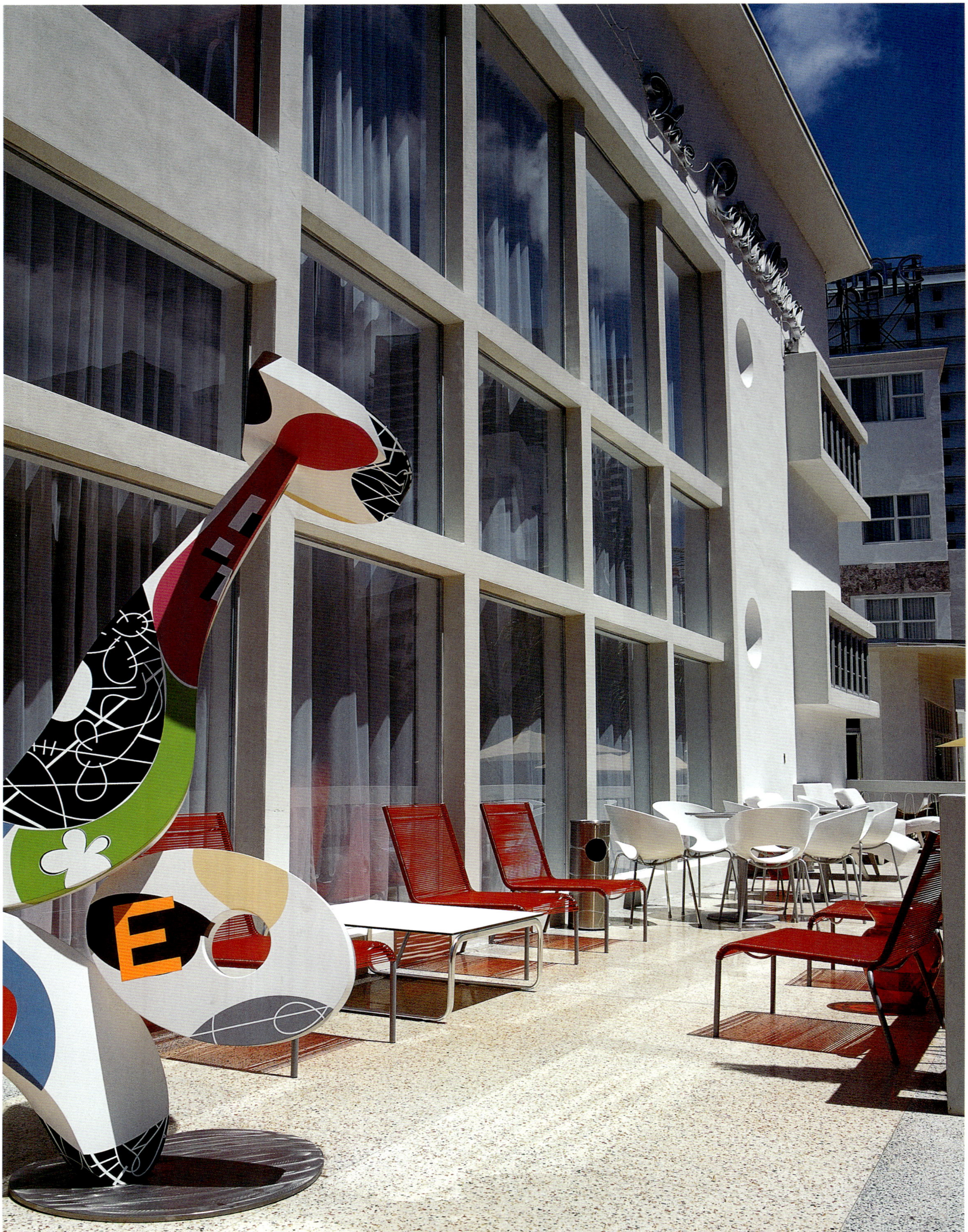

In 2004, Glazer and his partner bought the Catalina and renovated it, in a scant three months, back to its original 1940s splendor. An early example of what came to be known as "MiMo" (standing for "Miami Modern") architecture, the Catalina was built in 1947 and is famous for its open-to-the-street two story glass façade on the west side of Collins Avenue. Along with its architectural renovation in 2005, the Catalina has added to its 600-plus white-themed rooms the kind of hip amenities that have become synonymous with the South Beach lifestyle: in-room massage services, flat-screen TVs, upscale bathrooms with spas, passes to South Beach clubs, and even services for guests accompanied by their pets.

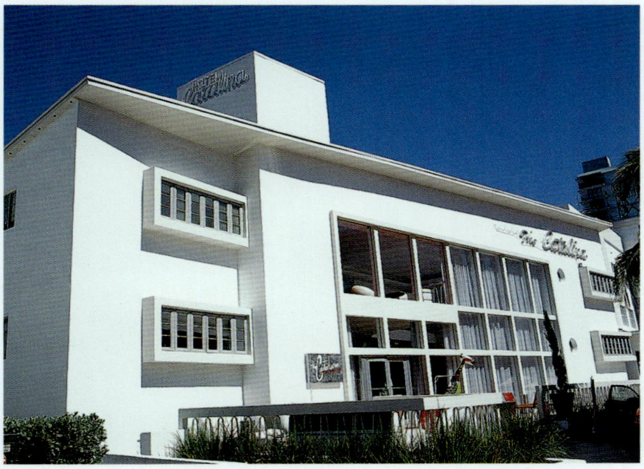

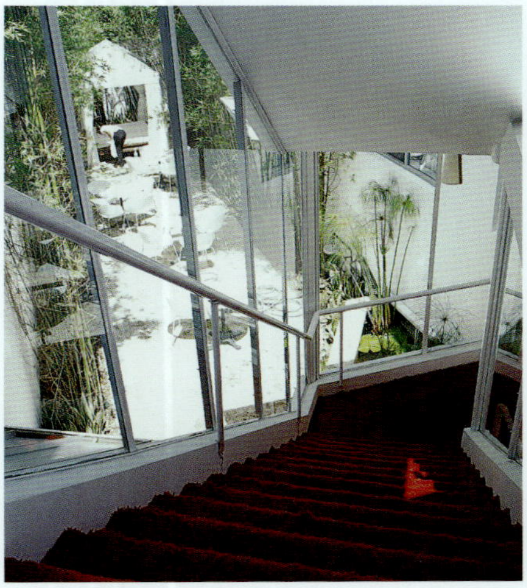

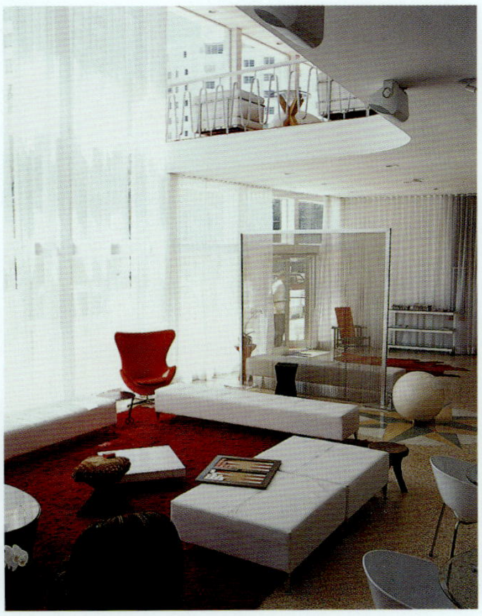

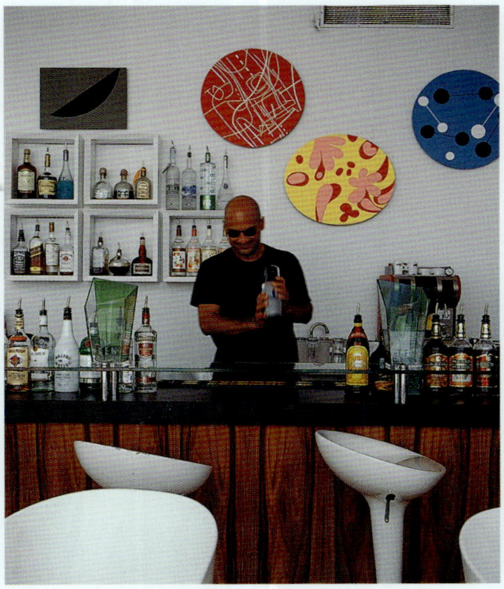

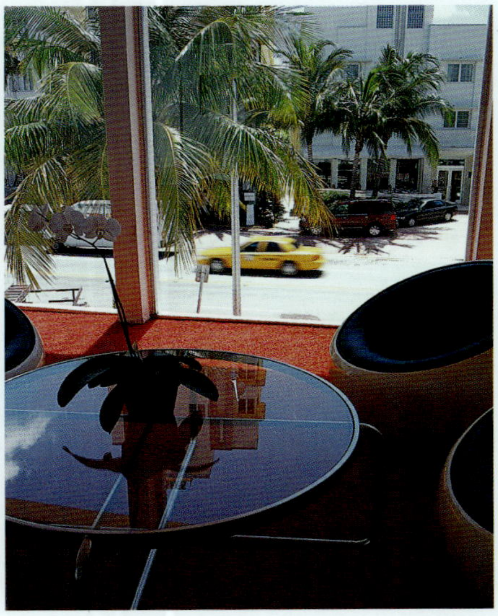

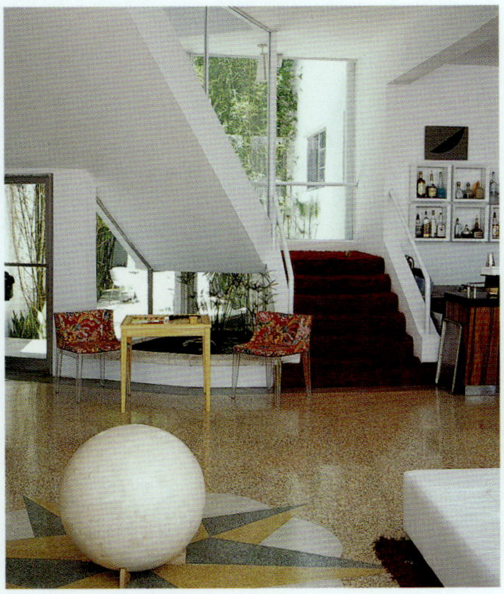

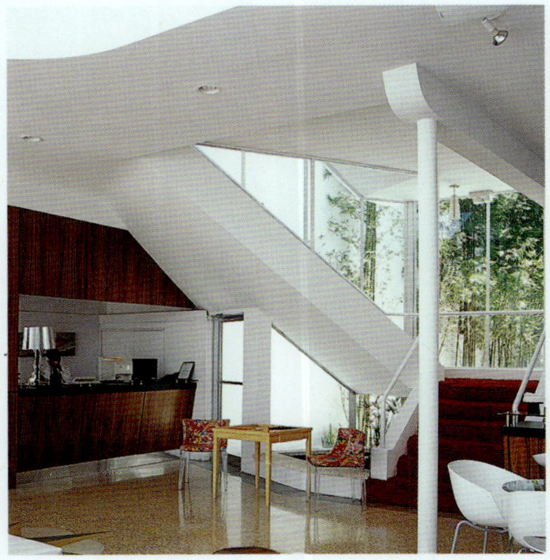

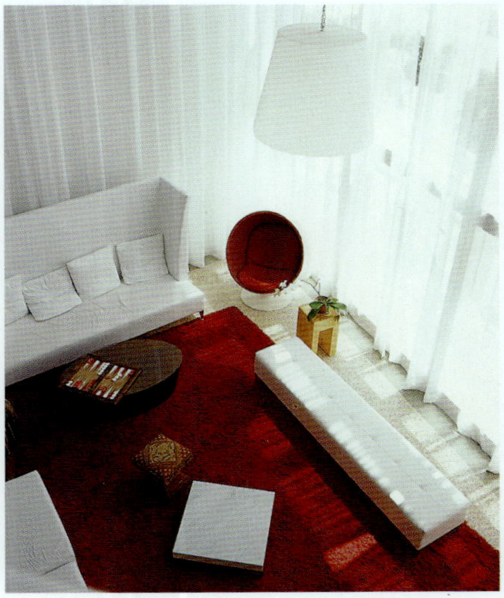

Glazer, an avid surfer and diver, would rather frolic in the ocean than frequent the South Beach clubs, though he does enjoy regular visits to one of Miami Beach's signature restaurants, The Forge on 41st Street (also known as "Arthur Godfrey Road," after a MiMo era entertainer).

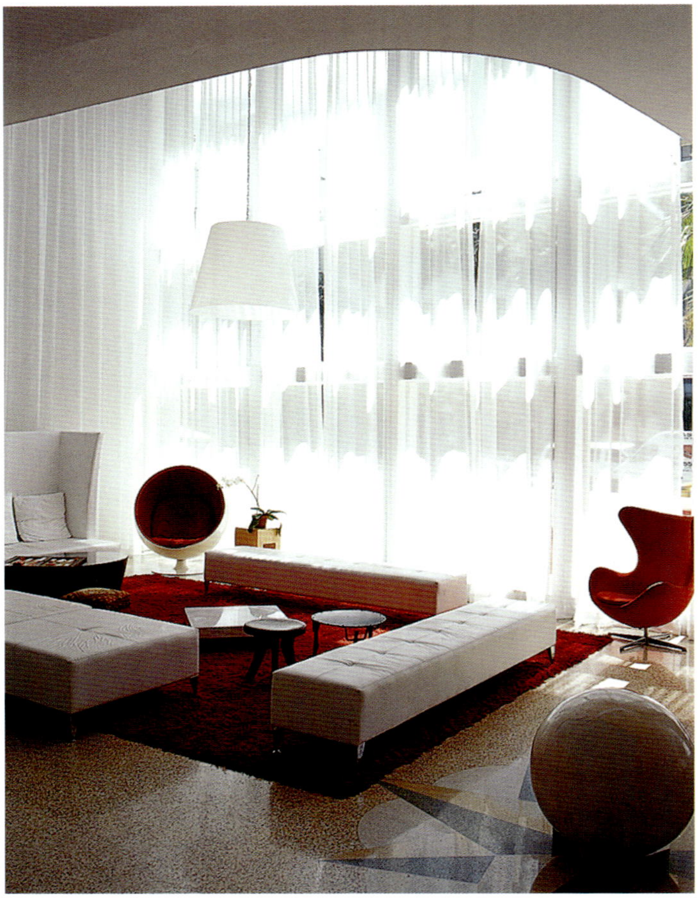

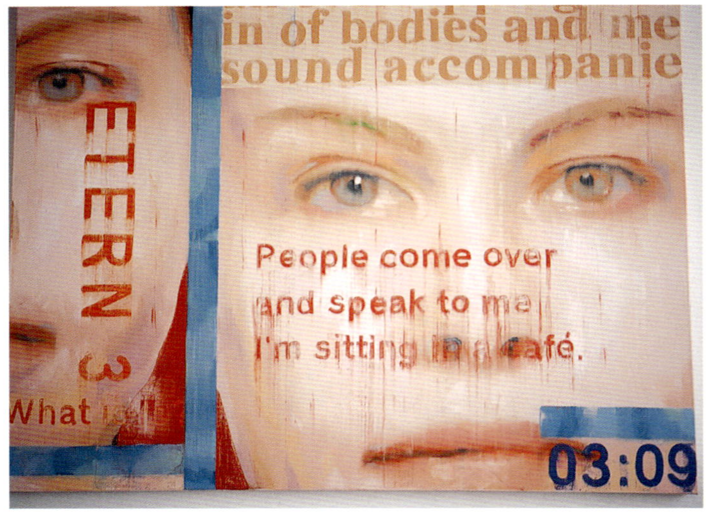

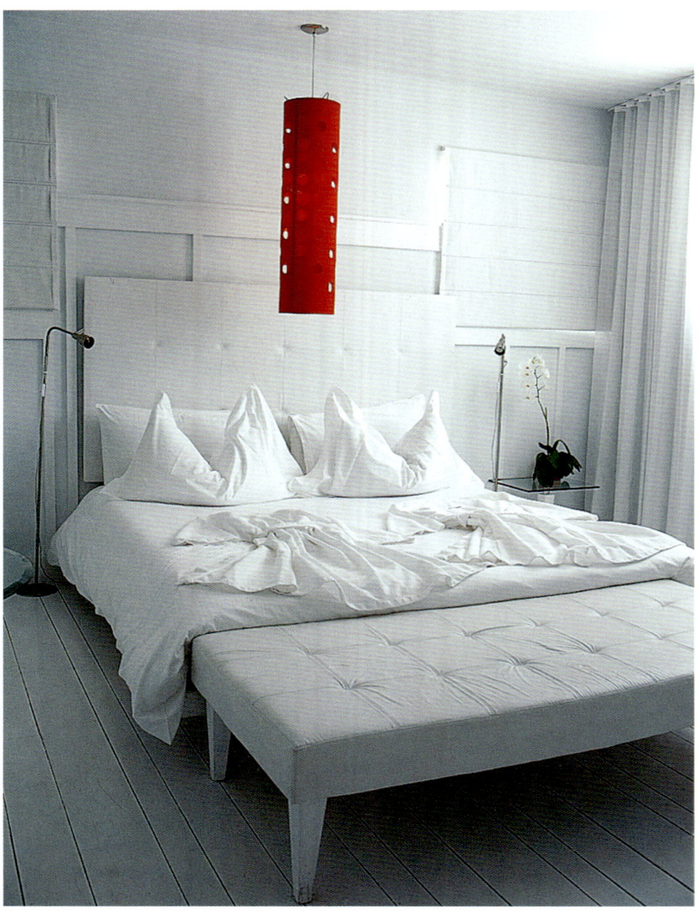

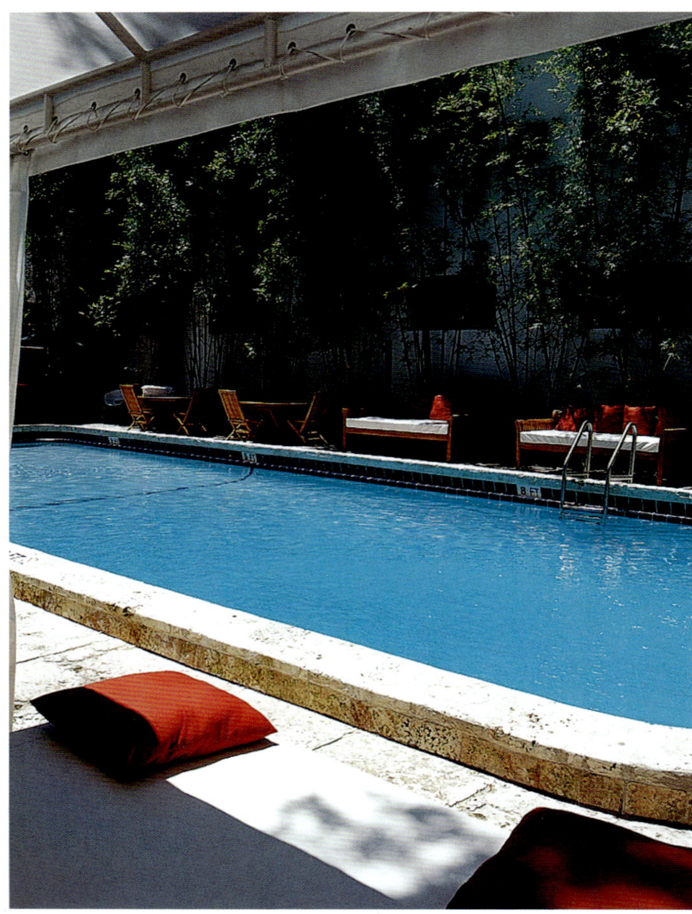

Chapter 16

THE MOST PLEASURABLE URBAN EXPERIENCE

CHAD OPPENHEIM AND THE MONTCLAIR

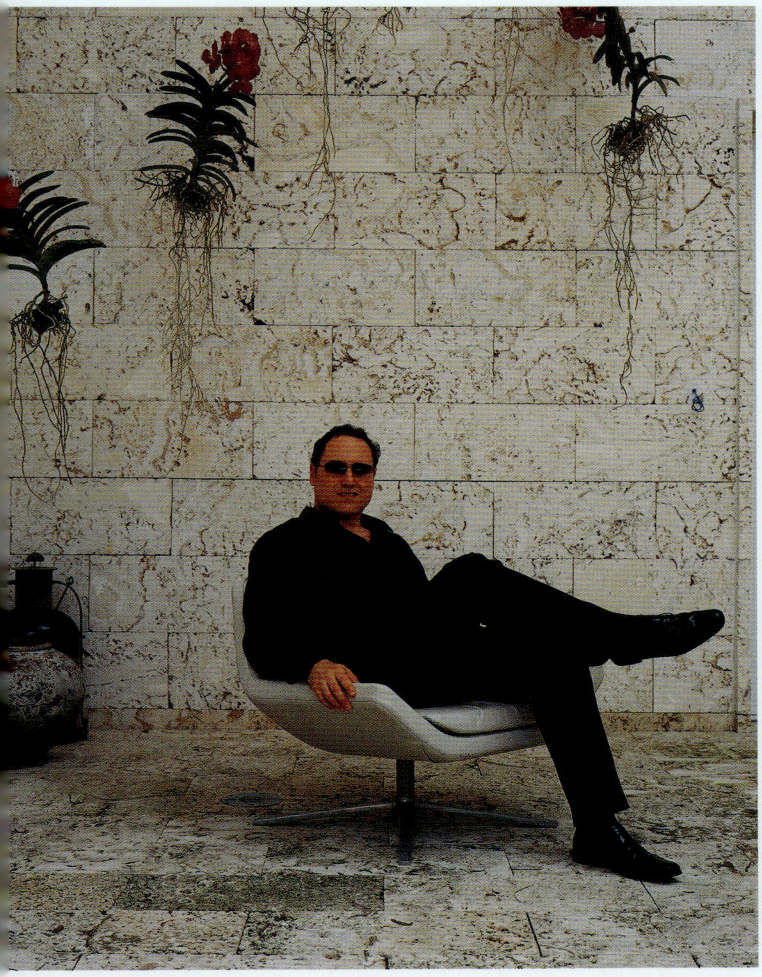

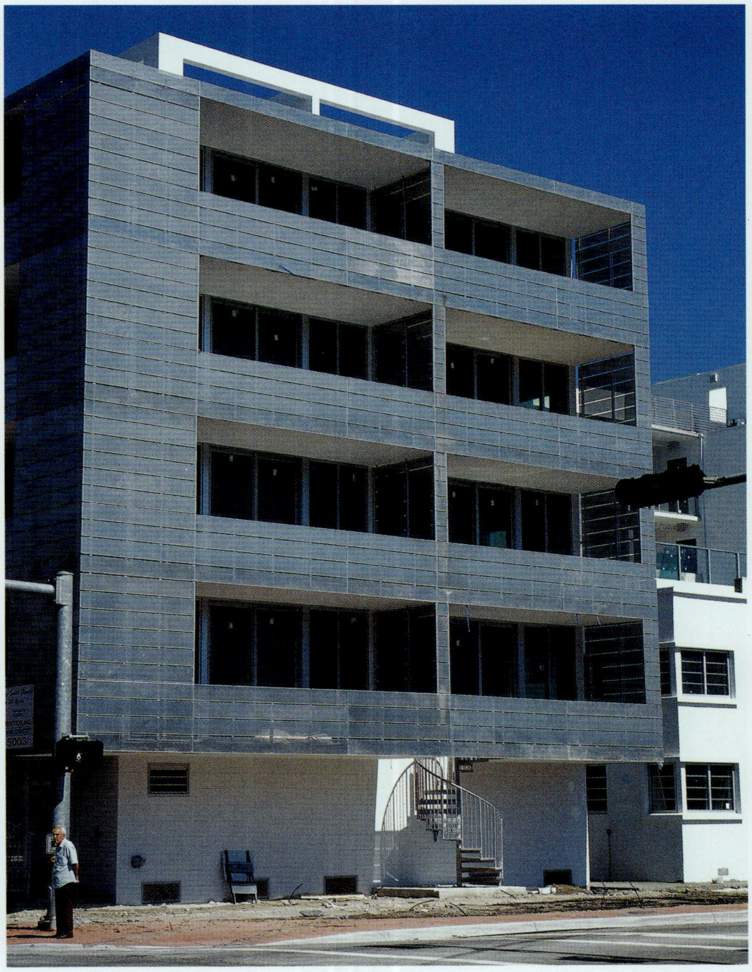

The boy-wonder of Miami's new architectural generation, thirty-something Chad Oppenheim has already lived in more countries than most people ever visit. And like a lot of very talented people in South Beach, he has made a name for himself without playing the nine-to-five game that restricts mere mortals. At this writing, Chad was working on no less than eighteen separate projects within shouting distance of South Beach. One of his most audacious and successful is the metal-clad Montclair condominium, one block north of Lincoln Road.

A native of New Jersey, Chad now makes his home on one of the beautiful islands that dot the west end of South Beach.

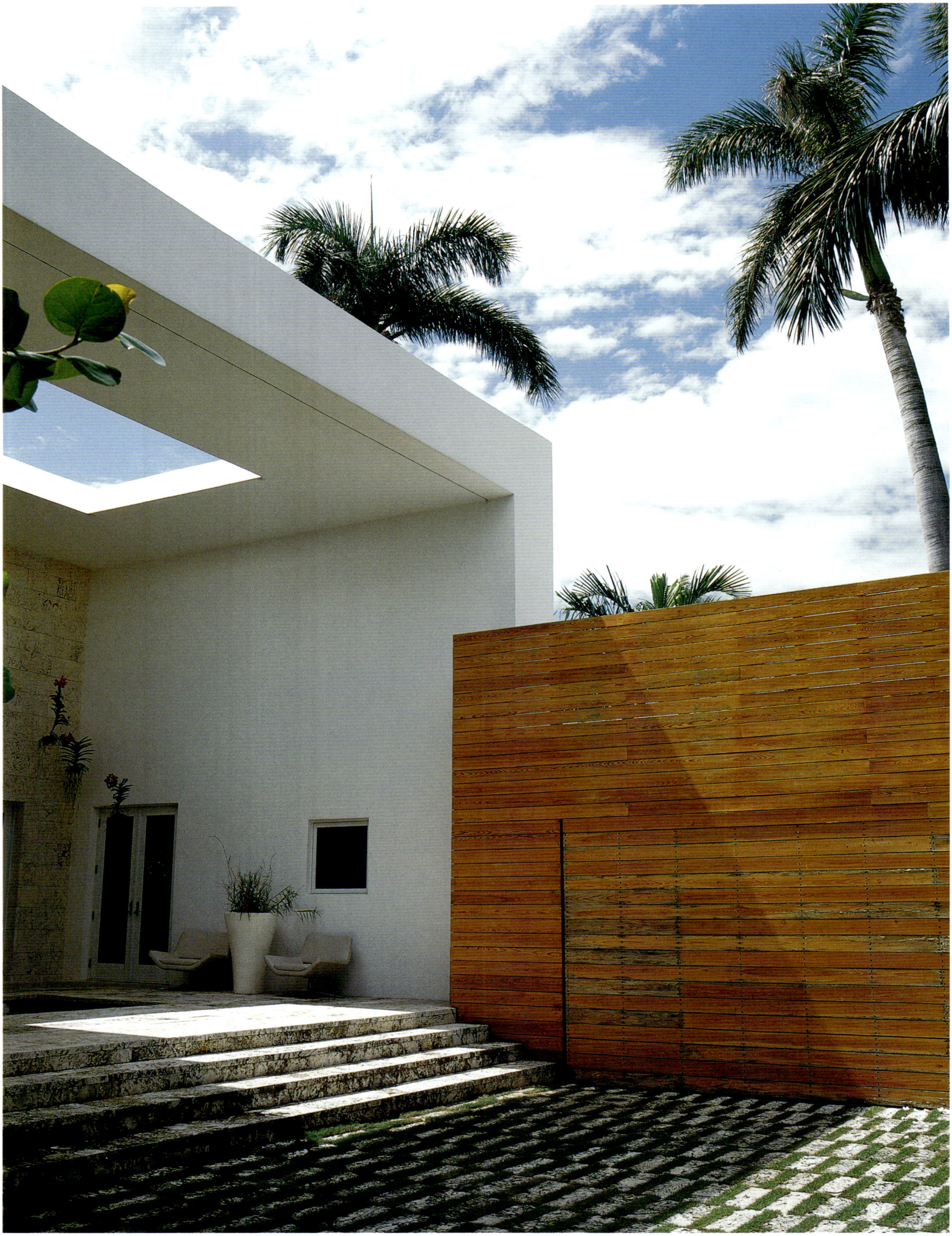

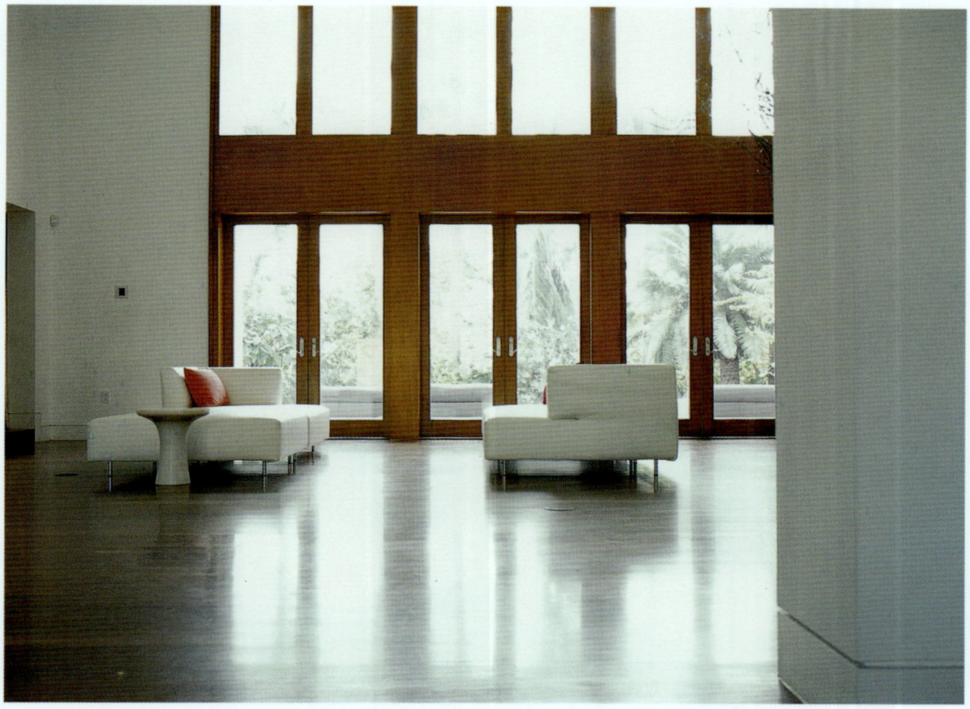

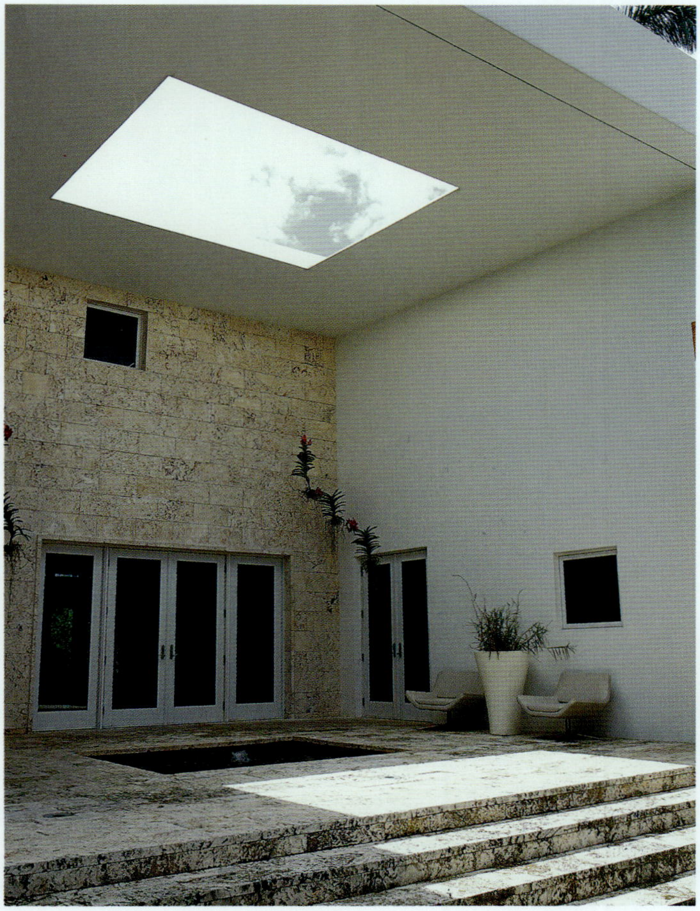

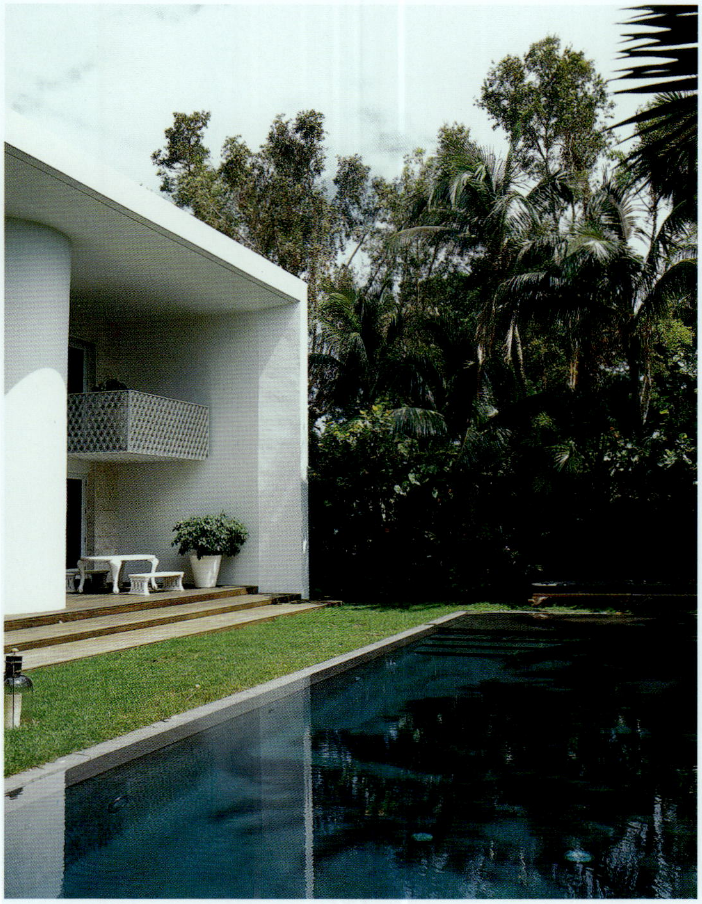

When not changing the skyline with his architectural brilliance, Chad can often be found biking or playing in the surf. His one sentence summary of the South Beach experience: "The city is all about the ocean."

Chapter 17

FRESH OUT OF THE WOMB

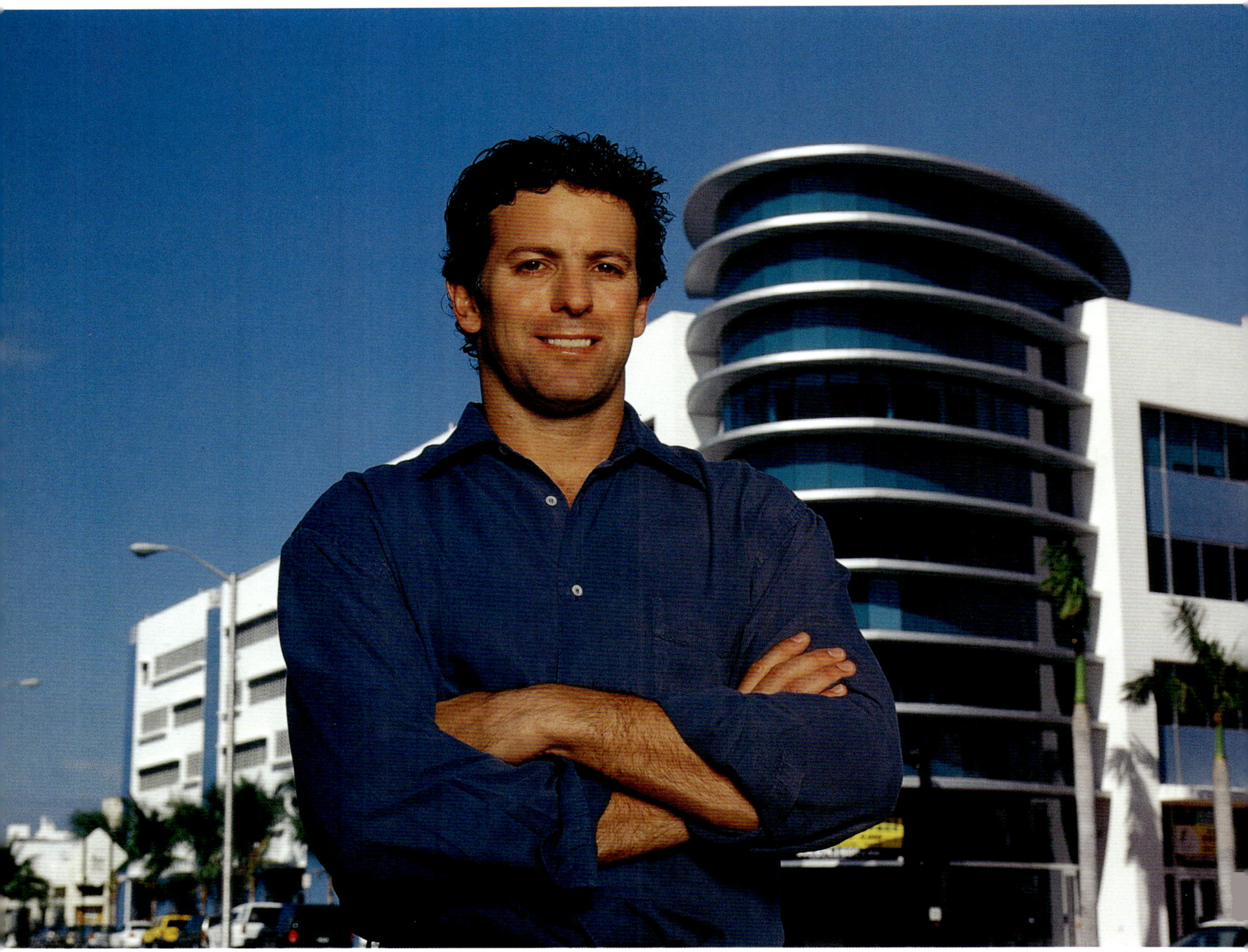

Photo by Simon Hare

SCOTT ROBINS

Doesn't everybody in South Beach actually come from New York? Sometimes, just when it seems that way, we're reminded that some of the most important and prominent individuals on the South Beach scene were actually born in Miami. A good case in point is Scott Robins, pictured here with one of his most recent South Beach projects, the office building at 555 Washington Ave.

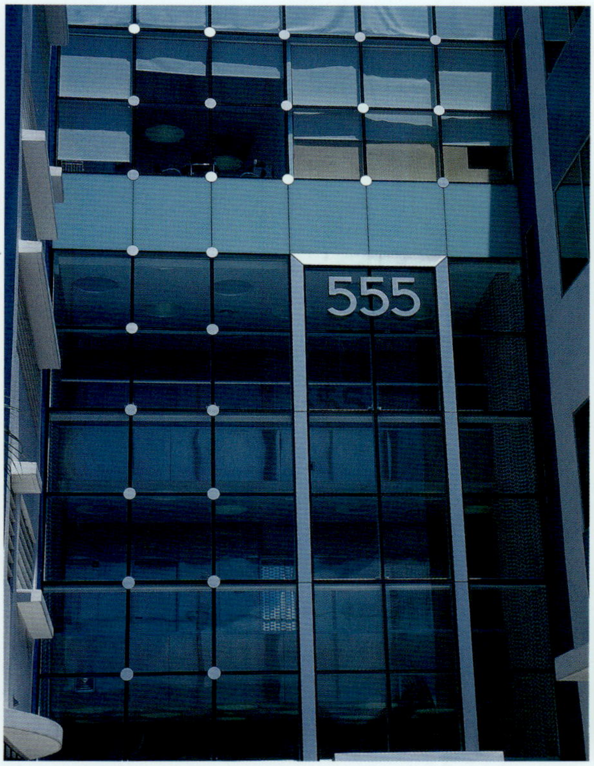
555

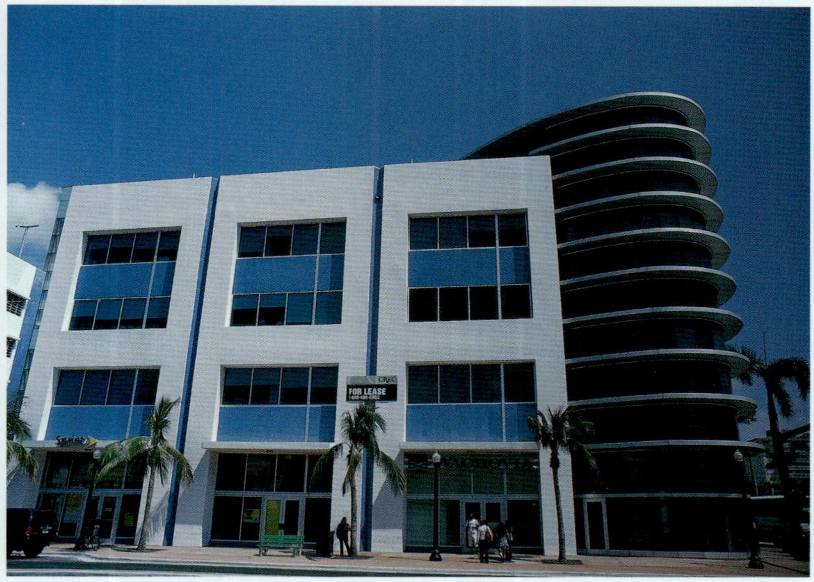
FOR LEASE

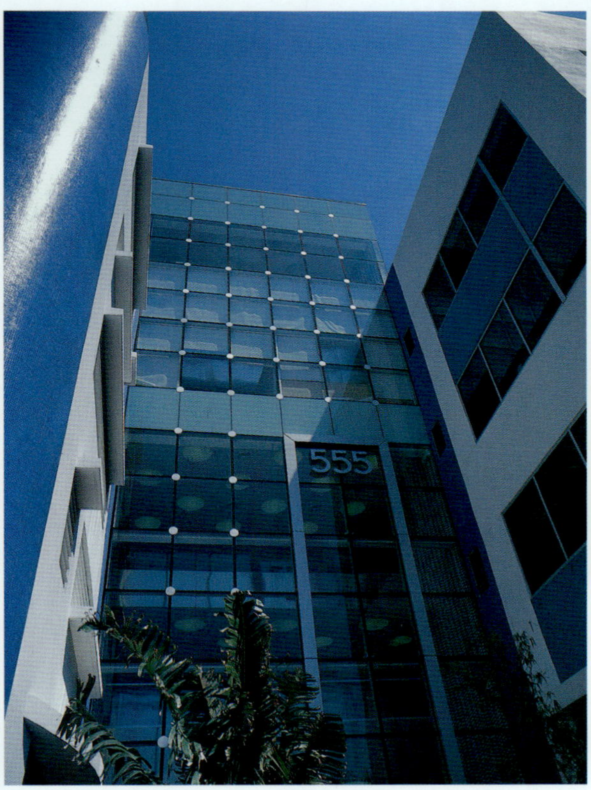
555

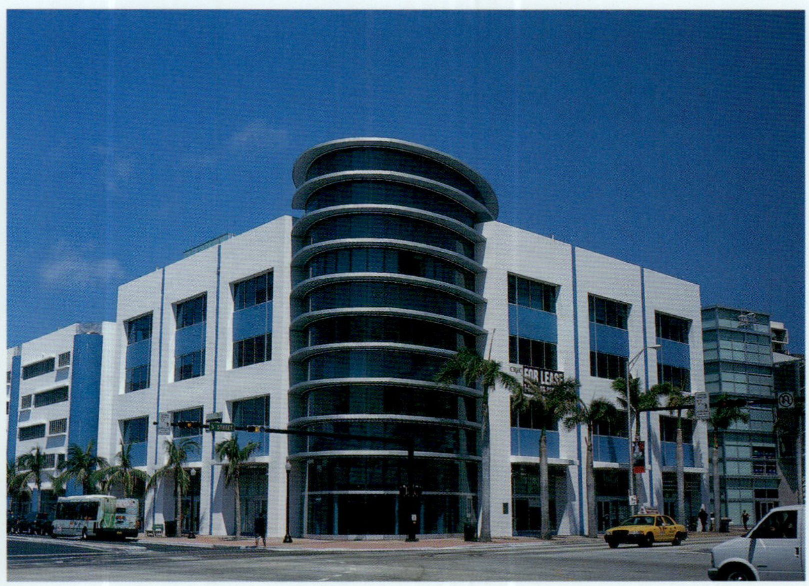
FOR LEASE

Robins has been a risk-taker since his days in the Dacra Companies (with his brother Craig), during the early South Beach renaissance. He has been an indispensable part of the South Beach scene ever since he arrived—as he puts it, "fresh out of the womb."

Also pictured is Scott's fabulous re-do of the "FinFed" (short for "Financial Federal") building at 743 Washington Avenue. A perfect example of MiMo (Miami Modern) architecture, this building originally housed a bank. Now, in keeping with the building's sensuality and with the sexiness of South Beach in general, its offerings include fine French lingerie.

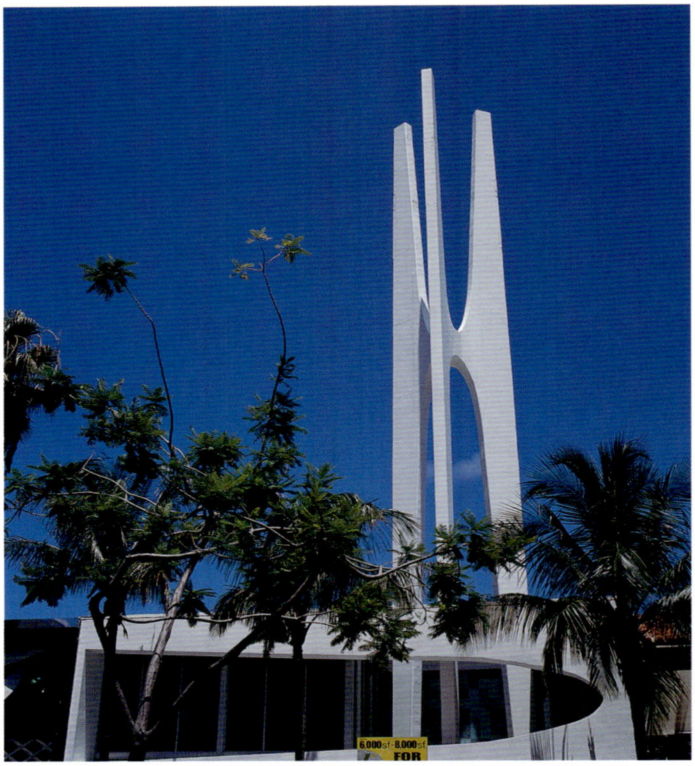

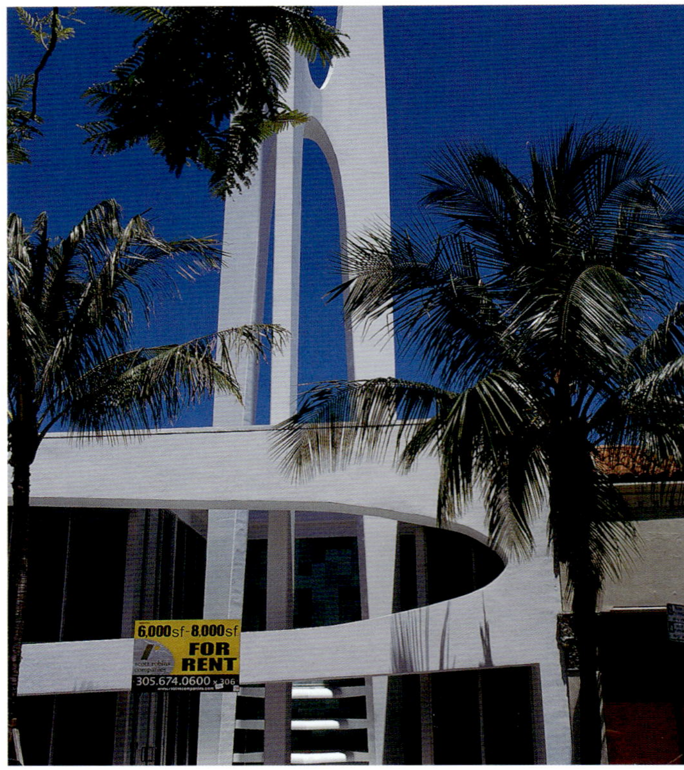

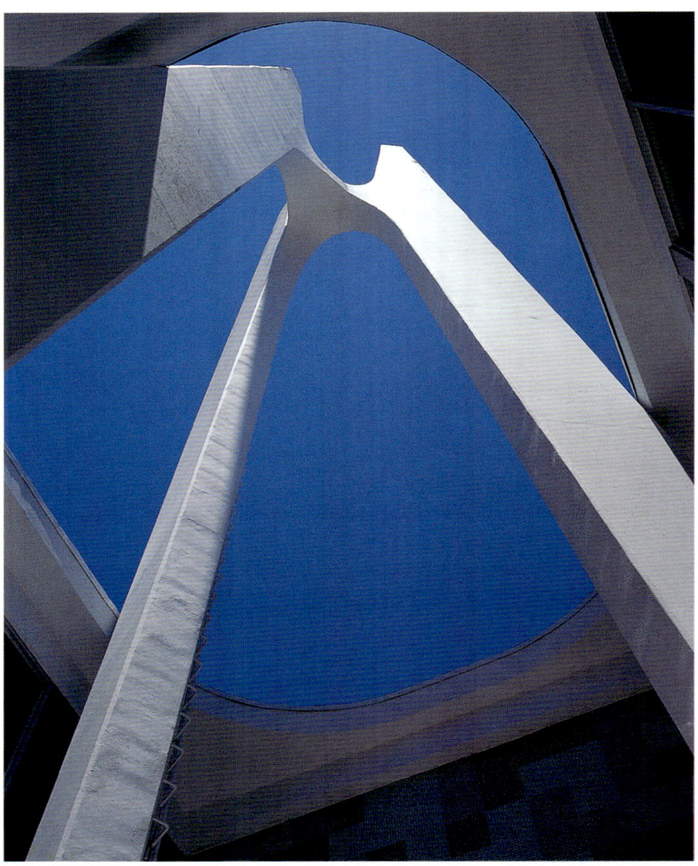

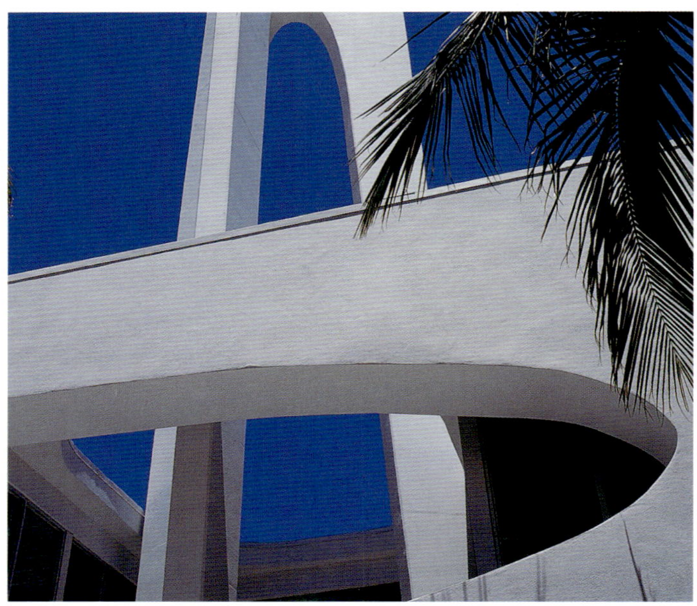

Scott has never lost his appreciation for what most people love about the Art Deco District: "People watching." And, when asked the simple, but inevitable, question of what he loves most about South Beach, Robins gives us a simple, but inevitable, answer: "The Water."

Chapter 18

STRIKING PAIR

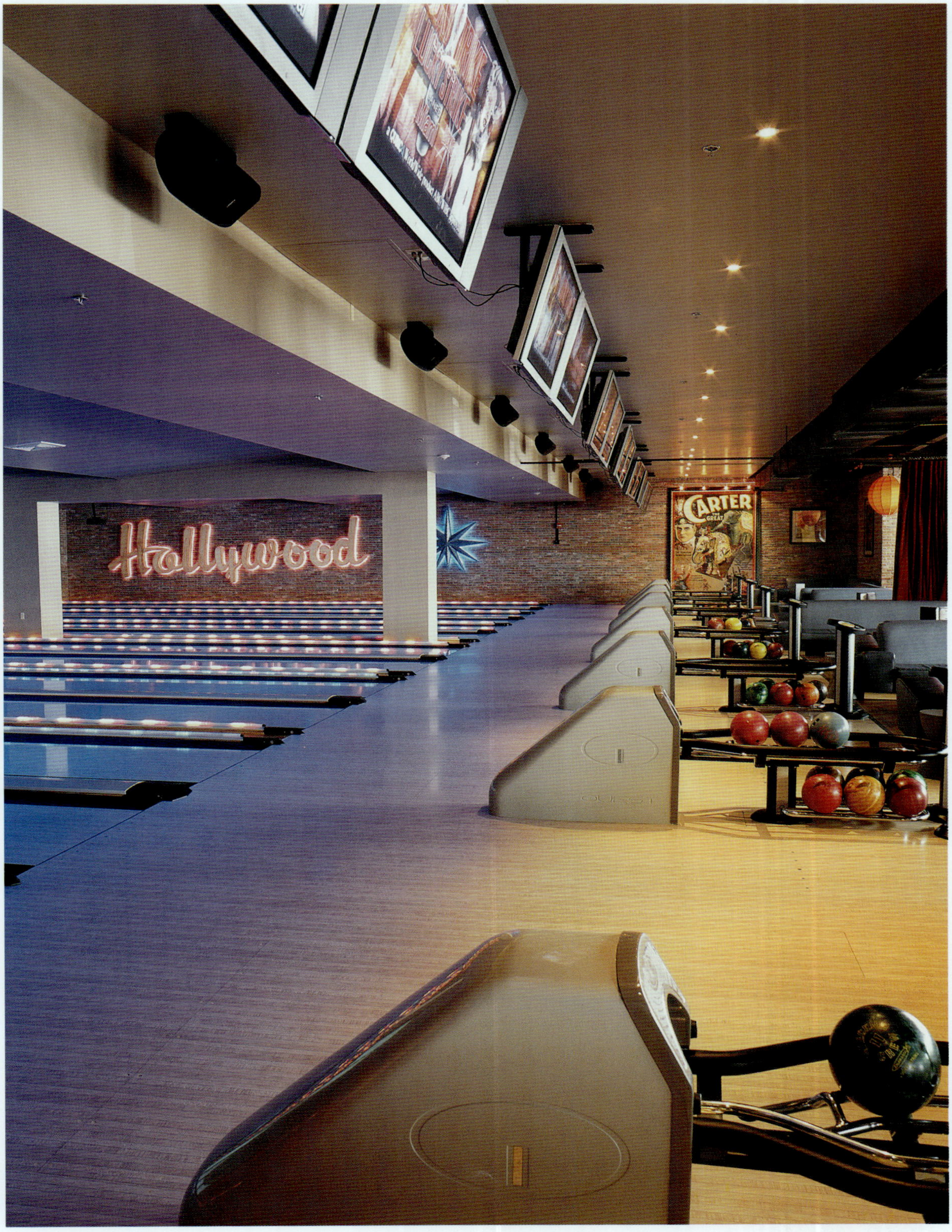

Brian Elias and Lucky Strike Lanes

Doesn't anyone in South Beach have a "real" job? Well, yes and no.

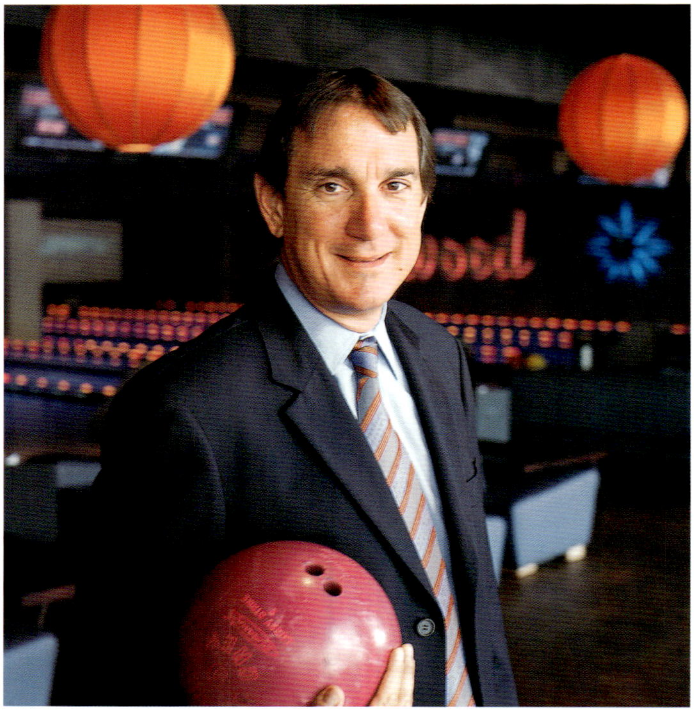

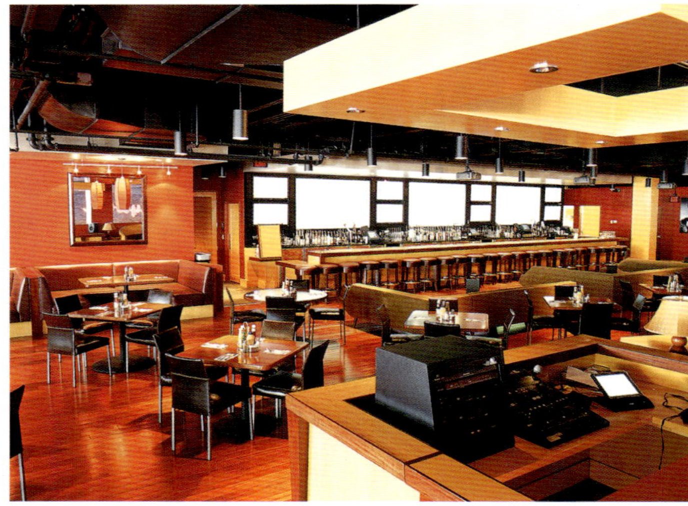

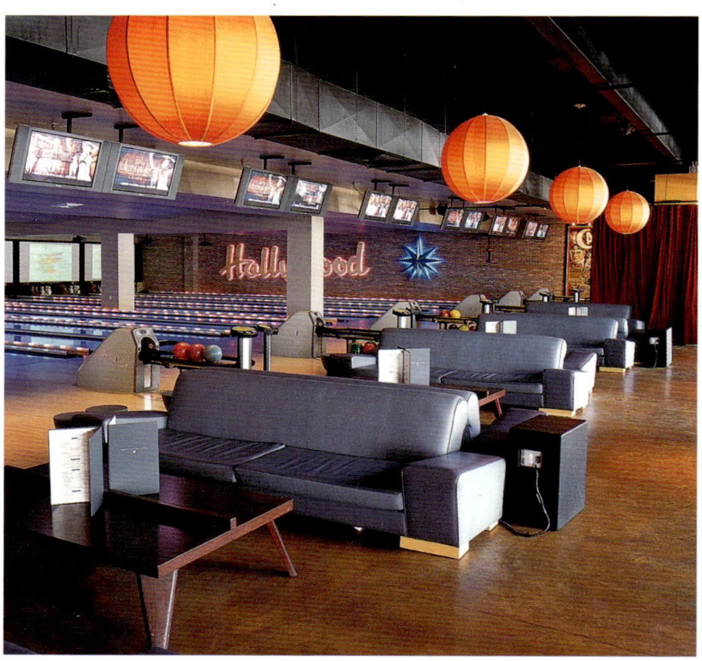

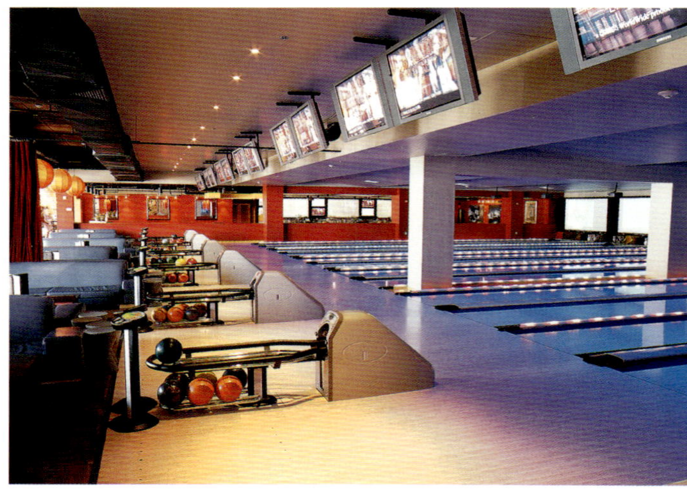

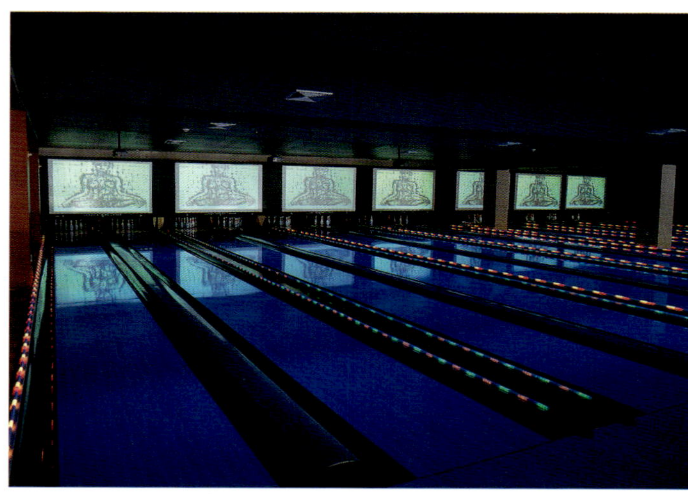

Brian Elias is a lawyer by day—a courtroom litigator, no less—but sheds the three-piece suit for a drink and a pair of bowling shoes by night. As part owner of the fabulously successful "Lucky Strike Lanes" just off Lincoln Road at Michigan Avenue, Brian has brought yet another delightful pastime to South Beach. Not an ordinary bowling alley, mind you, but more like a South Beach club where they happen to have bowling lanes.

After years of living in other Miami-area locales, Brian, who came from Minnesota to Miami as an infant, says "I have found my permanent home."

Brian's roots here go beyond the glitz and glamour of the South Beach lifestyle, no matter how much he enjoys the "night life options." He most values "the substantial relationships that I have developed and the comfort level that gives me no matter where I go."

Chapter 19

SOUTHERN OUTPOST FOR AN EMPIRE

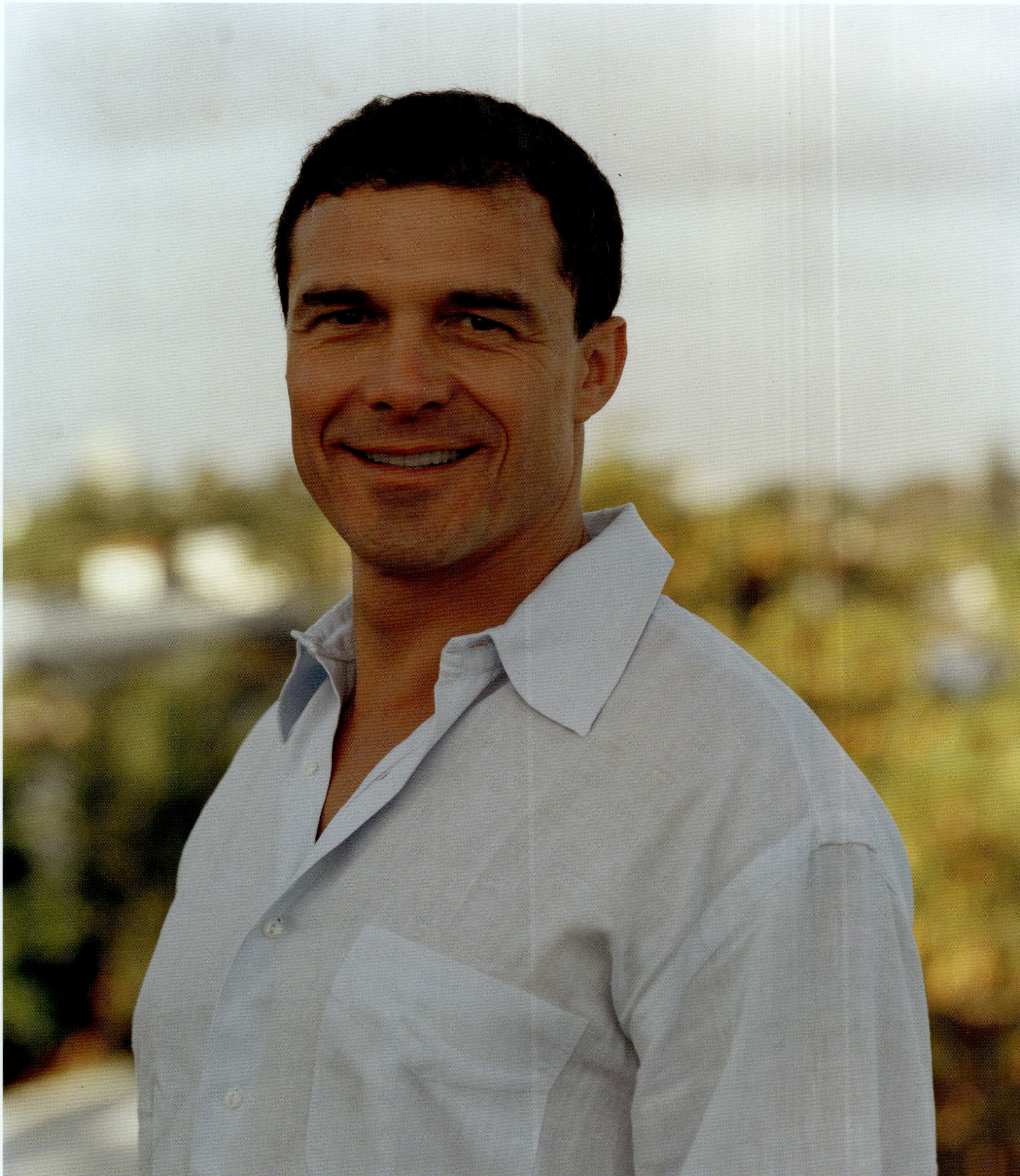

André Balazs, Lido Spa and the Raleigh Hotel

Having conquered the most demanding and *uber-hip* hotel territories of Los Angeles and New York, André Balazs entered the South Beach scene with his 2002 purchase of the Raleigh Hotel at 1775 Collins Avenue. Balazs, who earlier saved and reinvented Los Angeles' Chateau Marmont and other signature hotel properties on both coasts, is a Boston native who has made his mark as a hotelier in every city that has attracted his business and personal interest. He still divides his time among Los Angeles, New York, and Miami, where he recently purchased and redesigned the former Lido Spa Hotel—which he has renamed the "Standard Miami," after his Los Angeles hostelry of the same name.

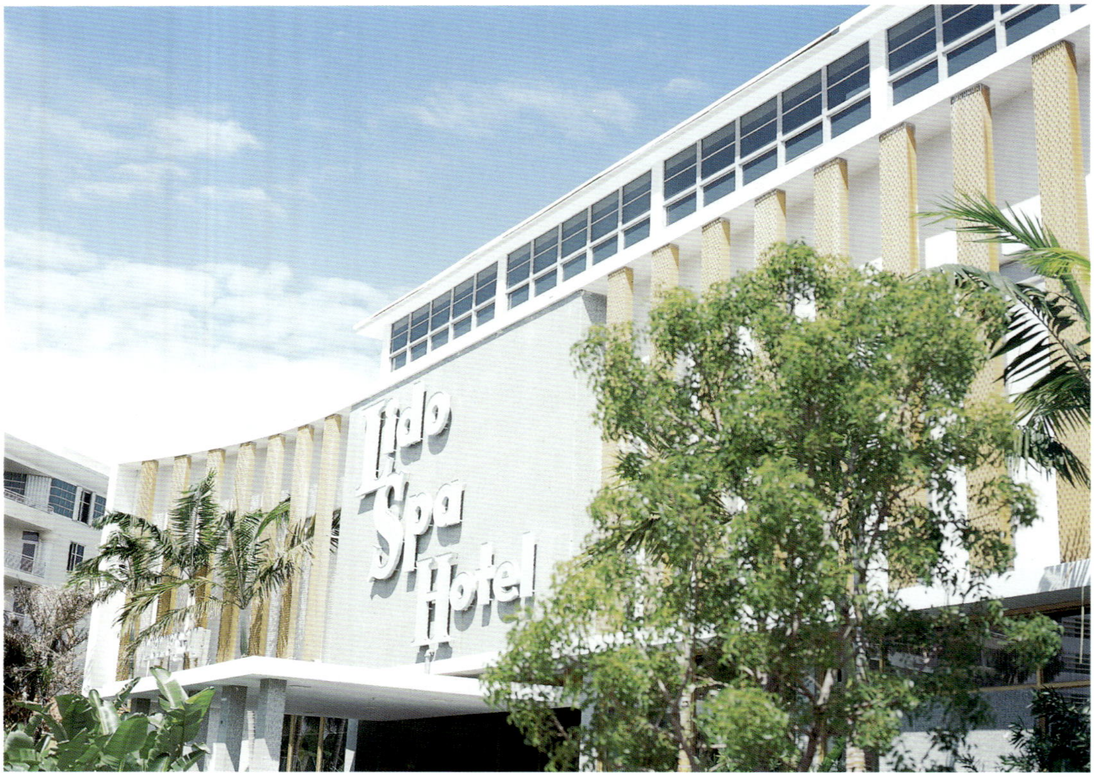

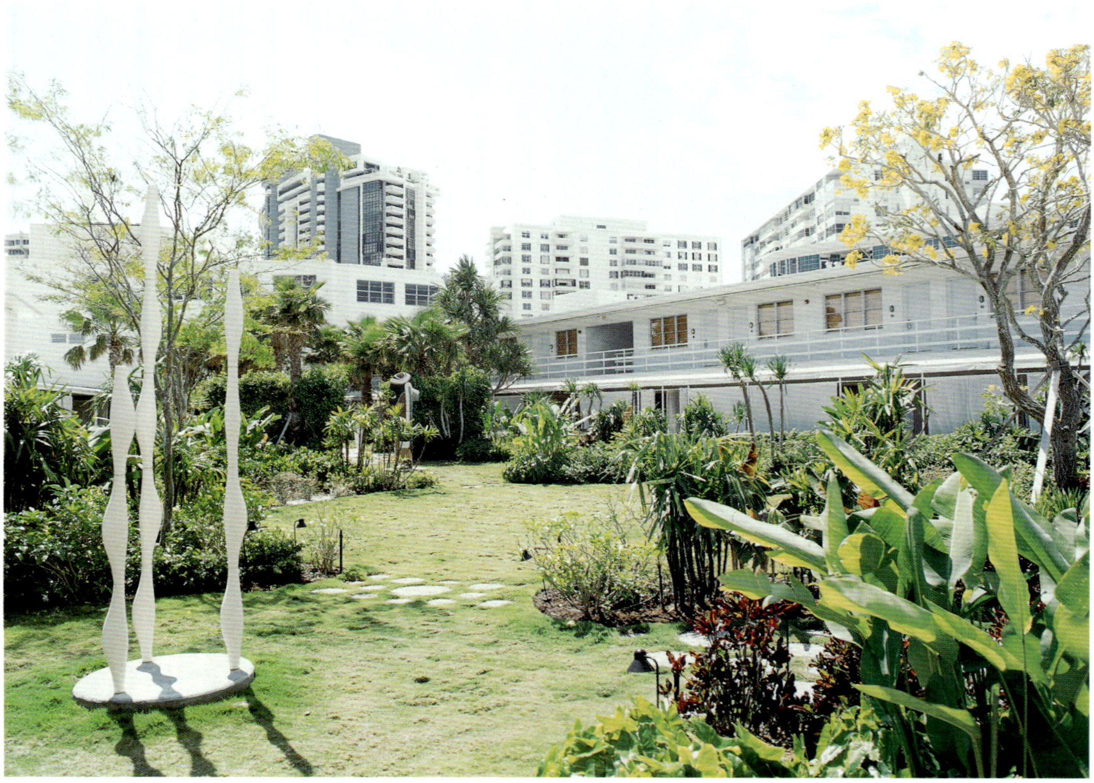

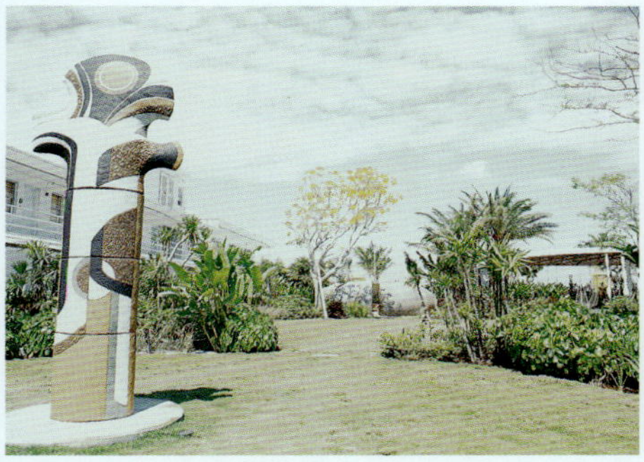
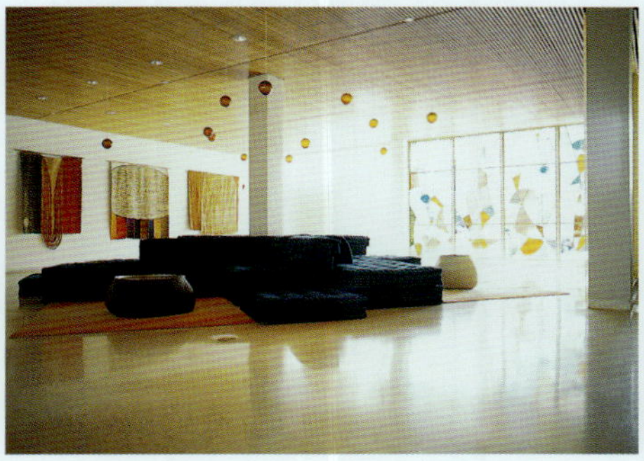
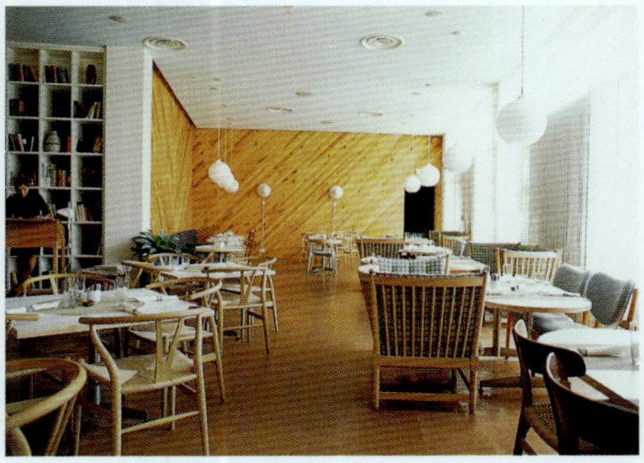
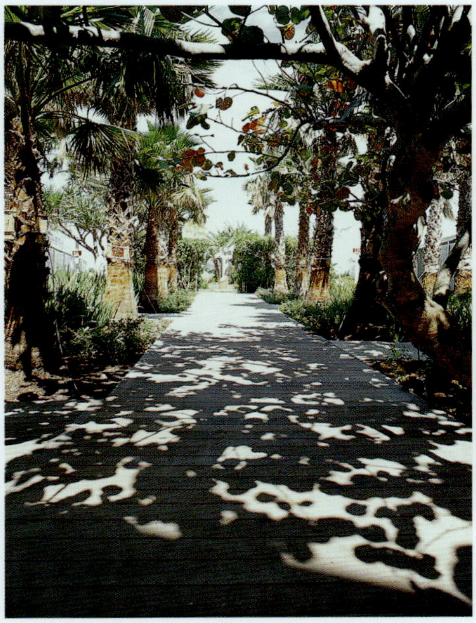
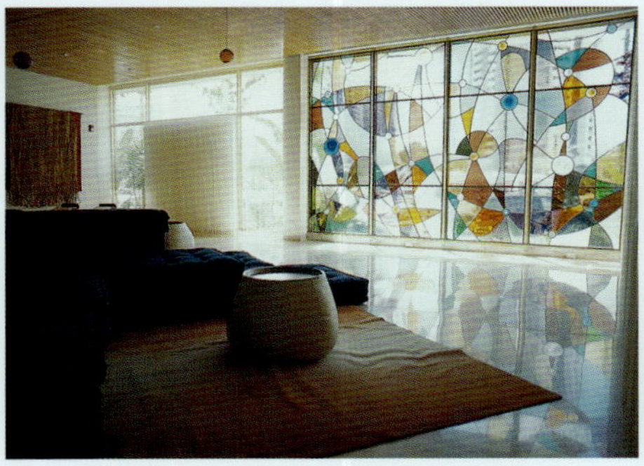
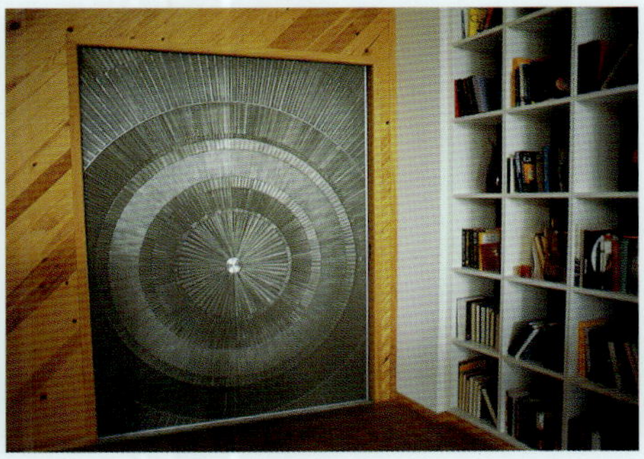
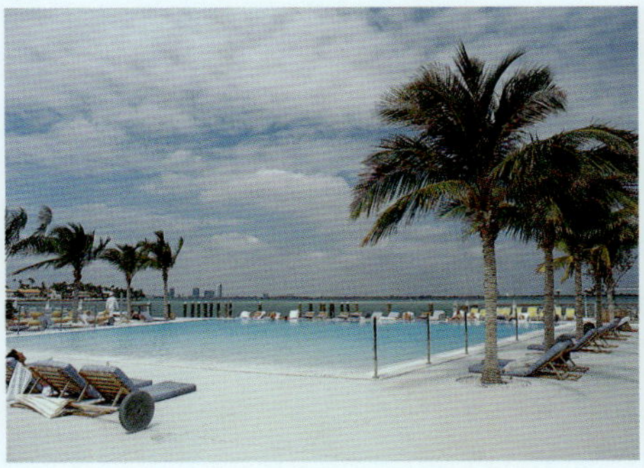
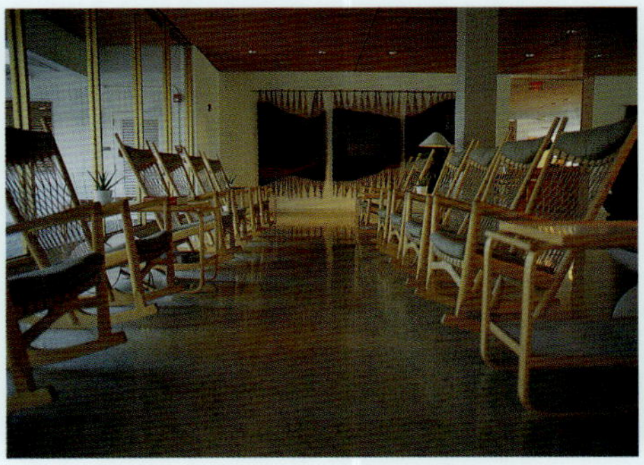
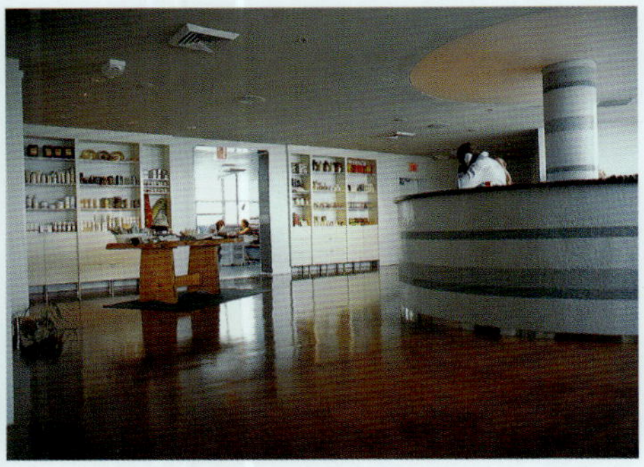

Balazs calls Miami a "multicultural metropolis," but he has a very simple, yet characteristically SoBe pleasure to recommend to a first time visitor to South Beach: "Swim in The Raleigh pool at dawn."

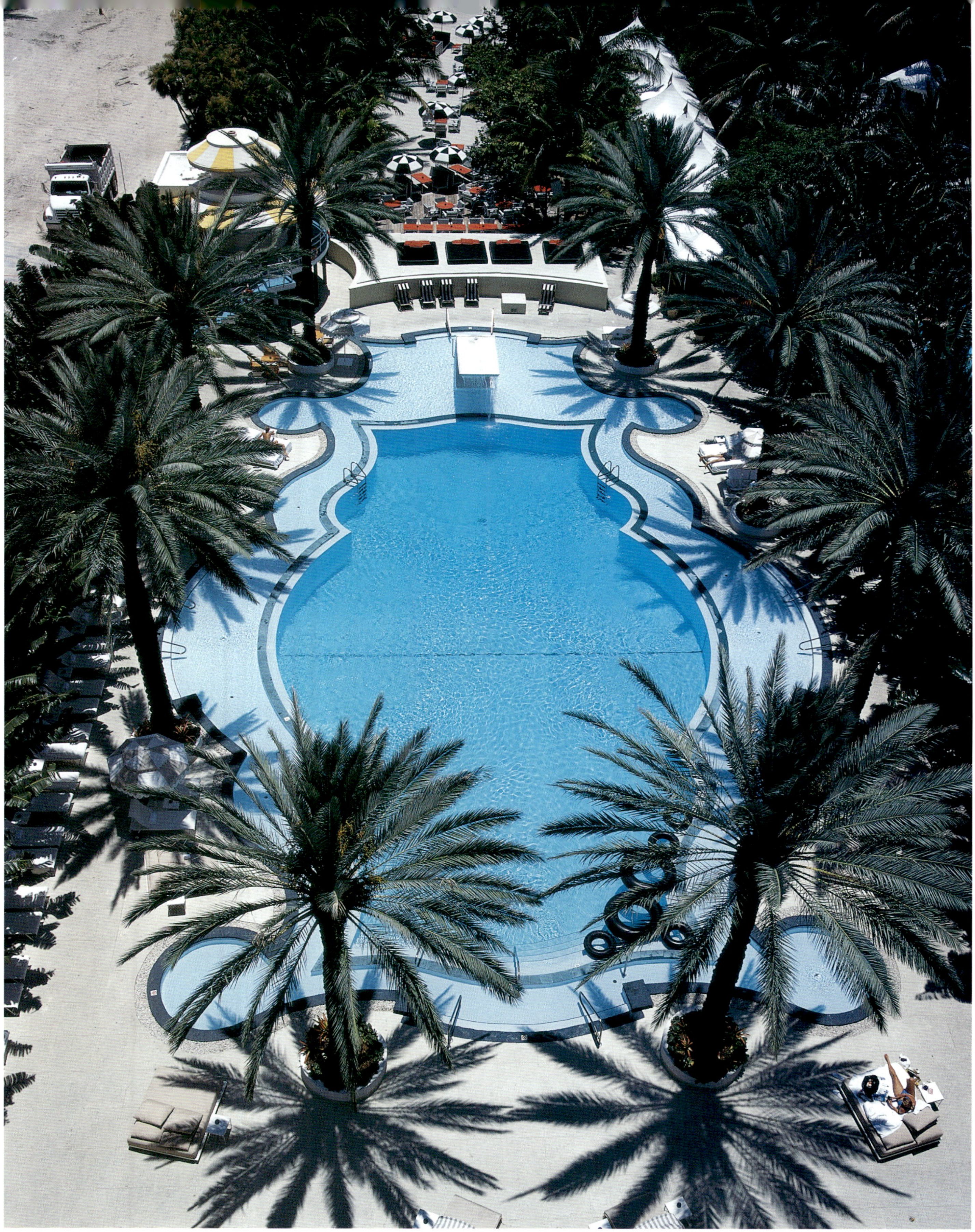

And, if you're lucky enough to be a guest at The Raleigh, we'd recommend the same, particularly following a night of South Beach subtropical adventures.

Chapter 20

DUTCH TREAT, ANYONE?

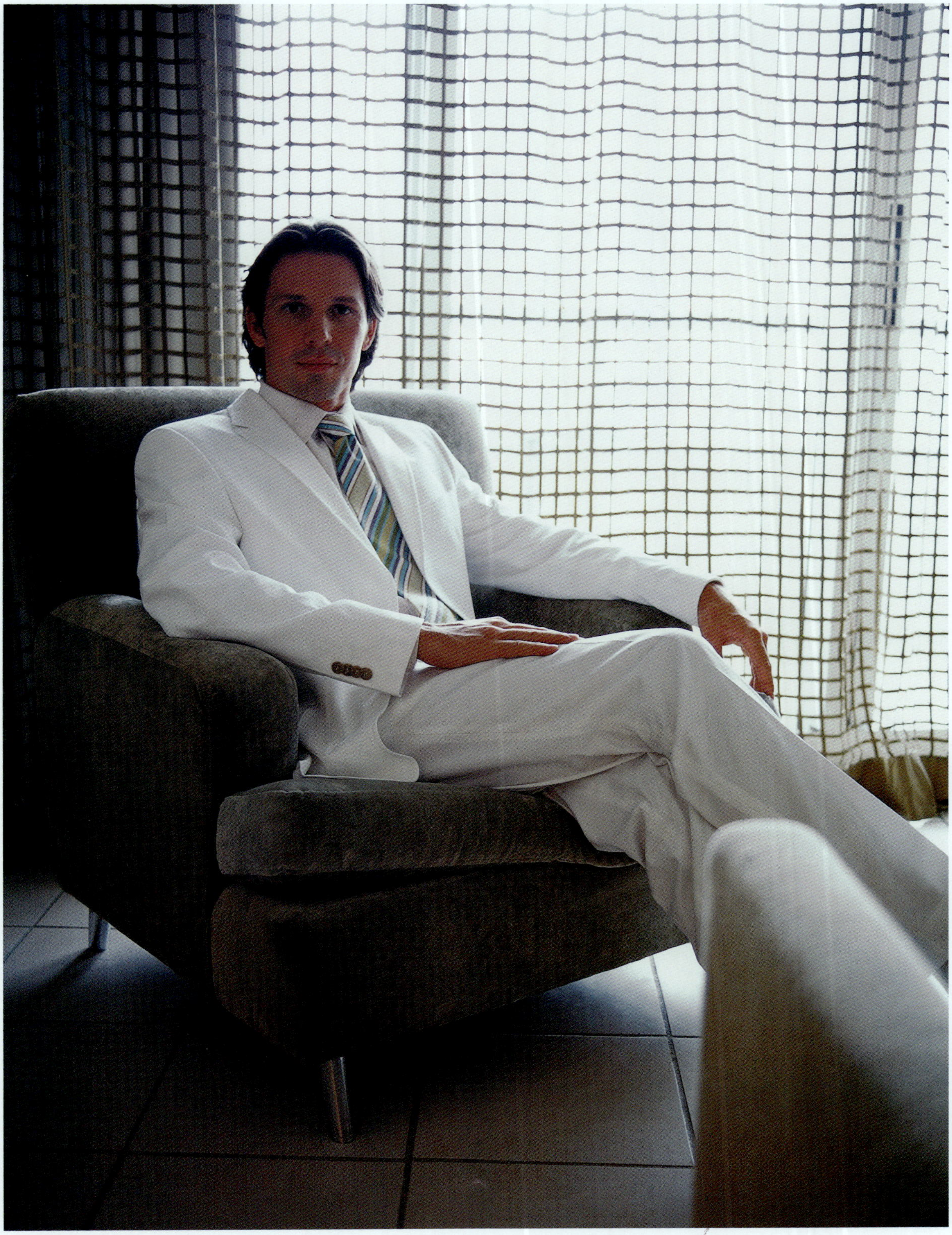

MARTIN KREDIET AND THE RALEIGH HOTEL

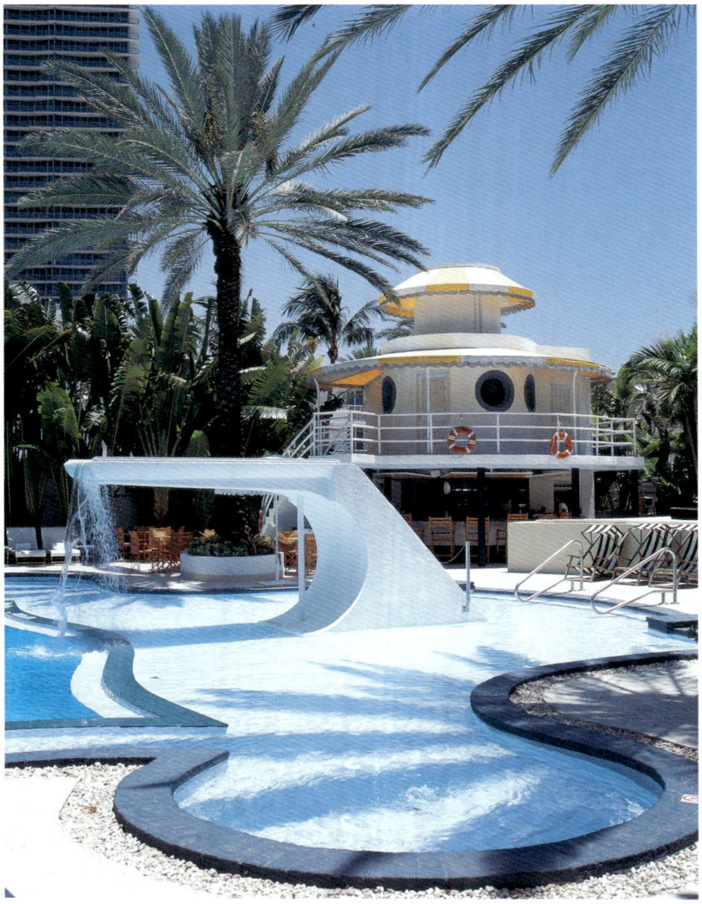

Ya "gotta" love the Dutch. (They're the ones from Holland, aka The Netherlands, but the people are never called "Hollish" or, except by an occasional Brit, "Netherlanders.") They live by holding back the sea in Northern Europe, raising tulips and terrific produce, and maintaining the world's most freewheeling major city (Amsterdam), all while washing their windows more than any other nation on Earth. They also produce people who are beautiful both inside and out.

Such a man is Martin Krediet, whose movie-star good looks have not prevented him from being known as one of the flat-out nicest people in South Beach. Before coming to SoBe, this native of the Dutch town of Den Helder was brought up on the Caribbean island (and former Dutch colony) of Curaçao, its own sort of paradise.

Martin is the Sales Director of the Raleigh Hotel, at 18th and Collins, a spot where celebrities gather for a little peace and quiet at the beach.

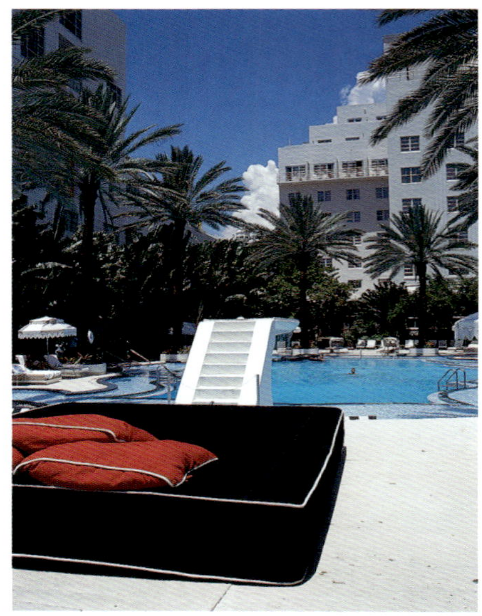

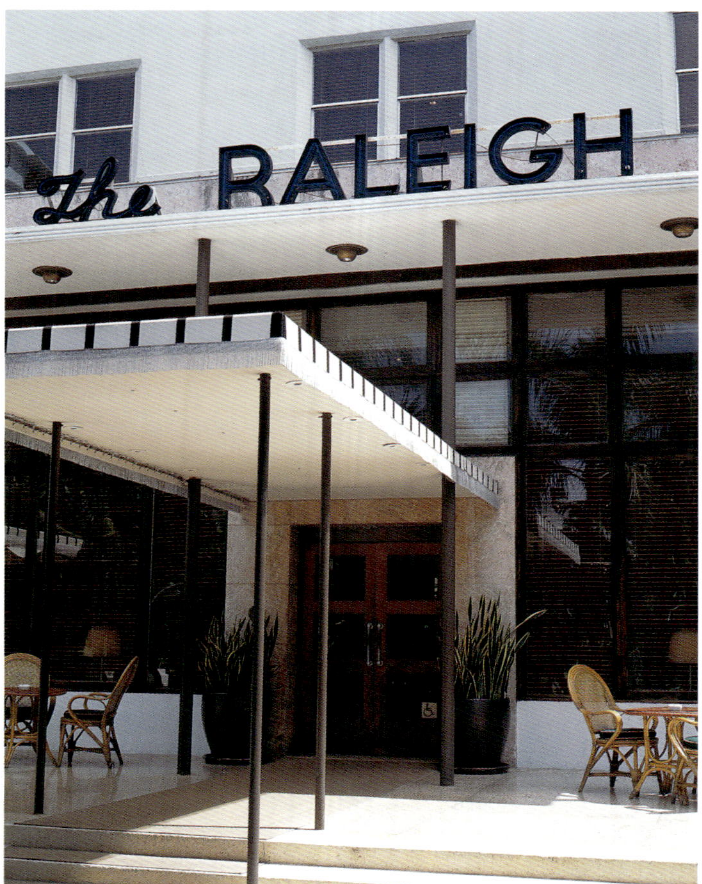

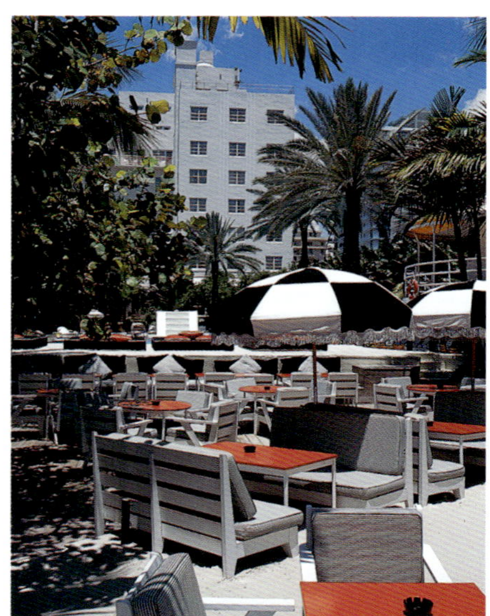

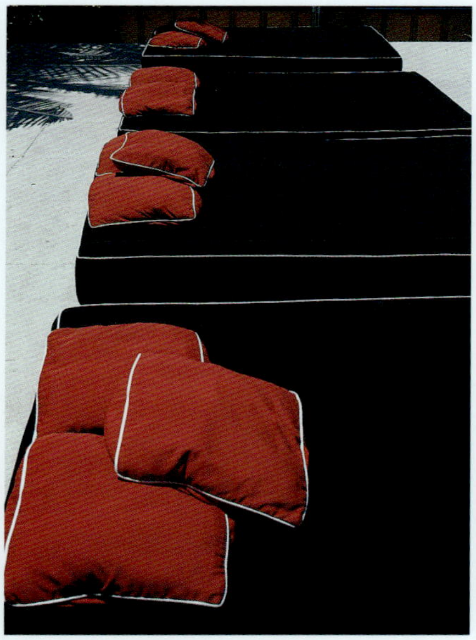

What tempted Martin to trade one paradise for another? "The South Beach Buzz!" says he. Aside from staying at the Raleigh and eating at its gourmet restaurant, Martin (like others in this book) feels that the best way to appreciate his latest paradise is by boat. Maybe that's the Dutch background in Martin, seeing as the Dutch have always been a seafaring people. Martin also echoes those who say that the best budget buy in South Beach is whatever it takes to snag a table at one of Lincoln Road's outside restaurants. From there the (more or less) free "people-parade" is worth a lot more than the price of admission.

The Raleigh Hotel, where Martin works, has become a signature hotel for "South Beach Hip." Built in 1940 and designed by architect L. Murray Dixon, the Raleigh is no architectural pretender. It really is an Art Deco gem. As long ago as 1947, the Raleigh was famous for its uniquely shaped swimming pool, which LIFE M*agazine* (the king of magazines in 1947) called "the most beautiful pool in the world." Today, the beautiful design of the pool is enhanced by the celebrities and assorted beautiful people who tend to stay and hang out at the Raleigh.

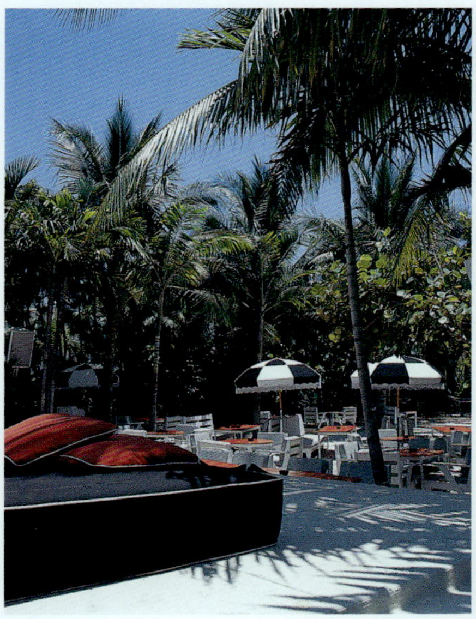

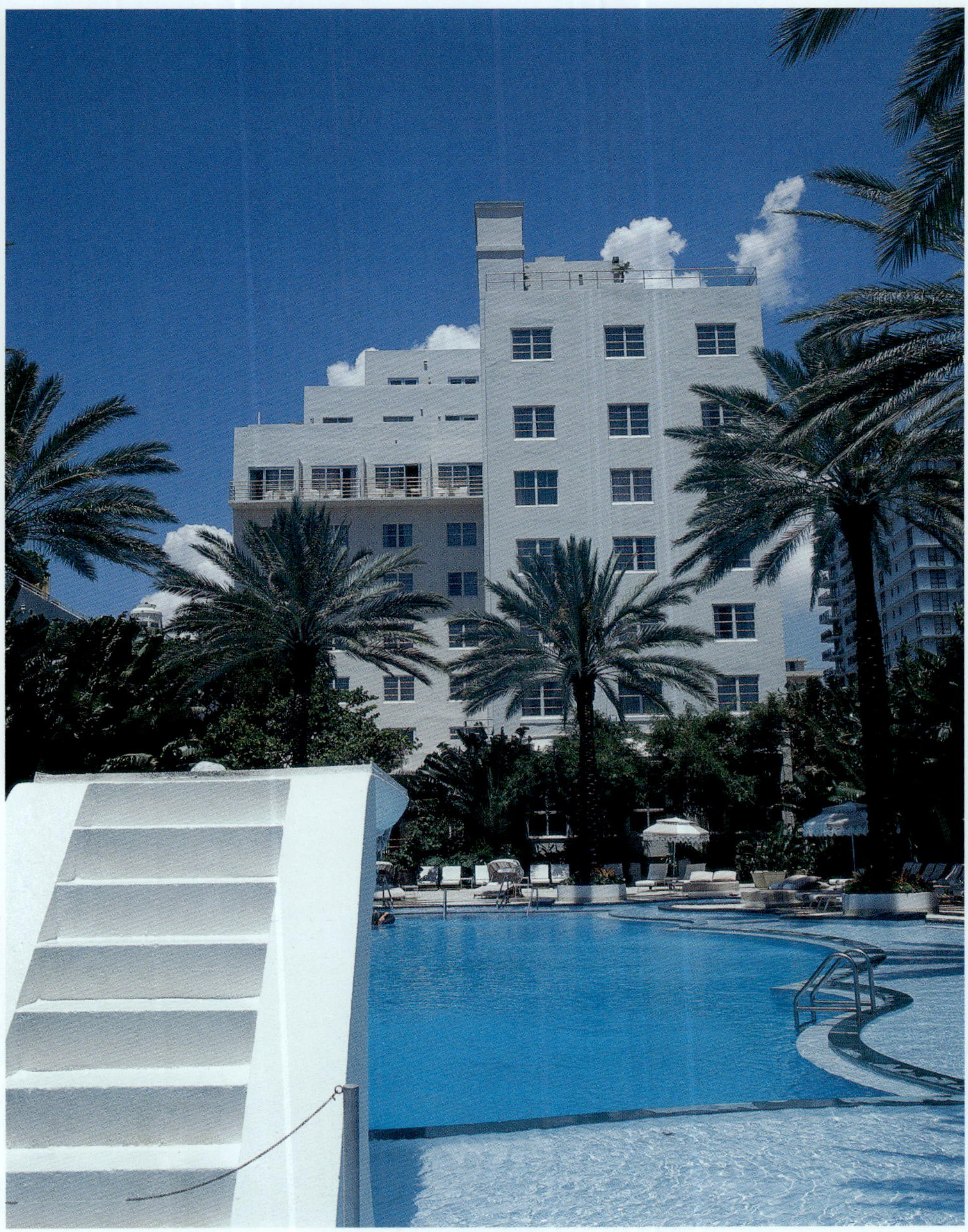

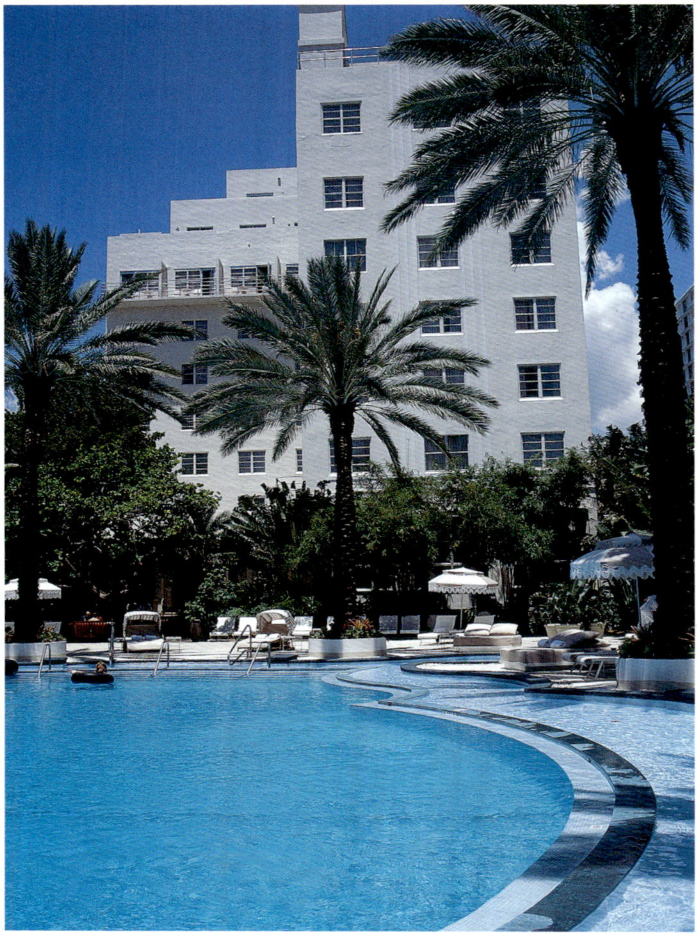

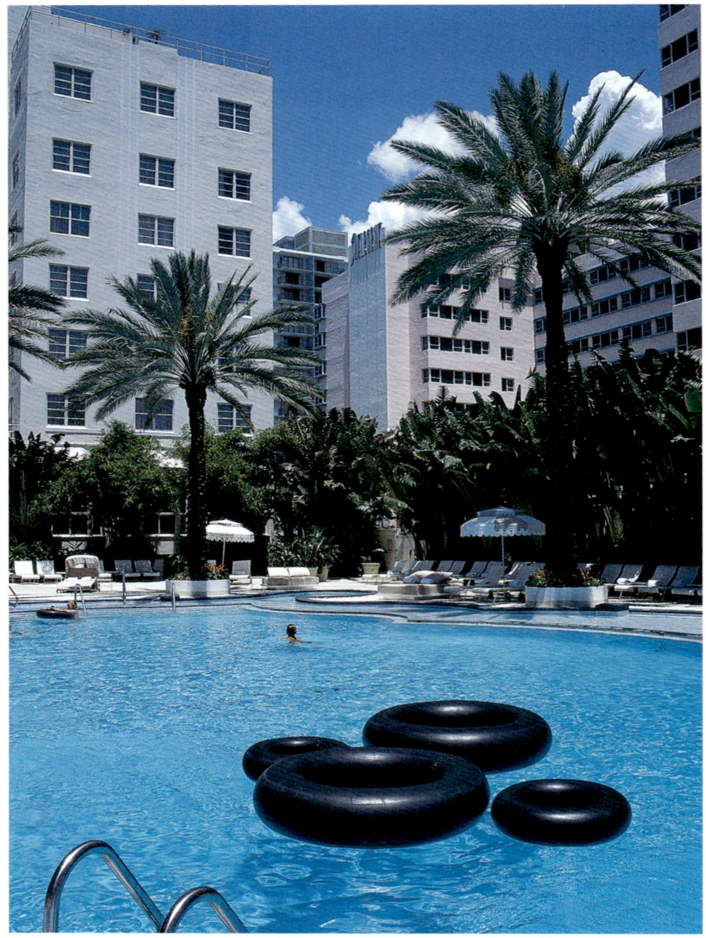

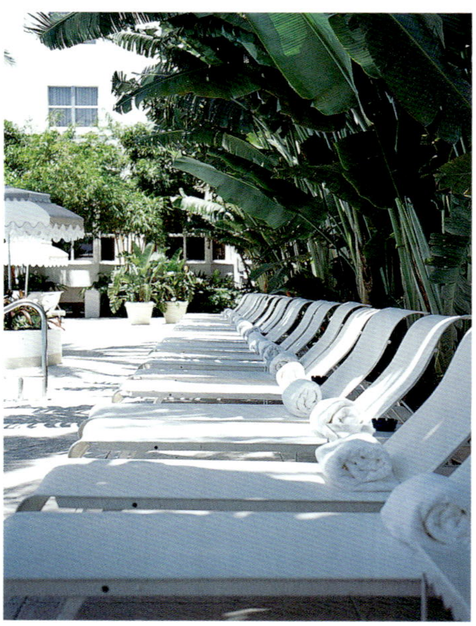

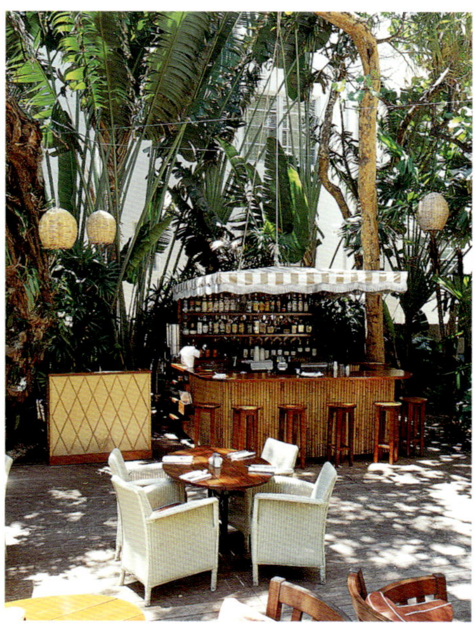

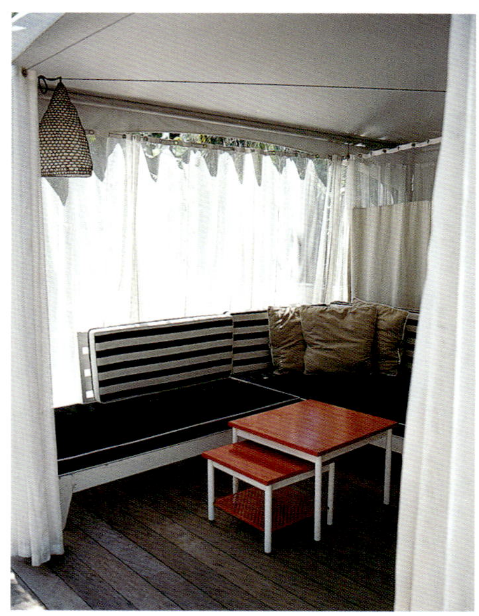

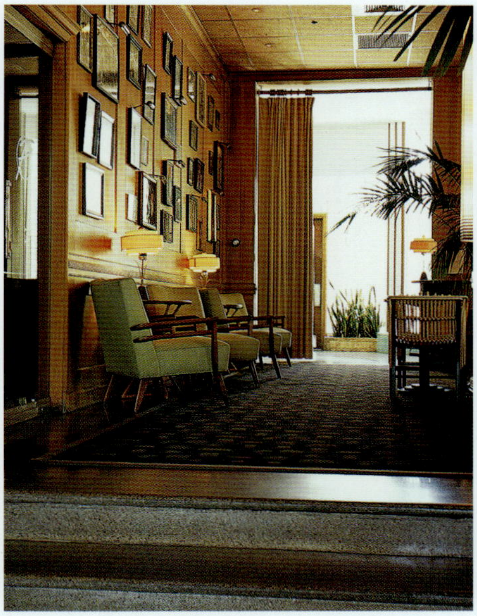
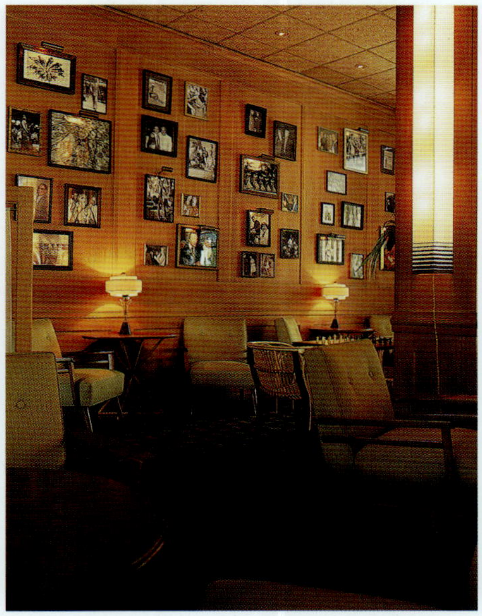
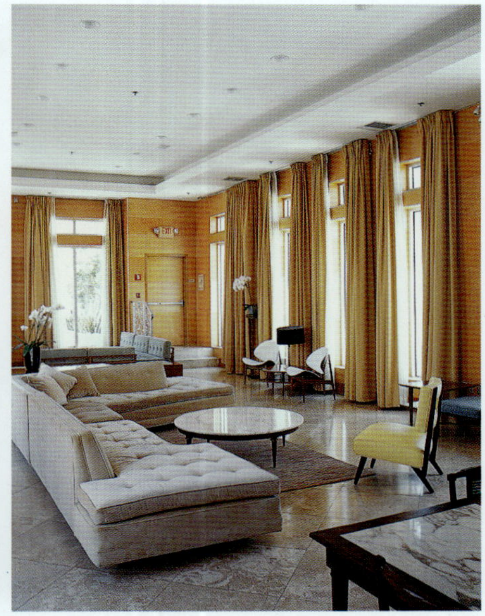
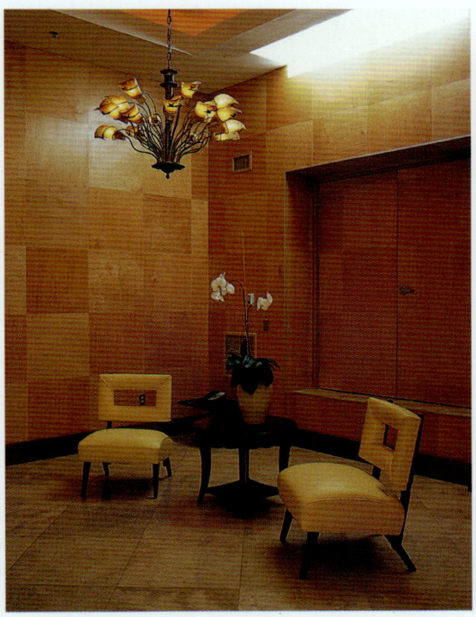
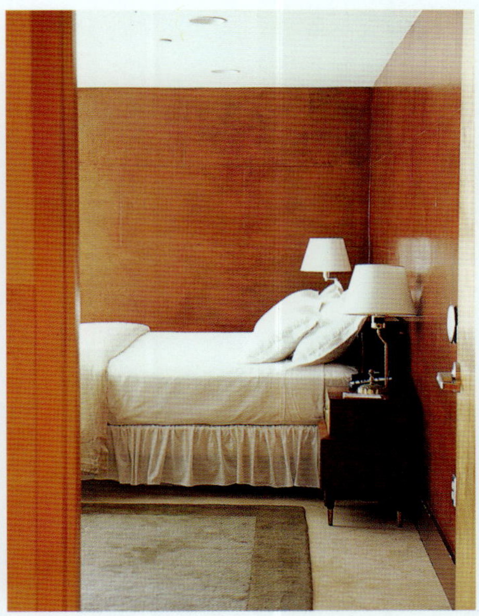
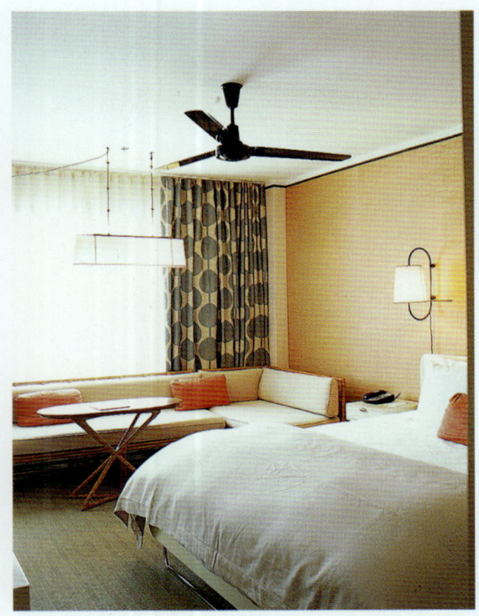

Which brings us back to Martin Krediet, who, even in the midst of such beauty, looks forward to the next treat that South Beach has in store. As Martin says, one of the most precious blessings of the South Beach life is "never having two days be alike."

Chapter 21

PUTTIN' ON THE RITZ

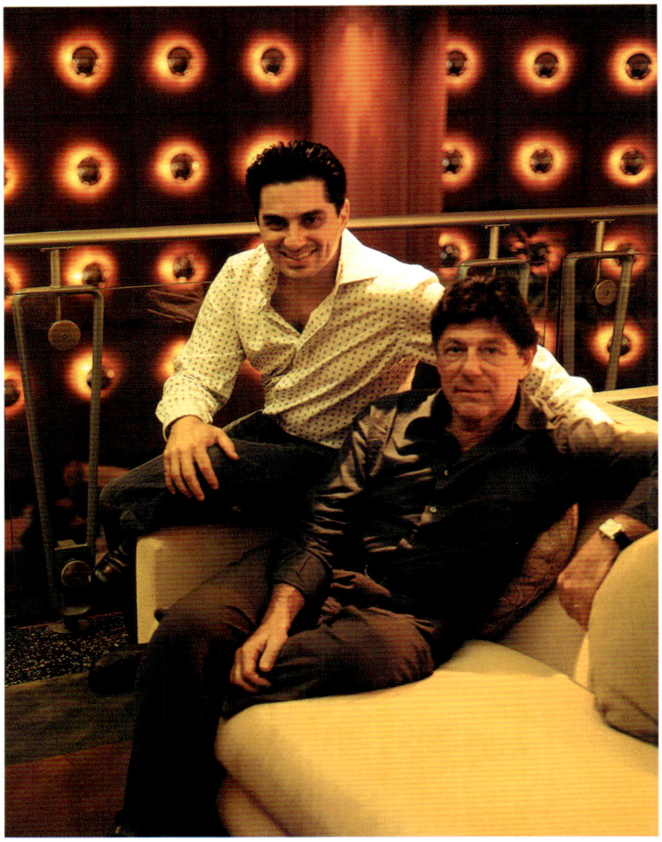
Photo by Richard Cordero

DIEGO LOWENSTEIN AND THE RITZ-CARLTON

Another living testament to the international character of South Beach, Diego Lowenstein (shown on the left in the photo, along with his father) is an Argentine native who oversees his family's real estate interests in the U.S. It may be the "ever-changing" nature of his adopted home town that fascinates Diego the most, but it is the consistent luxury and attention to detail of his flagship property, the Ritz-Carlton South Beach, in which he takes special pride (after his three beautiful children, of course). Among other things, the Ritz-Carlton is noted for its exquisite integration of details derived from the Art Deco di Lido Hotel structure that once occupied the new hotel's site.

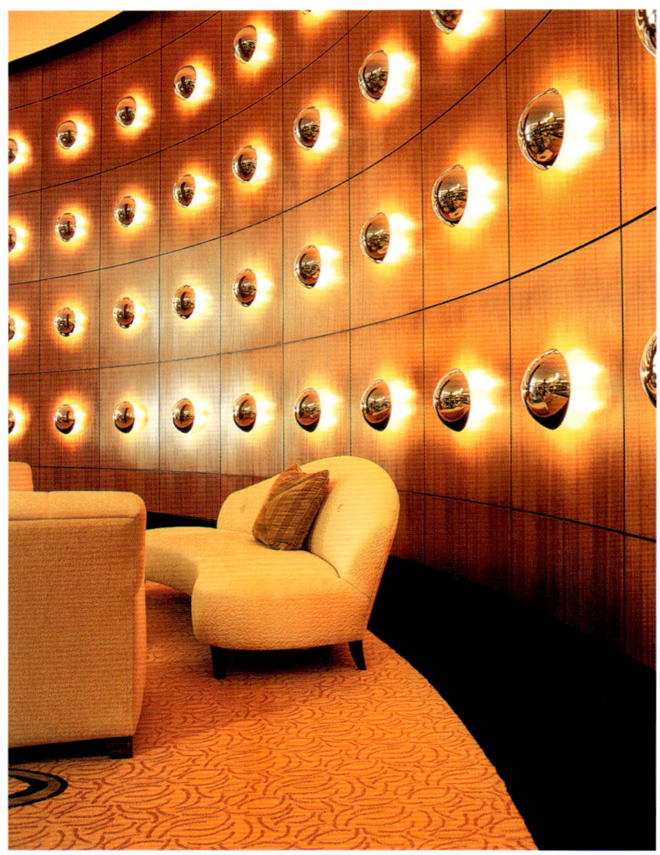
Photo by Richard Cordero

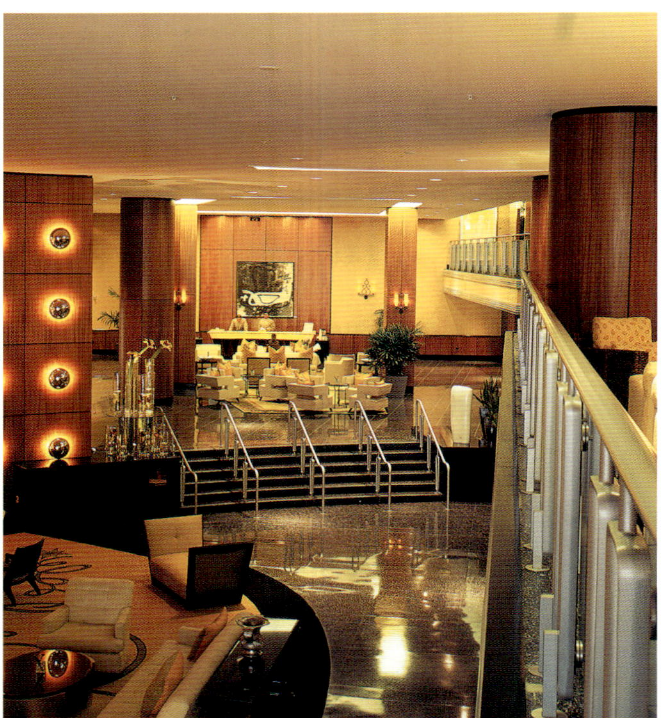
Photo by Richard Cordero

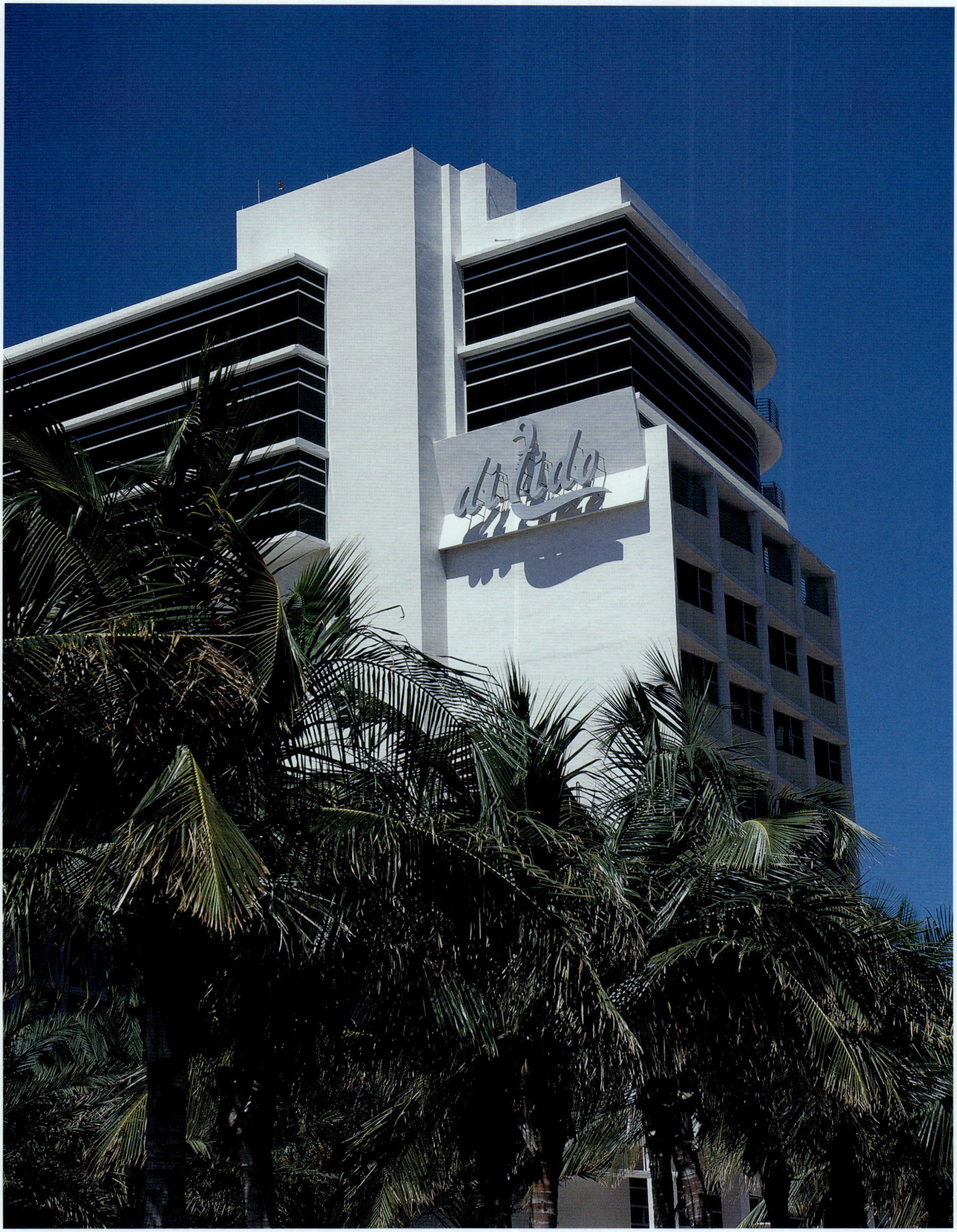
di Lido

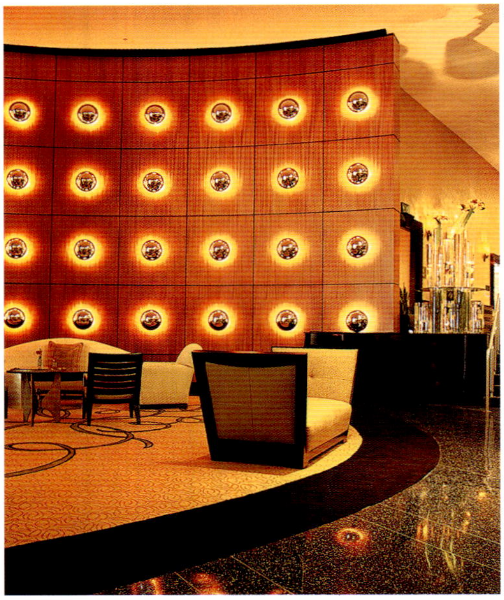

Photo by Richard Cordero

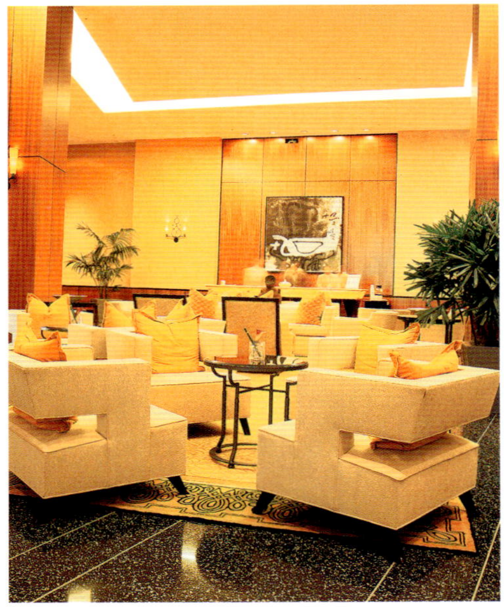

Photo by Richard Cordero

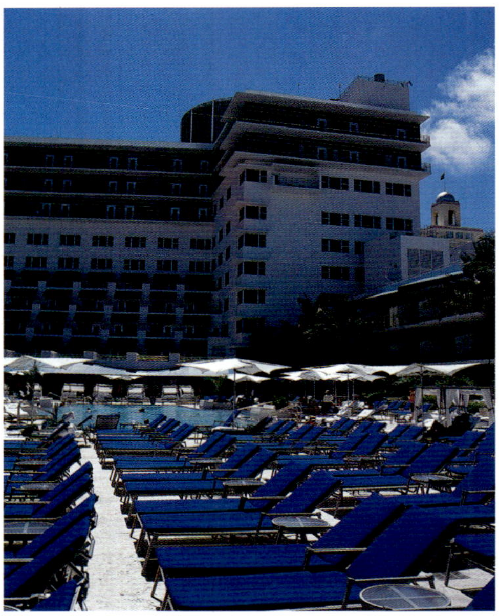

Photo by Richard Cordero

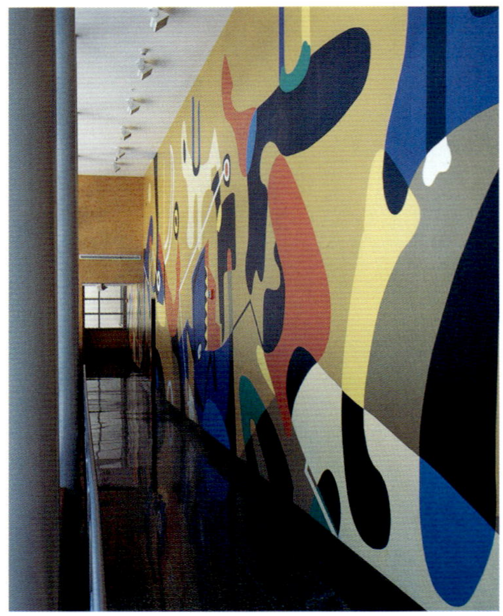

Photo by Richard Cordero

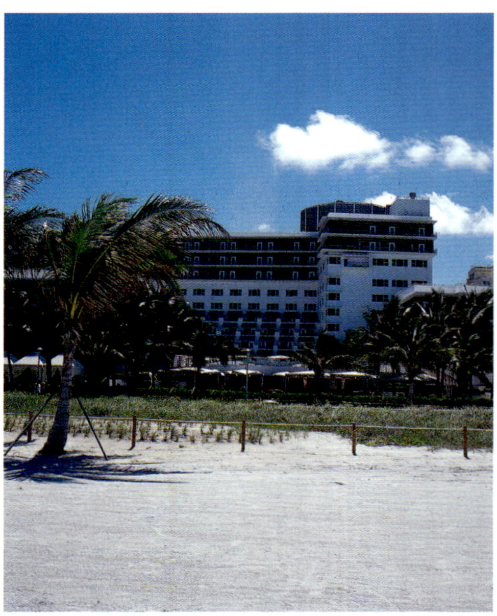

Photo by Richard Cordero

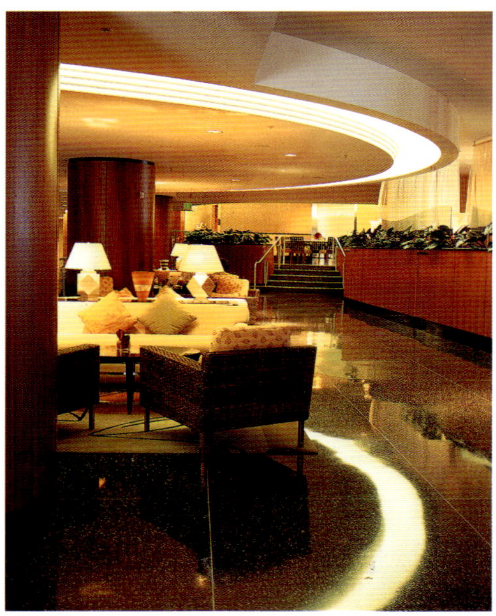

Photo by Richard Cordero

Like so many others with substantial real estate and other interests in South Beach, Diego still hasn't lost his taste for some of the simpler pleasures—the fact that "the city feels more like a town," and the never-ending "people-watching" opportunities along the Lincoln Road Mall. Though he hails from Buenos Aires, one of the great metropolises of the Western Hemisphere, Diego has fallen in love with the "diverse group of people who live in and visit Miami Beach."

Chapter 22

The Sensual Setai

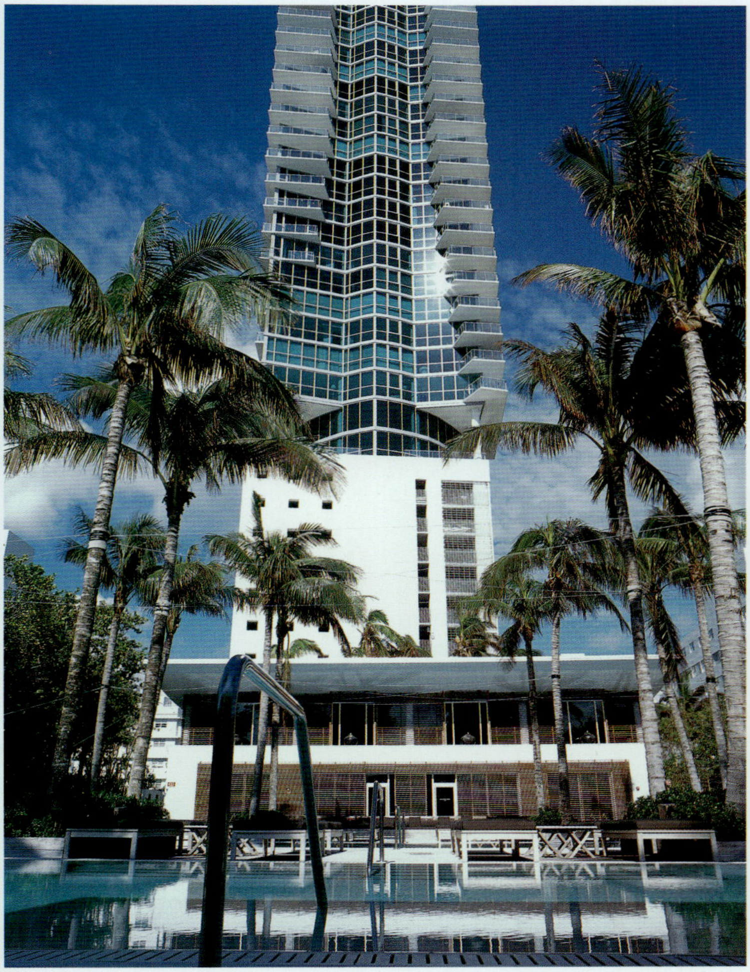

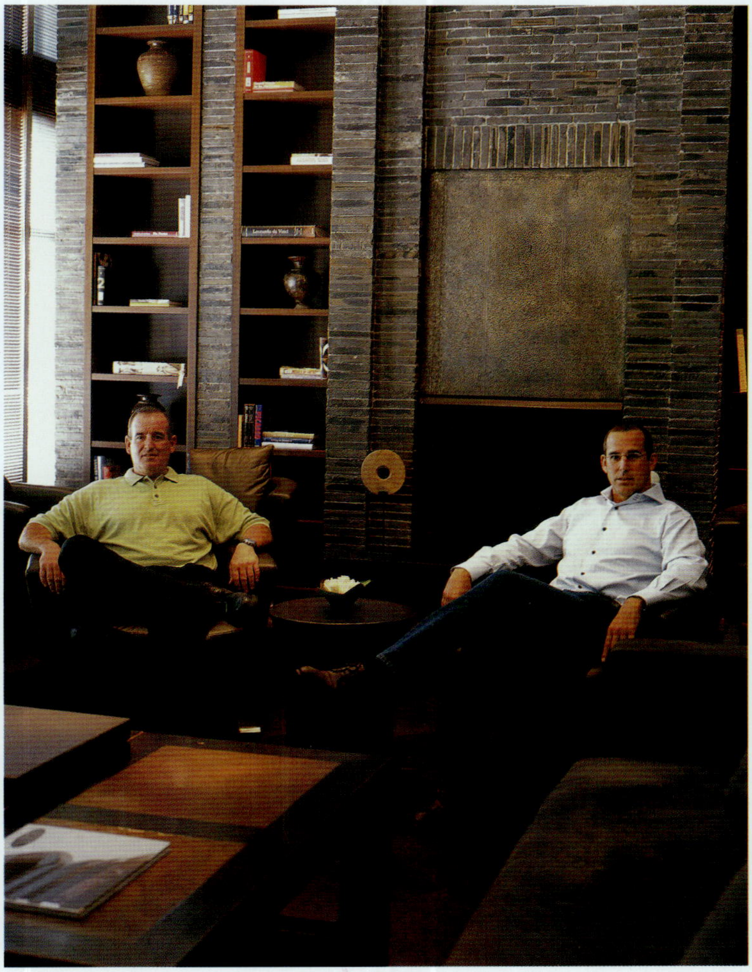

Jonathan Breene and John Conroy

What do you get when you take one young high-end real estate developer from New York, mix in a counterpart from Brisbane, Australia, add the spices of the mysterious East, and then heat gently to a South Beach simmer? If you're in Miami, it adds up to an internationally known five-star hotel and residence called the "Setai" (for which, we are told, there is simply no word in English). Soaring forty stories into the unbelievably blue sky on the Atlantic Ocean at 20th Street, the Setai, which opened in 2004, is a monument to the vision of John P. Conroy, Jr. (the New Yorker on the left) and Jonathan Breene (the Australian on the right).

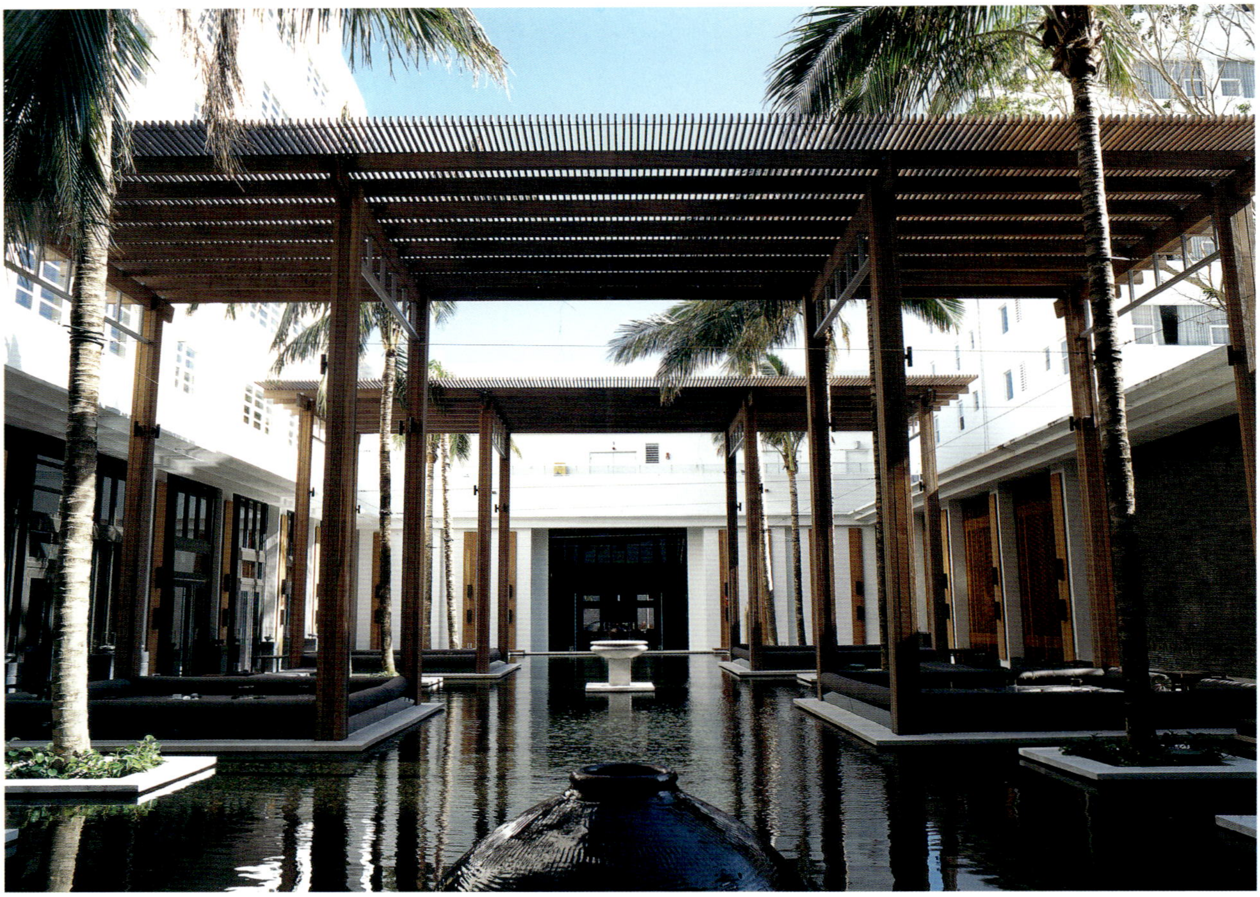

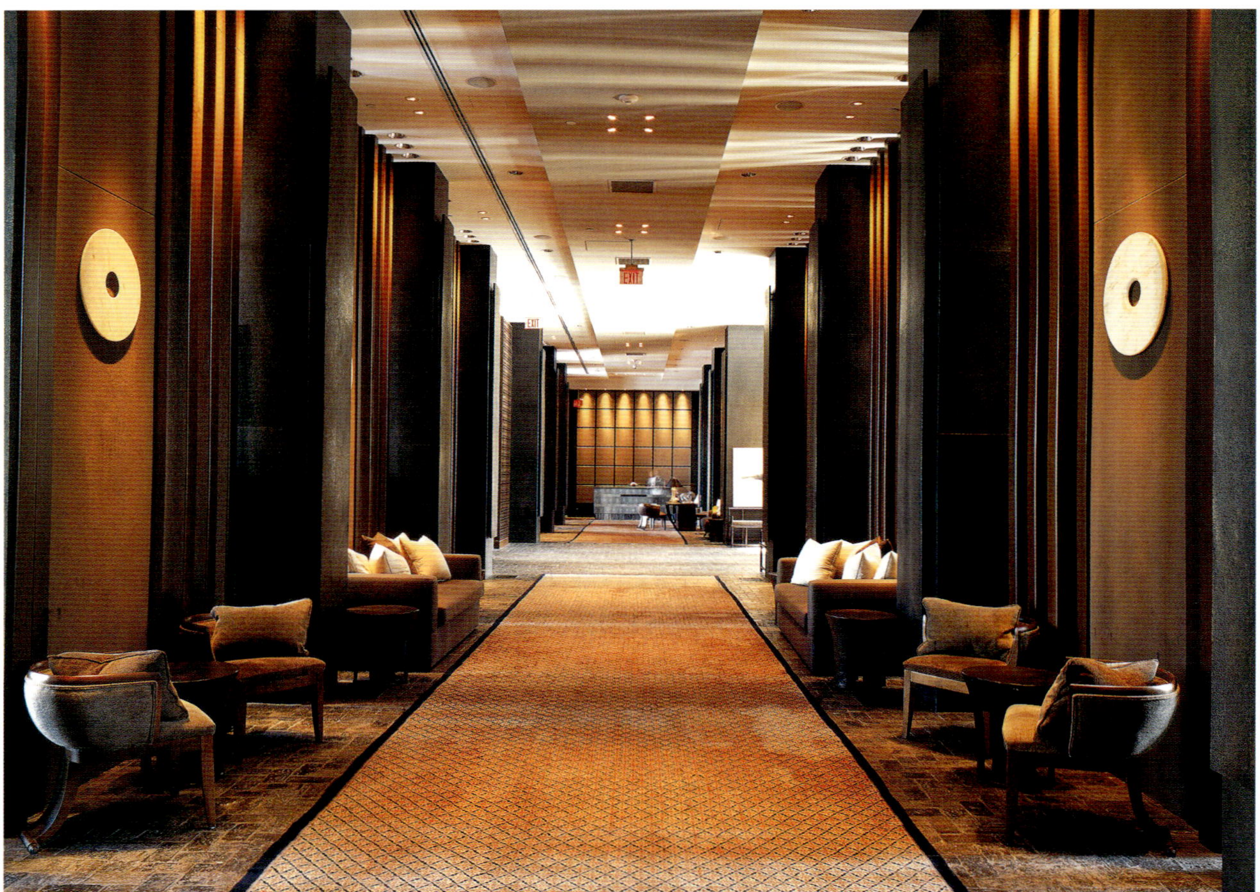

The Setai has already sparked a renaissance of the surrounding neighborhood (one of the most recent South Beach areas to throw off its "sleepy" period) and raised the ante for the ideal of the sophisticated SoBe luxury hotel. And it has done all this while creating an atmosphere of tranquil glamour for those lucky enough to be hotel guests or owners of one of its condominium residences.

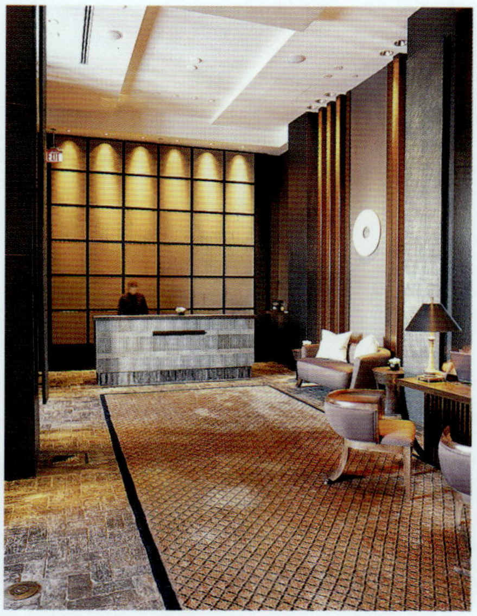

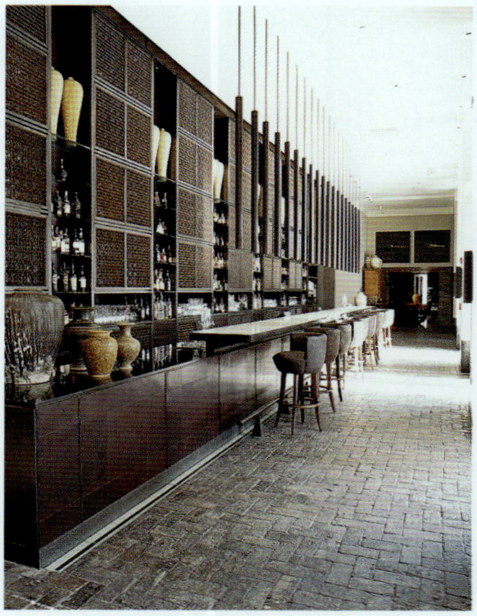

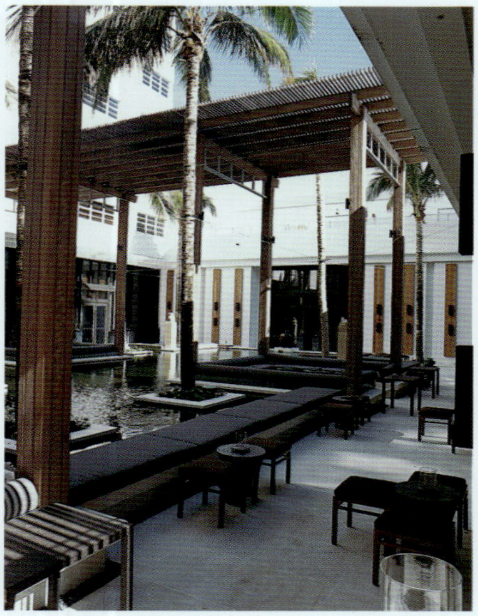

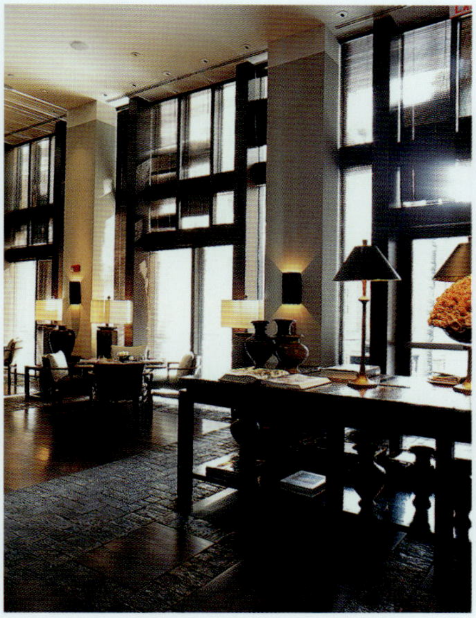

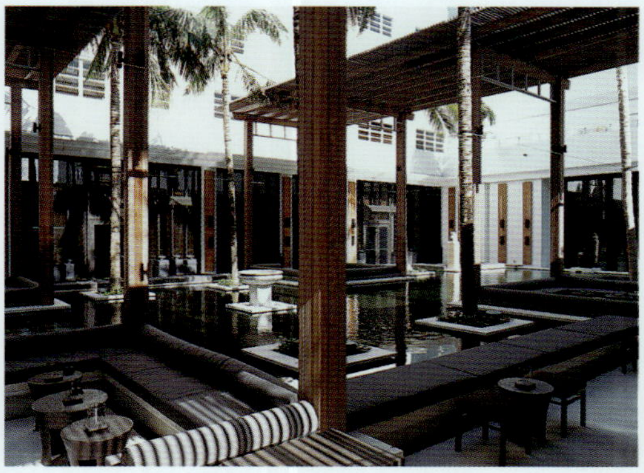

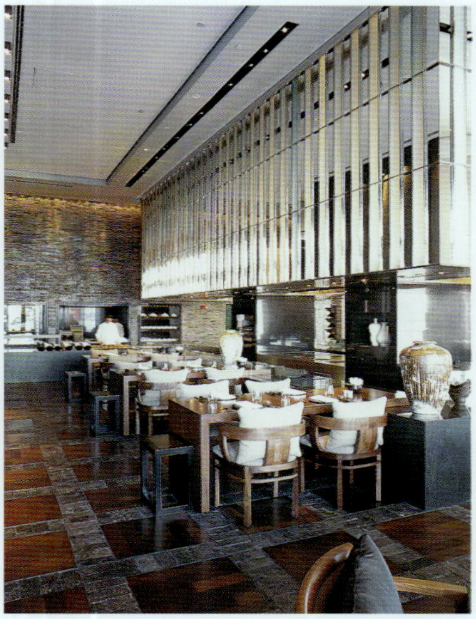

It's no wonder that Breene and Conroy have collaborated so successfully on their real estate venture. They are "attached at the soul" when talking about their adopted paradise in South Florida, with a mutual fascination for the exotic mix of human and natural wonders that make up the South Beach experience. Their pride in the Setai is matched by their common attachment to the sensual pleasures of palate and people that inhabit their new neighborhood. From the simple treat of "running at the water's edge" (Breene's favorite pastime) to "the international, cosmopolitan lifestyle" beloved by Conroy, this successful team of developers has raised the bar a notch in the South Beach hotel game.

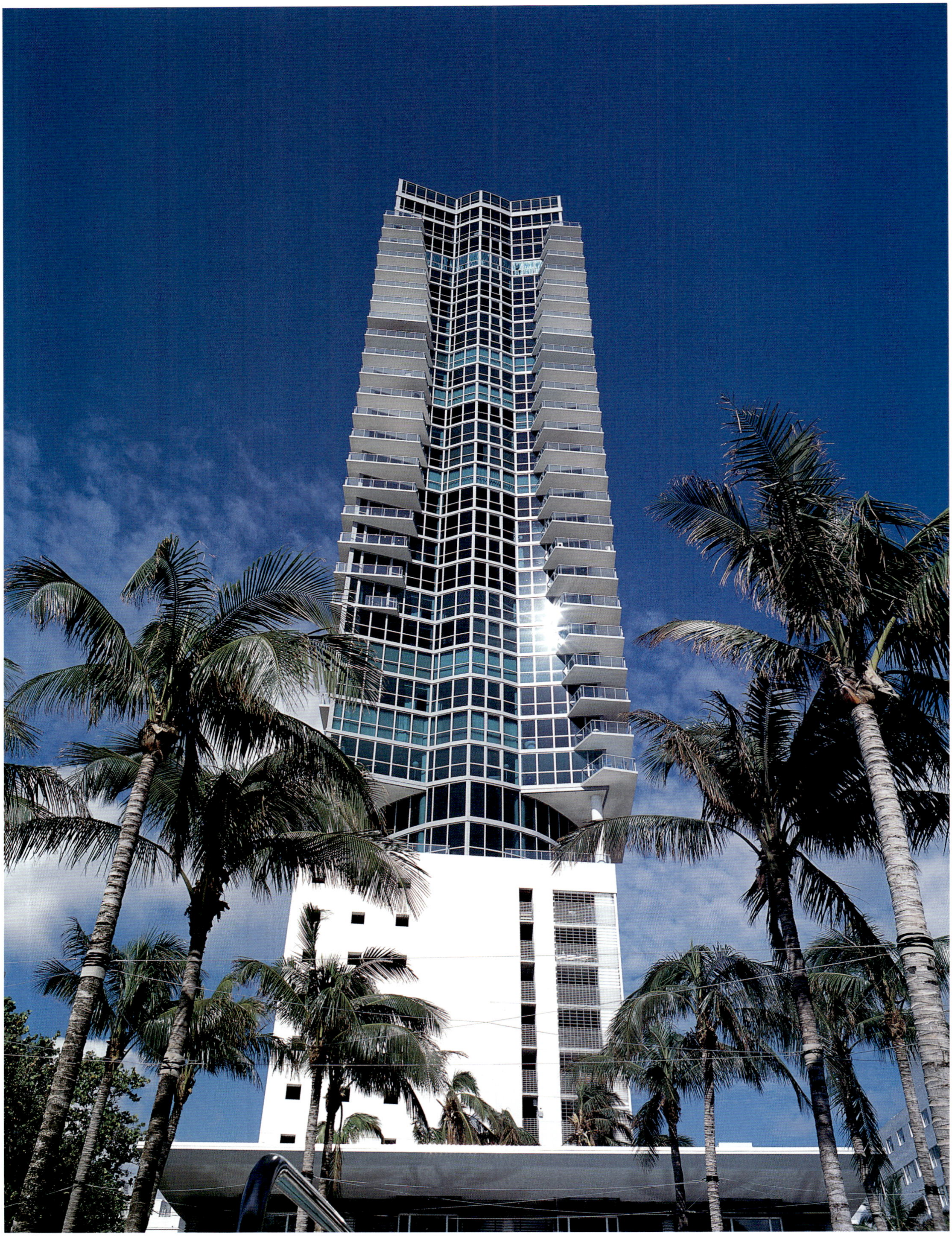

Chapter 23

Healing and Hip

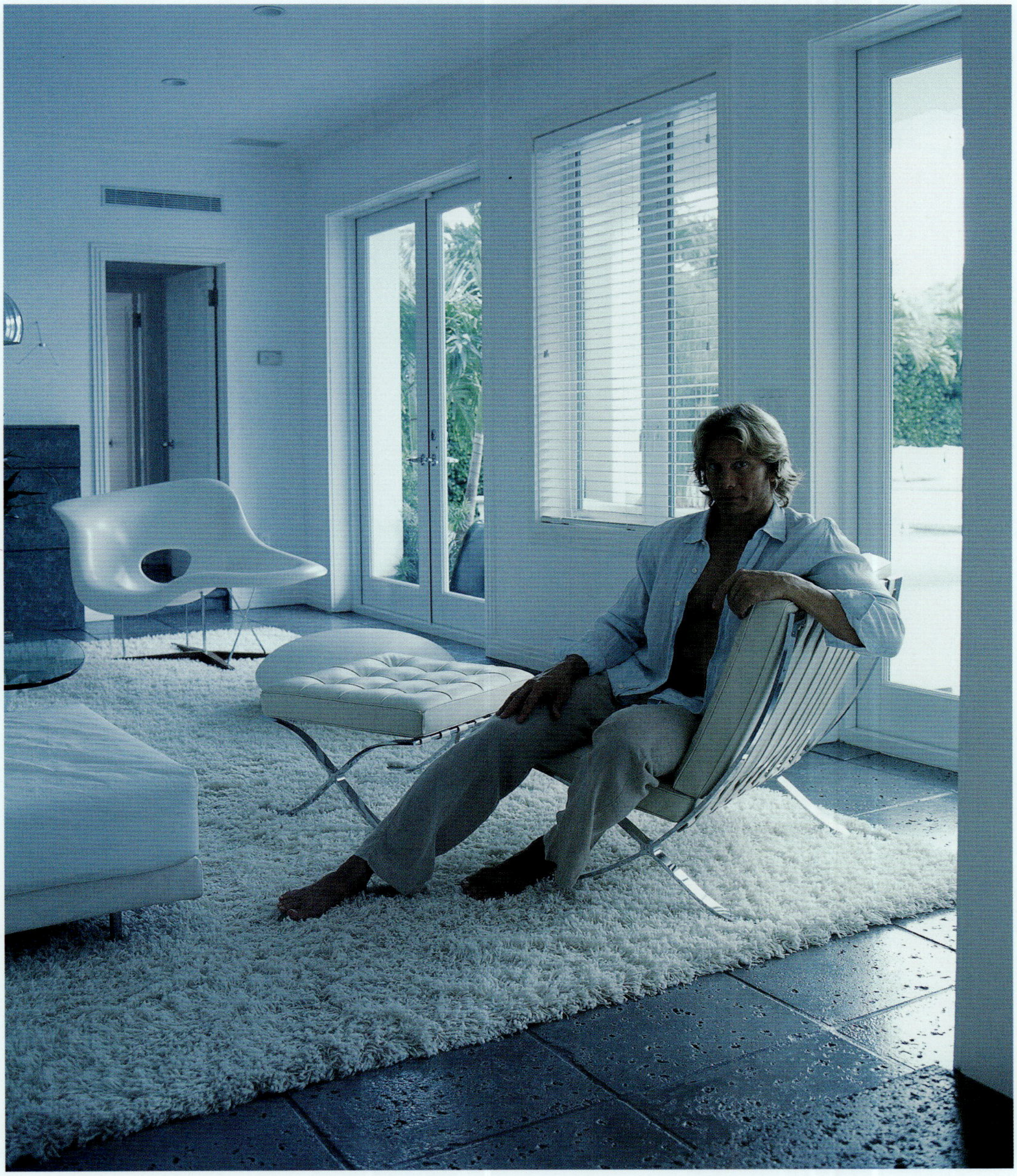

Dr. Robert Henry

Does your medical doctor look like this?

Does ANYBODY's real medical doctor look like this?

Only in the movies and in beautiful South Beach.

Dr. Robert Henry came to Miami twenty-three years ago from New York City to study at the University of Miami's Medical School. He practices medicine as a neuroradiologist at the Jackson Memorial Medical Center by day.

By night and during his days off, Dr. Henry does what a lot of Miami Beach's socially active residents do: When he isn't at ultra-fun locales like Lucky Strike, which is a twenty-first century bowling alley combined with a South Beach style nightclub, he relaxes at his ultra-modern residence (pictured here).

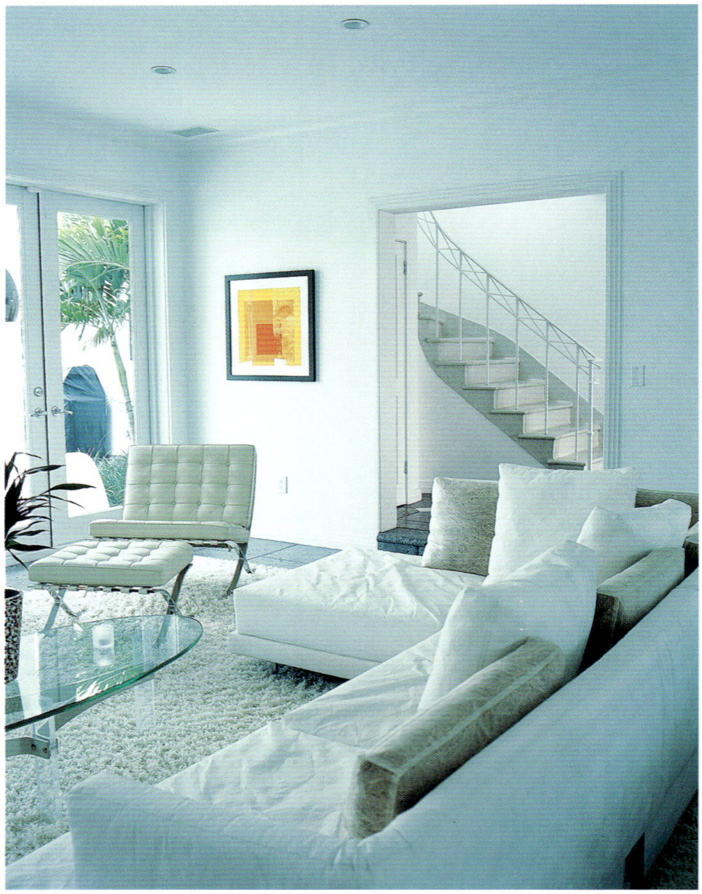

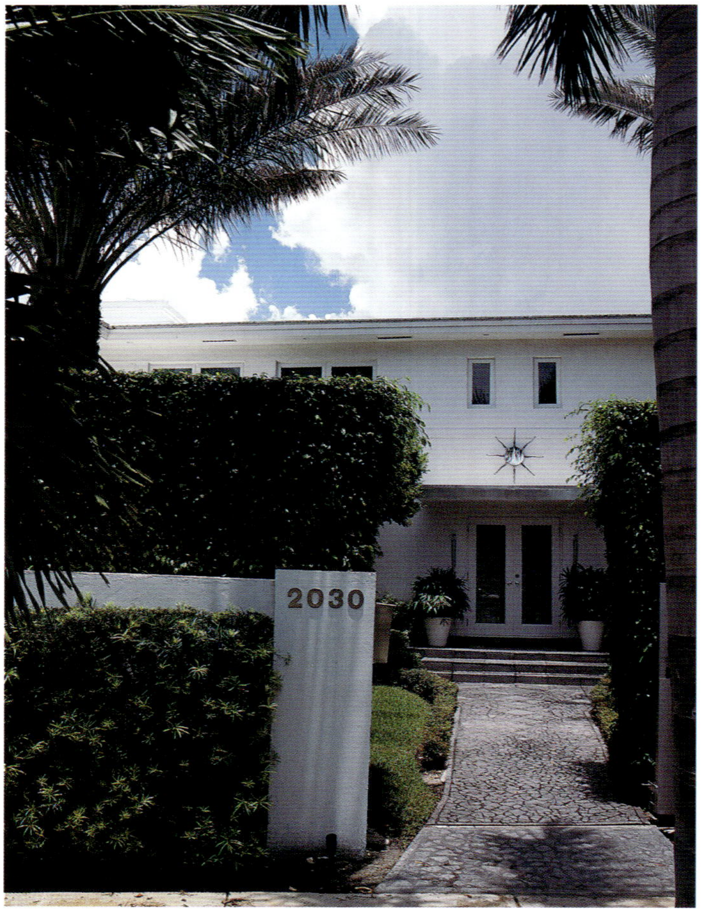

2030

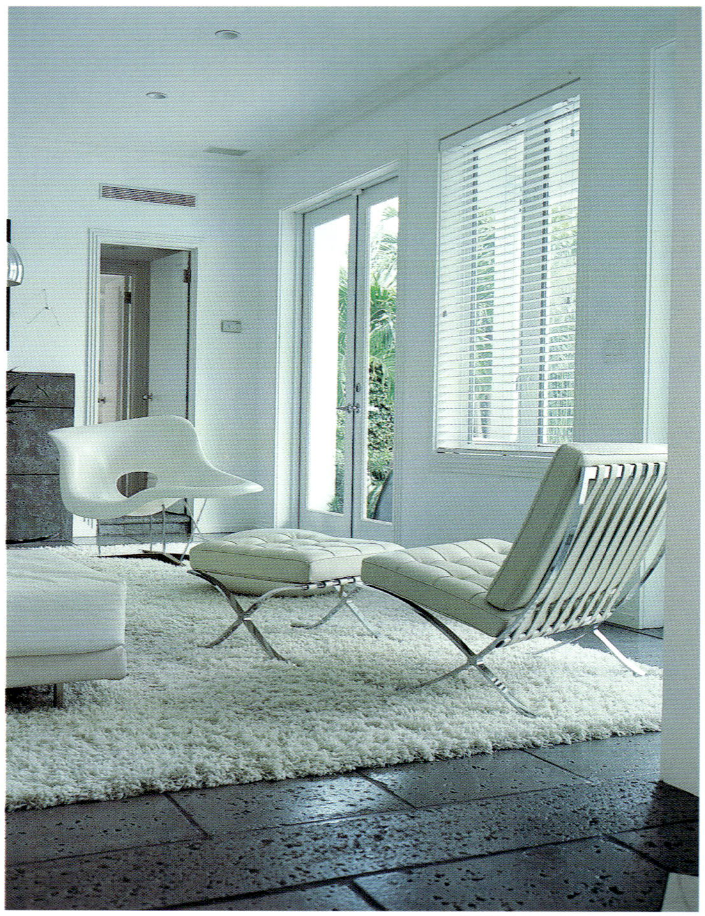

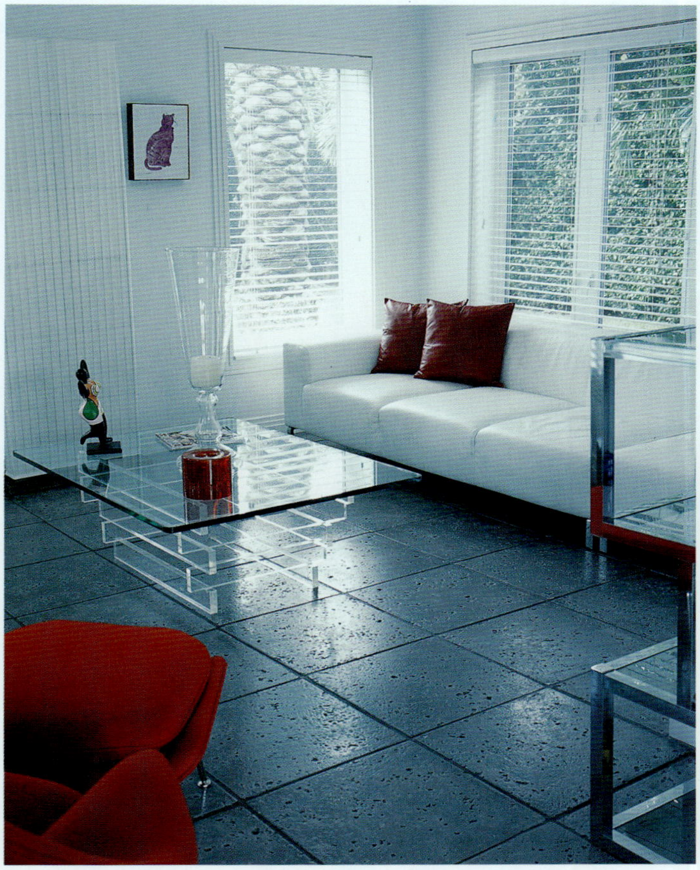

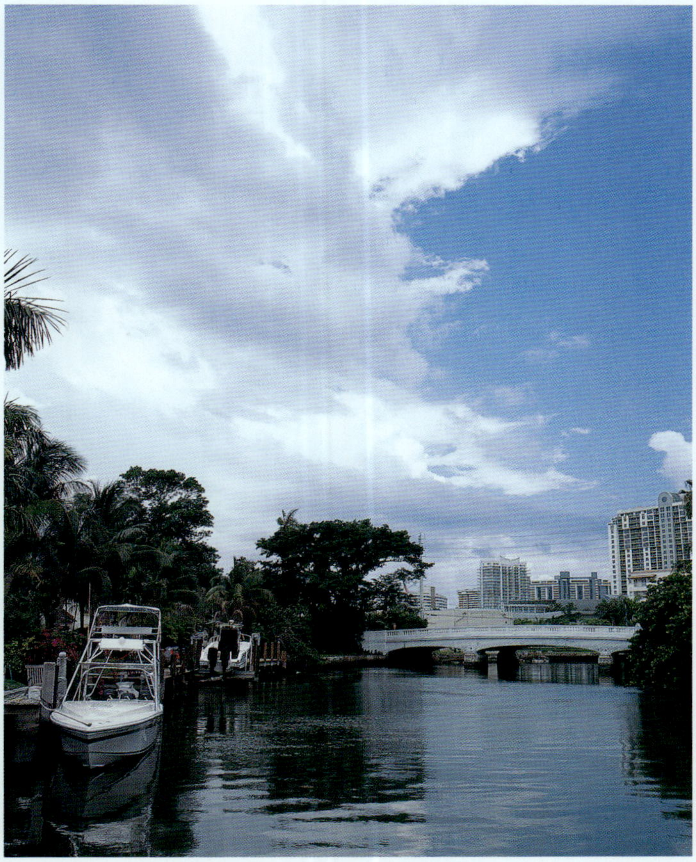

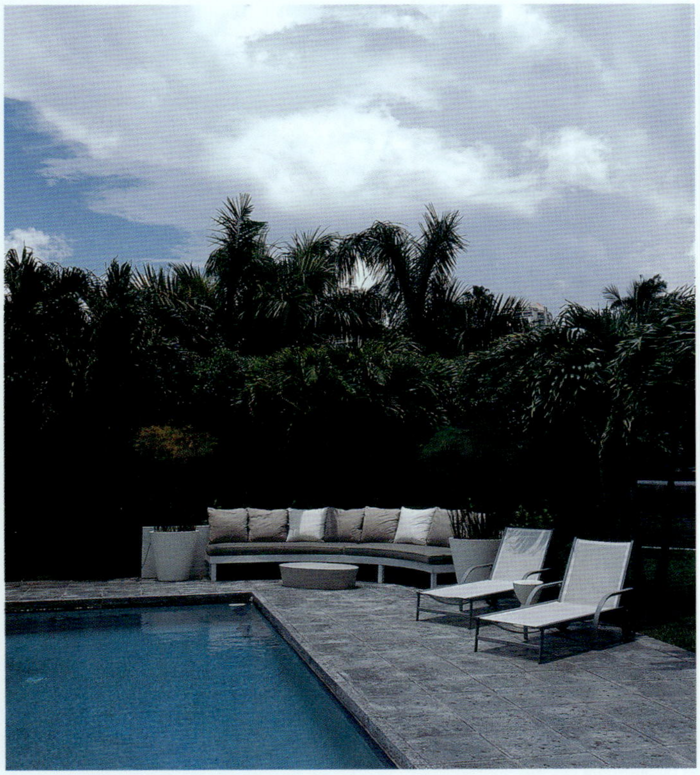

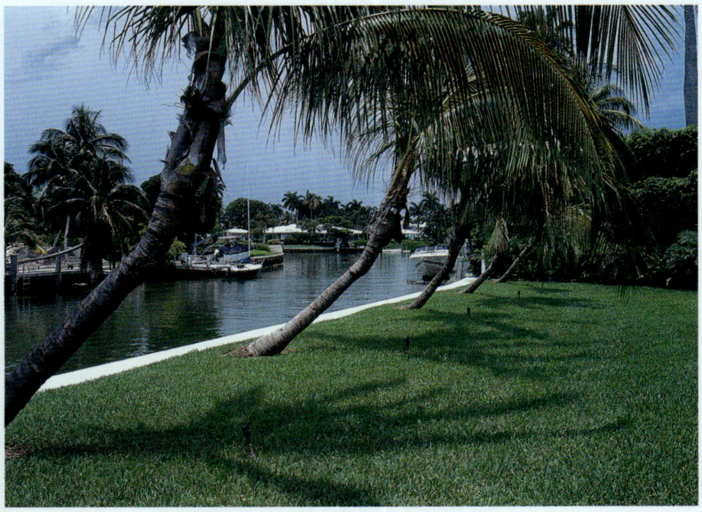

Like most other South Beach personalities, Dr. Henry hasn't forgotten the "sheer physical beauty" of his natural surroundings.

He recommends that a first-time visitor just "walk the city, both daytime and night," to appreciate its special allure and atmosphere. And he knows that South Beach can be best appreciated in hip-but-simple ways, like staging a gourmet picnic feast (with a good bottle of wine from South Beach's Epicure Market, of course!) at sunset on the beach at South Point with a few of his best friends. His life in South Beach feels like being at "the epicenter of what's happening both socially and culturally in the world."

With physicians like Dr. Henry in attendance, getting sick on South Beach might prove to be more fun than partying anywhere else.

Chapter 24

MODEL MAGAZINE MOGUL

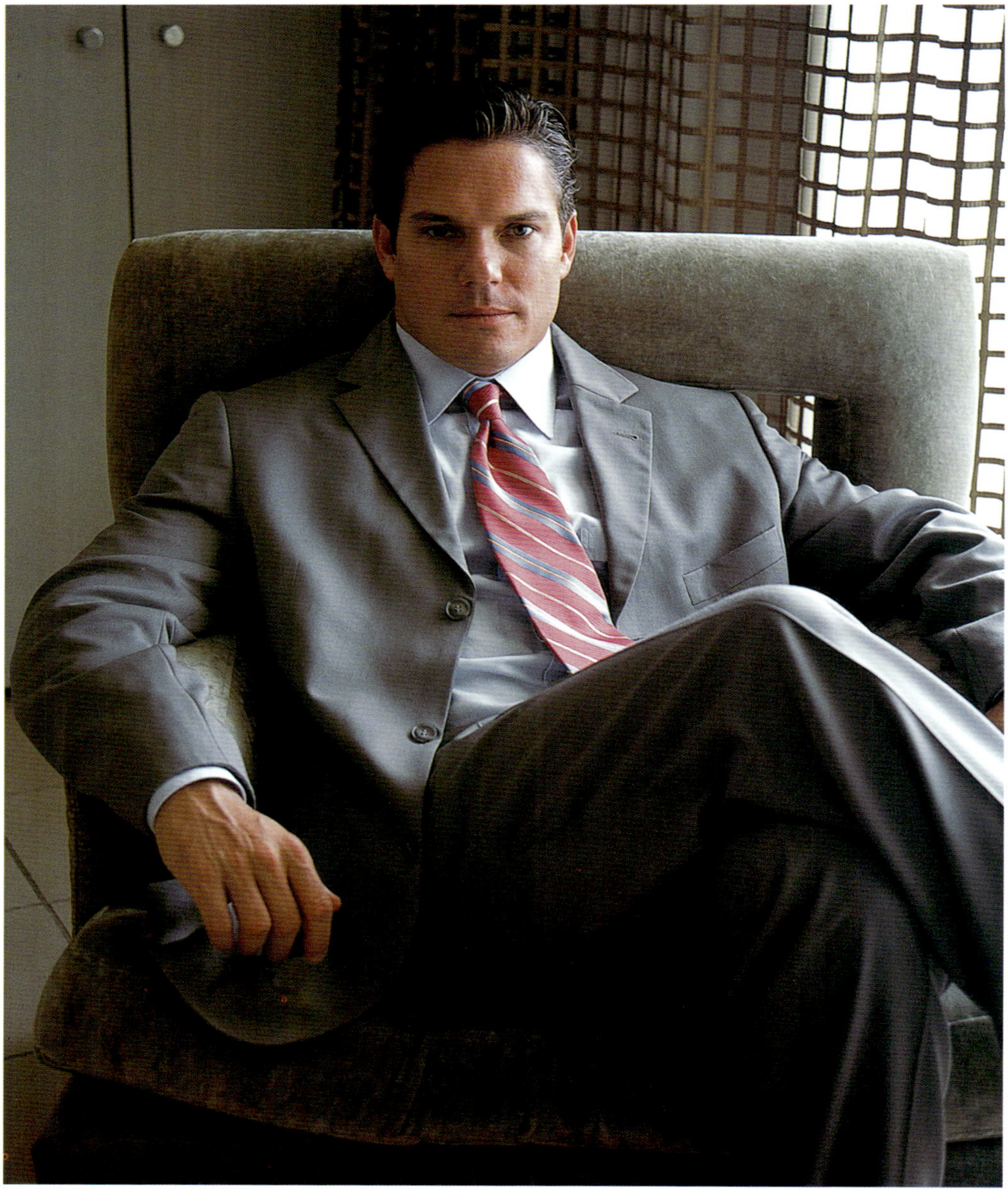

ALAN RANDOLPH AND OCEAN DRIVE MAGAZINE

Known until recently as "that big-shot banker with Hollywood good looks," Alan Randolph is now President of the famous South Beach publication, *Ocean Drive Magazine*. Notwithstanding his tender age, Alan is more than the chief executive of the magazine, which has come to symbolize the "SoBe" lifestyle. He is also a major civic leader, including a stint as Chairman of the Chamber of Commerce while he was Vice-President at Mellon National Bank. His combination of business hustle and after-hours glamour is symbolic of the new South Beach, where he has been making his living and loving since 1990. Like so many others, Alan came to South Beach from the more traditional American environment of Enid, Oklahoma. What does he love the most about his adopted seaside city? The "people, weather, and lifestyle" of course.

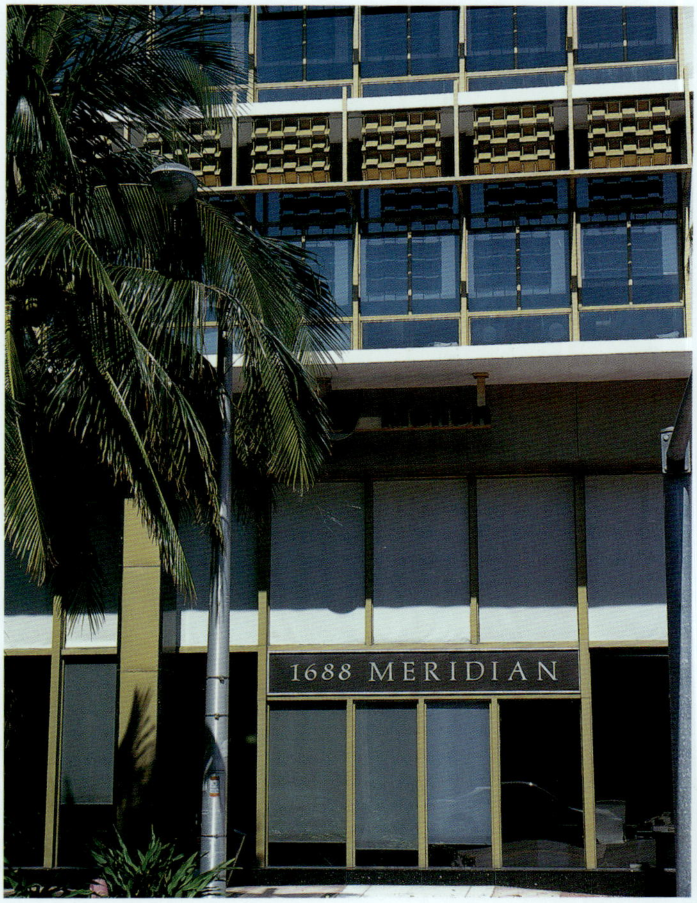

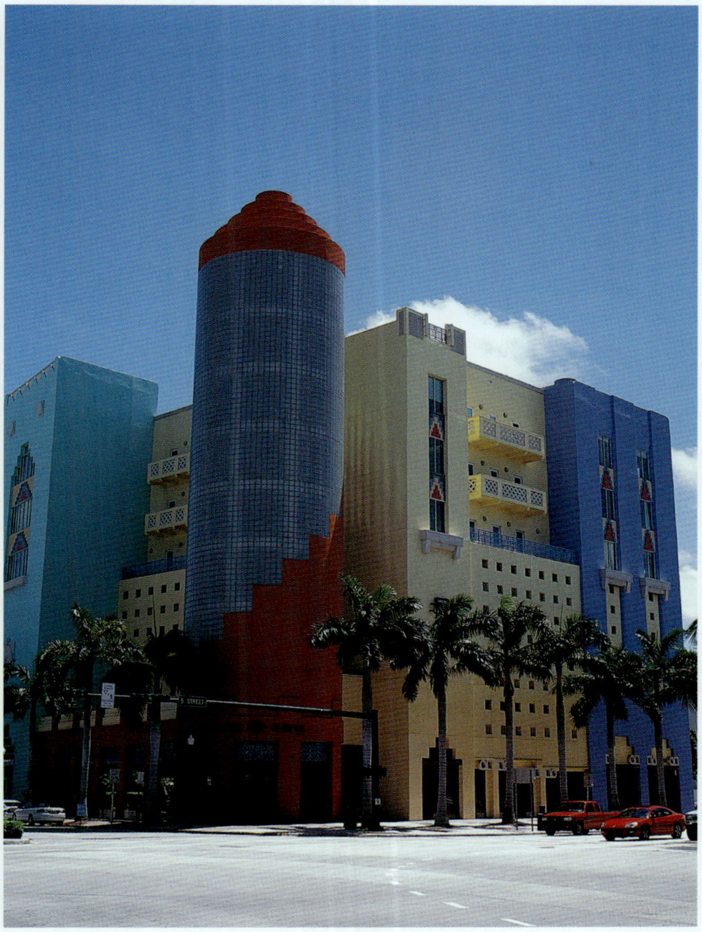

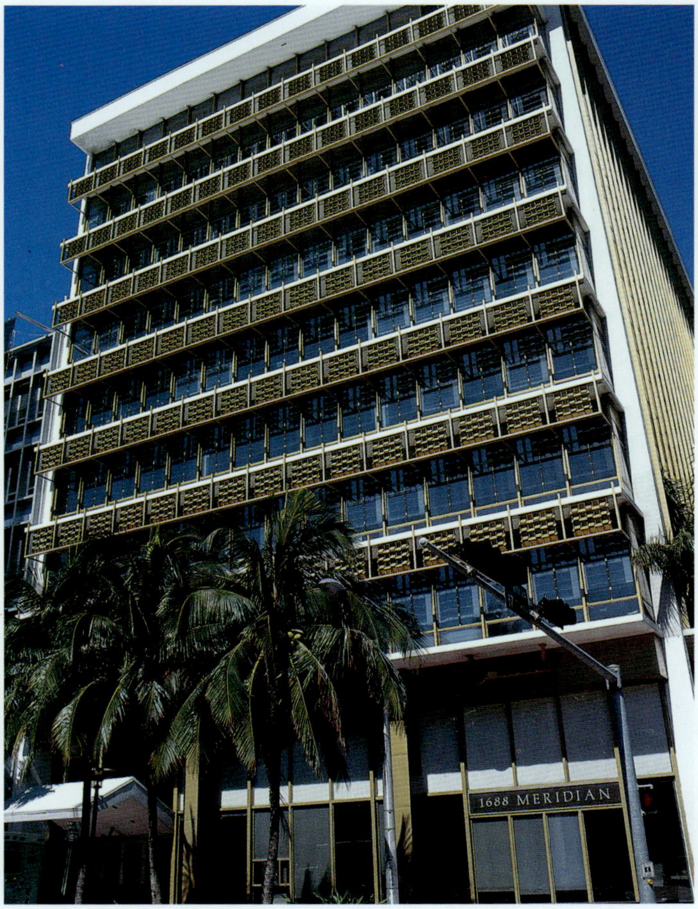

During most business days, Alan can be found in and out of his office at the magazine's South Beach headquarters at Fifth Street and Washington Avenue, located within one of the area's most colorful façades. Other days, he is overseeing and representing the Ocean Drive empire while jetting his way to Las Vegas or New York. By night, Alan is a familiar sight at South Beach's finest restaurants (his favorite? "Prime 112" on Ocean Drive), and wee-hours clubs. His advice to first time South Beach visitors includes getting used to the late-night hours here, where the evening starts at 10 PM and flows on until dawn.

How does he do all this and still get enough sleep to do justice to his former-model good looks? Alan's not telling, but with all there is to do in South Beach at any time of the day or night, who needs to sleep?

Chapter 25

THE TOWNHOUSE HOTEL

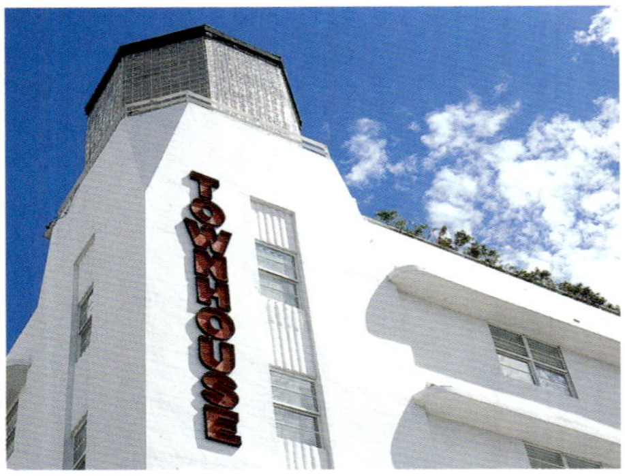

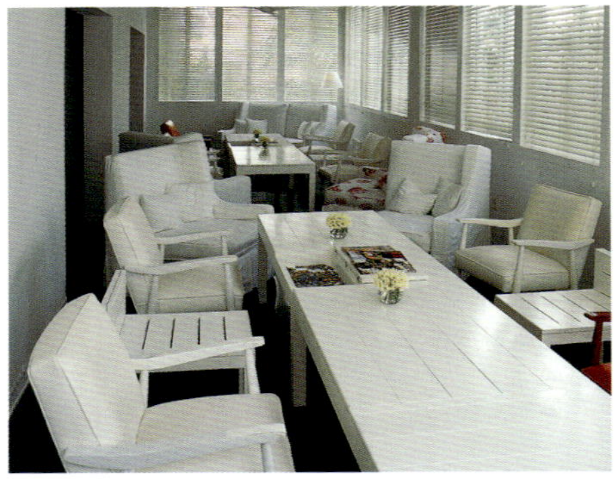

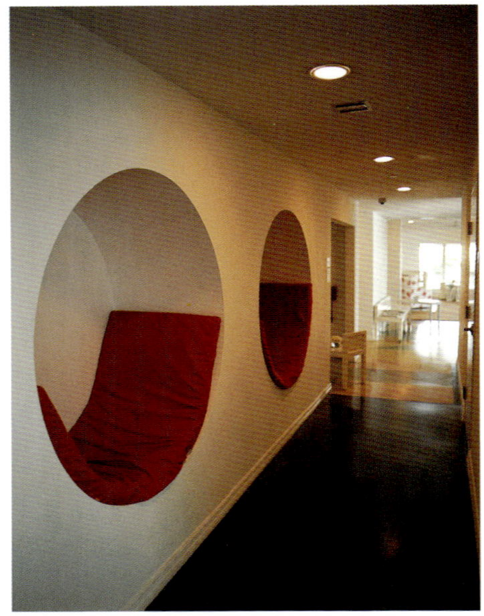

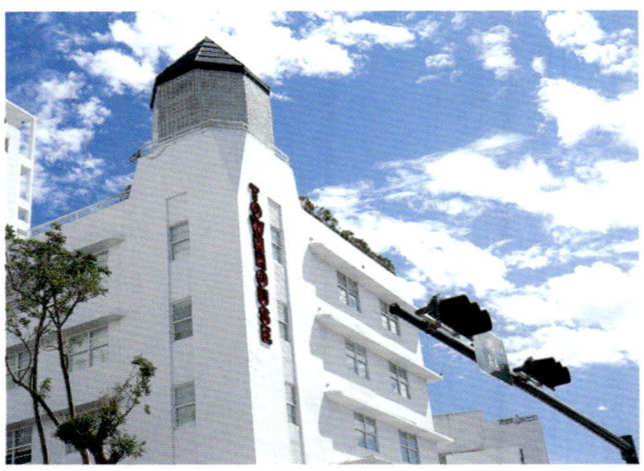

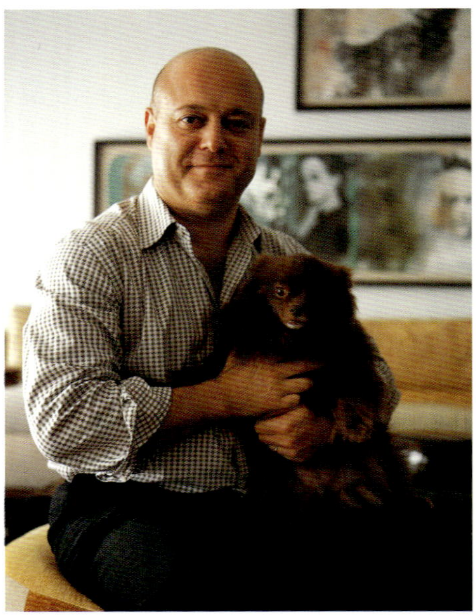

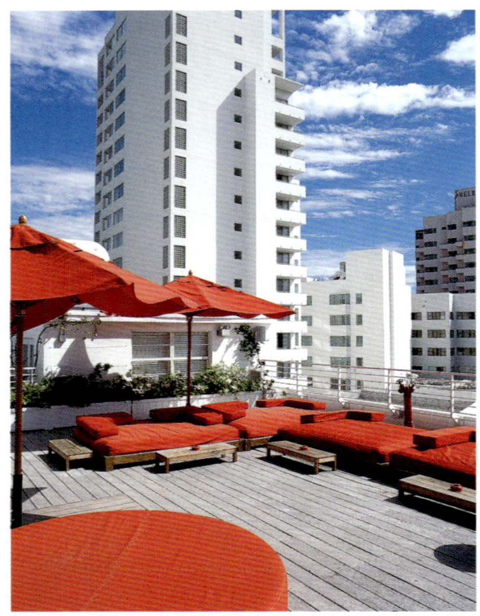

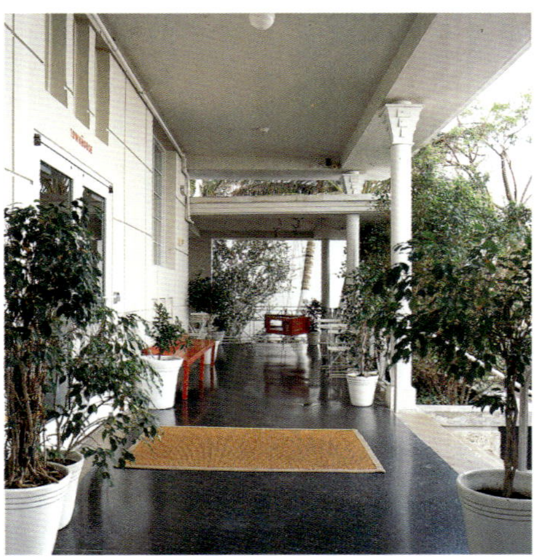

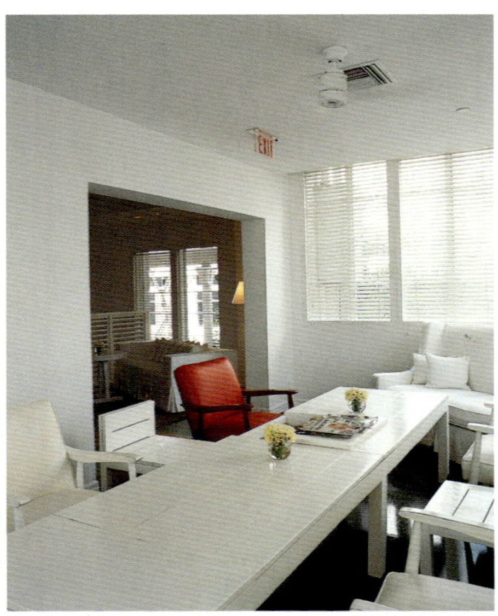

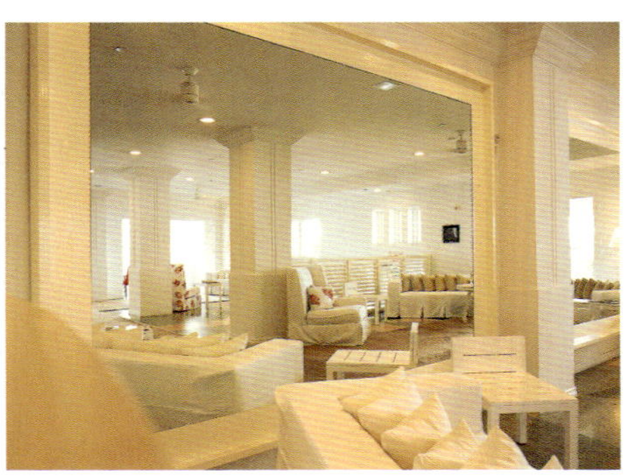

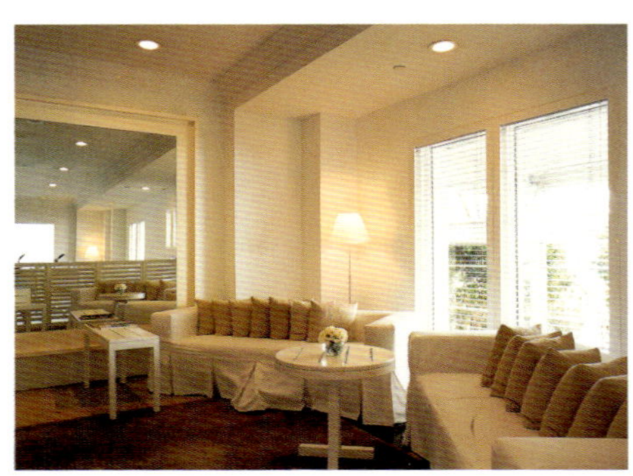

AMIR BEN-ZION

An Israeli native who lived in New York for twenty years before heeding the siren song of South Beach, Amir Ben-Zion is now firmly planted in all the good things that SoBe has to offer. In addition to his ultra-chic hotel creation, the Townhouse at 20th and Collins, Amir has brought us sophisticated dining with an East Asian flair. His "Miss Yip Café" just off Lincoln Road at Meridian (with its very hip lounge "Buck 15" on the second floor), is thought by many to serve the best Chinese fare in town, and his Bond Street sushi restaurant, located within the Townhouse, actually improves upon traditional Japanese themes with its own South Beach dishes.

On top of all of that, well, at home Amir is on top of just about everything. His spacious mid-Beach penthouse crib accounts for what he sees as the coolest thing about his life in Miami Beach: "My view."

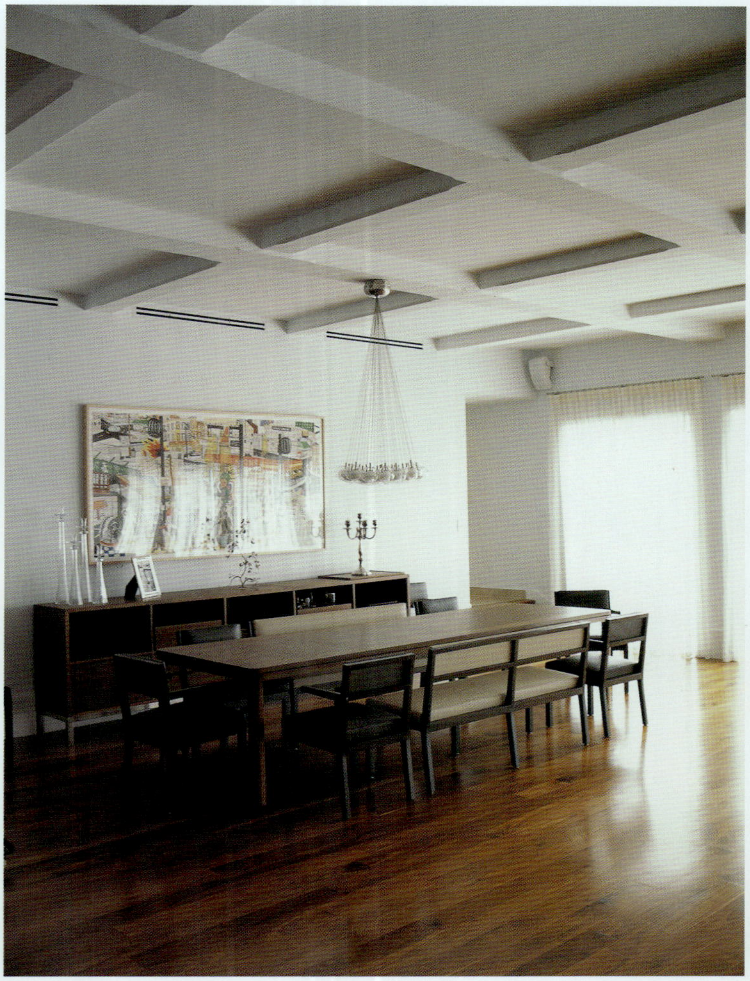

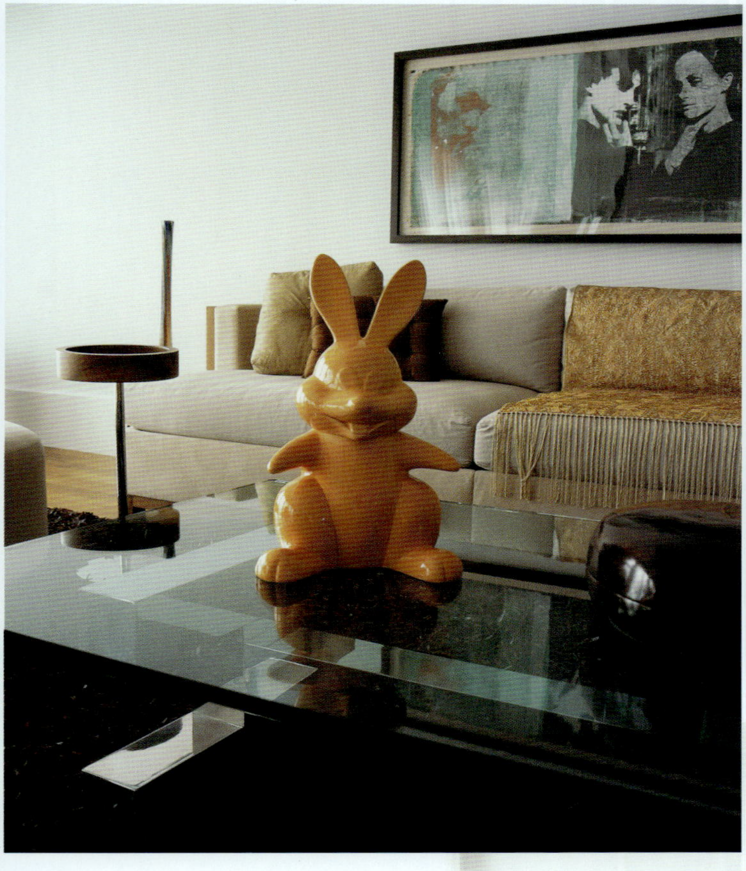

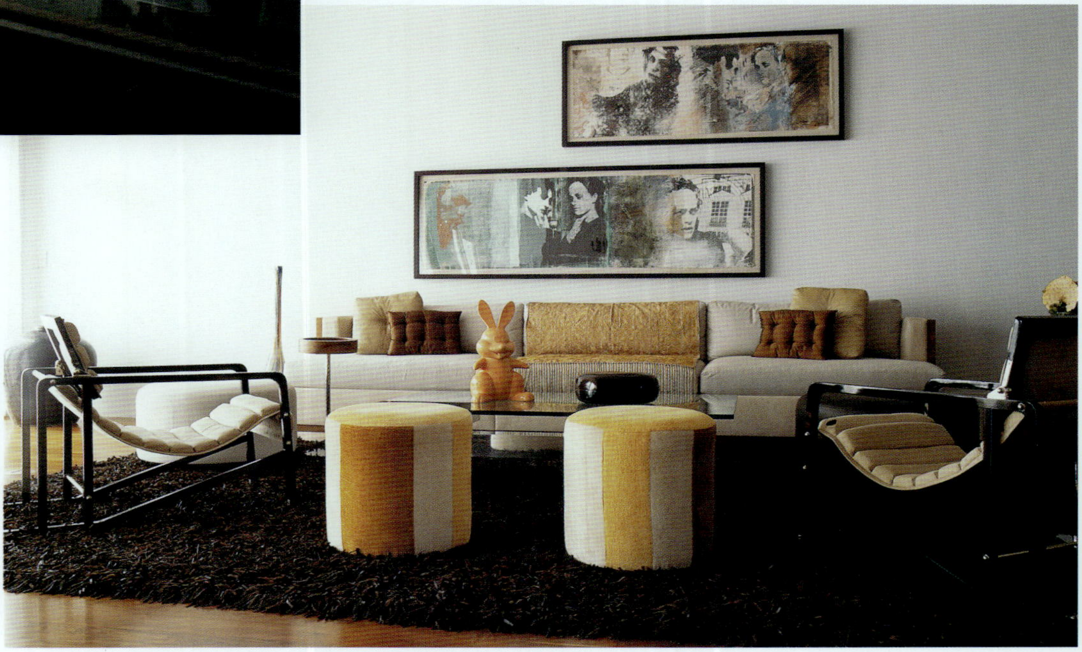

Chapter 26

ART, LOVERS

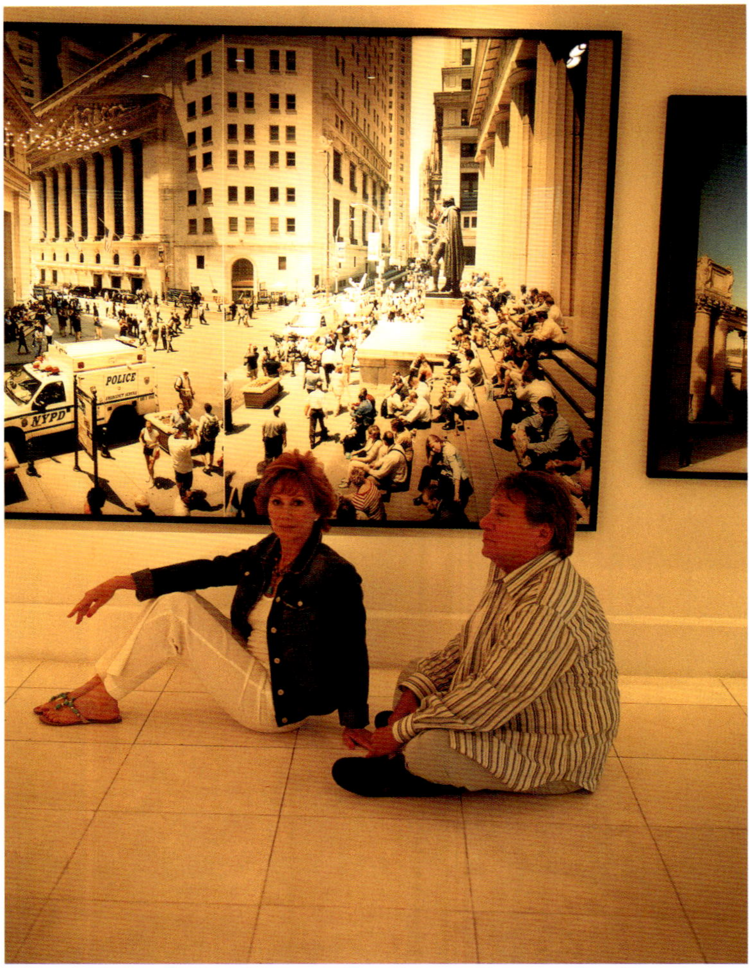

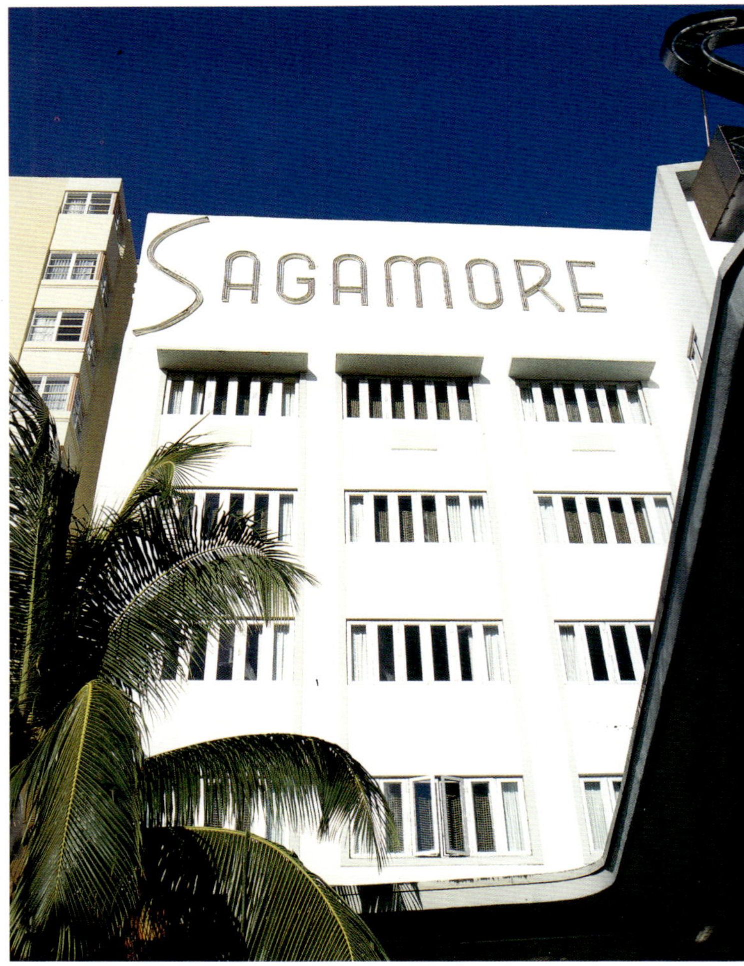

CRICKET & MARTY TAPLIN, AND THE SAGAMORE HOTEL

At 1671 Collins Avenue sits one of the hippest hotels in the new South Beach. It is, in fact, as much of an art gallery as it is a hostelry. It is the brain-child, and the love-child, of Cricket and Marty Taplin.

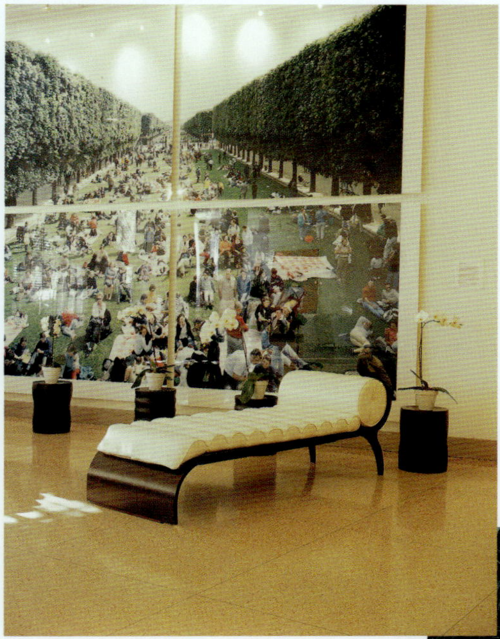

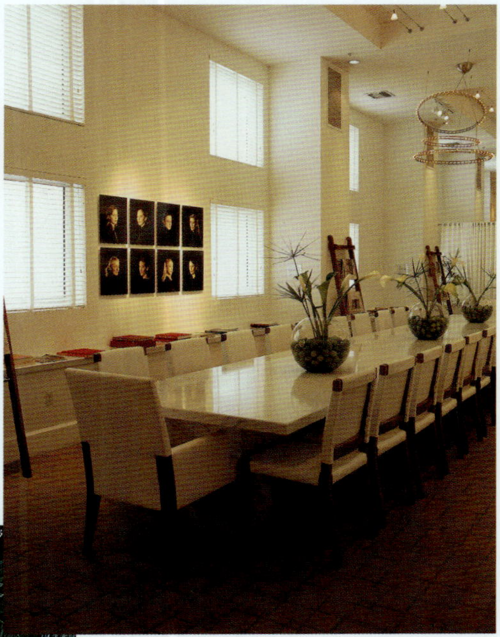

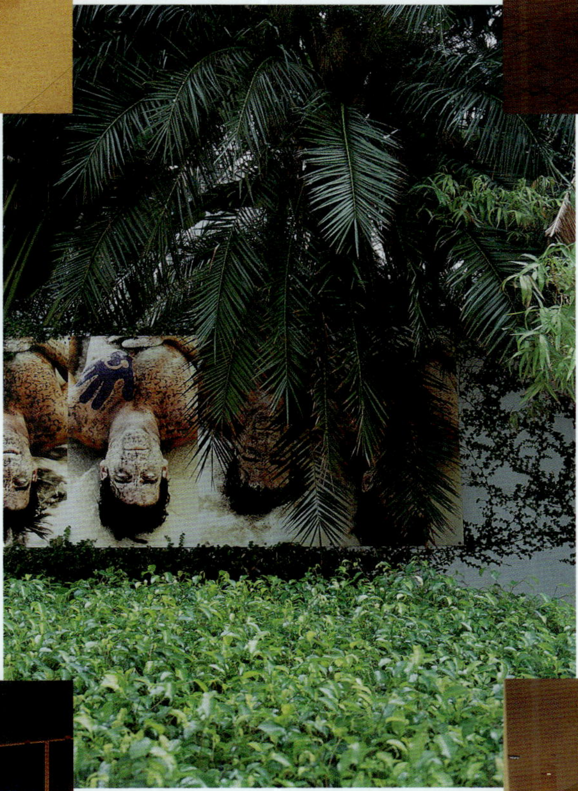

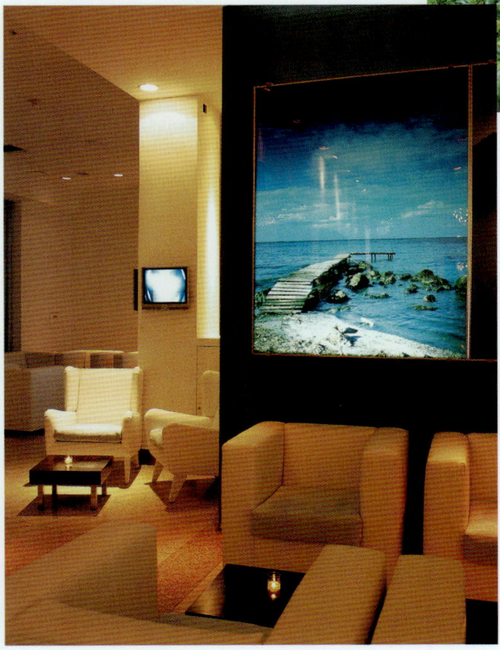

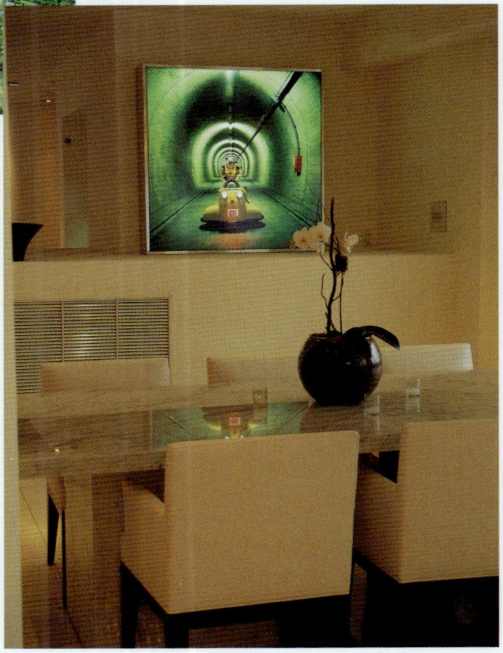

Cricket, who moved to South Beach from further up the Florida coast, is the avant-garde part of this dynamic duo, while Marty likes to present himself as the conservative, sensible anchorman. Together, they have taken the 1948-era Sagamore Hotel and turned it into an art-gallery-with-suites-attached for an overnight stay (not to mention "Social Miami," the Sagamore's hot new restaurant).

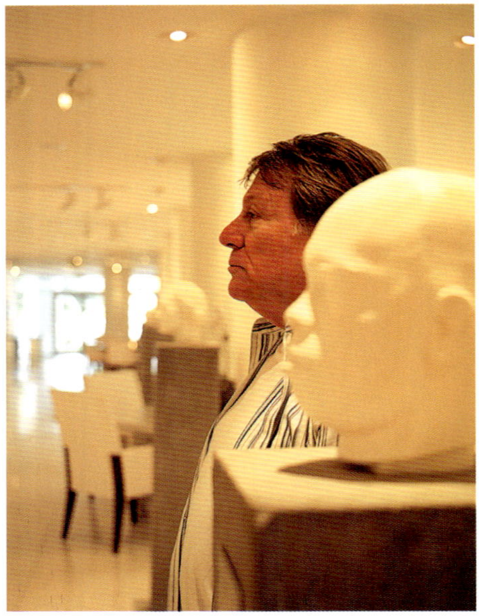

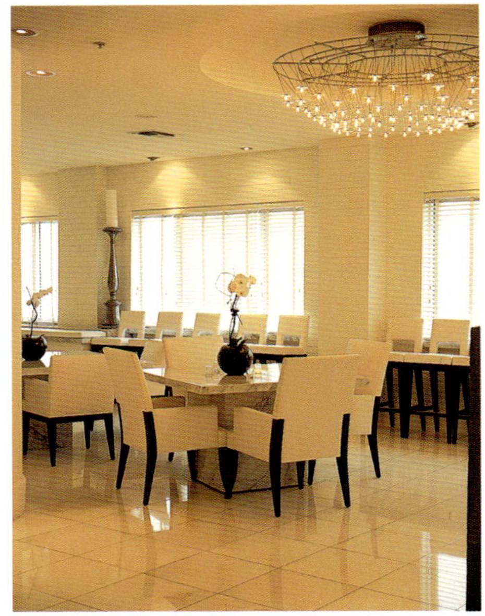

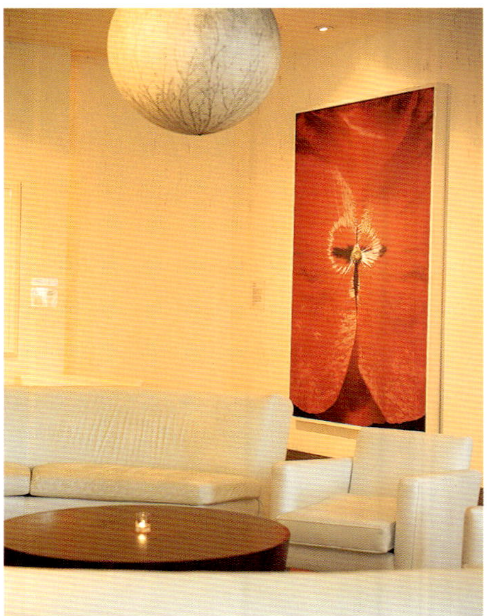

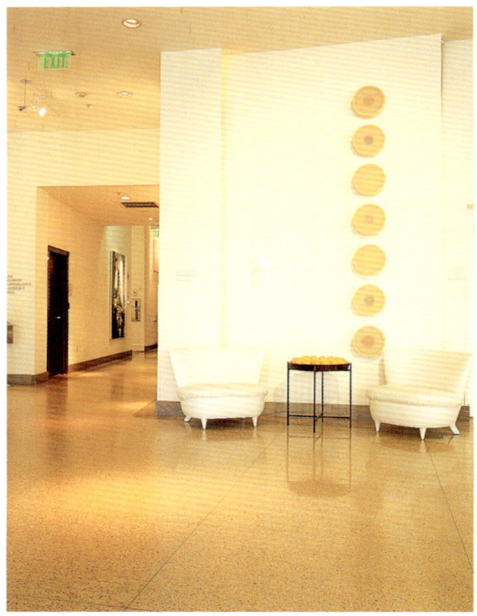

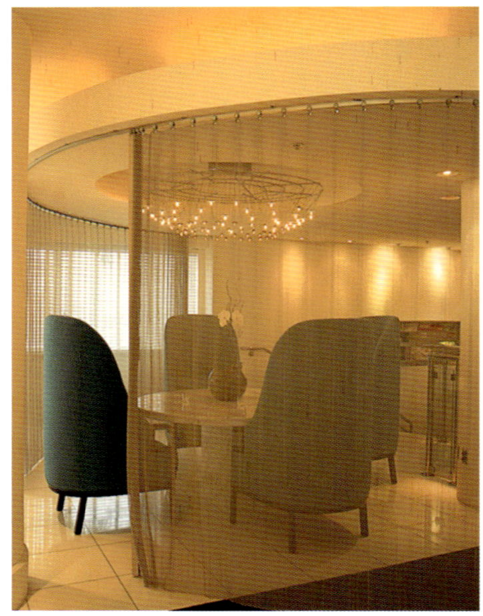

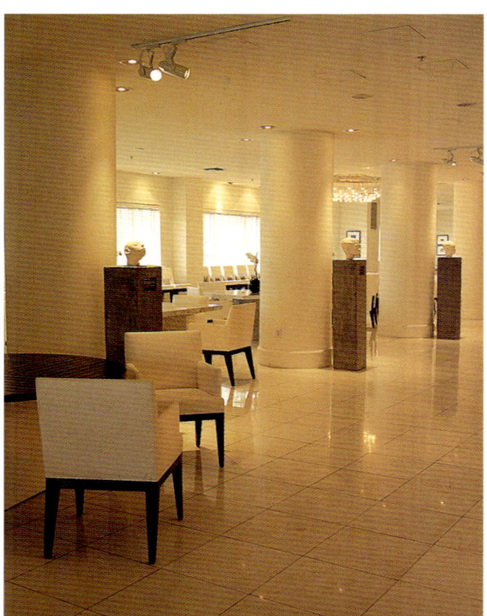

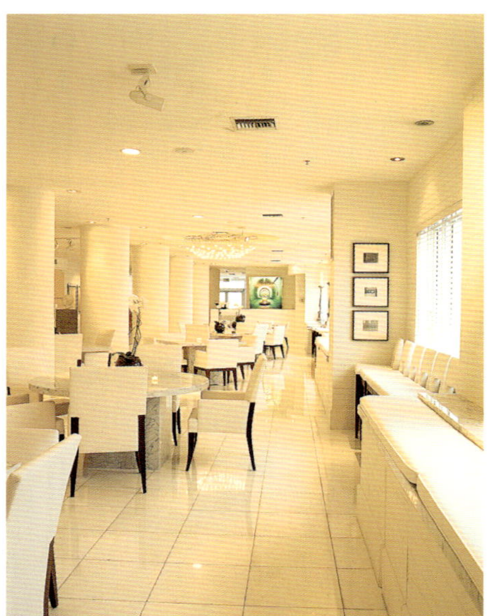

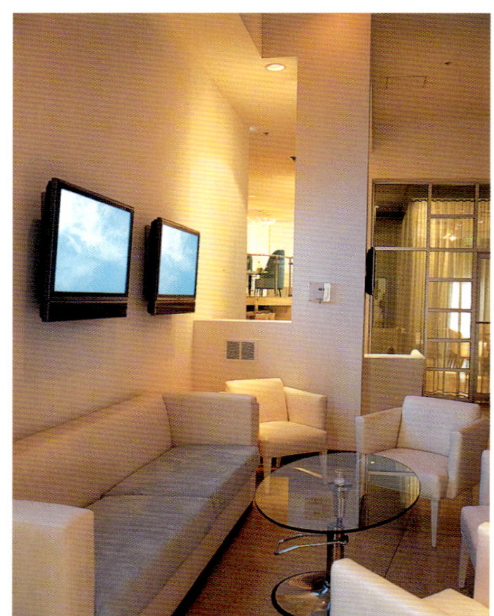

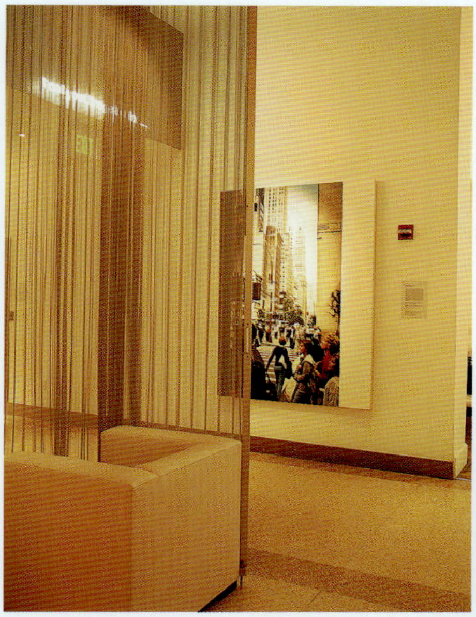

The word "fun" pops up frequently in their vocabulary, and like South Beach and merrymaking, they are the perfect fit. Well-known for finishing each other's sentences, they also know how to realize their mutual desires. Imagining a dream of unlimited material resources, both Cricket and Marty would spend everything they had on the same lucky beneficiary: Cricket. And what is it about her South Beach life that Cricket most loves? "Being with my husband..." A neat coincidence indeed, since Marty's favorite life-experience consists of "the fun opportunities I can share with my wife."

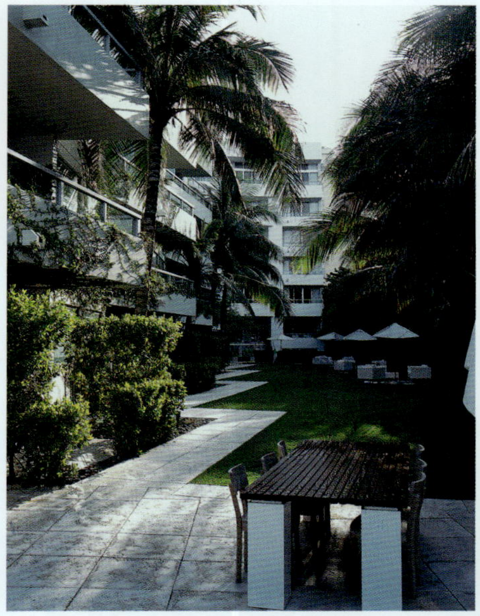

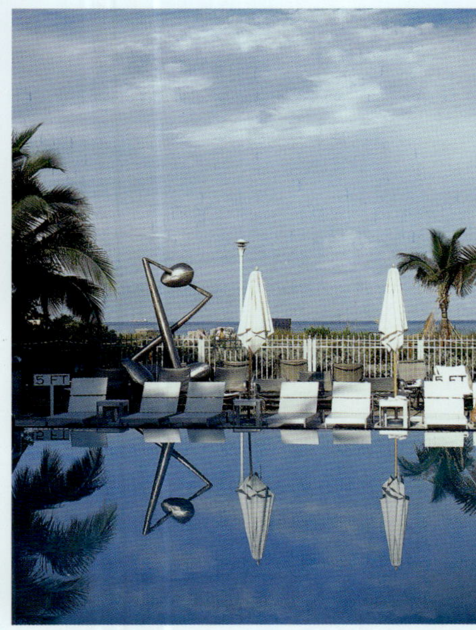

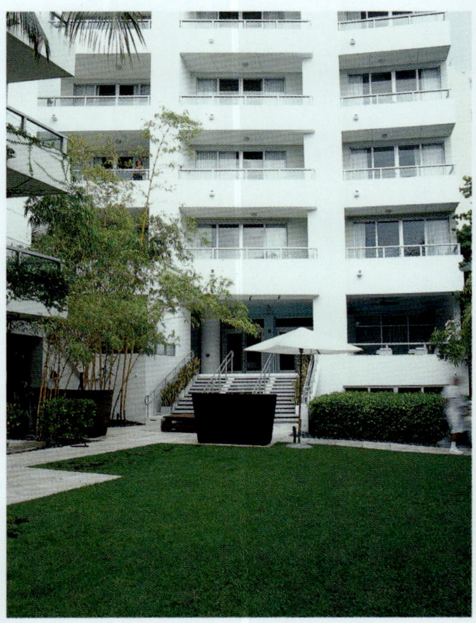

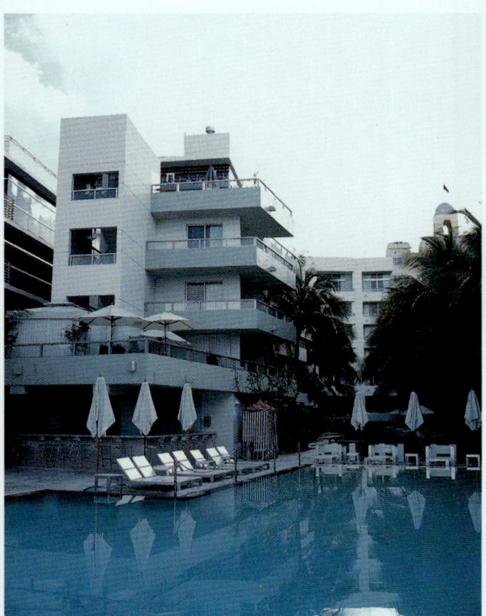

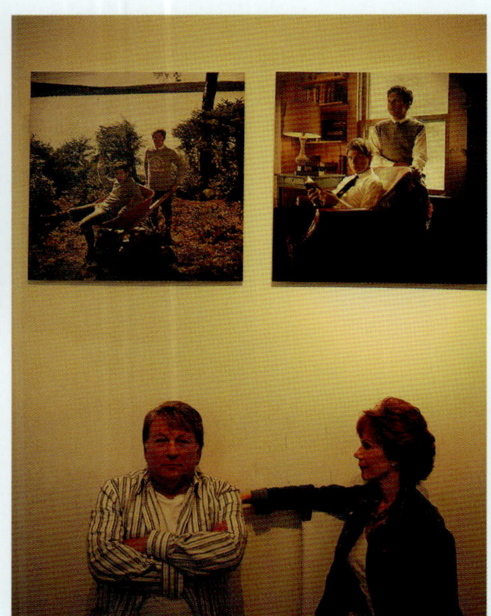

Chapter 27

ON TOP OF THEIR WORLD

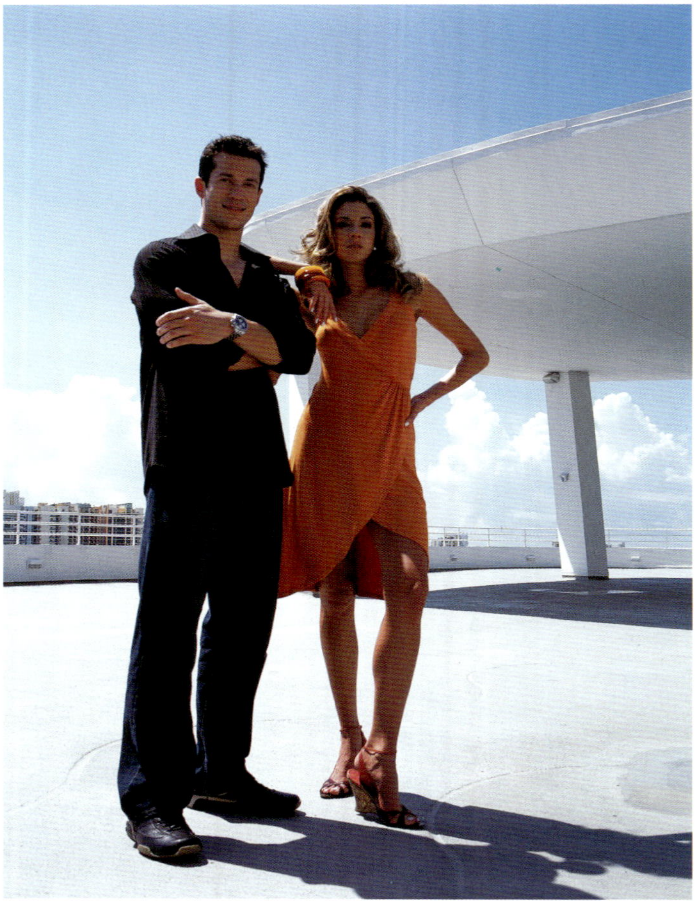

KATRINA CAMPINS AND BEN MOSS

An example of "the new South Beach power couple," Katrina and Ben have everything going for them—youth, looks, brains, fame, business acumen, and a marriage to match.

Katrina, like her husband Ben, is an honors graduate of the University of Miami, and is now a premier South Beach real estate professional and owner of the Campins Company. A few years ago, she took some time off from her real estate activities for a featured role on NBC's hit series *The Apprentice* with Donald Trump. A native Miamian, the fully bilingual Katrina is a natural attention-getter, whether speaking before groups of other leading real estate professionals or continuing her television and modeling career, which has led to the covers of numerous glamour magazines, including *People* magazine.

Ben, who came to South Florida as a child from Virginia, co-founded the Campins Company, which is now housed in one of Lincoln Road's signature structures, The Sony Building. The Sony Building stands at 605 Lincoln Road, home of one of the premier pedestrian parades in the world.

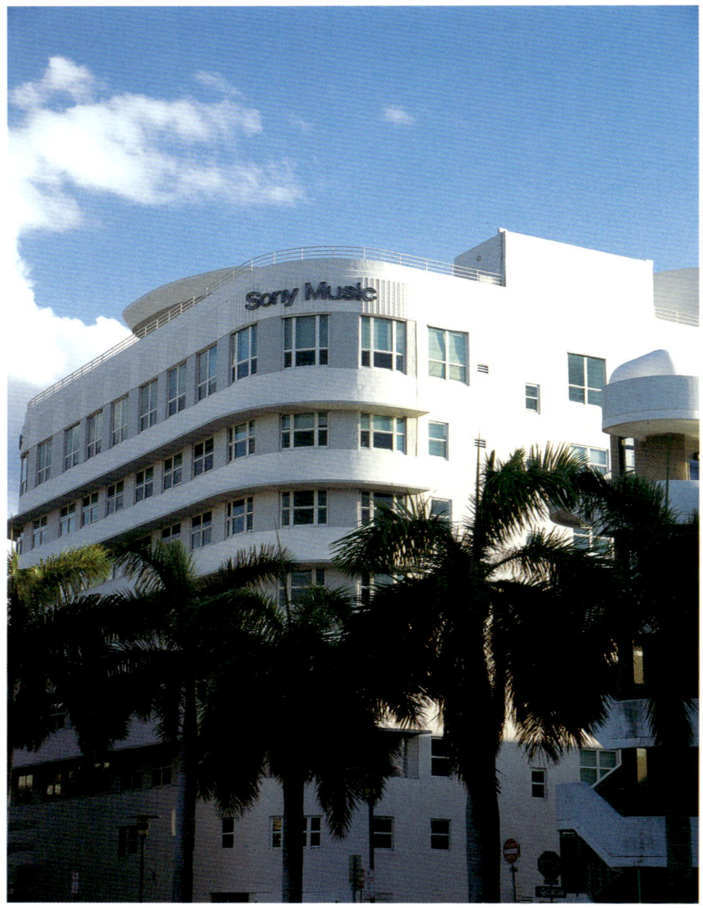

Ben's prescription for the first-time visitor to South Beach? "Have dinner at an outside table on Lincoln Road and people-watch."

Some of these photos were shot on the famous 10,000 square foot roof of The Sony Building, which Ben and Katrina helped to convert from leased office space to one of the most sought after office condominiums in the country. Naturally, the Campins Company was among the first owners of space after the building was converted. The roof of The Sony Building, with its signature whimsical concrete "umbrella," has long been THE South Beach venue for album-launch and other music industry events.

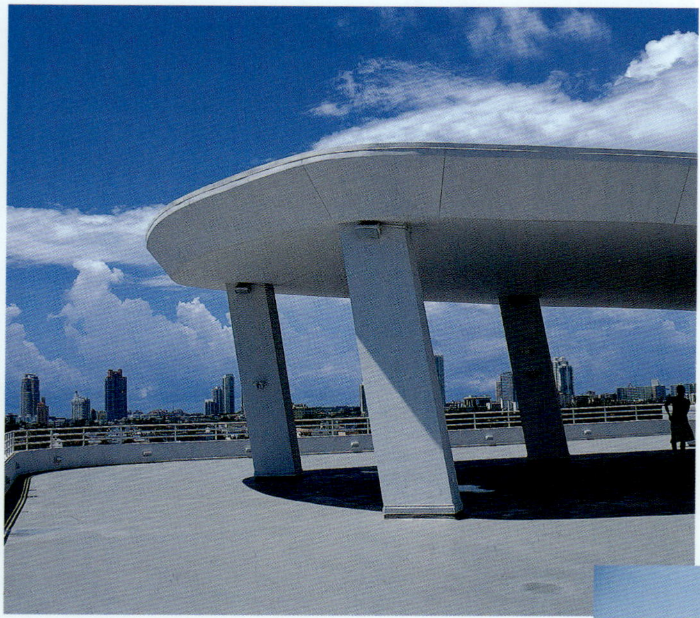

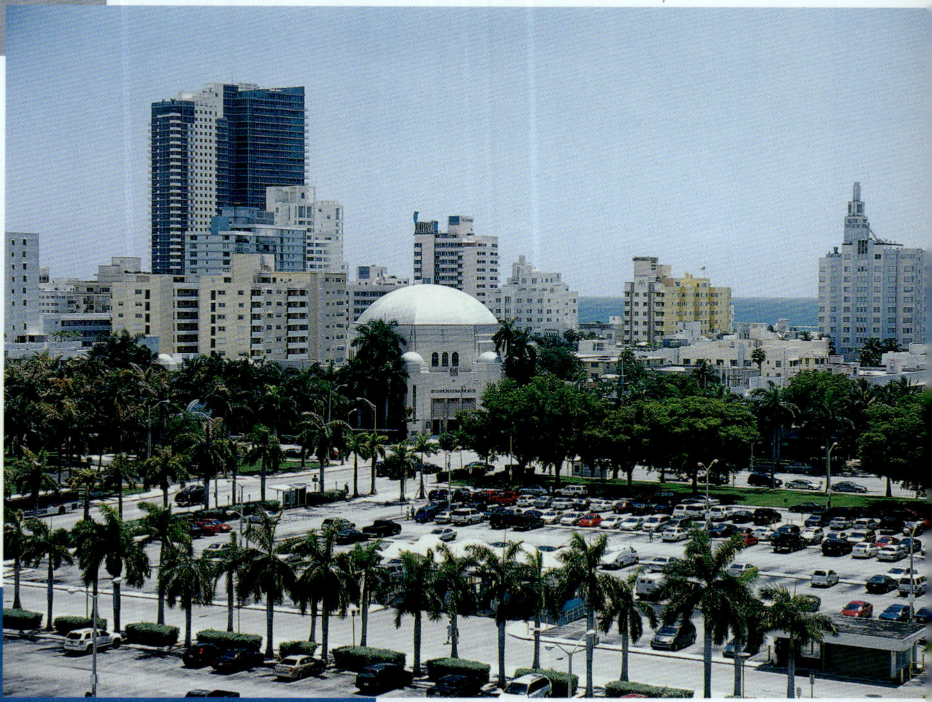

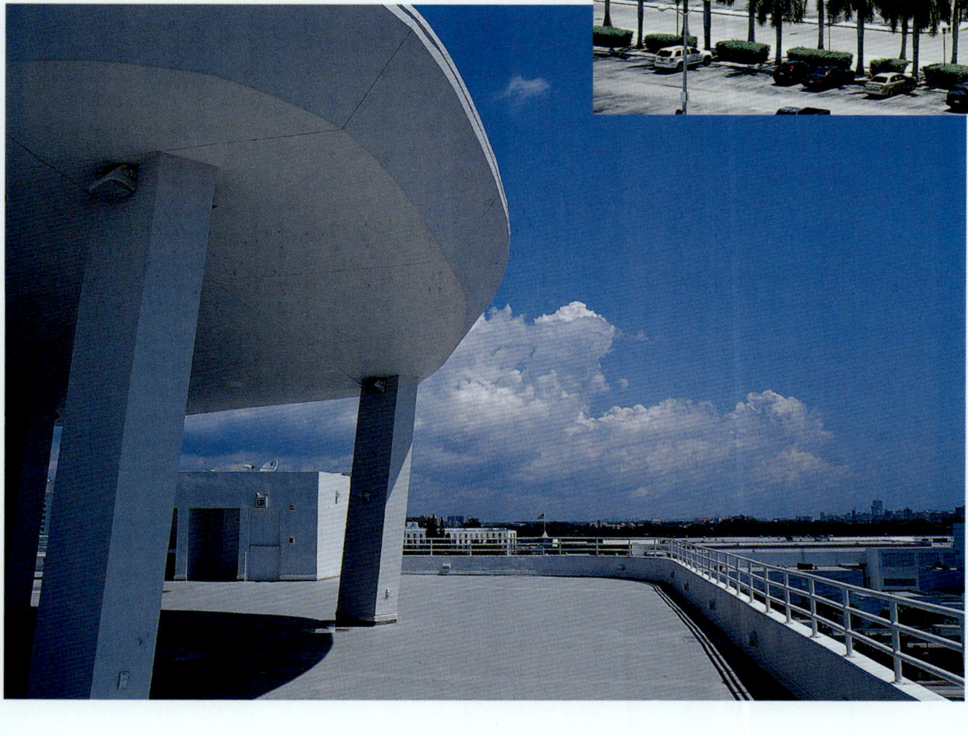

Chapter 28

THE WOLFSONIAN

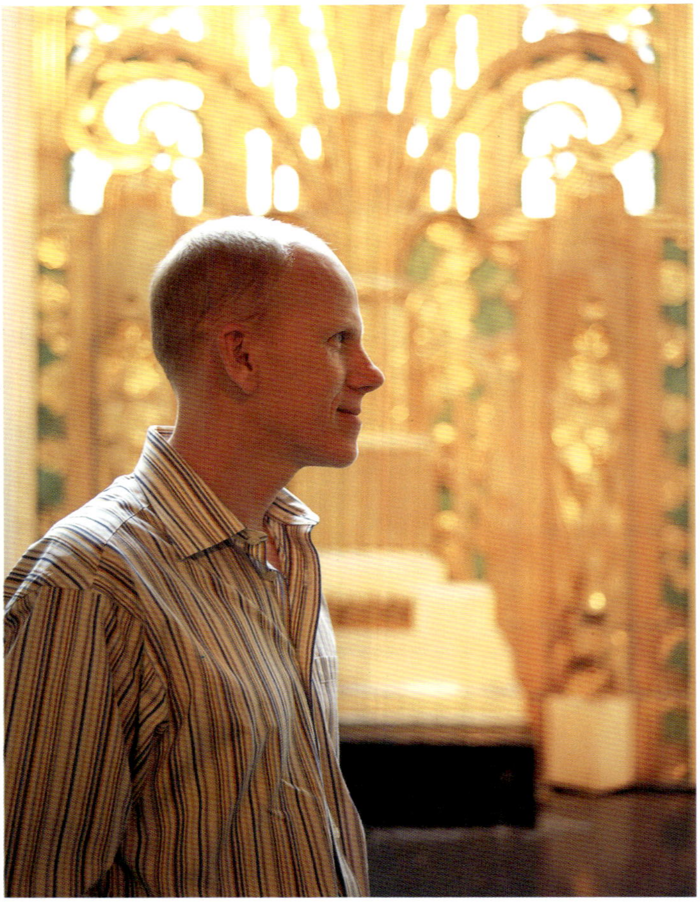

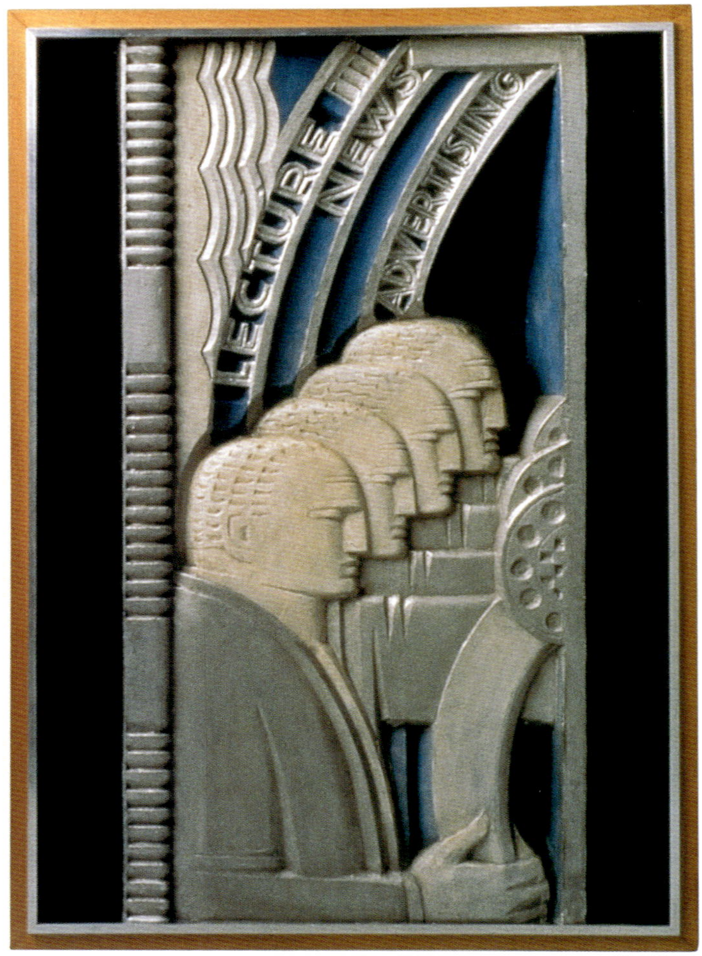

MICHAEL HUGHES

Having fled New England's winters for the gentler clime of South Florida, Malkovitch look-alike Michael now finds himself an essential ingredient in the success of the Wolfsonian Museum, which he describes as "an amazing institution."

Michael qualifies as a genuine expert on the culture and architecture of Miami Beach, having been an Art Deco tour guide and currently in charge of Visitor Services at the Wolfsonian, a "museum of Propaganda Arts" housed in a building that was originally built as an Egyptian-Deco structure for a storage facility, of all things.

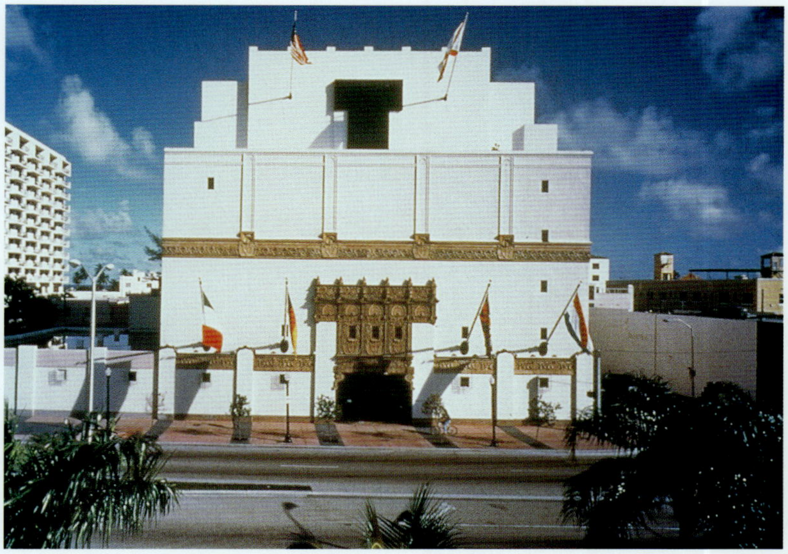

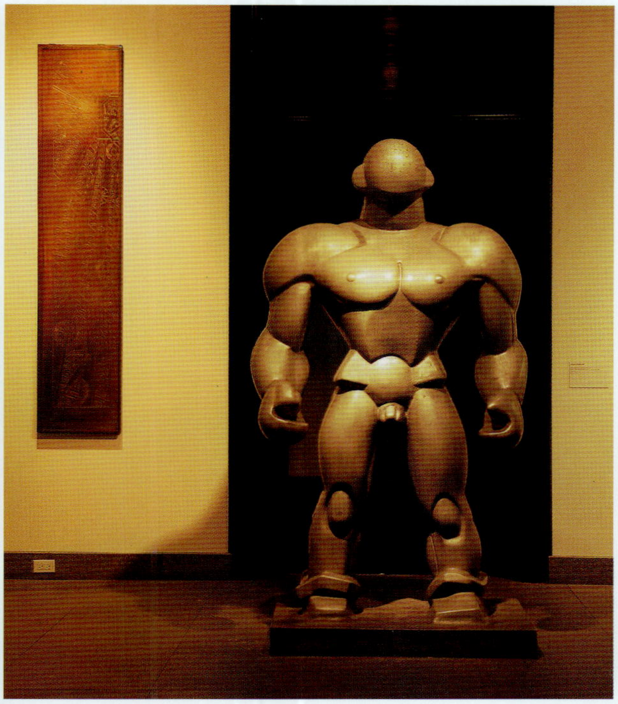

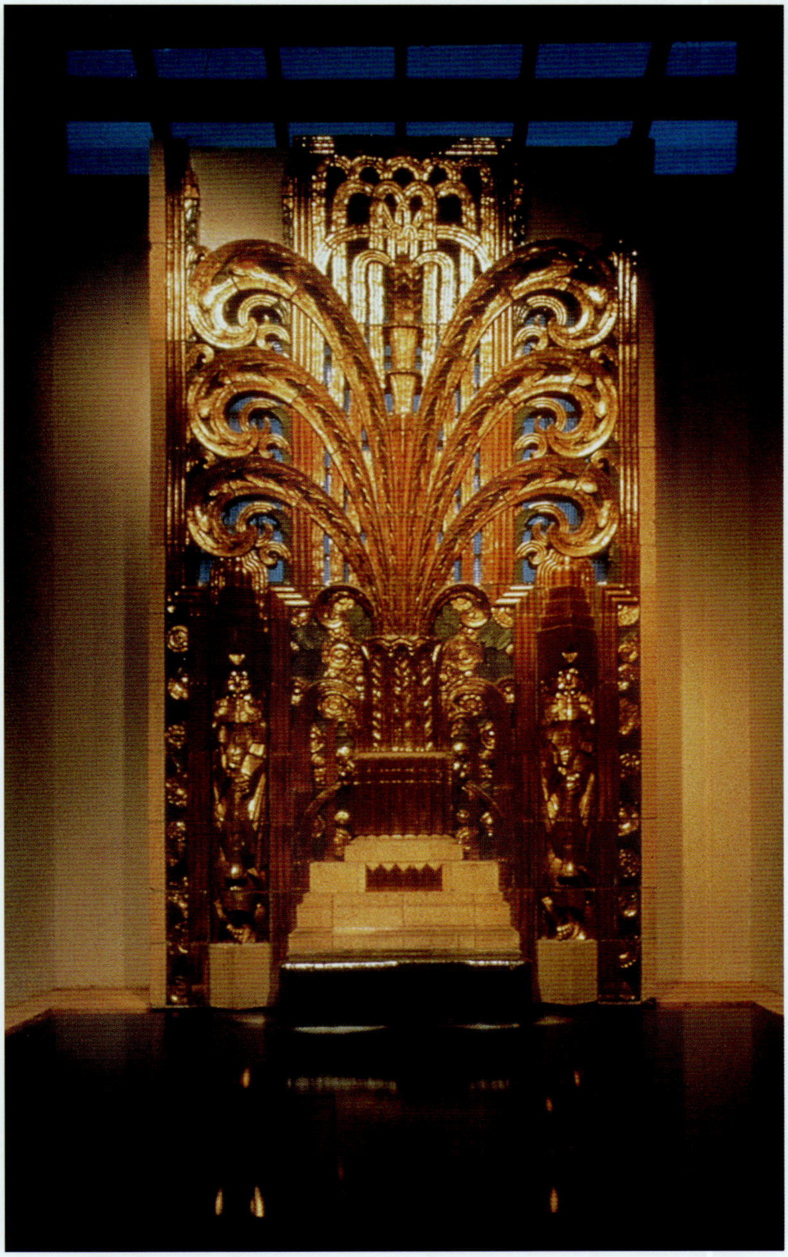

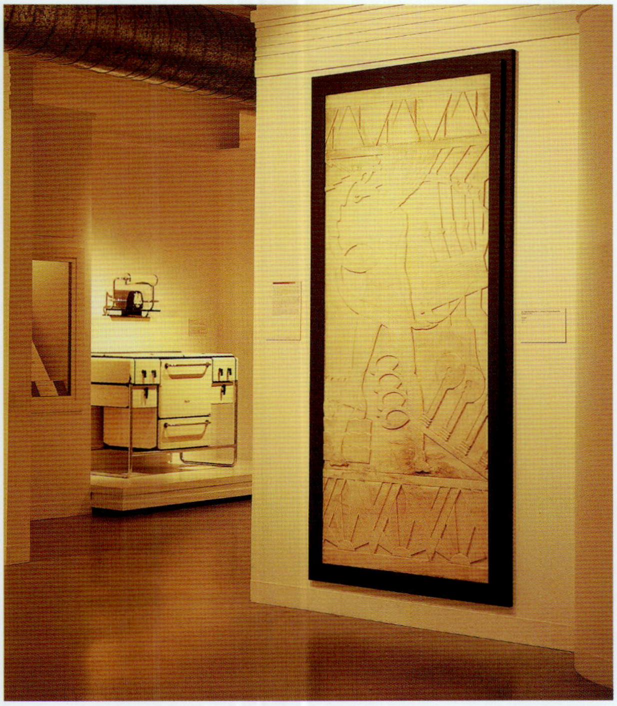

Like so many others, Hughes' original reaction to South Beach was "the incredible sexiness of the place." Michael's idea of the *sine qua non* for the first-time South Beach visitor is to relax at South Point Park (at the tip of South Beach), logging a "weekend afternoon spent watching the cruise ships go out; Joe's take-away (at 11 Washington Avenue); feeling romantic…" For those seeking a more sophisticated experience, he recommends "lunch at the Delano with cosmopolitans, then a cab ride home."

Chapter 29

THE ARTIST AND THE BASS MUSEUM

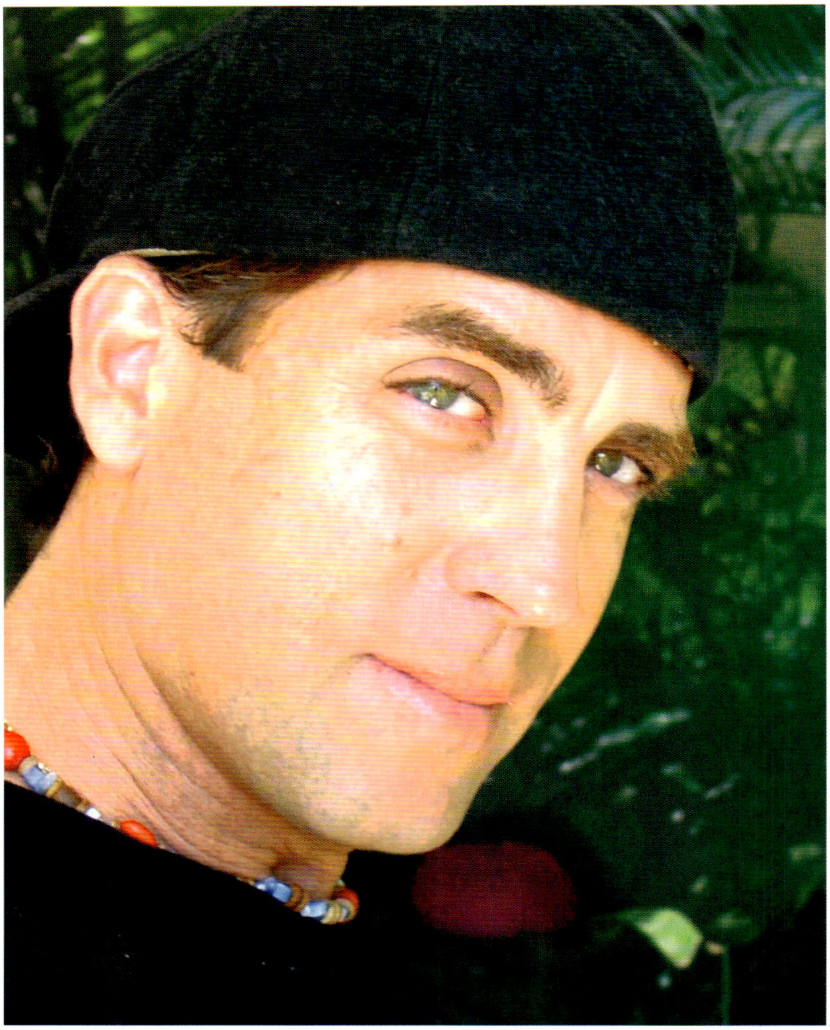

CARLOS BETANCOURT

Question: Which city has the best-looking multi-talented visual artist with Cuban parents and a background in Puerto Rico?

Answer: Miami Beach, because we have Carlos Betancourt.

A perennial name on lists of "beautiful people," "influential artists," and "future masters," Betancourt opened his first Miami Beach studio in the 1980s on then-decrepit Lincoln Road. His work has spanned the gamut from brilliant early furniture designs to his edgy photographic art of more recent years, including a signature façade-covering photograph (see following page) displayed at South Beach's Bass Museum of Art.

Throughout it all, Carlos has maintained his artist's love affair with Miami Beach.

He urges a first-time South Beach visitor to take a "morning or afternoon walk down the beach, alone," because "you cannot avoid to be filled with joy." He leavens his swirling life as a celebrity artist with "going out on my boat to read the morning paper while letting the boat drift on the bay...always discovering a new canal, new vistas, new sunsets." His talent is, he says, fed by "the sand, the ocean, the light, the freedom" of Miami Beach. A visual artist is Carlos, but one who can say it with beautiful words as well.

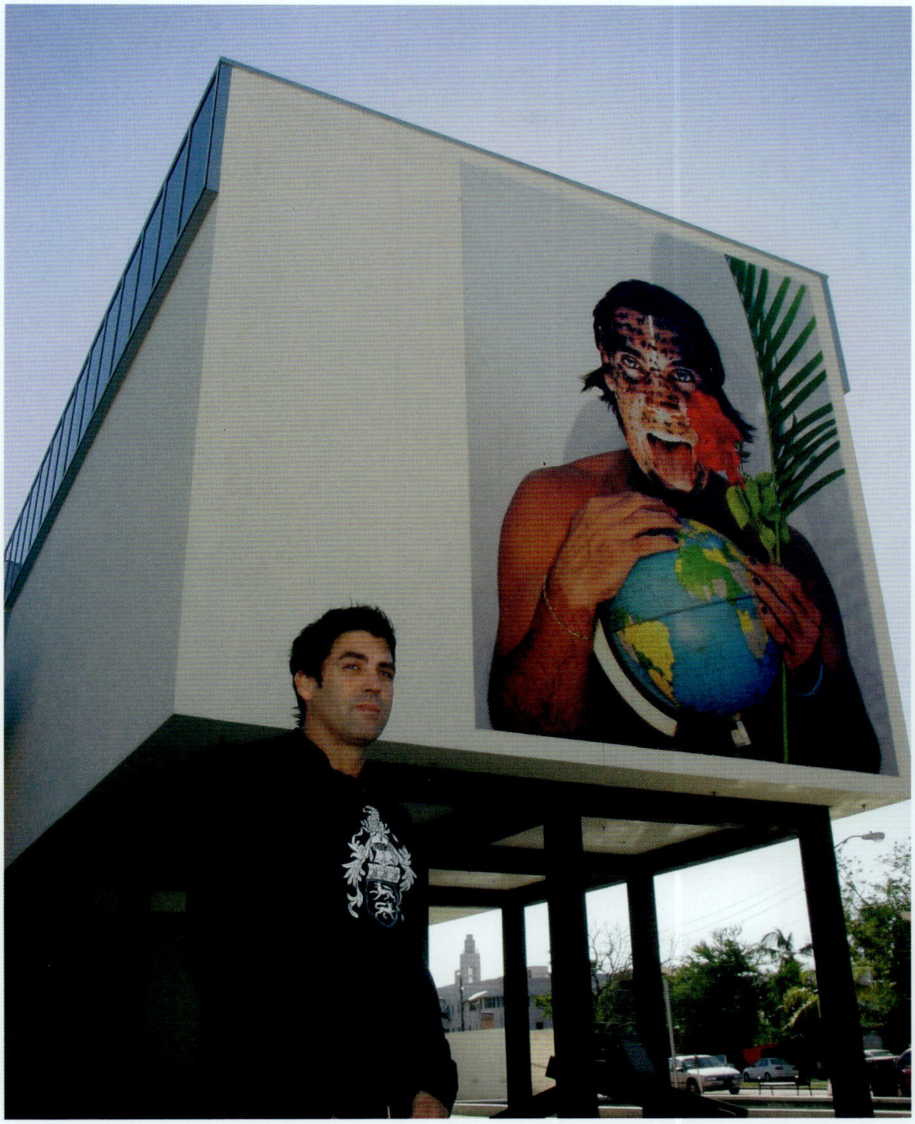

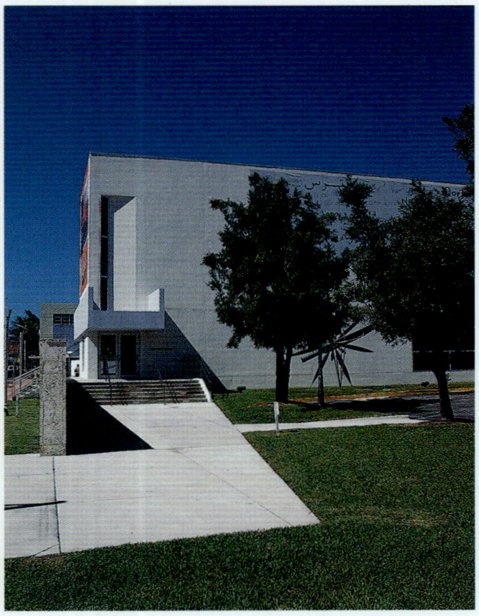

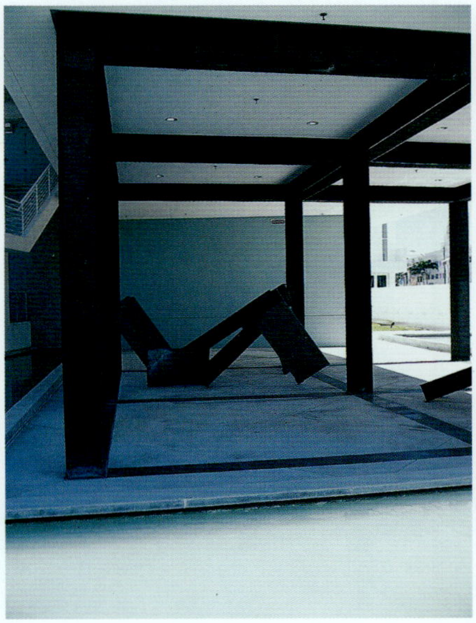

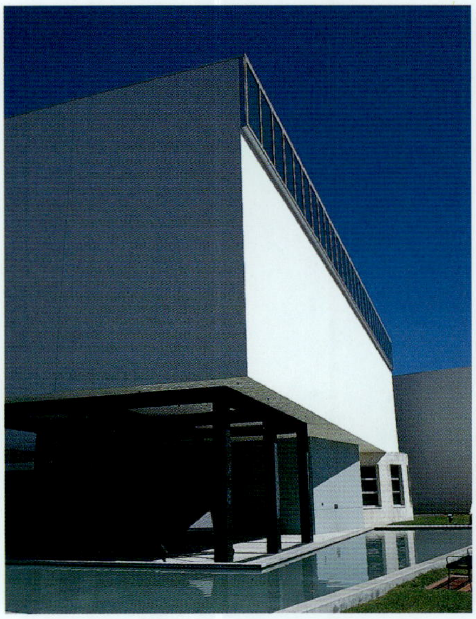

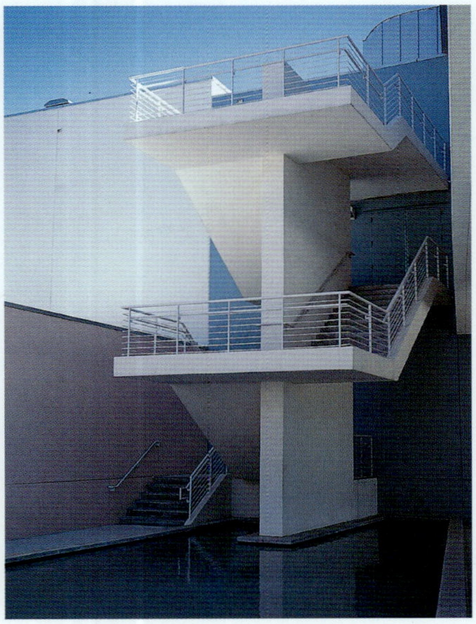

Chapter 30

Versace's Architect

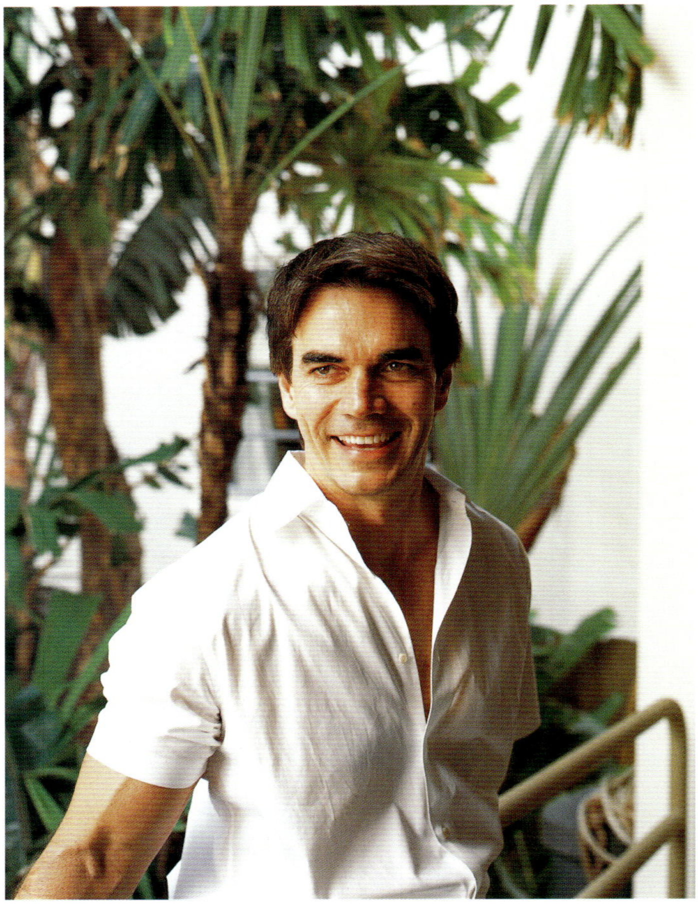

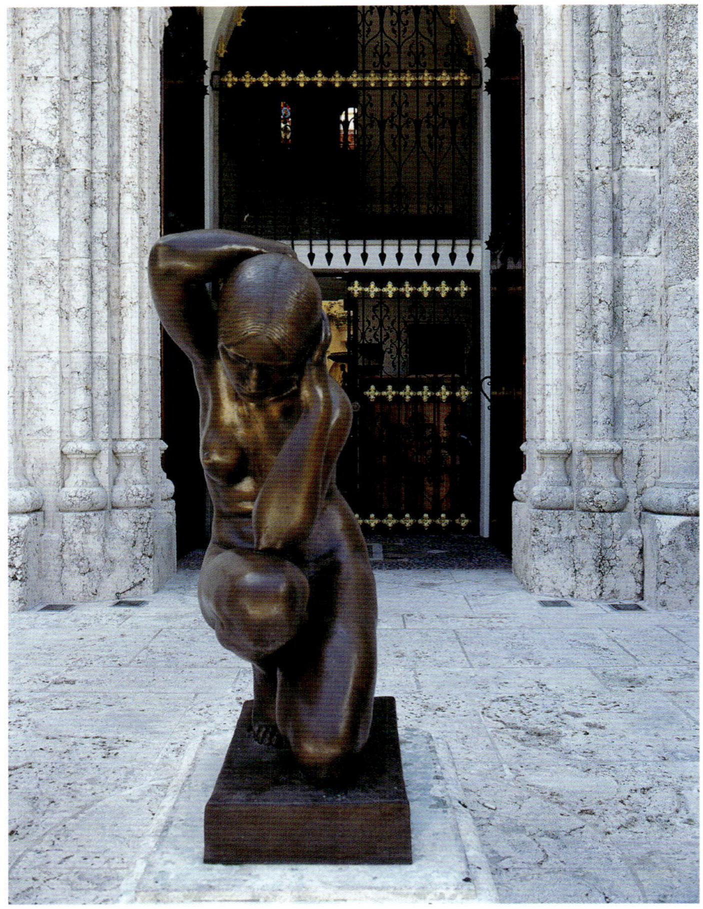

Peter Hawrylewicz

Among the Chicagoans who regularly escape to the warm climes of South Beach is Peter Hawrylewicz. He's been doing so for more than a dozen years, beginning with his celebrated remodeling of the mansion that came to be known as the home of fashion legend Gianni Versace.

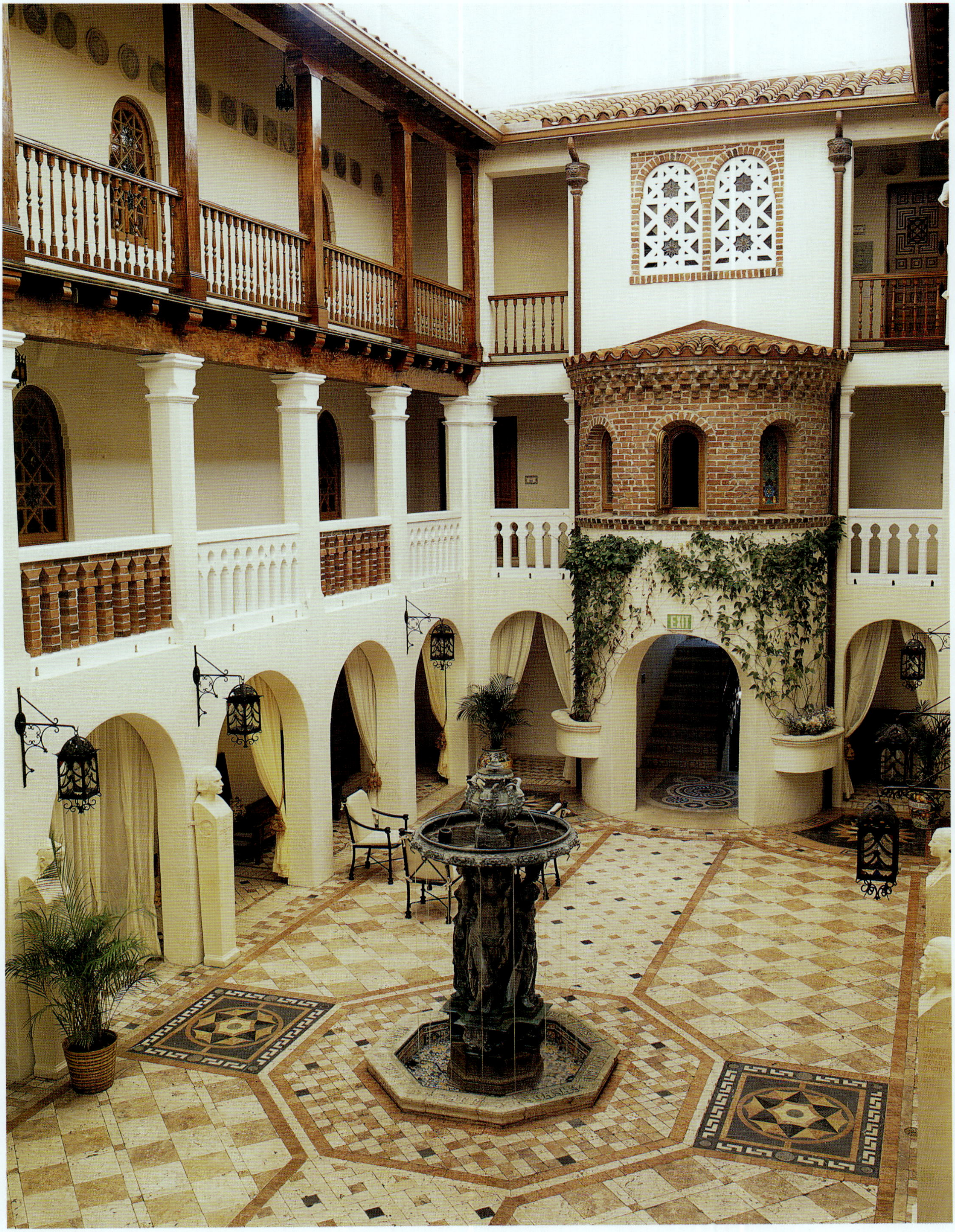
EXIT

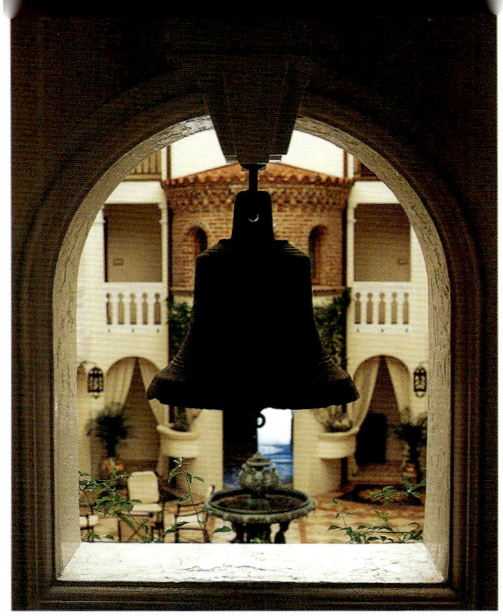
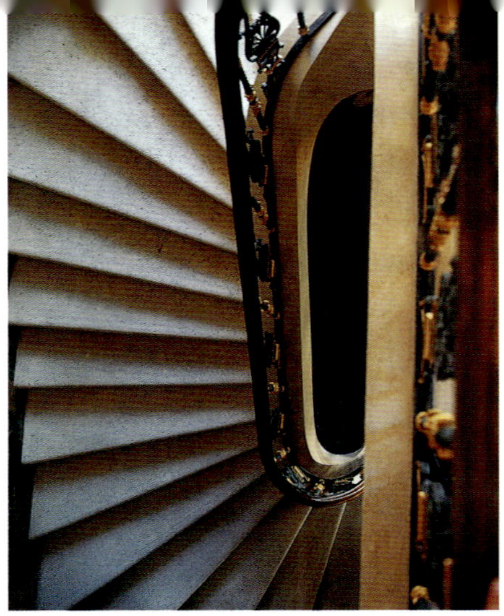
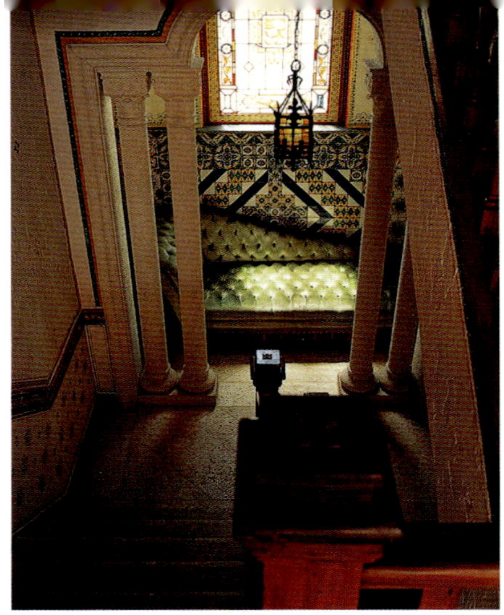
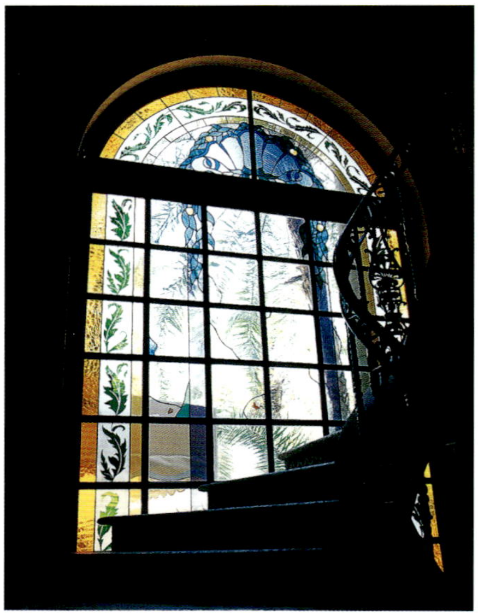
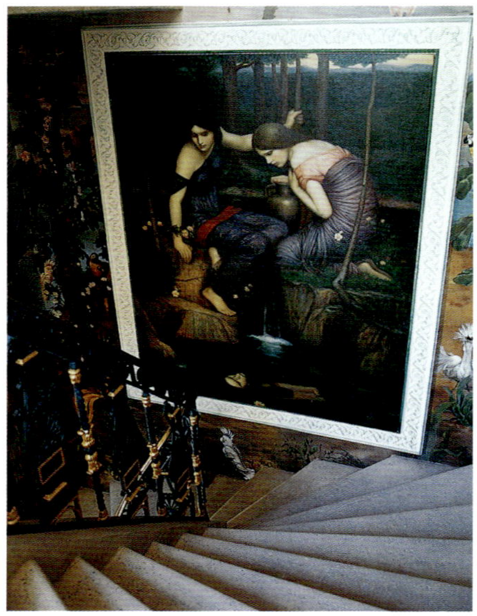
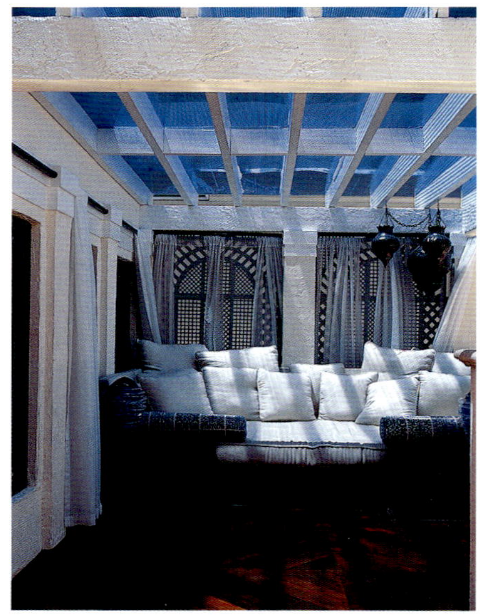
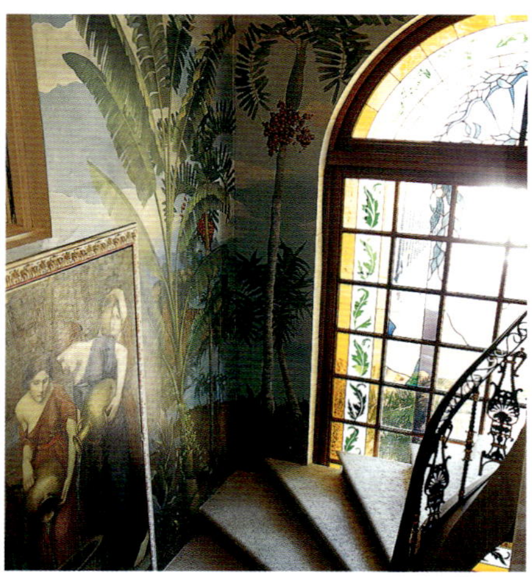
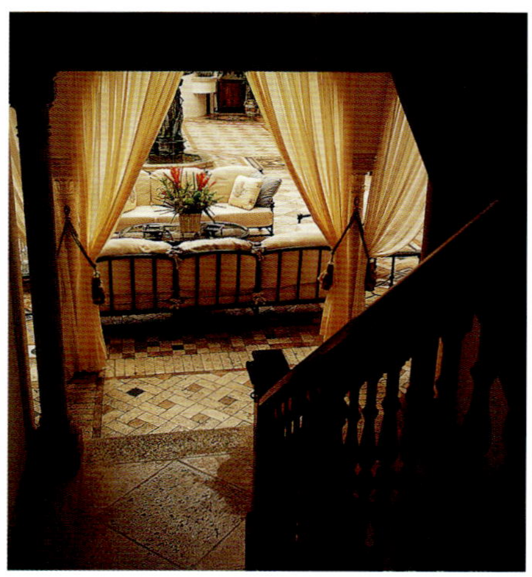

Perhaps most telling—about both Hawrylewicz and Miami Beach—is the architect's description of what he would do on the day he lived the fantasy of unlimited money to spend. We'll let him speak for himself, since we could not have said it any better ourselves:

"Throw a party, a big party. Maybe a boat party where all the guests are on boats…an armada that would fill the bay. There would be barges piled with food, drink and entertainment; waiters and waitresses would dart about on jet skis. Gold coins would litter the sea floor to encourage bathing and frolicking. Giant hot air balloons in the shape of Esther Williams suspended in various dives would provide sporadic shade in the day and continuous fireworks would provide light at night. President Clinton would make a short toast and we would all feel inspired and sane again. Cher would enter on a flotilla from one end of the bay with Elton John playing the piano on a regal barge from the other end. They would meet in the middle and sing their siren songs until we all crashed, only to be gently wakened by a kiss from the early morning Miami sun."

Wow.

Chapter 31

A ONCE AND FUTURE KIND OF PLACE

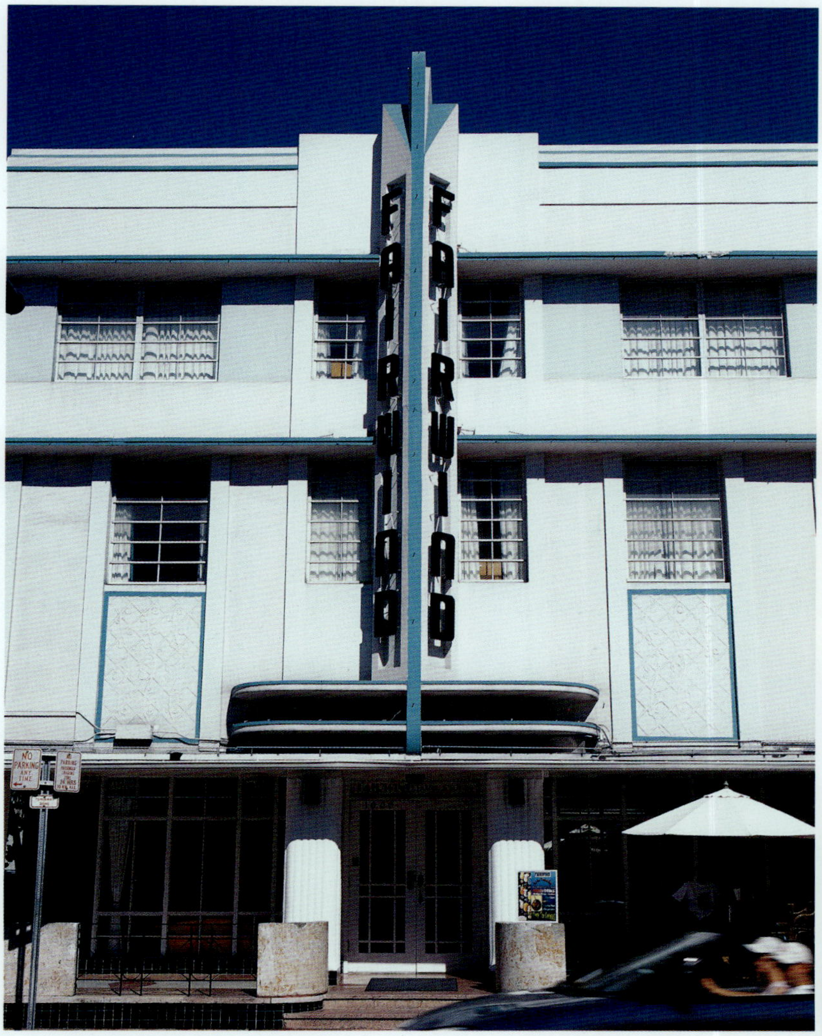

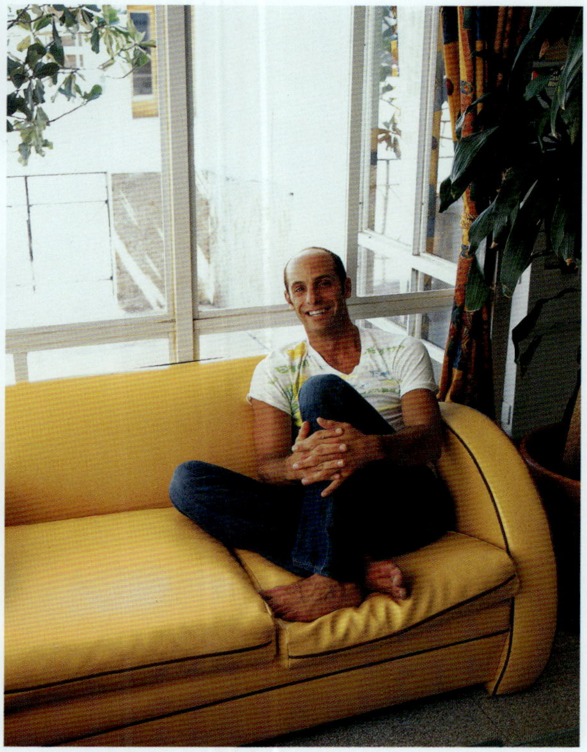

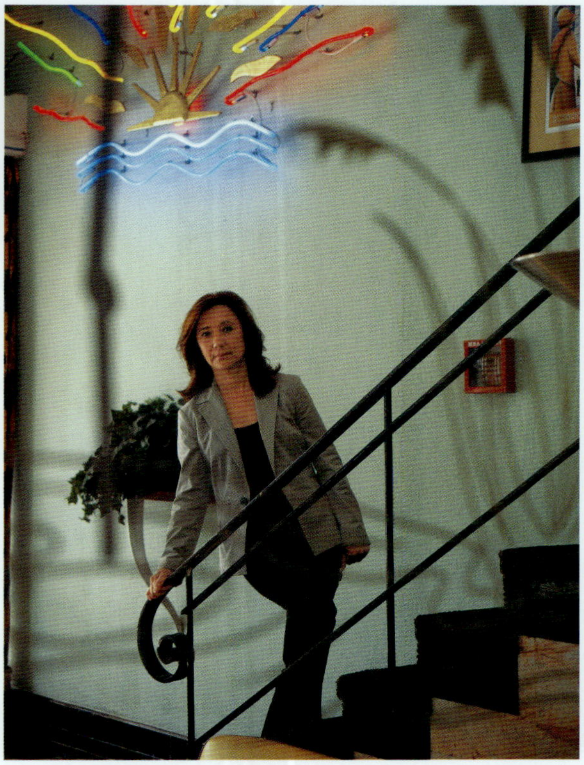

THE FAIRWIND HOTEL, MICHAEL COHEN AND CLAIRE CALLEN

Like the faces in this book, the façades of South Beach's buildings have stories to tell. The Fairwind Hotel, at 1000 Collins Avenue, is a great example. Once operated by his family's World War II generation, the Fairwind (previously known as the "Fairmont") is one of the reasons why native New Yorker Michael Cohen always felt "connected" to South Beach. And now The Fairwind has found its way into the loving hands of Claire Callen, born many thousands of miles away in Yokohama, Japan.

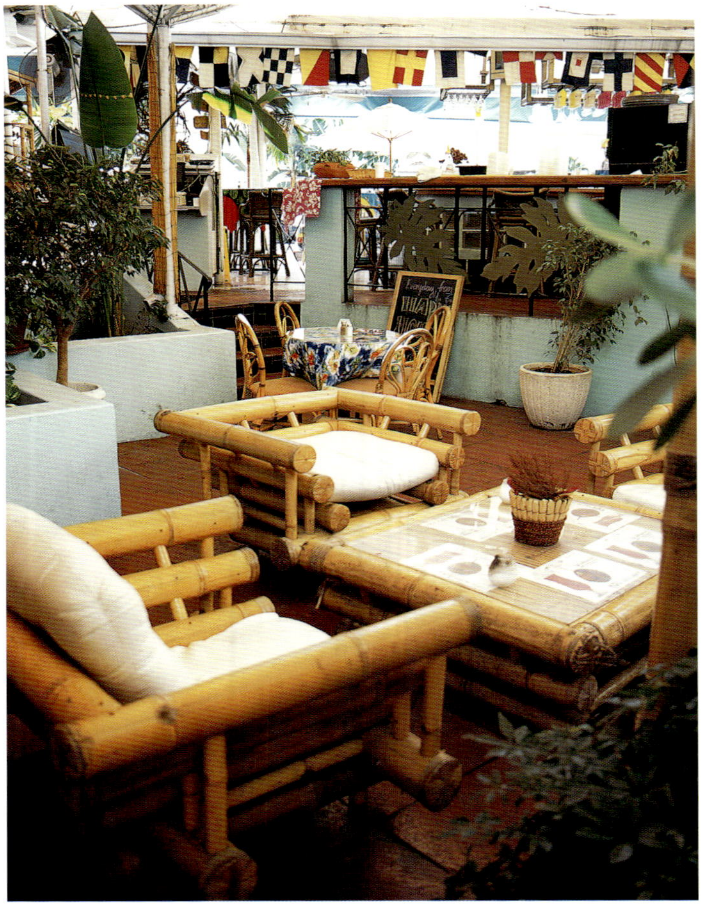

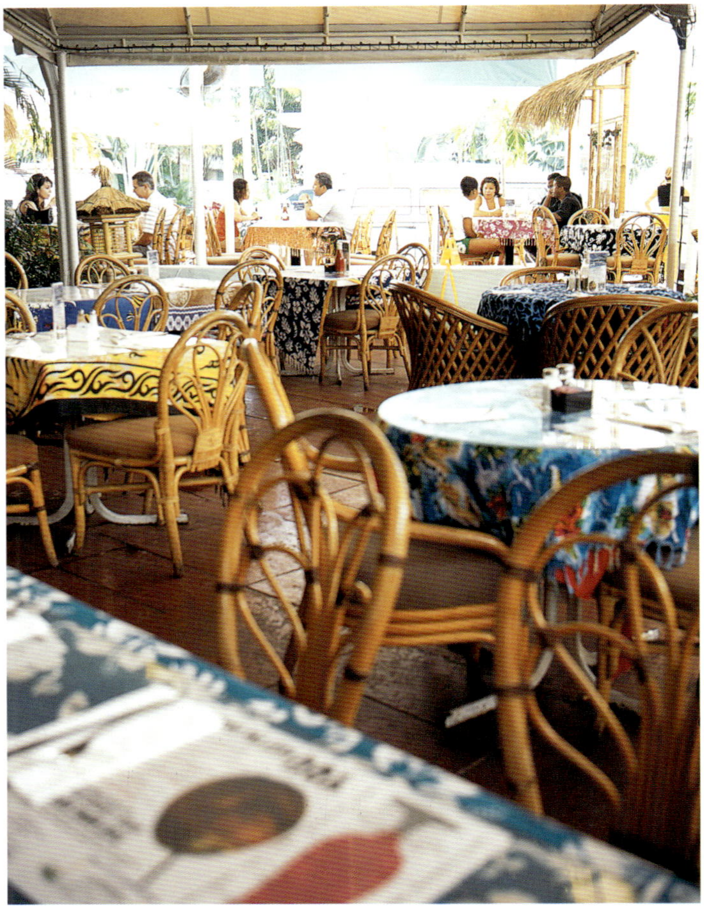

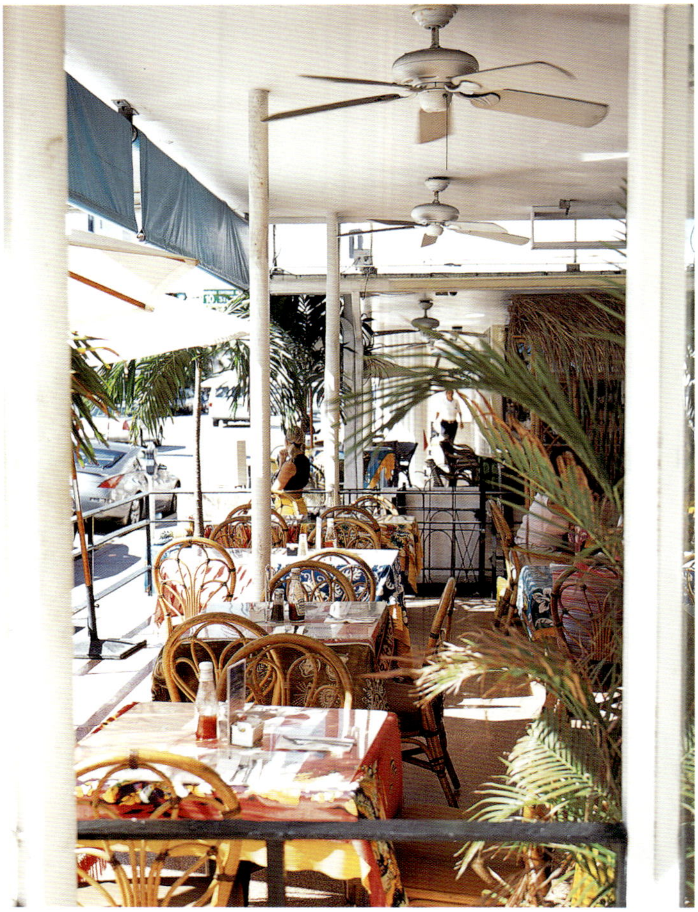

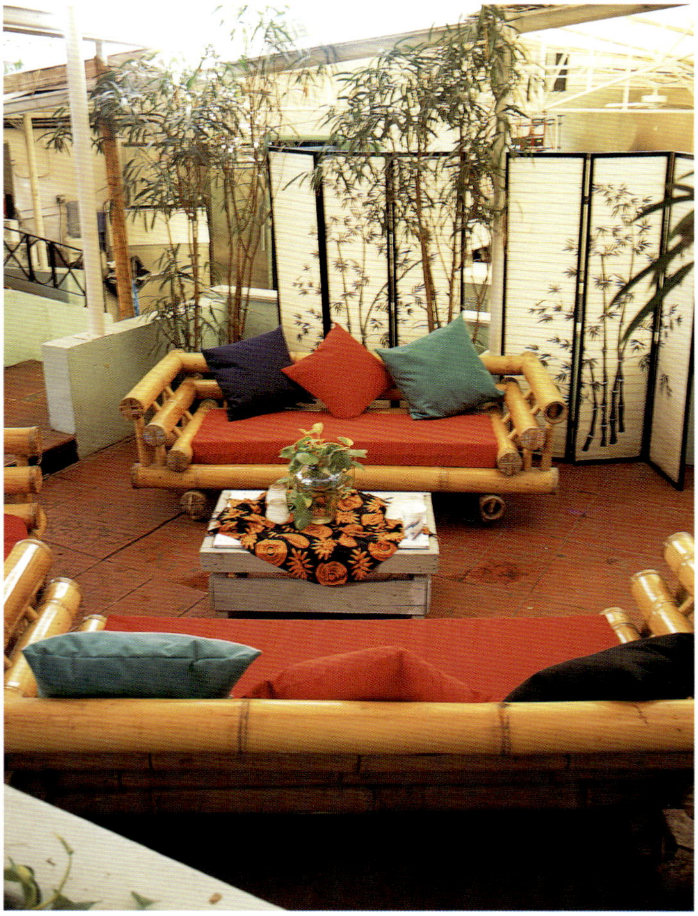

Built in the heart of the 1930s Art Deco period, the Fairwind sits at the geographical center of the Historic District. In the heat of the post World War II "discovery" of Miami Beach (largely a result of military people who were stationed here returning for a permanent dose of its beauty), Michael's forebears arrived to make their way in the real estate and hospitality industry. One of their properties was the hotel at 10th and Collins, then known as the Fairmont. Michael, an entertainment journalist based in South Beach, now lives a twenty-first century version of his ancestors' experience in the new South Beach.

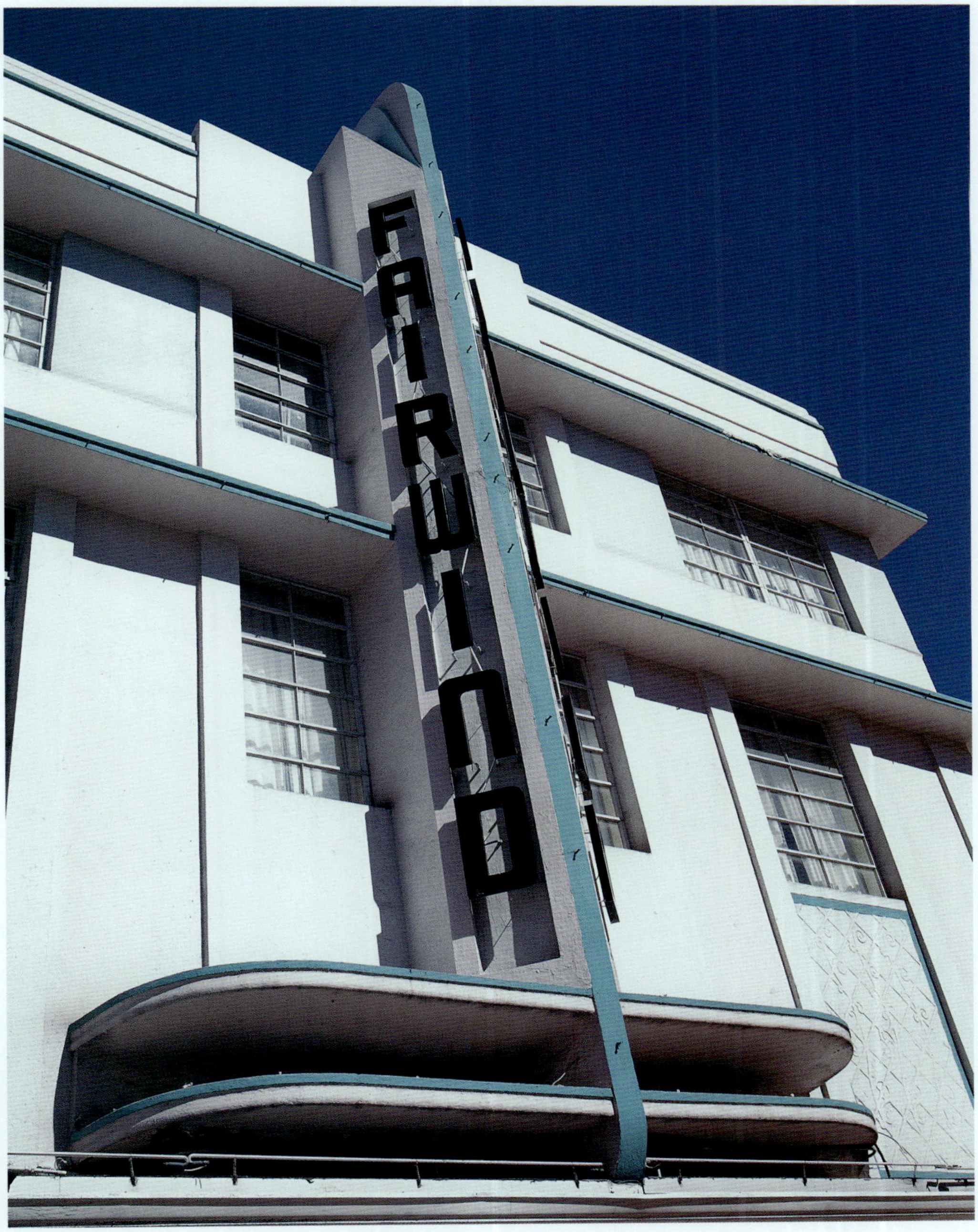

Claire Callen's journey to the Deco District began on the other side of the globe, where her New York City-born father and Japanese mother met and fell in love during the American occupation of Japan. Cornell-educated Claire, who moved to Miami during the 1990s for business reasons, is a prominent face in today's South Beach real estate and hotel scene (and an indispensable figure in the relationship between Florida and Japanese business leaders). From her office in Lincoln Road's Sony Building, she manages her family's extensive real estate holdings in the Southeastern United States, among them the same hotel that Michael Cohen's grandparents managed two generations earlier. Travel though she must to oversee her real estate responsibilities, Claire, like so many of South Beach's other faces, says that the coolest thing in her life is to "travel to many different cities but to come back" to Miami Beach, which she calls "Nature's spa." Amen.

Chapter 32

Haute Heritage

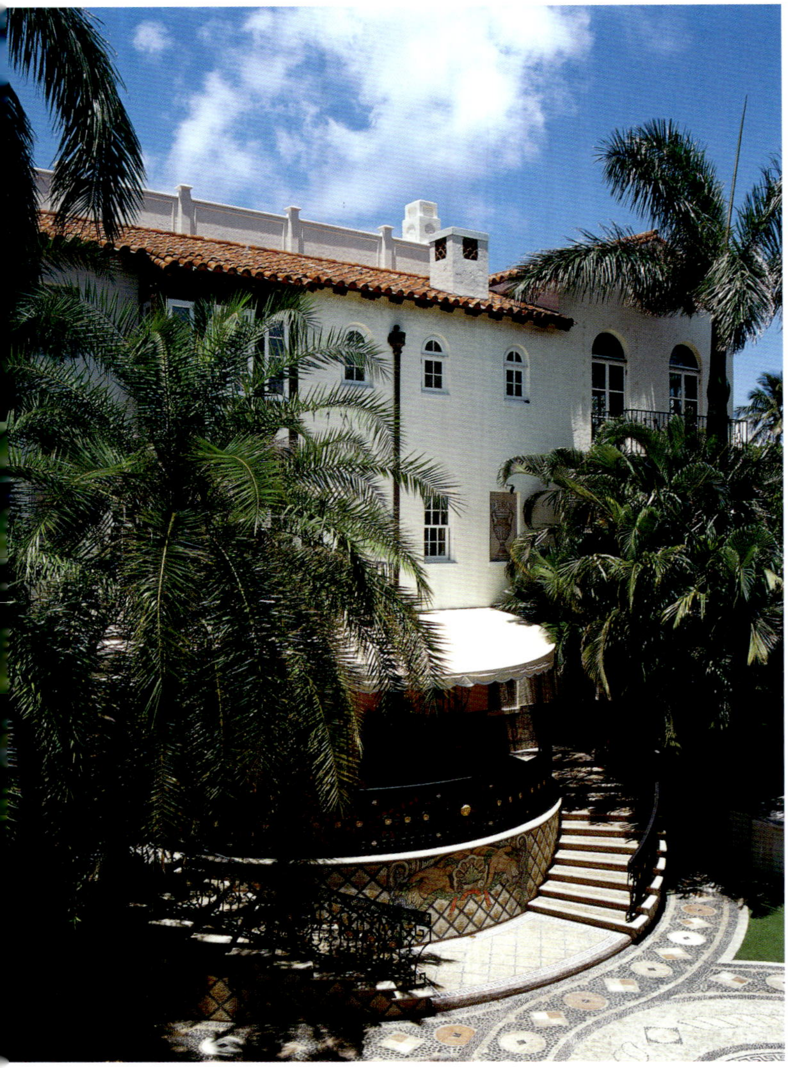

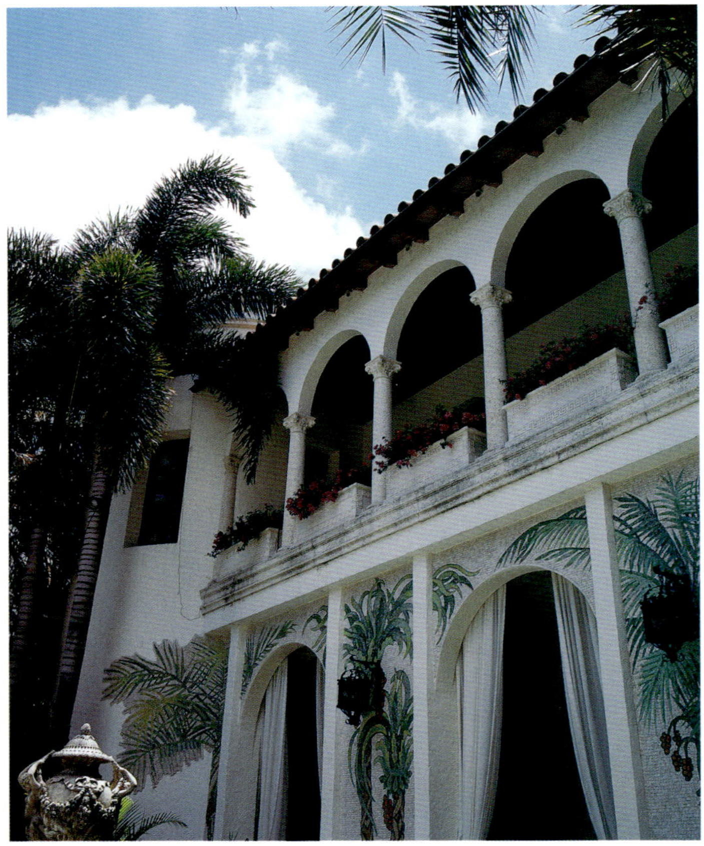

Peter Loftin and Casa Casuarina

Standing guard at the center of the ten-block strip that defines the magic of South Beach, Casa Casuarina, at 1116 Ocean Drive, is a structure with fascinating tales to tell. Built in 1930 as the beachside mansion of a wealthy industrialist's son, Casa Casuarina has been, from the beginning, something special. For starters, it epitomizes the Mediterranean Revival architectural style that is the "second style" of the famously Art Deco South Beach neighborhood.

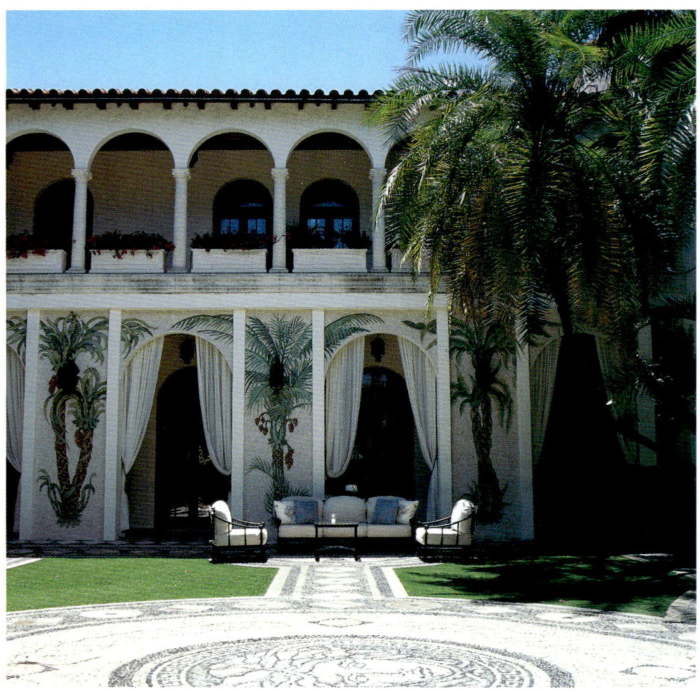

It was built, in fact, to duplicate the architecture of a Santo Domingo mansion built by one of the sons of Christopher Columbus. Its lovely name—Casa Casuarina—was later changed to "Amsterdam Palace," but NOT, as you might think, in homage to the city of Amsterdam. Rather, it was in homage to its then-new owner, whose name was Jacques Amsterdam.

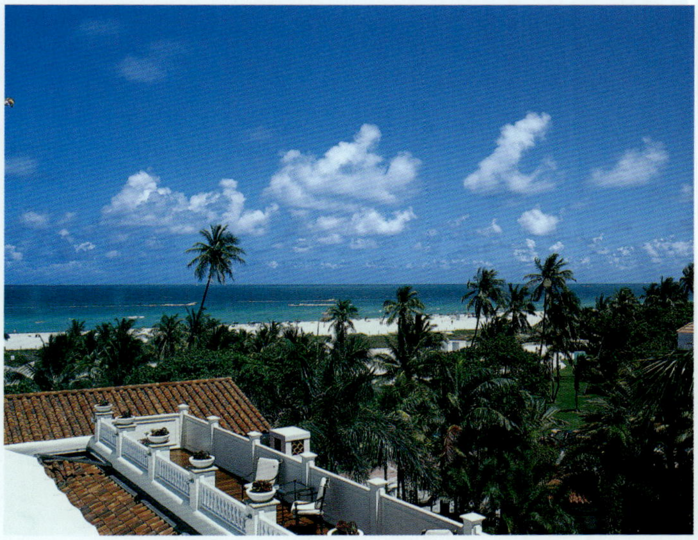

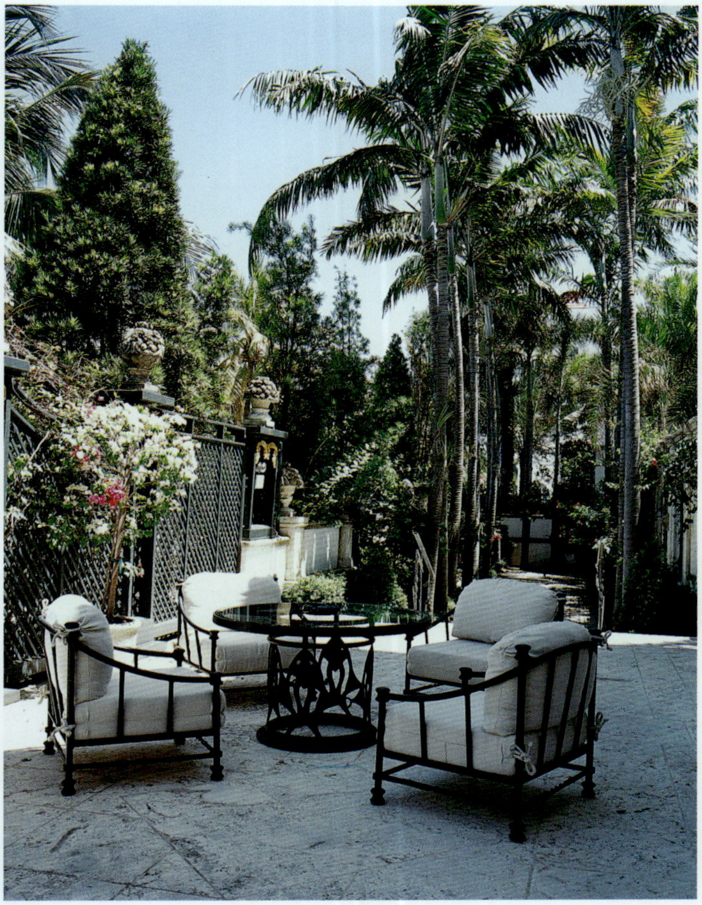

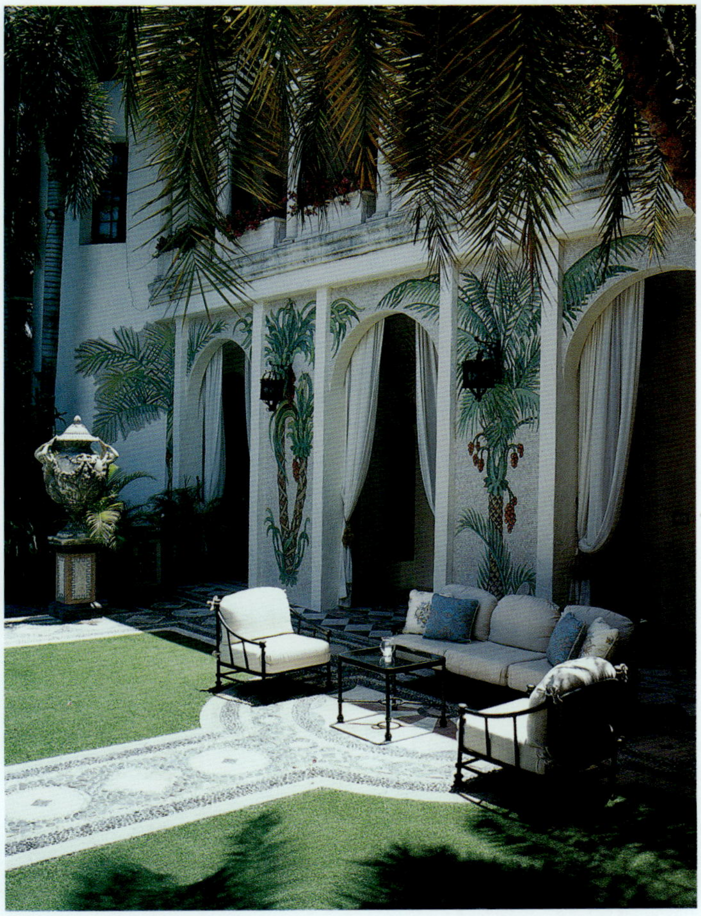

Casa Casuarina's colorful line of owners reached a zenith in 1992, when world-famous fashion designer Gianni Versace spotted it and saw through its dilapidated condition to a vision of oceanfront splendor that soon became reality. After five years of hosting the world's most beautiful people in this, one of the world's most beautiful spots, Versace was tragically murdered on the steps of his own dream-house. Several years later the property was purchased by Peter Loftin, a modern-day wealthy industrialist.

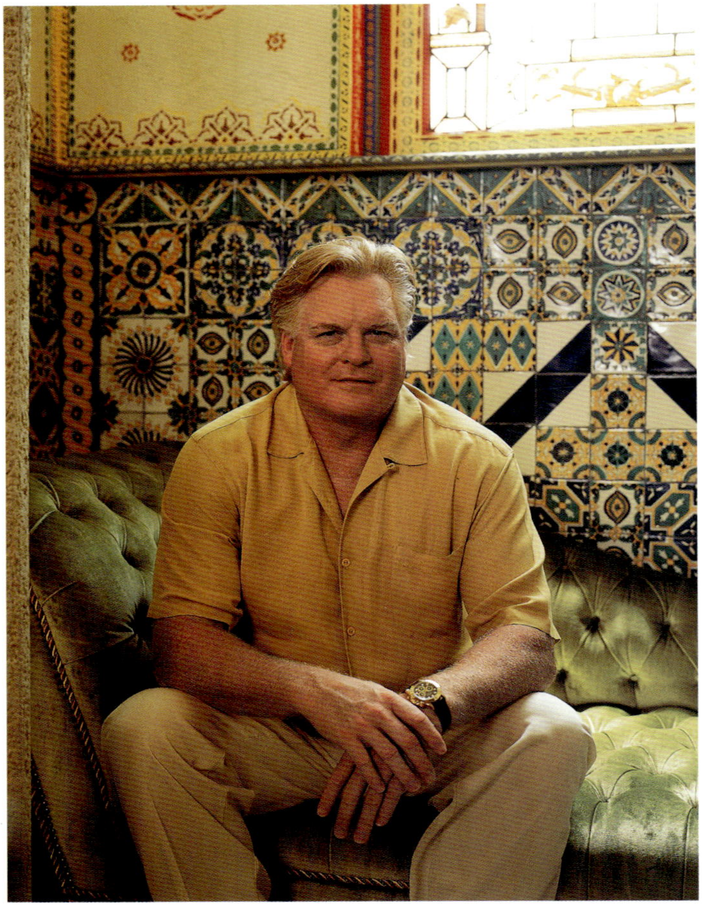

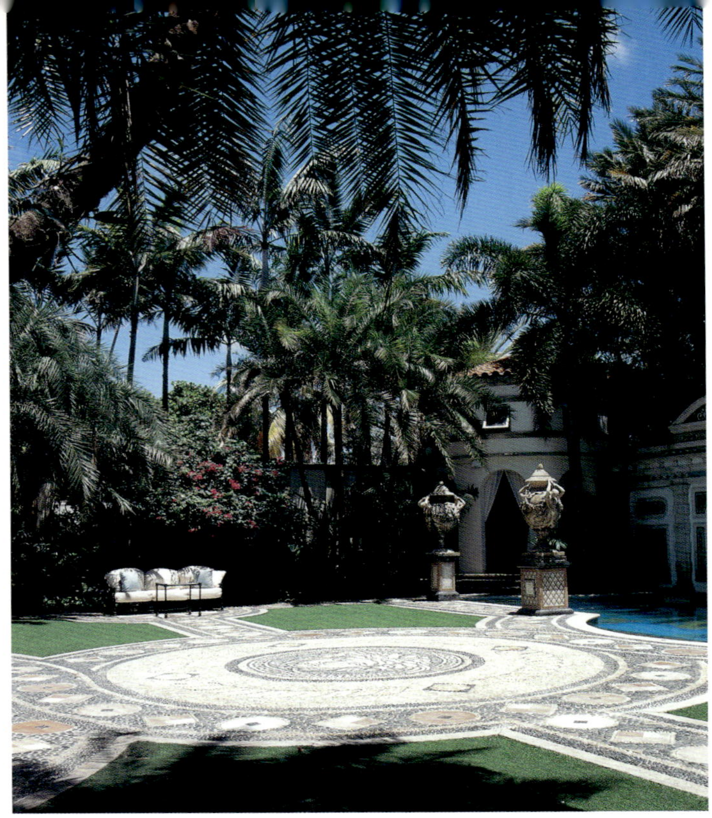

Currently, Casa Casuarina has resumed its place as one of the world's most desired addresses, this time as an elegant private club and hostelry. Loftin has been careful to retain much of the energetic opulence that Versace created in the house, and he has preserved its architectural heritage.

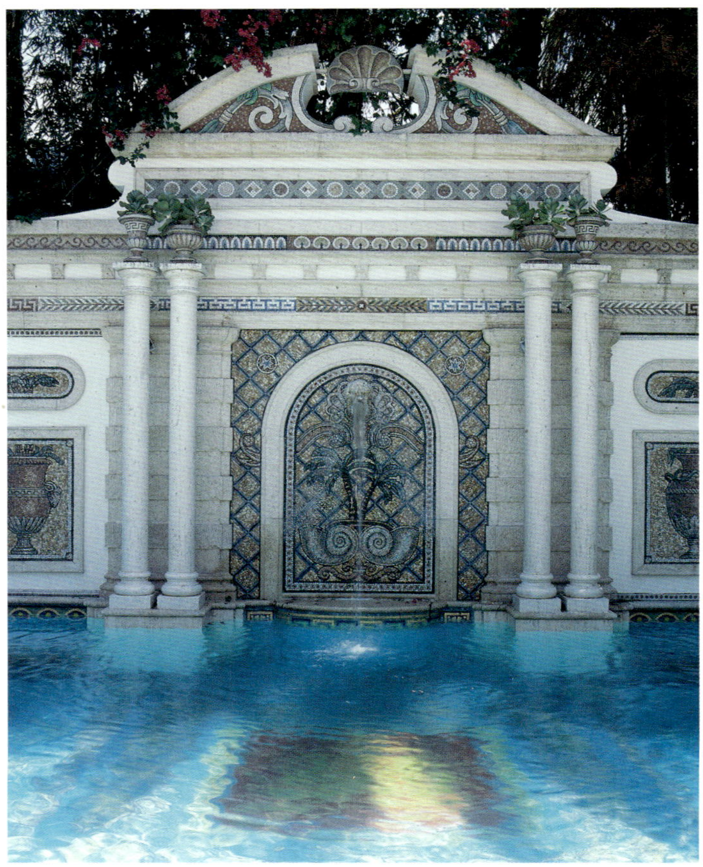

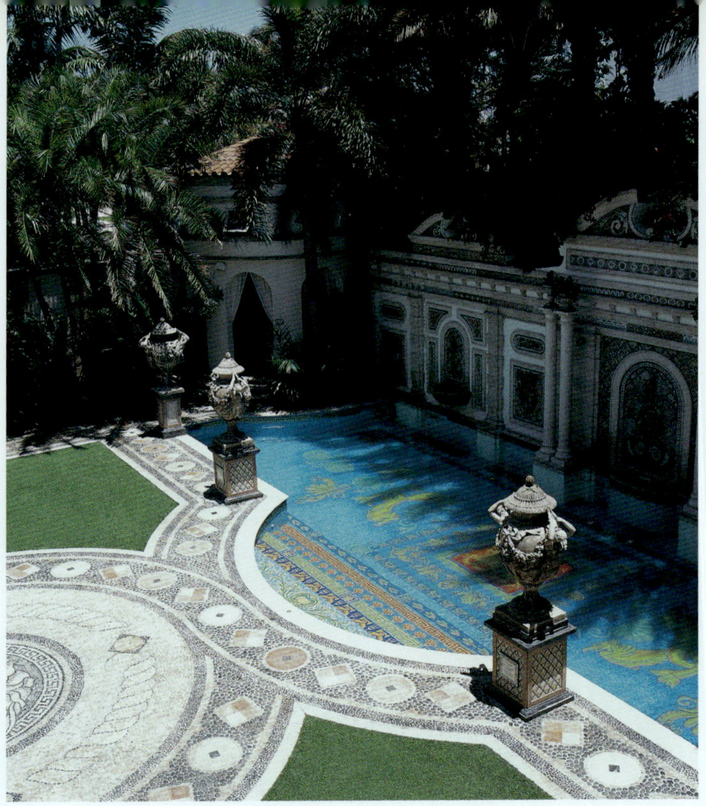

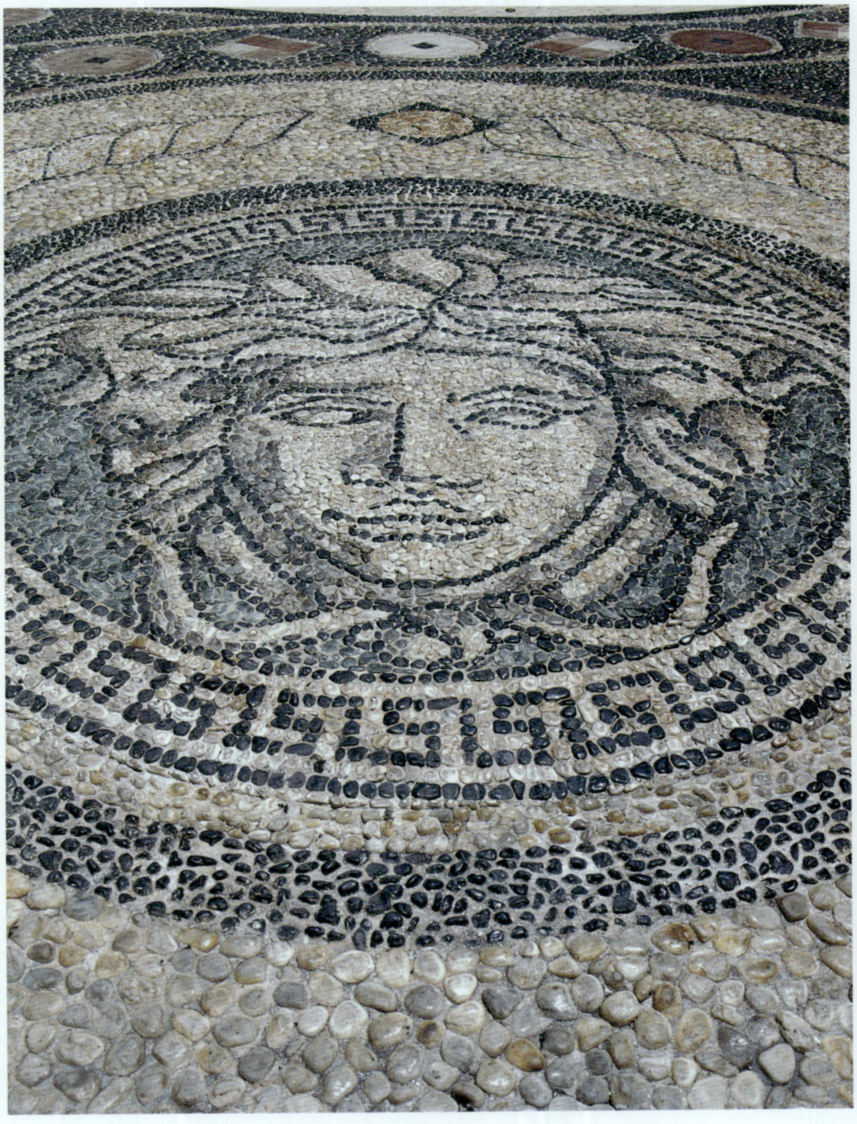

Loftin calls it "a haven, a refuge, and home-away-from-home." Now in its fourth quarter of a century, it is safe to say that Casa Casuarina has and will see more of its haute brand of life, one that could exist only in South Beach.

INDEX

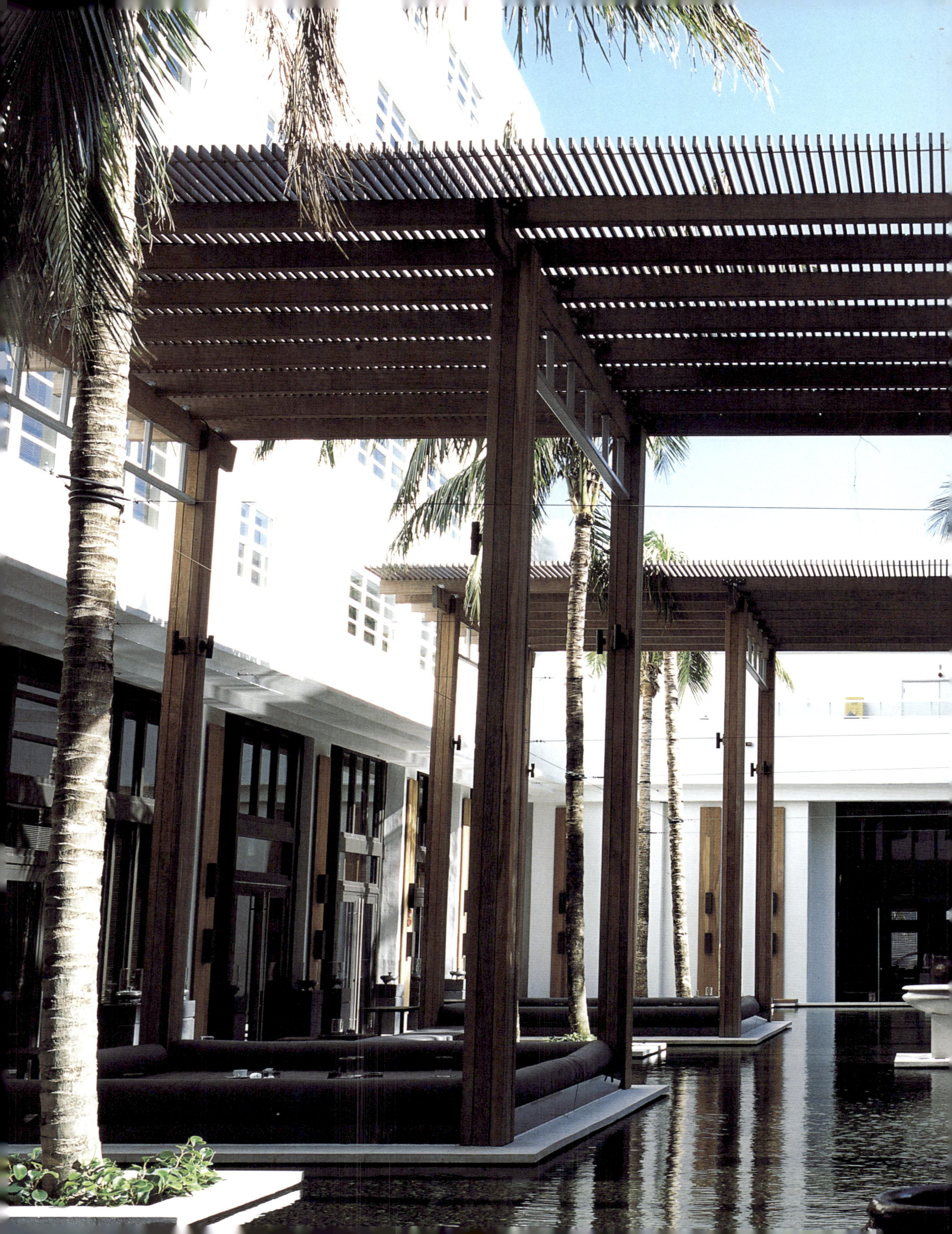